DENIAL
AND
DECEPTION

DENIAL
AND
DECEPTION

AN INSIDER'S VIEW OF THE CIA

MELISSA BOYLE MAHLE

NATION BOOKS
NEW YORK

DENIAL AND DECEPTION
An Insider's View of the CIA

Published by
Nation Books
An Imprint of Avalon Publishing Group Inc.
245 West 17th St., 11th Floor
New York, NY 10011

AVALON

Copyright © 2004, 2006 by Melissa Boyle Mahle

First trade paper printing January 2006

Nation Books is a co-publishing venture of the Nation Institute
and Avalon Publishing Group Incorporated.

CIA's Publications Review Board has reviewed the manuscript
for this book to assist the author in eliminating classified information
and poses no security objection to its publication. This review, however,
should not be construed as an official release of information,
confirmation of its accuracy, or an endorsement of the author's views.

Library of Congress Cataloging-in-Publication Data
is available

ISBN: 1-56025-827-6
ISBN13: 978-1-56025-827-8

9 8 7 6 5 4 3 2 1

Designed by Pauline Neuwirth, Neuwirth & Associates, Inc.

Printed in the United States of America
Distributed by Publishers Group West

To Dick and Hana:
Thank you for loving me even
during all the times I was not there
to give a good-night kiss or to mend a skinned knee,
or to do the normal daily things a wife and mother does.

As this book was going to press, the CIA insisted on a number of changes to the typeset pages. We have chosen to indicate the parts of the book so censored by blacking out the relevant passages. Previous CIA redactions resulted in rewritten passages or a note in the book that the Agency had requested the change.

—The Publisher

Contents

Preface

THIS BOOK OFFERS an insider's view of the Central Intelligence Agency (CIA) in the 1990s, the strengths and the weaknesses, and how we contributed to the intelligence failure of September 11. This book was written in part to answer the question of why the CIA failed to anticipate the attacks. An analysis of the performance of other agencies in the intelligence community in regard to September 11, 2001, is outside the scope of this book. As the findings of the congressional inquiries indicate, there were significant lapses on the part of the FBI, the National Security Agency, and the Department of Defense. It is not my intention to downgrade the importance of these failings in the overall context of the examination of what went wrong. They deserve equal scrutiny, but elsewhere. I chose to focus on the CIA, the organization that I know best.

I began thinking about writing this book in mid-2001, before the terror attacks. At the time, I was assigned as a recruiter for new staff employees for the CIA Directorate of Operations. In the Recruitment Center, I spent my days talking with young people interested in joining the CIA. They were enthusiastic, inquisitive, and demanding when it came to knowing just what is the real CIA. The most frequent complaint I heard was about the dearth of publications that described the CIA in the 1990s and 2000s. There were lots of books about the Office of Strategic Services and the CIA in the 1950s and 1960s. There are scholarly books that examine the role of intelligence and the uneasy relationship of intelligence in democratic society. There were exposés of questionable authority and the occasional memoir of a senior CIA officer. The most recent general book, which the CIA recommends to applicants, *Inside the CIA* by Ronald Kessler, was almost two decades old. The applicants wanted to know more about the current culture of the CIA and the strengths and weaknesses of the organization. This book was written in part to answer these questions, especially in the context of the CIA's capabilities immediately preceding September 11.

My biases are simple: I believe in the mission of the CIA and support the courageous men and women who dedicate their lives to achieve this mission. I am not blind to the warts of the Agency and of the intelligence community, and I am not afraid to be labeled a critic with an ax to grind. I believe that sunshine—not secrecy—is the way to address and fix the problems. There are those within the Agency who consider insiders writing about the CIA as apostasy. I agree, if the purpose is for self-aggrandizement or to sling mud out of pure spite. My purpose is neither. Instead, I hope that the book adds to an understanding of what happened in the CIA in the run-up to September 11 and that it adds to constructive debate about the important issues of adapting our intelligence community to meet the new security challenges of a new global reality where electronic and physical borders are growing increasingly porous.

Several notes on the text may be helpful. The CIA and the intelligence community love acronyms. I know that most people find them annoying and confusing. Therefore, I minimized the use of acronyms. The intelligence business has its own jargon, which I elected to keep. I provided a glossary of terms used in the book for the aid of readers not familiar with the jargon. In the text, I put jargon in quotations to indicate specialized meaning. I have limited references to keep things simple. It should be understood that statements related to events inside the CIA are based upon my personal knowledge of events, unless otherwise footnoted. Finally, this book is a product of myself and offers my interpretation of events, errors included.

I want to thank those individuals who aided me in writing this book. There are many Agency officers, who for cover reasons must remain unnamed but not unappreciated, who helped in different sections of the book. They know who they are. Some triggered memories by providing their own. Others challenged my assumptions and pushed me into deeper analysis. Many provided me with moral support to finish when the prospects seemed so impossible. I thank the CIA Publications Review Board for its professional comportment. They have a difficult job of determining what is truly classified and what is not, balancing the need to protect sources and methods and the need to be a part of our open and democratic society. I would also like to thank John Lehman, family friend and willing editor, who took what I thought was a final draft and remade it into acceptable prose.

I want to thank my family for their support and understanding. My husband, Dick, patiently listened to me ramble on about the book, always saying something clarifying and motivating me to finish. My daughter, Hana, would lose her mother days on end when I was in a writing mode. At her tender age, she did not understand what I was doing, but knew that it was important. To help me, she would write quietly in her own book, at her small desk next to mine. Thank you, Hana, for being you, making me laugh, and making me keep my perspective during trying times.

PART 1

SEPTEMBER 11, 2001

"The deliberate and deadly attacks, which were carried out yesterday against our country, were more than acts of terror. They were acts of war. This will require our country to unite in steadfast determination and resolve. Freedom and democracy are under attack. The American people need to know we're facing a different enemy than we have ever faced."

PRESIDENT GEORGE W. BUSH
September 12, 2001

1
Intelligence Failure

UNITED STATES OF AMERICA, 2001: On September 11, 2001, terror came to the United States. At 8:45 A.M. American Airlines flight 11 crashed into the North Tower of the World Trade Center in New York City. At 9:03 A.M. a second hijacked plane, American Airlines flight 175, flew into the South Tower of the World Trade Center. Forty minutes later, American Airlines flight 77 took a chunk out of the Pentagon. A fourth hijacked plane, United Airlines flight 93, plummeted into the ground, southeast of Pittsburgh at 10:10 A.M. It was 1:04 P.M. when U.S. president George W. Bush announced that the U.S. military had been placed on high alert and declared, "Make no mistake, the United States will hunt down and punish those responsible for these cowardly acts." Meanwhile, air traffic was shut down; international flights diverted to Canada; border crossing security placed on high alert; and federal and state government offices closed around the nation. On that terrible day, 3,016 fathers, mothers, sons, and daughters died as a result of the attacks. Within twenty-four hours of the first strike, Americans were asking why the CIA and Federal Bureau of Investigation (FBI) failed to anticipate a terrorist operation of this scale.

Accusations of intelligence failure dominated news headlines and policy debates in the weeks and months that followed. Intelligence failure is an extremely sensitive issue for the CIA. An intelligence failure writ large means the Agency failed in its mission. Nobody likes to hear they have failed—especially the dedicated men and women of the CIA.

CIA RECRUITMENT CENTER, VIRGINIA, 2001: For me, it started as a routine morning at the CIA. Walking through the halls toward my office, I could see the usual hectic activity of CIA officers preparing for the morning staff meetings. During the night hundreds of cable message and intelligence reports had arrived from overseas stations, some requiring immediate action and response. Important intelligence, operational, and support-related accomplishments of the previous day, and requirements/problems for the current day are the standard agenda items for the morning staff meetings. Directorate of Intelligence analysts were mulling over new developments, thinking about current intelligence and spot-reporting requirements for the day. Some Directorate of Operations officers were focusing on new operational developments in their region, while Directorate of Science and Technology scientists and engineers were working on their latest gizmo to advance technical collection. Mission Support computer gurus were taking calls from frustrated employees complaining of system slowness or nonresponse.

I arrived at my desk at 8:00 A.M., mentally preparing for a scheduled telephone interview with a New Yorker interested in employment opportunities with the Directorate of Operations. Although employed in personnel recruitment, I was not a personnel recruiter in the classic sense, but rather a trained assessor of people and recruiter of spies. This assignment was an enjoyable and welcome break from my primary occupation as an operations officer from the Directorate of Operations, Near East Division. After ten long years of back-to-back foreign assignments, my batteries needed recharging. Long hours, stressful living and working environments, and personal sacrifices had taken their toll. Talking with young people about the Agency, the fabulous opportunities and daunting challenges felt odd at first, since in days past I had to deny my CIA affiliation. Now I gave public presentations, visited university campuses, and interviewed people, talking up the CIA, telling "war stories" about my life in the CIA. Of course, I used a fake name and I dissembled when asked sensitive questions. With each presentation I was reminded why I joined the CIA in the first place and committed my life to public service and keeping the nation safe. I was looking for a few good men and women to join me and my colleagues in our secret world of espionage. Not just anybody has the right stuff to be a spy. My job was to find them among the thousands of applicants seeking employment with the CIA.

I filtered out the background noise of CNN from outside my office. CIA officers are addicted to CNN and never turn it off. We are all news junkies. We like to know what's happening, as it is happening. We also like the fact that we frequently know the story behind the story, chuckling when CNN gets it wrong, or cursing when they cover a story that is supposed to be a secret. Breaking news gets our attention, especially when it alerts us to some new development in our area of responsibility. Long ago, the CIA gave up trying to routinely beat CNN to a story. We are not in the business of headlines, but of intelligence.

I began the phone interview with a pleasant young lady who was so enthusiastic that I had to lower the volume of my headset. Nervous applicants often shout or whisper. I prefer the shouters because at least I can hear enough to make an assessment of the individual. I began my normal regime of questioning, designed to draw out information on how much thought went into the decision to apply to the CIA—was it on a whim or did the applicant do his or her research? I asked about her educational and professional background, assessing her ability to talk about herself in an articulate, but concise way. Is she persuasive? Is she interesting? Would an agent warm to her, or write her off? Applicants tell me that they are fascinated by the world and foreign affairs. It sounds good, but it's hollow if it's not demonstrated by foreign work and educational experience and a substantive knowledge of what has been on the front page of the international section of the newspaper for the past two months.

Because the volume of my headset had been turned down, I became aware of the background noise in my office suite. The clamor had grown abnormally loud. I put the applicant on hold and wandered into the office of another recruiter, also a Near East Division officer. It was 8:55 A.M. CNN was broadcasting. Time stopped as I saw the image of a smoldering tower. The announcer was repeating what little he knew. A plane had flown into the tower. There was commentary on how this could have happened. I stopped listening because in my bones I knew. I went back to my neglected applicant, still on hold. As she was in New York, I asked her exactly where she was calling from. She was in Midtown, calling from the privacy of her office. I told her about the incident and asked her what she could see from her window. She was responsive, but clearly confused and wanting to get back to the interview. I brought the interview to an end quickly, in part because I had heard enough and in part because I knew there was other work to be done. I worked counterterrorism issues for many years. I knew an attack when I saw one. I also knew that terrorists frequently plan multiple attacks on the same location to maximize casualties. I was not surprised when the second plane hit. Instead, I felt a deep sense of institutional and personal failure.

The order to evacuate all government buildings trickled down just before noon. There were reports of missing airplanes and concerns that other government facilities would be attacked. I was in an obscure building far away from CIA Headquarters. I had no fear about my own well-being. My colleagues in Headquarters were in a different situation. Langley was a choice terrorist target as we knew from past threat reporting. Despite this, many did not want to evacuate. We simply were not trained to evacuate our posts in times of crises. Most were ordered to leave, but a few in the Counterterrorism Center stayed behind.

I packed my gear and headed to my car. The scene before me was surreal. CIA security forces had deployed, establishing a perimeter around our up-until-then low-profile building. Combat vests and submachine guns transformed our friendly SPOs into a formidable-looking force. Directing traffic with an M4, an SPO cleared me through the growing traffic jam exiting the controlled-access area. Gone were their usual smiles.

Traffic was at a crawl as I cut through residential areas, meandering my way back to my Fairfax home. Federal and state employees had been sent home as a security precaution. As my car inched forward, I observed the outpouring of American patriotism and resolve. Time and time again, I watched men and women pull into their driveways and disappear into their homes, only to reappear moments later unfurling the Stars and Stripes. Watching my community rally around the flag on this awful day cut through my emotional wall of steel and reduced me to tears. Two hours later, when I finally reached my home—a journey that in normal times took twenty minutes—I, too, raised the flag.

LANGLEY, VIRGINIA, 2001: A day later, a visibly strained and embattled Director of Central Intelligence (DCI), George Tenet, addressed Agency officers over the CIA intranet. His clothes were rumpled; dark circles accented his piercing black eyes. The trademark cigar, never lit but always in chewing distance, was nowhere in sight. His demeanor was serious, with more than a hint of anger. We gathered around the circuit TV, anxiously waiting for a message to guide us out of our collective shock. He told us that there had been no intelligence failure, that the Agency had been working hard against the threat of al-Qa'ida and had in fact warned senior levels of the U.S. government of the likelihood of an attack. He rallied the troops to be proud, vigilant, and flexible to the calls of the "needs of the service."

What I found remarkable about Tenet's address was the total denial of failure. He continued to deny failure five months after the attack when he gave testimony before the Senate Select Committee on Intelligence. On February 6, 2002 he said, "Whatever shortcomings we may have, we owe it to the country to look at ourselves honestly and programmatically. But when people use the word 'failure'—'failure' means no focus, no attention, no discipline—[they] were not present in what either we or the FBI did here and around the world."[1]

Tenet's performance provoked public debate on whether the director was lost in reactionary denial, or whether the denial was part of a strategic game plan of bureaucratic survival (his and ours). There would be no public mea culpa from Tenet. Obviously, something went wrong; why could the CIA not admit this?

Traditionally, the CIA has been reluctant to admit failure in public because of its culture and history. Our mantra, "Deny Everything," is bred into our bones. To the public, it seemed once again the CIA was circling the wagons, deaf to calls for accountability. But the CIA's exterior stone wall should not be confused for internal denial. In reality, there was real turmoil on the other side of that wall, because while we were reluctant to mouth the words "intelligence failure," many CIA officers were grappling with the hard questions.

We had been working hard against al-Qa'ida for years. Dedicated and highly skilled officers had been working day and night, taking risks, professional and personal, fighting al-Qa'ida. We had done our best, but our best had not been enough.

Were the September 11 attacks the result of an intelligence failure? If indeed there was an intelligence failure, why and how did it happen? Who should be held responsible, institutionally and personally? What changes need to be made to ensure that it does not happen again?

The Joint Congressional Committee on September 11 was supposed to answer these questions. Instead, it produced a nine-hundred-page report that fell short in the most critical area: understanding the nature of the threat and why the U.S. approach had failed to counter it. The committee chalked up September 11 to "missed signals"—hardly a satisfying explanation to what is the worst disaster to strike the United States in recent history. Trains are derailed because the engineer misses signals. An orchestra reverts to cacophony when the string section misses the conductor's signal. Critical infrastructure of cities is not shut down because of missed signals. The military does not fail to show up for a war because of missed signals. The president of the United States does not fail to keep his nation safe because of missed signals. The committee's findings beg another look—specifically, a deeper look at the CIA—at what we did and did not do, and why.

As I grappled with these questions, I embarked on a little self-education, probing the history of the CIA to better understand what the CIA mission was and what an intelligence failure was. I found that the history contained some important keys to understanding the peculiarities that I observed day to day inside the Agency. The organizational fear of failure had roots in the fact that the CIA was established as a result of failure. This made us obsessed with mission achievement: getting the job done at any and all costs so that failure could be avoided. The obsession was intensified by the stark reality of a stacked deck: the knowledge that the CIA, with its dysfunctional structural design, was not actually given the tools necessary to achieve its mission. Finally, the CIA's unwillingness to share—its go-at-it-alone preference—was born out of the bureaucratic infighting that accompanied its creation and molded its development within the intelligence community.

Most of all, the Agency's history provided a context to evaluate its performance in terms of expectations and capabilities.

The CIA predecessor organization was created because of a failure of similar magnitude to September 11. On December 7, 1941, carrier-based Japanese airplanes conducted a surprise attack against U.S. forces at Pearl Harbor, killing 2,409 Americans and destroying numerous U.S. fighting ships and warplanes. The intelligence failure was attributed to two critical weaknesses: the United States did not have any spy networks in Japan, and there was no mechanism within the U.S. government to assemble and assess the information the disparate arms of the U.S. government had collected on Japanese actions and intentions. To redress this, William "Wild Bill" Donovan formed the Office of Strategic Services in 1942 as a wartime intelligence agency whose mission was to collect and analyze strategic information and to plan and direct special services (covert operations) as requested by the U.S. Joint Chiefs of Staff.

When the war ended, the Office of Strategic Services was dissolved as quickly as it was created. President Truman was sensitive to popular fears that the Office of Strategic Services would take on domestic responsibilities and evolve into a Gestapo-like organization that would threaten the civil liberties of the American people. The images of the wartime atrocities and oppression of the Gestapo were too fresh in the memories of Americans. The Office of Strategic Services, an organization created to meet wartime needs, did not seem well suited to peacetime America. The Office of Strategic Services officers packed up their desks and went home to their prewar lives as lawyers and journalists, professors and chefs. However, Washington of the 1990s was much like Washington of the 1940s: nothing is over until the fat lady sings, and she had not yet begun to warm up her voice.

In postwar policy circles, there was a growing consensus that the United States needed a centralized intelligence capability to warn against future attacks. The fear of establishing an American Gestapo was a powerful dynamic in shaping the debate on the type of intelligence organization the United States needed, but not strong enough to stop it. Bureaucratic interests of the military, State Department, and FBI played powerful roles in determining what would be created. These agencies were interested in preserving their departmental intelligence offices. A new and strong central intelligence organization represented a bureaucratic threat to their independence and power—a potential loss of turf, funding, and influence in the worst-case scenario. Therefore, they refused to support a strong centralized organization along the lines of Donovan's suggestions: a new agency that would take the lead position in the intelligence community. They also did not want to cede power to one of the existing national security departments, since this would have altered the existing bureaucratic balance. Instead, they opted for the lesser of two evils: to create a new agency, central in name but weak in structure and authority.

In 1946, Truman created the Central Intelligence Group and the National Intelligence Authority. The National Intelligence Authority, which was made up of the secretaries of state, war, and navy, as well as a presidential representative, supervised the Central Intelligence Group, thus ensuring that the new intelligence organization could be kept controlled. The organization was supposed to be small and was supposed to concentrate on providing summaries of current events to the National Intelligence Authority and the president. It was a weak organization by conception, designed to be dominated by the existing bureaucratic powers. The triumvirate had won, and Donovan had lost—or so they thought.

The CIA replaced the Central Intelligence Group with the stroke of Truman's pen when he signed the National Security Act of 1947 into law. Donovan had won Truman over on the need for an independent civilian intelligence service that answered to the president, not to the triumvirate. Much to the chagrin of the other powers in the budding intelligence community, Truman gave the CIA broader authorities. The CIA was charged with coordinating the foreign intelligence effort, correlating and evaluating intelligence, and performing such other functions and duties related to intelligence affecting the national security as the National Security Council may, from time to time, direct.

While the CIA was envisioned as a clearinghouse for intelligence, its weak structure guaranteed that it would have difficulty functioning in this capacity. The CIA had no means to make the other intelligence community agencies hand over their products. In a culture where information is power and influence, these agencies had many bureaucratic interests encouraging them not to cooperate.

Rather than complacently becoming a bureaucratic dwarf, the CIA forged its own path, scratching out turf in areas of little to no interest (at that moment in time, at least) to the other members of the intelligence community. The CIA started by seizing upon the emerging threat of an activist Soviet Union in Europe. Given that the predicting and warning mission of the CIA was considered primary, and that the other agencies were not sharing their intelligence willingly, the CIA quickly developed a collection capability, which was not part of the 1947 authorization. Human intelligence—in other words, running agents to collect information clandestinely—was the first capability to be developed. Technical collection followed quickly as the CIA pioneered overhead reconnaissance programs. Analysts took the CIA "raw intelligence" reports and created "finished" reports for policymakers, adding their analytical assessment on what the information meant. While the CIA analysts did draw on intelligence from other agencies, they were from the outset heavily dependent upon CIA-produced raw data. The CIA exploited a niche by expending the vast majority of its resources on collecting and analyzing intelligence on Soviet plans and intentions. While the CIA eventually grew into a worldwide organization, the Soviet account always remained the inner sanctum, regardless of the directorate.

The growth of the covert action arm of the Agency was also a result of the bureaucratic interests of the intelligence community and the growing threat of the Soviet Union. While competing agencies were shutting the CIA out from their proprietary interests, they had no strong objection to the CIA engaging in covert action overseas. The Soviet Union was taking over Eastern Europe, and Communist sympathizers seemed poised to win elections in Western Europe, particularly in France and Italy. The Communist influence needed to be counterbalanced and disrupted. With a realization of the threat posed by the Soviet expansionist plans, the CIA reconstituted its covert action capabilities by hiring former Office of Strategic Services officers. The CIA began to wage Cold War battles against the Soviets and their surrogates around the globe. The CIA authority to protect—that is, undertake covert action—was found in the catch-all phrase of "other functions and duties" of the National Security Act of 1947.

Fifty years later, when I joined the Agency, the mission remained the same.

Prediction. Warning. Protection. It's a pretty clear mission. But what about mission failure—what constitutes failure, specifically, an intelligence failure? The term is inexact. Not knowing something is not necessarily an intelligence failure. For example, failure to know in advance the final negotiating position of Israeli Prime Minister Ehud Barak at Camp David could not be considered an intelligence failure, because Barak had not himself established real red lines for negotiations until after Camp David. Failure to know days in advance that Saddam Hussein would invade Kuwait could not be considered an intelligence failure, because Saddam decided to attack only on the day of the invasion. It would be a stretch to label these as failures because there were no facts to collect and assess—that is, no hard positions or no exact dates. The information must be reasonably *knowable* if not knowing is to be considered an intelligence failure.

Order of magnitude is also important. In the real world of international politics, there is much that happens that remains unknown to the United States. While knowing the details of how the beautiful Queen Noor exerted so much influence on the late King Hussein of Jordan, effectively engineering a palace coup from the harem on his deathbed by placing her firstborn son in the line of succession (displacing the sons of the king's other wives), would make fascinating reading; not knowing does not constitute an intelligence failure. Jordan remains a close ally of the United States, regardless of who the crown prince is. Although it is an interesting story packed with bedroom politics and royal intrigue, it falls below the "who cares" threshold, generally considered to perch at the level of issues that impact U.S. interests. From a national security perspective, the threshold is higher yet, pegged to issues that pose a potential threat to U.S. interests, facilities, and citizens. Therefore, to be considered an intelligence failure, the issue must be significant in terms of national security and have an impact upon U.S. interests, facilities, and citizens.

Intelligence failures can occur at different stages of the process along the continuum of prediction, warning, and protection. Some failures are analytical, leading to wrong conclusions or predictions. Some failures are in collection, giving analysts inadequate grist for the mill. Others are failures to protect, whether attributed to imprecise intelligence or ineffective covert action. Normally, it is a number of little failures that *cluster into an enormous failure.*

As I pondered the details, I realized that the September 11 attacks fall into this category. The CIA has a clearly specified counterterrorism mission spelled out in Presidential Decision Directive-35 (PDD-35). Second, the CIA had been authorized by the president and the National Security Council to wage a war against terrorism through the use of covert action tools. Therefore, the CIA had a mission to predict, warn, and protect the United States from acts of terrorism. For my boss to say that the CIA met its mission because it predicted and warned policymakers of the al-Qa'ida threat is insufficient. The statement neglects the third part of the CIA mission: taking appropriate action to protect national security.

Examining what the CIA knew and did not know and what the CIA did and did not do, it became clear to me that the September 11 attacks fall firmly within the bounds of an intelligence failure. The CIA had the mission. The intelligence was knowable. The threat to U.S. interests was significant. What the CIA did not have was the capabilities.

In the following chapters, I endeavor to explain how and why the Agency failed to accurately predict the nature of the threat, comprehensively warn of the breadth of the threat, and effectively disrupt planning, preparation, and execution of the attacks.

If September 11 was the only intelligence failure on the books in recent years, I might be willing to make excuses or to claim unique extenuating circumstances. However, it was not. There had been a series of intelligence failures, and those failures fit a predictable pattern—especially with the advantage of hindsight—of insufficient human reporting sources, uncritical analytical thinking leading to groupthink and mirror imaging, and, worst of all, being tricked by denial and deception operations. It was shades of Pearl Harbor all over. But more to the point, when looked at systematically, it is possible to see significant trends in organizational development and behavior in the 1980s and 1990s that created an environment in which failure became inevitable.

Organizational Development. Organization Behavior. Pretty dull stuff. So let's put theory behind and talk about people: the men and women of the CIA. Real things happened in the decade that changed the way we thought about our jobs in general and our roles in particular inside the organization. We adopted new limitations, some self-selected, many imposed from above or from outside the organization. This, in turn, influenced how we viewed national security threats and the tools thought appropriate to counter them.

The paramilitary capability withered away, both organizationally and conceptually. Not only could the CIA no longer wage clandestine wars, but most officers did not even think of it as an option. Officers and management became so risk-averse that we became afraid to do the hard parts of our jobs. Clandestine officers stopped recruiting. The Agency had been cut to the bone and did not have enough people and money to meet our mission. Tenet refused to go to the mat with the Clinton administration to wage a real war on terrorism. Keeping one's job and winning bureaucratic turf battles was more important than achieving the mission writ large. Because of an FBI-CIA sandbox fight, Khalid Shaykh Muhammad escaped capture in 1996, leaving him footloose and fancy free to revamp his disrupted airplane-hijacking plan into the September 11 plot.

Organizational stovepipes made us think in linear patterns when we should have been building asymmetrical analytical models. African hands were not talking to experts on Sunni extremism, who were not talking to Asian hands, who were not talking to experts on Shia extremism. They should have been, and the cost of not doing so was that the CIA remained analytically stuck in the assessment that Usama bin Ladin is a terrorist and al-Qa'ida a terror group. While the CIA was thinking small and compartmented, al-Qa'ida was developing and spreading a new, global ideology that defied CIA traditional assumptions based on old models of sectarianism, nationalism, and terrorism, and defied CIA ad-hoc operational tools.

The DCI did not put forth a strategic assessment that would be produced and endorsed by the intelligence community as its collective view on al-Qa'ida. The absence of a National Intelligence Estimate meant that the intelligence community, specifically the DCI, was unable to focus policymakers and the nation on an existential threat. Without the focus, there could not be an integrated strategic counterterrorism policy. Without the focus, the war on terrorism was at best a big effort from a small part of the intelligence community and at worst, empty rhetoric.

That something was amiss was not lost on CIA management. The al-Qa'ida file is a poignant case study. CIA management knew there were serious problems affecting its ability to get on top of the target, but did not or could not move fast enough to overcome them. Problems within the CIA had been allowed to fester for years. These included risk aversion, staffing problems, and vertical stovepipes. Other problems are structural in terms of how the intelligence community is set up and managed, with the DCI unable to move the intelligence community at will to refocus and concentrate its efforts. Finally, there are the inevitable political problems—the intelligence community does not exist in a vacuum, but in the context of national politics and national leadership.

The failure was not the CIA's alone. The attacks of September 11 were collective failures of the intelligence and policy communities. The hard fact is that the CIA did more than any other U.S. agency against al-Qa'ida before September 11. It just wasn't enough.

The following is the tale of the CIA told from an insider's perspective—from the lens of looking at the world from the inside out—warts and triumphs together, with a modicum of perspective that hindsight provides.

PART

2

THE WEBSTER YEARS
(MAY 26 1987–AUGUST 31, 1991)

"I have a deep and abiding faith in this country and in its Constitution and in its laws. I think that no one has the right to hold public office unless they are committed to the faithful observance of those laws and who insist upon the faithful observance of those laws."

WILLIAM WEBSTER
Confirmation hearing, 1987

2
Iran-Contra Legacy

SEVENTH FLOOR, LANGLEY, VIRGINIA, 1987: It is impossible to write about the arrival of William Webster at the CIA in terms of an event of one day, a new face appearing behind the DCI's massive desk, with business continuing as usual. A better description is to say that there had been a nuclear explosion, named Bill Casey and Iran-Contra, and in the fallout came Judge Webster.

William "Bill" Casey died before the Cold War ended and before the 1990s began. However, his legacy lingered for many years, especially during the troubled early 1990s. I joined the Agency in the last months of Casey's tenure and never met him. Yet his imprint was so strong that I felt like I knew him personally. I cut my operational teeth on Casey stories. Casey is still remembered as a true leader, more than a decade later. There are many who did not like the path down which Casey led the CIA, but how he did it still evokes positive responses from Agency employees. More than anything, we remember the Casey era as a time when the CIA's *esprit de corps* was high and the mission firmly held.

Casey had the president's ear and the Agency flourished as a result of their relationship. He was a member of the Reagan cabinet and conferred regularly with Reagan on national security matters. What Casey said mattered; therefore, the CIA mattered. The CIA grew 33 percent during the Casey era, as the ranks were filled with more operations and paramilitary officers to fight the "Evil Empire."

The Directorate of Operations loved Casey because he was a man of action. His history as an Office of Strategic Services officer gave him instant credibility among the old boys leading the Directorate of

Operations. Casey held Congress in low regard, another trait the directorate loved. The Directorate of Intelligence was a little less enchanted, given Casey's penchant for toying with—or one might say skewing—the intelligence the directorate produced, to fit his (and President Reagan's) view of the Soviet Union.

Casey firmly believed the ends justify the means, and mission accomplishment was everything. The mission in Casey's time was battling Communism. Casey did not want to contain Communism, he wanted to wipe it off the face of the earth. Total victory demanded total commitment and a willingness to play hardball. A classic Casey operation was mining the harbors of Nicaragua. Yes, it was a bit extreme, but more to the point, it was effective at shutting down the ports, placing tremendous financial pressure on the pro-Soviet Sandinista government, part of the greater plan to destabilize the government. If Western ships were damaged, it was their governments' fault for not supporting the economic sanctions against Nicaragua, reasoned Casey. Allies should not be allies only when it is financially convenient.

Keeping Congress in the dark on certain CIA activities, such as the CIA role in arms for hostages and aid to the Contras, because of presidential wishes, did not pose an ethical dilemma for Casey. That those activities might also be illegal did not pose an ethical dilemma; they were conducted for the sake of national security at the direction of the U.S. president. In Casey's mind, the CIA was above the law when it came to protecting national security. Casey never wanted to hear why the CIA could not do something, from either his own officers, Congress, the Pentagon, or the State Department. Rather, he really wanted to hear how it could be done—or, better yet, that it had been accomplished. Casey pushed everyone's envelope. When he did not get what he wanted, he simply detoured around the obstacle.

The consequences of Casey's management style would reverberate through the CIA for years after his departure, particularly in the form of the Iran-Contra scandal. The actual events of Iran-Contra took place before my time; I just lived through the fallout. Because the scandal enveloped the Agency for such a long period, all officers became steeped in the lore of Iran-Contra.

NICARAGUA, 1984: Support for the Contras started modestly in the late 1970s before ballooning into a massive covert operation in the early 1980s. The CIA recruited, trained, armed, funded, and provided moral support to Nicaraguan groups—known collectively as the Contras—opposed to the left-wing Sandinista government. To support the covert action program, the CIA ran a large and complex operation, using staff officers, employing "contract" paramilitary officers, and operating proprietary companies for infrastructure requirements and other needs. For example, the CIA owned a sizable clandestine air fleet for moving people and cargo.

The CIA was running a full-scale war under cover of a covert operation, with appropriate presidential findings: secret legal documents signed by the president authorizing the CIA to engage in specific covert activities. Support to the Contras took place within the context of the Cold War—more specifically, the tense years of the Cold War under President Reagan. Though there were many other significant counterinsurgency programs against the Soviets and their satellites in the late 1980s, none captured Casey's fervor or imagination as the Contra program. The Sandinistas were playing footsie with the Soviets in the U.S. backyard. Was it to be Nicaragua today and Mexico tomorrow? Not with Reagan at the helm and Casey at his side.

Congress and the American people did not like what they saw. From the congressional view, overthrowing a democratically elected government—even a leftist one—was against the interests of the United States. In late 1984, Congress passed the Boland Amendment, which banned any U.S. agency or entity involved in intelligence activities from supporting the Contras.

The Boland Amendment, and the many subsequent amendments to it, reflected a Congress hedging its bets. While Congress did not like the CIA war-*cum*-covert action in Nicaragua, Congress did not want to take drastic legislative action, stopping all aid to the Contras. If Nicaragua should fall under Soviet influence and become a base for the Soviet military, Congress would then be open to the charge of having been "soft" on Communism and responsible for placing U.S. national security interests at risk.

Therefore, Congress pursued a middle course, stopping certain kinds of support but permitting others. Overt humanitarian assistance was eventually authorized, some military training continued, and so on. The legislation was complex and conflicting in some cases, evoking disagreement among congressional staffers and lawyers on what was and was not authorized in terms of aid to the Contras and under what circumstances. In 1985, when rumors began to surface in the press and around Washington that government officials continued to be involved in military resupply to the Contras, Congress did not investigate rigorously, thus sending mixed messages on congressional attitudes.

The congressional legislation shut down a large portion of the CIA covert action program to the dismay of the Reagan administration and Casey in particular. They did not want to abandon the Contras and permit a Communist victory in America's backyard. Conversely, the White House was also not willing to wage the domestic political battle by taking the issue of the Communist threat in Nicaragua to the American people as a strategic challenge the United States must battle.

Instead, the White House opted to take a very politically risky path of running an off-the-books covert action program out of the National Security Council. While the CIA maintained certain infrastructure, much of the supply infrastructure was spun off to the National Security Council and to "The Enterprise", a "private" group of its creation. Heading up this effort was Lieutenant Colonel Oliver North, a National Security Council staffer, retired Air Force Major General Richard Secord, and former CIA employee Felix Rodriguez, operating under the alias of Max Gomez. Casey put the three together; if his Contra program could not get around congressional obstructionists, then he would do an end run, enabling North to do so, with the CIA dovetailing their activities on the fringes.

The Reagan administration skirted the law and the intent of Congress through its interpretation that the National Security Council was not an intelligence agency and therefore not proscribed from assuming from the CIA the military support role to the Contras. North funded the operation through donations from foreign governments and private individuals. Government officials outside the National Security Council, notably State Department officials, assisted with fundraising from foreign governments. Casey played a key but shadowy role in drumming up funds for the Contras from his intelligence contacts around the globe, especially the Saudis. In 1984 and 1985, the Saudis contributed $32 million for the Contra program. Funds were channeled to the Contras by North through "The Enterprise".

Institutionally, the CIA was no longer directly supporting the military resupply effort, but not all activities in support of the Contras stopped. The CIA was authorized to conduct certain activities on the ground in Central America. Field officers had to navigate under unclear guidance on what was and was not permissible, forcing them to work in a very gray environment. It was not unusual for field officers to refer certain support requirement questions back to Capitol Hill to obtain validation. It is impossible to run an operation referring everything back up the chain for approval. So CIA field officers made many calls themselves. Given the knowledge that the DCI and the president were supportive of an activist program, line calls went in favor of action. Certain field officers crossed the line on their own accord, in order to do what they thought was wanted by their managers, and believing the activities were necessary and legitimate in the battle against the Communists.

While information on the National Security Council program was held tightly in Washington, in the field, among the players, it was not. Agency officers were instructed to give the North operation wide berth; but in reality, this was very difficult in the field because many of the Contra players were involved in both operations—that is, CIA and National Security Council initiatives. CIA leadership at Headquarters was knowledgeable of aspects of the National Security Council operation—especially the fact that "The Enterprise" took its orders from the National Security Council, with Oliver North being the first-line contact.

BEIRUT, LEBANON, 1984–85: Across the ocean, the United States had a different kind of a problem: terrorism. In 1984, seven Westerners, including two Americans, were kidnapped by Lebanese and Palestinian terror groups. One, William Buckley, was the CIA chief in Beirut. In 1985, four more Americans were kidnapped. The terrorists were not a motley group with an annoying kidnapping habit, they were a formidable threat to the U.S. government. In 1983, a car bomb blew up the U.S. embassy in West Beirut, killing 63 and wounding 120 people; more than a few among the dead were CIA officers. Six months later, a car bomb decimated the U.S. Marine headquarters at the Beirut airport, killing 241 Marines. The continued kidnappings and the inability of the U.S. government to free the hostages showed the situation was deteriorating.

Who was behind the bombing and kidnapping campaign? Imad Mughniyah of Hizballah, various Palestinian terrorists, al-Quds Forces (an Iranian intelligence group), and the Iranian Revolutionary Guard Corps (IRGC) were the names that surfaced most frequently. Despite significant U.S. government intelligence resources being transferred to collect against the threats emanating from the Baqaa Valley, the perpetrators remained elusive.

TEHRAN, IRAN, 1985: Even though the mullahs still held the upper hand, the U.S. hard-line policy of regime change and containment toward Iran, inaugurated after the 1979 Iranian revolution and the taking of U.S. diplomats as hostages, remained steadfast despite few signs of success in the intervening period. For a change, though, promising rays of light were coming from Tehran. Iranian "pragmatists" and "radicals" were engaged in a struggle for control. Ali Akbar Hashemi Rafsanjani, speaker of the Iranian Parliament, had recently emerged into the consciousness of the West. He was calling for an end to Iran's isolation from the world community and was working actively to improve Iran's image. He conducted a world tour and attempted to downplay Iran's participation in terrorism in hope of winning greater support for its position in the war with Iraq.[1]

More immediate to the United States, Rafsanjani had personally intervened in freeing hostages taken in the TWA 847 hijacking in June 1985. In one of the more bizarre hijackings, two Lebanese Shi'ites commandeered the flight shortly after takeoff from Athens, and over the next three days, the aircraft, with hostages aboard, shuttled back and forth between Beirut and Algiers, releasing some passengers at each stop. The hijackers executed Robert Dean Stethem, a twenty-three-year-old Navy frogman, in front of the other hostages and dumped his body on the Beirut tarmac. Thirty-nine hostages were held for seventeen days before being released in Beirut, with Iranian and Syrian help. The hijacking was prime-time news. Images of the pilot through the window of the cockpit with a gun to his head were engraved upon the collective memories of Americans. And when it was over, the hijackers held a press conference on network news, spouting their ideology, triumphing over the U.S. humiliation.

In 1985, the Reagan administration began to review its policy in light of internal Iranian developments, regional issues, and Cold War policies. At the center of the U.S. debate was the issue of Iranian support to terrorism, whether it had been static or declining, and what would be the likely future trend under a new, more pragmatic government. With the right incentives, would Iran really abandon its renegade behavior and want to rejoin the international community, or would it continue state-sponsored terrorism, albeit more clandestinely?

Iran remained embroiled in a costly war with Iraq—a war that would turn out to be the longest conventional war of the previous century, costing the belligerents millions of petrodollars and hundreds of thousands of lives—and the United States knew that Iran was in desperate need of military equipment. The United States was already deeply involved in providing weapons and other military support to Iraq while vigorously working the international community in various diplomatic initiatives to deny similar support to the Iranians.

Iran was also an important player in Lebanon and had influence—if not control—over Hizballah. American hostages continued to be held in Lebanon, many held by Hizballah, as pawns in the complex Lebanese/Israeli/U.S. political and military confrontation. To Reagan, the hostage issue was the most important aspect. He was rightly fixated on the release of the American hostages and could not understand why such a powerful country as the United States could not find and free them. The CIA was taking tremendous heat from Reagan on its inability to find the hostages.

Casey was not one to accept failure lightly. The hostage situation was personal for him. He and Buckley were buddies, and Casey probably felt some guilt at not being able to find and free him. A channel to Buckley's kidnappers indicated they were willing to trade Buckley for Mustafa Youssef Badreddin. Badreddin was one of the so-called Kuwait 17, seventeen people arrested and convicted by the Kuwaitis for the bombing of the American embassy in Kuwait in 1983. Badreddin was the brother-in-law of Imad Mughniyah, a Hizballah military leader and the suspected mastermind of the Lebanon kidnapping spree. The problem was that the U.S. government had a policy—often repeated—to not negotiate with terrorists. If a trade took place, the policy would be undermined and a dangerous precedent would be set. Knowing that Americans would be trade currency, terrorists would be motivated to increase kidnapping operations.

Casey was not just thinking about Buckley and Iranian terrorism; he was thinking about Communists. Casey requested a Special National Intelligence Estimate (SNIE), in which the intelligence community warned about increased Soviet influence in Iran. The SNIE recommended a new approach to Iranian policy, including improved Western relations, to cut out the Soviets, and an elimination of restrictions on weapons sales to Iran. Casey pushed for the SNIE to be adopted as a National Security Decision Directive— that is, new marching orders for the national security community. According to the report of the Independent Counsel for Iran-Contra, in the context of rethinking Iranian policy, the U.S. government approached the Israelis to share information on Iran. This started the Israeli wheels moving.

WASHINGTON, D.C., 1985: Summertime in Washington, a time when an oppressive humidity lulls life within the Beltway to a dull hum, is not usually a season for new initiatives. Yet, this is when the arms deal with Iran was born. David Kimche, a secretive figure within the Israeli intelligence world, approached administration officials with an outside-the-box proposal. He came with an offer to introduce U.S. officials to some "Iranian oppositionists" who wished support from the United States and proposed engineering the release of the American hostages as a demonstration of their bona fides. The initial proposal of a unilateral demonstration of goodwill evolved into a quid pro quo of the sale of arms in exchange for the release of hostages.

Whereas the Contra program was off-line, the debate of the merits of the arms-for-hostages proposal took place as regular business, with all the seniors of the national security team weighing in. There was disagreement, but in the end, no one was willing to go to the mat to stop the arms deal. The summertime heat must have dulled the wits of U.S. policymakers when it came to assessing the downside of this initiative. While stating publicly that the United States would never make concessions to terrorists nor supply weapons to a rogue Iranian regime, the United States took the first tentative steps in that same direction.

Casey was a strong supporter of the proposal, despite CIA Iranian analysts' assessments that there was no such thing as Iranian moderates when it came to policy toward the United States. These same experts also argued there had been no real indication that Iran was moving away from state-sponsored terrorism, and its support to terrorism continued, although more clandestinely. Casey minimized the "analytical voice" of the CIA by compartmentalizing the operation and not reading in CIA Iranian analysts. The assessments of CIA counterterrorism analysts were promoted instead, since they fit nicely with the view of the National Security Council—that is, that Iran was moderating its support for terrorism.

TEL AVIV, ISRAEL, 1985: The Israelis received the go-ahead from Washington in August, authorizing Israel to ship American-made TOW (Tube Launched, Optically Tracked, Wire Guided) missiles to Iran with guarantees the United States would replenish Israeli stocks. The first shipment of 96 TOWs took place on August 20. No hostages were released. The Israelis were not deterred, and neither was Oliver North, who had become point man for the operation. On September 14, another 408 TOWs arrived in Iran. The Israelis passed along the U.S. request that if only one hostage were to be freed, it had better be William Buckley, the CIA station chief. The CIA wanted its man out first to validate Iranian bona fides.

BEIRUT, LEBANON, 1985: On September 15, American hostage Reverend Benjamin Weir was released by his Beirut captors. The CIA did not know that Buckley had been dead for four months—it would be a long time before the CIA learned the horrific details of his capture, interrogation, and murder. The terrorists would eventually send an audiotape of Buckley's last moments, moaning in agony as he died from the injuries they had inflicted.

The release of a hostage was a bittersweet moment for the CIA and the U.S. government. Perhaps the arms sales were working and Buckley would be released next. Optimism about the new policy was difficult to maintain. Acts of terror continued to intrude the daily consciousness, not to mention the front page of the national papers.

MEDITERRANEAN SEA, OFF THE EGYPTIAN COAST, 1985: Less than a month after the release of Reverend Weir, on October 7, Palestinian terrorists hijacked the Italian cruise ship *Achille Lauro*, sailing in the Mediterranean. Abu Abbas, a leader of the Palestine Liberation Front, masterminded the hijacking. U.S. citizen Leon Klinghoffer, a sixty-nine-year-old wheelchair-bound passenger, was executed during the operation and his body was dumped in the water. The terrorists were sending a message that they were serious and not to be toyed with.

As the ship was in Egyptian waters, the Egyptians negotiated a safe passage agreement with the hijackers, agreeing to transport them to Tunisia in exchange for the release of the hostages. In a daring counterterrorism operation, a U.S. military jet intercepted Abu Abbas and his team after they fled, forcing their plane to divert from the planned landing in Tunisia to an American air base in Sicily. Abu Abbas was turned over to the Italian government for prosecution, but internal Italian politics led to his release. Abu Abbas fled to Iraq and hid out under the protection of Saddam Hussein, beyond the reach of the United States. At that moment in time, Saddam was considered a U.S. ally; his refusal to hand over Abu Abbas apparently was taken in stride given Saddam's larger contribution toward containing (and bleeding) the Iranians.

TEL AVIV, ISRAEL, 1985: Meanwhile, the Israelis prepared for a third shipment—this time eighty Hawk missiles. It was on this third shipment that the CIA became involved. The Israelis encountered problems with the transport logistics and called upon the United States for help. To mask point of origin, Israel wanted the shipment to appear to originate in Europe, not Tel Aviv. The European country in question—its identity remains classified—was not cooperating, and was asking probing questions about the nature of the cargo before granting landing/transfer permission. The "nudge-nudge, wink-wink" that it was U.S. goods did not cut it, and the European country demanded an official note from the United States as to the purpose. As the onward destination was Iran, North could hardly say it was a shipment of arms. The cat would be out of the bag.

North called upon the CIA to arrange flight clearances through its channels, believing that the CIA would be more effective than the Israelis. As is typical in tightly compartmentalized operations, the left hand did not know what the right hand was doing. The CIA official on the ground in Europe was told his assistance was not required. The Israeli craft was forced to abort the planned delivery with eighty Hawks on board and returned to Israel. With the possibility looming of Israel missing its deadline for delivery in Tehran, an urgent request for help went to the CIA.

According to the 1993 Final Report of the Independent Counsel for Iran-Contra, CIA Air Branch reportedly provided one of its proprietary aircrafts—a plane secretly owned by the CIA and operated by a CIA front company—to transport "oil drilling equipment" from Israel to Tehran. A fiasco from the beginning, the operation had a sour end as well. There were only eighteen missiles delivered, and they were not the type the Iranians were expecting. They wanted I-Hawks, capable of shooting down planes at high altitude. What they got were standard Hawks, with the Star of David branded on their casings. Pissed would be an understatement for the Iranian reactions.

No hostages were released. And the CIA had a problem, a big problem. It had used covert action resources to support the shipment, without the appropriate legal authorization from the U.S. president, called a "finding." According to the Hughes-Ryan Amendment, the CIA has to obtain a presidential finding and notify Congress in advance of undertaking cover action operations. While in exceptional circumstances notification can take place after the fact, a presidential finding cannot be retroactive. Because of the administration's determination not to notify Congress, the CIA would not have to admit its wrongdoing immediately.

So the cover-up began.

WASHINGTON, D.C., 1986: Having started down the road, despite the mixed results in freeing hostages and stopping terrorism, the Reagan administration decided to stay the course, but to do so with more control over the process. The arms sales continued, but with new procedures that included direct CIA operational support. To get around the legalities—as no one wanted to brief Congress and admit the administration was selling arms to a state sponsor of terrorism—the CIA purchased the weapons covertly from the Department of Defense and then sold them to the CIA-handpicked middleman, retired Air Force Major General Richard Secord, the same Secord involved in North's "Enterprise" and aid to the Contras. Secord transferred the weapons to Tel Aviv, and from there to Iran. Covering its tracks, the CIA requested and received a presidential finding authorizing its covert action role, including its "illegal" support for the November 1985 shipment.

In February, the CIA entered into a direct negotiating role with the Iranians—significantly deepening the CIA role with the hopes of exerting better operational control. The CIA did not want to deal with Manucher Ghorbanifar, one of the Iranian intermediaries, because of past negative experiences with him. In fact, the CIA had issued a "burn notice" on Ghorbanifar—a notice to all field stations and some friendly liaison services stating that he was a fabricator and not to be trusted. CIA objections to Ghorbanifar would be overruled. A similar burn notice would go out on Ahmed Chalabi many years later, which, too, would be ordered ignored by the politicians—but that is another story.

A retired case officer, George Cave, was brought back from retirement to handle the negotiations and arms sales on behalf of the CIA. Cave, a senior officer, had extensive experience on Iran and spoke Farsi. Within the CIA, the operation was tightly held—run out of a vault away from other Iranian operations. Cave, Duane Clarridge and Clair George, and of course Casey, were the primary actors in the supersecret operation.

On February 18 a shipment of five hundred TOW missiles was delivered, and seventeen of the eighteen Star of David Hawks were backhauled. What happened to the other? Perhaps it had been used in a test fire. Perhaps it had been shipped to a lab for reverse engineering. No one seemed too concerned with this detail. A few days later, on February 27, an additional five hundred TOWs were delivered.

No hostages were released. Sucked in by Ghorbanifar's unending promises and the desperate hope that with a sufficiently sweet deal, the Iranians would produce and the hostages would be freed, the United States decided to press ahead. A delegation, headed by Robert McFarlane, flew to Tehran on May 25, carrying a belly load of Hawk spare parts. The deal offered was more Hawk spare parts, currently sitting in Israel, which would be shipped when the hostages were released. The delegation left with an empty belly load and a pit in their stomachs. The Iranians had only excuses.

Then negotiations turned ugly. The United States was pissed that the Iranians once again failed to deliver. The Iranians were pissed because they just learned they had paid up to six times the list price for the

TOWs and Hawk spare parts they had received. The United States decided to play hardball and refused to meet with the Iranians until more hostages were released.

BEIRUT, LEBANON, 1986: Father Lawrence Jenco was finally released by his captors on July 24, but the other hostages remained captive. Still, the United States decided to resume negotiations; no stone must be left unturned, it was thought. The myth of progress was shattered, however, when Frank Reed and Joseph Cicippio were kidnapped in September. The scoreboard was tied: two hostages released, two taken.

The program was not working as planned. Rather than cut their losses, the administration decided the problem was the channel—Ghorbanifar—not the concept. The day after Reed was taken hostage, the United States opened a second channel through a nephew of Rafsanjani. On October 28, an additional five hundred TOW missiles were delivered to Iran. On November 2, David Jacobsen was released.

Then all hell let loose.

SOUTHERN NICARAGUA, 1986: The C-123K was part of the accelerated resupply push for the late summer. Crews were making more sorties into both northern and southern Nicaragua, dropping food, supplies, and arms. On October 5, a cargo plane was loaded with lethal supplies when it took ground fire. As the craft was going down, one passenger jumped out and deployed his parachute successfully. The other two did not survive the crash. Eugene Hasenfus, the cargo kicker, found he had company in the jungle. The Sandinistas had discovered "The Enterprise" air routes from Ilopango air base to their drop sites and had prepositioned themselves with radar and antiaircraft. They captured Hasenfus and walked him out of the jungle, tethered in a noose. Then they interrogated him.

Hasenfus admitted he worked for the CIA resupplying the Contras. He named names and locations for their operations. In particular, he identified a "Max Gomez" as being the CIA man in charge of food, lodging, and their services for the operation's pilots and crews at Ilopango air base. The Sandinistas had caught the CIA's hand in the cookie jar.

In testimony before Congress, the CIA quickly denied that Hasenfus was a CIA employee. Technically, he was not. He was one of the guys living in the gray area. They also denied knowing who "Max Gomez" was and what private entity was behind the resupply effort. So began the false testimony.

BEIRUT, LEBANON, 1986: The Lebanese magazine *al-Shiraa* had a hot scoop. A source told their reporter about a secret visit to Iran by five American government officials. According to the magazine, the group, led by former National Security Council chief Robert McFarlane, had visited to arrange a deal to sell military hardware to Iran in exchange for Iranian cooperation in releasing U.S. hostages held in Lebanon. *Al-Shiraa* published the story on November 3.

The U.S. media picked up on the story. President Reagan quickly denied any involvement in the arms sales. After one week of failed damage control, the administration admitted that the U.S. government had entered an "arms-for-hostages" deal.

Who leaked the story to *al-Shiraa?* The speculation was that the Iranians did, to show their displeasure and to get them out of keeping their side of the obligation. Questions on the source of the leak quickly became irrelevant once Rafsanjani acknowledged the McFarlane visit.

The linkage of the two operations—aid to the Contras and the arms-for-hostages deal—took place through a back-channel funding scheme devised by Oliver North, illegally diverting millions of dollars in Iran arms-sale profits to the Contras. The diversion took place with the knowledge of senior CIA officers. While the knowledge was not complete, the CIA knew North was charging the Iranians far more than the CIA purchase price from the military. North had made repeated references to a reserve. By early October, CIA officers began expressing concern that there had been a diversion of profits to the Contras. CIA senior management, including Casey, his deputy Robert Gates, George, and Clarridge, were advised of the concerns. But CIA management took no action to report these concerns to appropriate authorities.

Efforts to cover up the story proved impossible. As a desperate act of damage control, on November 25, President Reagan and Attorney General Meese held a nationally televised press conference and disclosed the diversion. It was announced that those responsible for the breach of U.S. law had resigned or been reassigned.

SEVENTH FLOOR, LANGLEY, VIRGINIA, 1986: Casey had been behaving strangely for a month—strange even for Casey, recalled James McCullough, then-director of the Executive Staff. Casey was under tremendous pressure. Attacks were coming from Congress, the politicos, and the public, questioning his and the CIA's role in the Iran and Contra operations. Everyone was ducking for cover and not cooperating with the official investigation. The Reagan administration invoked the circuit-breaker mechanism, declaring that the president had no knowledge of the affair. Casey, who had always thrived in the heat of the battle, had lost his usual combativeness and seemed—well, tired.

Casey's testimony before Congress on November 21 had not gone too badly, considering that Casey had to admit to failing to comply with the Hughes-Ryan Amendment. He read his testimony blandly, mumbling through much of it, as was his wont. Casey thought the matter was over, all questions on the Iran operation answered—case closed, or so he told the entire leadership of the U.S. intelligence community that had assembled at a CIA training installation for a prescheduled management conference on November 23.

Casey's optimism seemed odd, given that his testimony had provoked a small storm among administration officials, with some accusing Casey of having intended to give—or indeed have given—false testimony in order to protect the National Security Council, specifically, Oliver North's role in the 1985 shipment of missiles. Casey did have a problem: the CIA had provided North assistance, at North's asking, without a presidential finding. How could he demonstrate that the role of the CIA was small, that they were sucked into it during a crisis, without placing blame on the National Security Council?

North was trying to distance himself from the missile deal, no doubt because he feared the other shoe would drop. When it did, everyone forgot about the illegal missile shipment and focused upon the larger illegality and the cover-up.

When Meese announced that some of the proceeds from the Iran arms sales had been diverted illegally to the Contras, the spotlight again focused on Casey. Why had Casey not mentioned it in his testimony four days earlier? The assumption was that Casey and the CIA had known and approved of the diversion scheme.

Casey had no opportunity to address these accusations. Although he was scheduled to testify before the Senate Select Committee on Intelligence on December 16, fate prevented him from doing so. The day before, an exhausted and gaunt Casey showed up for work, not in his normal uniform of a conservative suit and tie but in a sweater in lieu of a coat, according to James McCullough. Some of the old Casey was there, but not much. When given his draft testimony to review, he once again refused to apologize to Congress for omitting the diversion details in his prior testimony. It would be his last jab at Congress. Shortly thereafter, Casey was taken out of his office on a stretcher. The Georgetown University Hospital diagnosis came quickly: a malignant brain tumor. A very controversial figure passed away quietly in May 1987.[2]

The Iran-Contra scandal, as it became known, did not pass quietly, despite a continuing belief within the CIA that it would. The resulting investigations, public testimony, legal action, and press exposés, subjected the CIA and covert action policy to scrutiny to the nth degree. CIA officials were called to testify before intelligence oversight and investigative committees. The officials decided to do damage control by adhering to the cover story that the military resupply effort for the Contras was a private endeavor and that there was no CIA institutional involvement. They confirmed CIA support for the arms deals to Iran, citing the presidential finding.

The initial statements by Deputy Director of Operations Clair George and CIA Central American Task Force chief Alan Fiers were crafted in language that was technically correct, within the most limited reading, but misleading. The intent was to present the actions of the CIA as legal and to not steer the line of inquiry to either the National Security Council or the White House. Subsequent testimony evolved into outright lying. The truth had been splintered too much and there was no way out except to cover half-lies with new lies.

Because Congress had already established a track record of not vigorously investigating rumors of U.S. government support for the Contras, the CIA expected Congress to make surface inquiries but then drop the matter in due course, accepting the plausible deniability tactic for the good of the nation engaged in the Cold War. In the perverse in-house humor of the Director of Operations, while the Deputy Director of Operations was on the Hill testifying before Congress, disclaiming any knowledge "other than what is in the press" about former CIA officer Felix Rodriguez, operating under the alias of Max Gomez, Directorate of Operations officers in the know were sporting buttons saying, "Who is Max Gomez?" "I Am Maximo Gomez." The prevailing wisdom was that the storm would be weathered and all could go on to the more important task at hand: winning the Cold War.

The decision by the attorney general to appoint an independent counsel in December should have been sufficient warning to the CIA that the controversy was not just going to die on the vine. It was no longer a matter of congressional ire, but a full-blown criminal investigation. U.S. laws had been broken. The Constitution had been willfully subverted.

Casey died at an unfortunate time for the CIA, just as the Iran-Contra storm was brewing. There are many within the CIA who were certain if Casey had remained at the helm, he would have led the CIA through the troubled waters to bureaucratic safety. As a part of the old-boy network, he would have been protected and would have protected his own. Casey had clarity of mission and the personality to force his interpretation of mission down the throats of others, Congress included. As with great legends, the inconvenient negative parts were quickly forgotten, and Casey became the formidable icon against which we measured the following DCIs. Not surprisingly, the next few DCIs did not measure up.

SEVENTH FLOOR, LANGLEY, VIRGINIA, 1987: It was a difficult period when Judge William Webster assumed the helm of the CIA in May. Public congressional hearings were scheduled to start in two weeks. National Security Advisor John Poindexter and Oliver North would shortly be granted immunity and were scheduled to testify in public. The CIA was in crisis management mode. The web of half-truths spun by Clair George and Alan Fiers would begin to unravel. It would be clear that CIA officials had broken the law, were not cooperative with the congressional investigation, and had indeed given false statements while briefing intelligence oversight committees and during formal hearings. Webster quickly found that the scope of the CIA's problems was not limited to a handful of officers, but to an unusual culture within the Directorate of Operations.

3
Directorate of Operations

SACRAMENTO, CALIFORNIA, 1986: I confess that I joined the CIA as a result of a sudden opportunity rather than a burning desire to work in the secret world of spies. I had graduated from the University of California–Berkeley in 1983 with an undergraduate degree in Near Eastern Studies. My academic fascination with biblical and Egyptian archaeology, where I learned Arabic along with three ancient (read, dead) languages, was difficult to translate into a job, let alone a career, despite earning the highest blue ribbon of *summa cum laude*. I took whatever opportunities came my way.

In the summer of 1985, I went to northern Israel to work at the archaeological site Tel Dor. It was a long, hot summer in the trenches. I dedicated myself to what I thought was my calling, all while Israeli gunships buzzed overhead on their daily runs to and from Lebanon to lay waste to Hizballah fighters. I had one of those clarifying moments in life that summer. I realized I had no desire to spend the rest of my days digging in dirt, and I yearned to know more about the current conflict in the Middle East.

I also had something odd happen to me while in northern Israel. On the site, there were staff archaeologists who stayed the entire season and volunteer archaeologists who worked for shorter periods. I was an in-betweener—a volunteer who stayed the entire season. One day, I found I had a new bunkmate, a Frenchwoman. As there were few women working at the site, I was thrilled to have a bit of female companionship, plus the opportunity to practice my French. However, Frédérique was totally uninterested in associating with me; in fact, she seemed uninterested in digging as well—odd for a volunteer.

Several weeks later, Frédérique made a sudden departure. Shortly thereafter, our camp was crawling with Israeli security officers asking questions about this mysterious woman. We had little to say, since she had kept to herself. It turned out—and this I only learned later through press reports—that Frédérique was an agent of the French Secret Service, and she had been on a mission. Frédérique was part of the cell that executed the bombing of the Greenpeace ship, the *Rainbow Warrior*.

Frédérique, whose real name was Christine Cabon, had infiltrated the Auckland Greenpeace office, collecting intelligence on Greenpeace's plans to stop French nuclear testing at the Moruroa atoll in the South Pacific. After passing the intelligence to her handlers, Frédérique cleared out of the operational area—no doubt so that she would not be wrapped up if the operation failed or was exposed after the fact. Frédérique traveled to Israel and shared my camp quarters as French commandos planted explosives on the exterior hull of the *Rainbow Warrior*, scuttling the vessel on September 10, 1985. Fernando Pereira, the crew photographer and father of two young children, died in the attack.

The brush with the clandestine world made a subtle impression upon me that would come into play later. The more immediate influence was my growing interest in modern-day issues of the Middle East. I returned to the States and started taking graduate classes in international relations at night at California State University–Sacramento (CSUS). While at CSUS, my economics professor drew my attention to a recruiting poster for the CIA, suggesting it might be an interesting opportunity for a young Arabic-speaking graduate in search of a career. I took his advice and applied. Was the professor a spotter? Heck, I don't know. At the time, I did not know what a spotter was, or that the CIA recruited people by finding them rather than the other way around.

In 1985, the CIA was offering internships to graduate students planning to matriculate within one year. I was looking for a job and experience in something relevant to this century. I took their screening exam. By the end of the full day of testing, with hundreds of questions to flesh out my psychological profile and aptitudes, I simply did not know if I'd rather drive a fire truck or read a good book. I knew I loved my mother, but could no longer articulate why. My brain was scrambled. However, some of the questions captured my imagination and stayed with me over the years. For example, one question gave me a scenario that I was a cat burglar working a second-story job. I could take ten things with me on the job; what would they be? Yes, I had fun with these questions; I also just skipped over the math portion—if the CIA wanted a number cruncher, I was not their woman.

My responses must have met the minimum, and I was invited to Washington for more testing and interviews. I went and threw myself into the process. The remarkable thing was that I had no clue about the type of job for which the Agency was considering me. When one recruiter worried that I might be a "square peg trying to fit into a round hole," I insisted that I was not. In retrospect, I am amazed by my naïveté and willingness to throw myself into the great unknown. The job title "Case Officer" meant nothing to me, nor was it described in any detail because of secrecy requirements. What I liked was the description of the Directorate of Operations, living a life of adventure and intrigue overseas. I had romantic images of Frédérique, posing as an archaeologist by day while stealing secrets by night. I was assured by the recruiter that acceptance to the internship program meant smooth sailing into a thirty-year career of living life on the edge.

In the winter, the CIA called with a job offer—a dream job for a dreamer. I turned it down. By then, I had a better offer.

In the fall of 1987, I entered the graduate program at the School of International and Public Affairs at Columbia University. You see, I had come from a middle-class family. My parents, divorced since I was a wee baby, instilled a drive in me to aim high, work hard, and to not be put off by obstacles. My father in particular encouraged me to get a good education. His idea of a good education was an Ivy League school, if not his own alma mater, Harvard, then Columbia. He saw the Ivy League as a union card to greater opportunities. Without telling him or anyone else in the family that I had a choice to make, I pondered my destiny. I elected to take my father's advice, gambling that the CIA would wait. The recruiter was not pleased with me, telling me it was a one-shot opportunity—now or never.

As I was intent upon getting what I wanted—probably a trait that defines me best (my husband would call it sheer stubbornness, while I prefer the word "perseverance"—I kept in frequent contact with my recruiter, updating her on my studies and how the additional education only added to my credentials as an Arabist. Arabists were rare breeds in those days, as they are now. There were few individuals who could claim an in-depth knowledge of the culture, traditions, religion, and language of the Middle East. My self-promotion paid off. I joined the Agency in the summer of 1988 and then promptly went on leave to finish my graduate degree.

It was with great secrecy that I entered my life at the CIA. Secrecy would become a central theme from then on. My husband, Dick, and

I were married in a secret ceremony on Saint Patrick's Day in 1989. He needed to get his security clearance in process so that we would not be held up in our overseas processing; the obstacle was tying the knot officially. (Dad, please forgive us this minor charade. The big wedding before family and friends was in no way diminished by the technicality that we were already married.)

What I did not appreciate fully about my new career was how secrecy would totally permeate my life. Once inside the Agency, I learned just what a case officer did and just how the Director of Operations accomplished its business.

OLD HEADQUARTERS BUILDING, LANGLEY, VIRGINIA, 1987: Like me, before Webster arrived at the CIA, he knew little about the Directorate of Operations. This part of the Agency is shrouded in mystique and misunderstanding. In many ways, the Agency promotes misunderstanding by refusing to comment publicly on Directorate of Operations activities or to correct the public record on many flawed stories circulating about specific clandestine activities. This is due to the culture of secrecy, which is especially strong in the Directorate of Operations.

The reason for the secrecy, I quickly learned, is the protection of the directorate's human and technical sources and collection methods. Also, the mystique provides operational advantages in the field. The CIA has a reputation overseas of being all-powerful and all-knowing, as a benevolent party, or as a hostile force, or somewhere in between, depending upon where you are and with whom you are dealing. We field officers learned to use this amorphous image to our advantage to achieve our mission.

As Webster quickly learned, as did all previous and subsequent DCIs, the Clandestine Service, as the directorate is also called, is the source of most of the intelligence "flaps" within the Agency—and within the intelligence community, for that matter. The Directorate of Operations is the overseas arm of the Agency. Clandestine operators break the laws of foreign countries and, when caught, there is usually political blowback. Ambassadors are called in and read the riot act ("demarched," in diplomatic terminology). Sometimes there is a public airing of accusations and denials. Whether guilty or not, one always denies—even if caught in the very act. Sometimes, there are expulsions of spies-cum-diplomats in a tit-for-tat cycle. Political relations, joint programs, cultural exchanges are frozen, canceled or whatever, to the consternation of policymakers, who generally find these situations embarrassing, ill-timed, and/or ill-conceived.

The blowback is not all political, but personal as well. The operations officer faces consequences at the hands of the foreign government, including being arrested, roughed up, interrogated, and hopefully thrown out or declared "*persona non grata*" (PNG'ed) fairly quickly. In the 1990s, most countries around the globe operated by "gentlemen's rules," which include not killing each other's operatives and releasing them after making the political point. This has not always been the case, as there have been more than a few CIA employees who wasted away in foreign prisons, subjected to inhumane treatment over prolonged periods. There are a few stars on the CIA Memorial Wall that pay silent homage to my colleagues who died in foreign prisons or at the hands of criminal elements. Terrorists, drug traffickers, and international criminal syndicates, needless to say, do not play by gentlemen's rules. Ask William Buckley.

Because the Directorate of Operations walks on the dark side, breaking laws, keeping in the shadows, Americans tend to be both intrigued by what the officers do and suspicious of their ethics. Policymakers continue to support the existence of the Clandestine Service, despite the flaps, because it provides a disproportionate amount of intelligence of critical value to meet national-level intelligence requirements. Incoming presidents quickly learned about and grew to depend on the Clandestine Service as a presidential action arm in executing foreign policy.

The Directorate of Operations that Webster took over was almost fossilized in terms of structure and tradition. It was run by Cold War warriors, the good-old-boy network that earned their spurs fighting the Communists. Its mission had remained virtually unchanged for forty years.

The core mission of the Directorate of Operations is the clandestine collection of human intelligence (HUMINT)—in other words, the primary source of the intelligence is a person or persons. The directorate does that by recruiting, handling, and debriefing agents with access to intelligence. This was my job as a case officer—or as it is called now, an operations officer. The directorate will use technical means of collection that are facilitated by human sources, such as audio operations and telephone taps (bugs) planted in target locations. Officers break into or otherwise gain access to the contents of secured facilities, safes, and computers; we steal, compromise, and diddle foreign cryptographic capabilities in order to make them exploitable by U.S. agencies that collect signals intelligence. We will also work with foreign intelligence agencies to run all types of operations. The directorate protects its operations and defends the government from other intelligence services by engaging in counterespionage activities, including the aggressive use of double agents and penetrations of foreign services. We secretly emplace and service sensors that collect signals intelligence (SIGINT) and measurement and signatures intelligence (MASINT)—the telltale emissions spewed by communication transmissions and nuclear and chemical materials. The information that is of intelligence value is put into raw intelligence reports that are disseminated to designated consumers.

Intelligence is divided into two broad categories: foreign intelligence and counterintelligence. Foreign intelligence includes—but is not limited to—plans, intentions, and capabilities of foreign governments and organizations that are hostile to the United States or that pose some kind of threat to national security. Classic foreign-intelligence topics are Russian's weapons of mass destruction development programs, political and military developments in China, and terrorist operational planning. Foreign intelligence collection priorities change in response to consumer requirements. At the beginning of the 1990s, the directorate's collection requirements were guided by the Cold War.

Counterintelligence is information on what foreign governments and organizations are doing against the United States, such as plans and operations to compromise U.S. national security through espionage, "double-agent" operations, sabotage, and information warfare. The Agency spends considerable resources on counterintelligence and counterespionage operations and countermeasures. There is more to the subject than ferreting out "moles," or penetrations of U.S. government agencies, although these cases receive a lot of public attention. The meat-and-potatoes of counterintelligence work is the recruiting of foreign intelligence officers, collection of intelligence on operational methods of foreign services, and the protection of Agency operational methods and U.S. government secrets. Every field station has counterintelligence on its Operating Directive, which are the written marching orders that guide and prioritize all station operational activities.

It is the counterintelligence cases—spy versus spy—about which we operations officers really get excited. Working against a Russian or Chinese intelligence officer is about as challenging as it can get. In an elaborate fencing match, each professional spars with the other, probing vulnerabilities, countering intellectual arguments and ideological premises, assessing whether the other is a good recruitment target. A recruitment approach (also called a "pitch") to an unwilling candidate can lead to embarrassing diplomatic "flaps," increased harassment in the country of the target's origin—or, worse yet, a counterrecruitment pitch from the intelligence officer. The counterintelligence operations that I ran were by far the most exciting and challenging parts of my operational career. These are also the ones that are the most highly classified—the ones the CIA would never permit me to describe, except in the vaguest of terms.

Counterintelligence operations are a real wilderness of mirrors. Nothing is as it seems. The last thing an operations officer wants is to be pitched by a foreign intelligence officer. Office of Security will suspect the worst. The presumption is that you were pitched because you were vulnerable to recruitment, regardless of the fact that the pitch was declined and reported to security. If an operations officer pitches a foreign intelligence officer and he agrees without first presenting a litany of objections or reservations, then the foreign intelligence officer is presumed a "dangle." The CIA will spend the next umpteen years testing the source to disprove the assumption the operation was controlled by the foreign intelligence service from the very beginning.

Proponents of the spy versus spy game note the operational windfall resulting from significant recruitments of foreign intelligence officers. Opponents criticize it as an egotistical mind game and waste of resources, because the fruits of the game are usually limited to operational issues, not foreign intelligence useful to the policymaker. Yes, but I must say it is fun. It is the stuff of Tom Clancy novels.

In addition to collecting intelligence, the Directorate of Operations is also charged with conducting covert action on behalf of the U.S. president. Covert action operations are normally well-guarded secrets within the Agency, rarely discussed in detail in public. Covert action is the most politically sensitive of all CIA activities, because it involves taking action that may be acceptable to the serving U.S. president but not to future presidents, Congress, or the general public. The presidential finding authorizing the covert action often is written in fuzzy terms to give the president future political deniability.

In conducting covert action (and foreign intelligence) activities, the directorate uses methods that are not generally acceptable within the framework of American society. We steal secrets by bribing foreign officials. We overthrow foreign governments hostile to the United States by funding, training, and arming insurgency groups. The directorate also thwarts radical leftist groups by funding, training, and arming foreign government paramilitary groups. We frequently form relationships with less-than-respectable people to do less-than-respectable things. Although Americans accommodate the existence of the Clandestine Service for the sake of national security, there are always concerns, just below the surface (or sometimes above), that the CIA might employ these "dirty-trick" methods at home, against American citizens.

Directorate of Operations recruits go though paramilitary training on air, land, and sea operations to learn such basic skills as weapons handling, navigation, and survival. I was taught to parachute, sling cargo, set up landing zones, conduct ambushes, and navigate by compass or landmark through the swamps of the tidewaters. The understanding was that at some point in my career, I might need to "bug out" of a country being overrun by hostile forces, or use a weapon in a hostile environment, or provide ground support to a military effort.

Being prepared was a basic teaching point that I took to heart. I remember when I first arrived at a new assignment in a Persian Gulf country—the CIA would prefer that I not say specifically where—shortly after the Gulf War. I was given a bug-out kit during my first day in the office. That night I unpacked it in my temporary quarters. It was a large backpack full of the usual stuff: flashlight, flare, emergency medical kit, MREs, shortwave radio, a compass, and maps. I unfolded the maps for familiarization. One was a map of the waterways in case I opted to bug out by boat. The other confused me because I did not immediately find an easy reference point. When my eyes focused upon the city of Bandar Abbas, I realized I had a land map of Iran. After pondering the likelihood of my choosing to bug out through Iran—a country where I definitely would not have been welcome—the next day I asked that Headquarters provide alternative maps.

All Directorate of Operations officers, at multiple points in their careers, will work on covert action programs; there is not a special category of officers designated to covert action only. The goal was to familiarize in order to prepare for eventualities, as opposed to create paramilitary officers out of all recruits. Paramilitary officers are a specially designated career track within the Directorate of Operations, trained specifically in paramilitary skills. Career paramilitary officers would go through more extensive training, versus familiarization; invariably, they are recruited out of the U.S. military.

Frequently, covert action programs are controversial or become controversial at a later date. Many of the biggest scandals leading to public criticism of the CIA have been caused by covert action activities, Iran-Contra being a good case in point. I used to joke with my colleagues that it would simplify matters if at the time we were assigned to a covert action program, the letter of reprimand should accompany the orders, as receipt of one seemed inevitable.

When Webster arrived, the Directorate of Operations was organized primarily in geographical line divisions, as it had been the decades previously. The world was divided up into regions: Africa, Middle East and Southeast Asia, Asia, Soviet and Eastern Europe, Europe, and Latin America, National Collection and Foreign Resources. The CIA was a worldwide organization, with a physical presence in capitals and key urban centers around the globe. The division chiefs, who called themselves "the Barons," treated their areas as their own personal fiefdoms and, when united, laid claim to more raw power than the DCI could ever claim. The chief Baron was the Deputy Director of Operations, the DDO.

Webster would introduce a new challenge to the Barons by the creation of interdisciplinary centers focused on issues. It was not a brand-new concept; Casey had created the Counterterrorism Center in 1986. Webster established the Counterintelligence Center, the Counter Proliferation Center, and began the bureaucratic process that led to the Counter Narcotics Center, which was formally stood up one month after his departure from the CIA. Not only did Webster take authority and responsibility away from the Barons, but he also took their funding and their personnel slots.

The geographical divisions and the issue centers would maintain a competitive relationship through the decade, but with the Barons keeping the upper hand. The Barons held the trump cards of controlling the field chiefs down to the lowly junior officer. We knew who controlled the assignments and the promotions: the Barons. When considering a choice between joining Near East Division or the Counterterrorism Center after completing my operational training, I was advised to select a geographical division if I had any aspirations for advancement.

If Webster found the Directorate of Operations structure difficult to change, he found a culture that was even more deeply entrenched. The culture had evolved because of the unique requirements of the work. Directorate of Operations officers are known for their flexibility, adaptability, and creativity, and their ability to lie. They are required to make decisions, based on knowledge and instincts, frequently without consulting others. When a field officer is out meeting with an agent, things happen requiring immediate response. Once operational, the field officer cannot "call home" and consult. Good judgment and confidence are required.

Mary, a colleague of mine at the Recruitment Center, used to tell job applicants a personal story to illustrate the point. She had a hotel meeting with an agent in a Latin American country. She walked into the hotel, wearing a business suit and carrying a briefcase, proceeding immediately to the elevator banks. As she waited for the elevator, there was a tap on her shoulder. She turned to discover hotel security. "Madam, are you staying at the hotel?" he asked politely. "No," she said, she was visiting a friend. "What is the name and room number of your friend?" Hmm, a persistent security officer. Mary knew that she had trouble, that she had been mistaken for a prostitute, despite her attire. In that particular country, there were few female businesswomen, and prostitution in hotels was common.

Mary provided a name and room number, which she made up off the top of her head. But then the security officer insisted on accompanying her to the room. Confidently, she agreed, and they rode the elevator together. She knocked on the room door, but no one answered. Relieved, she suggested that perhaps there was a mix-up with the room number. The security officer was not to be deterred and insisted on accompanying her down to the registration desk to check on the proper room. In the short elevator ride down, she quickly put together a new plan.

At the registration desk, Mary looked directly into the eyes of the young man working there, explaining she was here to meet her friend, but that the security officer had "some concerns." Her sweet smile and inquiring eyes masked the intense scenario gaming taking place in her mind at warp speed preparing her for all possible developments. The young man quickly checked the registration book and looked up with a serious expression on his face. "I'm sorry, but your friend has just checked out." Looking a bit embarrassed, the security officer excused himself. The young man smiled and wished Mary a nice day.

Mary exited the area, meeting aborted. While she conducted a surveillance detection run to check for hostile surveillance, she pondered what just happened. She had no need to use her improvised cover story—that she must have the wrong hotel—because the hotel detective did not say the expected—that is, that there was no one at the hotel with that name. Perhaps he also assumed she was a prostitute, and he did not want to jeopardize the kickbacks he received in brokering sexual services. Perhaps. She would never know. She would never use that hotel again. Nevertheless, being mistaken for a prostitute is far better than being suspected as a spy. Nerves of steel and a quick mind are the basic ingredients for a good operations officer.

The culture of the Directorate of Operations has been designated the cause of the directorate's failings and at the same time the basis for its successes. I believe there is truth in both. The culture fosters a worldview of ambiguity and situational ethics, where issues have various shades of gray rather than a black-and-white dichotomy. Truth, right and wrong, come in layers rather than finite blocks. It is a culture that provides the president with a flexible action arm—in other words, people who are willing to deploy at a moment's notice and undertake dangerous and risky missions. It is also a culture that breeds intense loyalty to mission, Agency, and commander in chief that encourages a deep-seated belief that overall mission requirements sometimes necessitate action beyond the limits of the law and norms of American society.

The Directorate of Operations is an elitist organization. From the moment of entering on duty, I was told (indoctrinated) that I had been admitted to an elite group, the best of the best. Operations officers held themselves a cut above the rest of the organization because of the difficulty of the job and the critical nature of the mission. Part of this is a legacy of the Office of Strategic Services days, where the battle was fought and won on the front lines. Officers are so focused on mission achievement that personal sacrifice to achieve mission is an expected standard. The personal sacrifices range from working extended hours and weeks without extra compensation, to long absences away from the family, to working in dangerous situations. Training reinforced this message, from the 24/7 training schedule to the high performance standards.

The time requirement was no exaggeration. During my time overseas, I worked day and night, often seven days a week. Family life had to be integrated into operational life if you had any hope of staying married, raising a family, and remaining overseas in operational positions. It would become so natural that I did not question it even in the most extreme circumstances. For example, while I was in labor delivering my first baby (the CIA has no maternity leave), I fielded calls on threat information from U.S. Secret Service agents who were in the country preparing for the visit of President Clinton to Gaza and Bethlehem. My baby was not one day old before I was back to holding security meetings to ensure a safe and successful presidential visit.

The CIA has one of the most intensive training programs in the world. When I entered on duty, the Career Training (CT) program (which is now called the Clandestine Service Training program) was [*number of months censored by the CIA*] long. My CT class was the last of the large classes, as the new-hire program all but disappeared in the decade that followed as a result of the post—Cold War demobilization. We were a proud group, young, smart, confident, and ambitious to make our mark, serve our country, and live a life of danger and intrigue.

The CIA put us baby spooks through the training wringer to make sure we had the right stuff. After a six-week orientation—death-by-wiring-diagram, we called it—the fun stuff began. The operations officers went through intensive operational training. We were told to forget about our families for months on end as we were whisked off to the "Farm," a "black" training facility, and taught the secret tradecraft of espionage. Months were spent on refining our ability to recruit agents, detect surveillance, and master clandestine communications methods. We spent days and nights on the streets of America practicing our skills. In our final exercise, we were put up against the FBI. With surveillance nipping at our heels, our instructors pulled all the tricks on us, testing our ability to think on our feet to deal with an "agent-candidate" going crazy in a public place after you pitched him—screaming, "You want me to be a SPY?!?" as Middle America looked on. Let me say there is nothing like the feeling of the FBI swarming around you, being thrown up against a car, and frisked as a prelude to a barrage of questions designed to break down your story and expose you for what you really are.

Operational training was the main part, but, as mentioned earlier, I also went through paramilitary training. Training segments were broken up with interim working assignments at CIA Headquarters. I lucked out with two great interim assignments: one working on Persian Gulf issues and the other in the Counterterrorism Center, working against radical Palestinian groups. All the while, we were drilled with the messages of institutional loyalty, secrecy, and excellence.

The term "needs of the service" has such cultural weight in the Directorate of Operations that few officers will ever question the call to service or sacrifice. The pay scale for the directorate lagged behind that of the others (and private industry) because officers are not the type to complain. Taking vacation—especially when overseas—is frequently discouraged. Most officers routinely exceed the number of leave hours they are allowed to carry over to the next year and are forced to forfeit the leave or donate it to the Medical Leave Bank once it was created in the mid-1990s.*

The mentality is that the officer's role is so critical that he or she cannot be spared for personal time off. There has just been a crisis, there is an ongoing crisis, or there is a threat of imminent crisis, any of which

---

* The Medical Leave Bank is a program that allows government officials to donate hours of annual leave (vacation time) to other officers who have long-term illnesses or family members with illnesses and have exhausted their own accrued sick leave.

might require all hands on deck, or so the thinking goes. Mission achievement might suffer. Those officers who could not or would not accept the expected routine and mind-set did not survive long in the directorate. Ten percent of my CT class did not make it through training. Those who did, like me, served with a minimum of complaints and felt personally fulfilled in their self-sacrifices.

As a result of this elitist self-identification, there is strong comradeship among officers. The system feeds upon itself, creating "true believers." Those who leave the service, and with the passage of time and distance become nonbelievers, are often surprised by the sheer intensity of the culture they left behind. I found that the culture truly enveloped me to the extent that the world outside-looking-in was very different than the world inside-looking-out.

While the CIA is a secret organization, the Directorate of Operations is the heart of secrecy. From the moment of the first interview, secrecy is inculcated into the recruit. Recruits are told that their discretion during the interviewing process will be assessed as part of their suitability for employment. The not-so-subtle warning is there: talk about the Agency as an applicant, and you will be disqualified. During the polygraph, applicants are questioned on who they have told about the application and why. At one time, Agency officers were forbidden to tell their spouses about the identity of their true employer. Times have changed, and the realization that secrets of such depth destroy marriages and render operatives less effective made the Agency change its policies. Now recruits are required to tell their spouses about their employment with the Agency, but not about the specifics of their work.

When I joined, I told only my husband-to-be. Just before going overseas, I told my father—who was totally thrilled by my career choice. I did not tell my mother, because I suspected she would never again sleep. When I did tell her—only after I left the Agency—the look on her face confirmed to me that I had made the right decision.

To the operations officer, guarding secrets means guarding lives—not only his or her life, but the lives of sources and colleagues. Officers are told that protection of sources and methods is the number-one priority, not the collection of intelligence. At a minimum, compromising sources and methods means potential sources—that is, candidates for recruitment—would not have the confidence to place their lives in the hands of the organization. At a maximum, it would be death to those who had already done so. It is hard to question the need to protect sources and methods. Without secret sources and secret methods, the directorate would not be able to function and fulfill its mission.

Protection of the lives of fellow officers is not taken lightly. We put our lives on the line running operations, and protecting our identity is integral to protecting the identity of the sources we run and the operational methods we employ. If an officer's cover is blown, those in close association with the officer can be put at risk. This is especially tricky when an officer undercover dies in the line of duty. If the Agency assesses that lifting the cover of the officer would jeopardize other officers or operations, the Agency will go to extreme lengths in the name of security, often causing hardship to the family of the deceased.

At the end of a career, the Agency decides whether to lift the cover of officers, permitting them to acknowledge their CIA affiliation. My cover was lifted. That does not mean I am no longer governed by secrecy requirements. I signed a secrecy agreement that gives me a lifelong obligation. For me, this is at times frustrating and maddening, especially given the circumstances that led to my departure. It was not a friendly departure. I made a mistake, to which I admitted freely, accepting responsibility for a poor decision. Just what transpired, and the unfairness of it all, has been classified secret by the Agency, or so I was advised in a very threatening letter from the CIA. At the end of it all, I was left wondering how the CIA can decide arbitrarily that personal aspects of my life are national security secrets.

While officers must accept a life of secrecy and learn to deal with the burden of living undercover, family members often are not comfortable or accepting of being told or telling lies to maintain that cover. Frequently, the family members are not told the circumstances surrounding the death or are provided a cover story—a lie, to mask the circumstances. Families are told that they cannot talk to the press, or anyone else for that matter, with the consequences being an "or else!" The Agency is very good at intimidating people to act in a certain way, with veiled threats of serious consequences. It is not surprising that family members of deceased CIA covert operatives become frustrated in their unsuccessful search for answers about their loved ones and also paranoid about actions the CIA could take against them if they choose to pursue their search.

The "need to know" principle is sacred within the Directorate of Operations as the element that governs who is read into secrets and who is not. The need to know principle is executed through a complex system of "compartmentalization." Officers are given access only to those compartments that contain cases on which they are working. There are "bigot lists" documenting who has authorized access. Compartmentalization can be horizontal, limiting access to one office but not another.

Compartmentalization can also be vertical, limiting access within a chain of command.

There is also the process of spoofing, which removes an operation from one bigot list to another, for security reasons, using false pretenses. For example, the bigot list for an operation involving the development of a Russian intelligence officer for recruitment might be relatively large. Once the Russian is recruited, knowledge of the recruitment needs to be minimized for security reasons. Many officers on the original bigot list will be told that the Russian turned down the recruitment pitch and the case is dead. In reality, the crypt (the internal operational alias assigned to an agent) for the Russian will change and there will be a new, more restricted bigot list authorizing access to the case information. So, in the name of security, we lie even to our colleagues!

Rarely will an officer push the envelope when running up to the silence of need to know. Officers are taught to accept the information barrier unless they have a compelling reason to know that had been overlooked by management. The self-discipline is what permits the system to work efficiently. Officers are inquisitive by nature, but we are taught to channel our questions.

The Memorial Wall is a perfect example of the need to know principle. The Memorial Wall is the CIA monument to those officers who lost their lives in the line of duty—not just Directorate of Operations officers, but officers from all directorates. The Memorial Wall currently has eighty five-pointed stars carved in a slab of Vermont Danby marble. The Memorial Wall is located in the grand foyer of the Old Headquarters Building at the Langley Headquarters. Officers stream by the Memorial Wall as they come and go from the main entrance to the building. Every May, the DCI holds a memorial service, paying homage to those officers who made the ultimate sacrifice for their country.

Attached to the wall is a locked glass case enclosing a book. The book has a line devoted to each star on the wall. Some lines include a year and the name of the deceased officer. Other lines include the year but nothing else. The omission of the name signifies that the officer died undercover and, therefore, the identity of the officer is classified. The first entry in the book is for 1950. The last is for 2003.

Whenever I would return to Headquarters from overseas, I would enter the Old Headquarters Building through the main entrance in order to collect my building access badge. I would always linger before the Memorial Wall and pay respect to my fallen colleagues, several of whom I knew personally. Although I knew the lore on several handfuls of the stars, the identity of most were clouded in secrecy even to me, and I did not dare to inquire because I did not have the need-to-know. The culture of secrecy had enveloped me completely.

As most Directorate of Operations officers are undercover, they tend to not associate closely with officers of the other directorates, most of whom are overt. It is awkward socially to have to create and maintain a plausible explanation for an association, especially in a mixed group, where some people are aware of your CIA affiliation, but others are not, and some are undercover, but others not. You spend all your energy guarding your cover rather than enjoying the social occasion.

The need to know principle creates the "us and them" mentality, further making the directorate insular. Officers tend to have limited rotational assignments outside the directorate, because they are not considered career enhancing. I, for example, had only one rotational assignment during my entire career. As an elitist organization, there is no desire to mix with non-elites. There is almost no rotation into the directorate by intelligence officers outside the CIA because of secrecy requirements. It is a perfectly closed society.

One aspect of Directorate of Operations culture that is rarely discussed internally is its situational ethics, and, when discussed, a specialized jargon has been developed to mask words with negative cultural context. We tell "cover stories," not lies. We motivate agents to "collect intelligence on their behalf"; we do not manipulate, trick, or coerce. We "assess and exploit target candidate's vulnerabilities"; we do not prey upon the weaknesses and entrap people by virtue of these weaknesses. We "collect intelligence"; we do not steal information. We "compensate" their agents; we do not bribe them.

This wordplay does not mean we are unaware of what we are doing, but rather we choose to—and are encouraged to—look at the matter with a different lens. Fundamentally, it comes down to the issue of means and ends. In order to be effective, officers must genuinely believe that the ends justify the means. Lying, stealing, and cheating in order to fulfill the mission of protecting national security is acceptable, if not meritorious. Within the Directorate of Operations, the situation is paramount. It is permissible to use these less-than-savory means in order to achieve the mission.

It was this aspect of the culture that gave Webster the most angst. In his view, operations officers lacked ethics. Agency officers were not bothered by using dirty tricks to accomplish their mission. There seemed to be no limit to what the Directorate of Operations was willing to do under the cloak of secrecy. The situational ethics in the office, in the conduct of business with him and with Congress showed that the officers could not be trusted. If it was okay to lie to an agent, it must be okay to lie to him and to Congress. Operational ethics offended his core beliefs in integrity, honesty, and public trust. It is this aspect of directorate culture Webster set out to change. To do so, he would have to throw out the dirty tricks, the traditional practices, and the cowboys.

4
Setting New Standards

SEVENTH FLOOR, LANGLEY, VIRGINIA, 1987: Webster's propriety, his image as a clean, impartial judge, was what appealed to Congress. His confirmation as DCI was a relative cakewalk. He quickly convinced Congress that he would remain independent from politics and do "the right thing." He was the opposite of Casey, the wily lawyer who was accused of playing fast and loose with the truth and the laws. Everything Webster did, he did so after studied consideration of legality, public trust, and effectiveness. He spoke the truth, and the truth was absolute. The Directorate of Operations' view of truth—that truth came in many layers and shades—was completely rejected by Webster.

In December, Webster would fire Deputy Director of Operations Clair George, who survived the initial internal purge after Iran-Contra (which can only be attributed to the power of the old-boy network). To Webster, George represented what was wrong with the Agency and with the Directorate of Operations in particular. Congress expected that Webster would be a salve that would penetrate deep within the organization, restoring its respectability—that Webster could and would fundamentally alter the culture of the Agency, as he had done at the FBI. Webster would work hard to do this. He set the standards high and was uncompromising when it came to ethics. He had no intention of being sucked into the old-boy system and kept himself separated from it. He would set the example of comportment by deed.

William Webster, or "the Judge," as he preferred to be called, never made the Agency his own; nor did the Agency accept the Judge into its ranks. Webster isolated himself on the Seventh Floor and passed judgments. He did not lead the troops, or really ever try to get to know them. He surrounded himself with his special assistants from the FBI, suggesting to CIA officers that they were not and never would be of Webster's ilk, but something dirty, something infectious, something to be kept at a safe distance. Webster managed—not led—the Agency from a safe distance through his special assistants and by memo.

Webster found the Agency confusing and secretive. His pet peeve was the use, or overuse in his considered opinion, of acronyms and cryptonyms—in Agency lingo, "crypts" are code words used to obfuscate what is actually being discussed. It was tradition within the Directorate of Operations to use crypts when referring to government organizations, including the CIA. Between the use of crypts and acronyms, officers could have complete conversations in this weird jargon, without ever using any real words. We would be completely understood by each other, while sounding like speakers of an unknown dialect to outsiders, as my husband was fond of pointing out. It made little matter to us that at times the identity of the organization was clear from the text, despite the use of a crypt. This was the language of insiders—spook-speak. Webster put the kibosh on the practice, dictating the CIA would henceforth be CIA in cable traffic and the FBI would be the FBI. Period. After Webster left, the tradition was slowly resurrected, showing just how strong the Agency culture is.

Webster also had no real interest in or knowledge of foreign affairs, the business of the Agency, causing him to have a credibility problem inside the organization. Agency officers are passionate about foreign affairs, and we talk about foreign affairs just for fun, over coffee with colleagues and on the tennis court with friends. To make matters worse, Webster came to the CIA directly from the FBI, the age-old rival, bringing his FBI people with him.

Webster was the ultimate outsider, and the CIA does not like outsiders. It was a bad start, from the first day in his new office. Ultimately, it meant Webster would only be tolerated—never embraced—despite all the good that he did for the organization.

OLD HEADQUARTERS BUILDING, LANGLEY, VIRGINIA, 1988: One of Webster's early initiatives was to improve the working relationship between the FBI and CIA. The two organizations had a long history of bureaucratic competition and conflict. The source is differing missions and cultures. As a law enforcement agency, the FBI is charged with arresting criminals and bringing them to justice. The FBI operates (or is supposed to) within the rule of law and claims the moral high ground for doing so. The CIA traditionally has been more focused on collecting intelligence for policymakers and subverting foreigners through bribery, blackmail, or psychological manipulation to spy on its behalf. The CIA "walks on the dark side" in order to protect national security.

Cultural stereotypes have led both services to look with disdain on the other. CIA officers see themselves as sophisticates involved in a complicated intellectual chess game with adversaries, using deception and "dirty tricks" as tools to mislead, disrupt, and master the enemy. FBI agents, as stereotyped by the Agency, are gun-toting grunts more interested in making busts for immediate gratification of bureaucratic kudos than contributing to the larger goal of long-term national security. FBI agents suspect that the CIA, pursuing its own questionable agenda, provides the FBI with less than the whole story. FBI agents question CIA officers' ethical standards. The presumption is that if CIA officers are willing to break foreign laws, then they are willing to break U.S. laws. Lying is a way of life to CIA officers, so expect lies.

These stereotypes are just that. The actual relationship between FBI agents and CIA officers depends upon the individuals involved. Those who made the effort to work well together and get along personally did so. Those who were suspicious or scornful had poor working relationships. In my career, I had both excellent and extremely confrontational relationships with FBI officers working on counterterrorism issues overseas. This, of course, led me to conclude that they—not me— were the problem!

Historically, the CIA has worked more closely with foreign intelligence and law enforcement services than the FBI. The CIA can more easily hand off cases for action to foreign governments without becoming embroiled in the taking down or judicial process, allowing the CIA to protect its sources and methods. U.S. judicial requirements governing discovery and the chain of evidence pose difficult challenges to the CIA when providing intelligence to the FBI. Under no circumstances does a CIA officer want to end up in a U.S. court testifying on a criminal case and be forced to discuss operational issues. The tension arises from the need of the CIA to protect its secrets (sources and methods), while the FBI wants to use the information to prosecute cases. Conversely, the FBI has been restricted in sharing information obtained from criminal wiretaps and grand jury deliberations with intelligence agencies. The conflicts are sharpest when domestic and foreign intelligence-gathering missions of the FBI and CIA, respectively, cross, creating turf battles.

Responsibility for counterintelligence was one of the most contentious areas. In 1985, the CIA suffered a massive loss of Soviet agents and technical operations targeted against the Soviets. The CIA concealed the 1985 operational losses in its Soviet Division from the FBI because of issues of compartmentalization and a belief that it was not a Bureau matter. Furthermore, the CIA had just gone through the unpleasant experience with the FBI on the handling of a problem former CIA employee, Edward Lee Howard.

Howard was a new case officer in the CIA Soviet Division. His first field assignment was in the inner sanctum: Moscow. In the months before his scheduled departure, he began "reading in" on the cases he was assigned to handle, learning the names and positions of his agents, their operational histories, and the type of intelligence they provided. He also had to complete special operational training given to officers serving in "denied areas." In the Internal Operations Course, case officers—now called operations officers—learned the finer points of spy tradecraft, including detecting and losing surveillance and impersonal communication.

Impersonal communication permits agents and handlers to communicate with each other without having physical contact. One form of impersonal communication tradecraft was the use of dead drops and vehicle tosses. An operations officer can pass materials to an agent indirectly by hiding the materials in some sort of packaging to disguise the content and placing the package in a location for retrieval by the agent at a later time. I would notify the agent that the drop site is loaded by placing a signal at a specific location checked frequently by the agent. The signal could be anything; frequently it is a chalk mark along the route the agent travels daily. The agent might also put down his own signal once he has retrieved the drop.

Drops also work in the reverse direction, with the agent making the drop and the operations officer receiving it. Dead drops require manually placing the disguised package in a specific place, something that takes time and visual privacy for a controlled few minutes for both emplacement and recovery. Done properly, a hostile intelligence service will never know that the handler or the agent committed an act of espionage.

A vehicle toss is quicker to place, with the disguised package being tossed from the window of a moving car into a drop zone. It can take longer to recover, because it is not at a specific location but in a larger area. Additionally, the package may roll, or the toss may be imprecise, thus placing the package outside the zone. There is nothing worse than the feeling you get when you go to retrieve a drop and do not find it immediately. Every additional second on site searching means another chance of being exposed.

As Howard was about to depart for Moscow, a last-minute polygraph test uncovered suitability issues, including petty theft and drug and alcohol abuse. He was fired abruptly in 1983. Wanting revenge, Howard volunteered his services to the KGB. Despite significant alerting behavior by Howard, the CIA did not uncover his treachery until 1985. Vitaly Yurchenko, a Soviet defector, provided details on a Soviet source who could be no one other than Howard.

The FBI, which was involved in the joint debriefing of Yurchenko, put Howard under twenty-four-hour surveillance. The CIA did not warn the FBI that Howard was expert at evading surveillance. Then again, it did not take expert credentials to escape from the FBI novices assigned to watch him. Using the oldest trick in the book, Howard used a dummy in his car to double for him. While his wife drove around the quiet Santa Fe streets seated beside the dummy, Howard slipped away from FBI surveillance in September 1985. He later resurfaced in Moscow.

Although the CIA never had a chance to debrief Howard, it assumed that he told the KGB everything he knew about Moscow operations. Besides compromising his agents, Howard was assumed to have exposed the tradecraft, permitting the Soviets to learn the criteria for site selection, signal types, concealment types, and operational flow parameters. The CIA blamed the FBI for letting Howard escape, calling into question FBI professionalism and suitability to conduct counterintelligence operations. It was one of many low points in the FBI-CIA relationship.*

In June 1988, Webster and FBI Director William Sessions signed a formal Memorandum of Understanding outlining in broad language how the CIA and FBI would work together on counterintelligence issues. The Memorandum of Understanding required the CIA to notify the FBI of "any other facts or circumstances which reasonably indicate that a present or former CIA officer or employee has engaged or may engage in espionage or a related offense, or conspire with others to commit such an offense."[1] Strained CIA-FBI working-level relation-

---

* In July 2002, Howard died in Moscow at the age of fifty, a broken and forgotten man. When I read his obituary, which was buried in the bowels of the *New York Times*, I wondered how many readers would notice and how many would care, let alone remember the terrible damage he did to U.S. national security.

ships would torpedo the effort at the director level to improve the coordination and cooperation between the two agencies.

The Memorandum of Understanding was disregarded by Soviet Division management, which by then knew the possibility—if not probability—that there was a mole in the division. Howard could not have known about all of the cases that were compromised. There had to be someone else. The Baron of Soviet Division simply refused to cede his authority on what he saw as an internal CIA matter. It would be six years before the full magnitude of this turf battle would be felt.

There was another reason why the tensions between the CIA and FBI were especially high under Webster. The Iran-Contra scandal remained a front-page issue. Even when Webster cleaned house, purging the rest of those officers involved in the scandal, the matter did not end for the CIA. The independent counsel had determined there were strong indicators to justify criminal investigations of CIA employees. With Webster's consent, FBI investigators were combing through sensitive CIA files in Langley, looking for evidence to put some of CIA's best and brightest behind bars. While the CIA was trying to resolve old problems, it was caught by surprise.

OLD HEADQUARTERS BUILDING, LANGLEY, VIRGINIA, 1989: When the Berlin Wall came down, the mood in the Agency was downright festive. The corridors were alive with people, talking, laughing, and swapping war stories. I was like a child among dancing adults— too inexperienced to understand the subtleties of the stories or their implications, but nonetheless enthusiastic to join in. There was champagne and a sense of camaraderie among the Cold War warriors. The good guys had won.

On that day, there was little talk about the future, as CIA officers were content to live in the moment. Never mind the detail that the CIA failed to understand that the fall of the Berlin Wall would lead to a complete collapse of the Soviet Union. No one—certainly not I—realized this great victory would usher in a decade of decline for the Agency. The decline would be across the board, in terms of budget, personnel, prestige, mission, and morale.

From its earliest days, the CIA has been focused on collecting intelligence on the Soviet Union and its satellites and countering the threat that their policies posed to U.S. national security. The CIA had developed an extensive infrastructure for collection and covert action throughout the world, designed to counter Soviet influence and provocation. Preferring backwater locations in the Third World, the CIA engaged the Soviets in Cold War battles employing surrogates in some cases, going mano a mano in others. Europe was the largest and most civilized battleground. In European bars, cafés, sex spots, and checkpoints, the spies and counterspies ran elaborate operations against each other to expose, exploit, and disinform the enemy.

Against Moscow, the CIA "Russia House" worked with great secrecy and with diligence to steal the secrets of Red Square. Operational methods used by the CIA were designed in this Cold War environment. The kind of agents the CIA had in the "stable of assets" were typically those who could either report on Communist activities, take direct action to counter Communist activity, or provide operational support for these offensive activities. The CIA view of the world was through a counter-Soviet lens. While the Soviets lost the war, the CIA lost its footings in the post–Cold War world.

The CIA began to drift. Its old mission was gone. Yet, we did not seem to be in any hurry to reorient ourselves to meet new challenges in the new unipolar world. We continued business as usual, collecting intelligence on the breakup of the Soviet Union, recruiting recently unemployed Soviet intelligence officials, and running proxy wars even though the Soviets were not playing anymore. It would take others—mostly critics of the Agency—to force the CIA to ask the hard questions as to what purpose it served. That would take time; in the meanwhile, the CIA focused on the crises that each day presented. In the unstable geopolitical environment, new and unanticipated intelligence collection requirements would pop up in remote areas or areas where the CIA had few resources. The Agency dealt with these in an ad hoc way, pulling people and resources from all over the Agency for immediate deployment to the crisis. Known as surge requirements, Headquarters would send out "volunteer cables," asking officers with specific skills to join one surge after another as the CIA deployed to support the military in regional wars and confrontations around the globe. Being an Arabist, I was immediately caught up in one surge effort.

KUWAITI DESERT, 1990: The campaign to expel Saddam Hussein's Iraqi armies from Kuwait did not start out very well, for the Kuwaitis or the Americans. The problem was that no one in a position of authority took Saddam's threats seriously. He was like a broken record, complaining about the Kuwaitis stealing Iraqi oil, pushing down the price per barrel, occupying islands Saddam considered part of historical Iraq. The United States, too, thought Saddam was posturing, bluffing to force concessions from the Kuwaiti shaykhdom. When Saddam sent his armed forces to the border, the United States interpreted it as upping the pressure, not a real deployment in preparation for war. Although CIA assessments considered the possibility of an invasion, the final assessments went the other way.

In the period just before the Iraqi invasion and through Operation Desert Storm, CIA officers undertook dangerous missions that made measurable impact and saved lives. CIA officers operated behind enemy lines to emplace sensors, set up stay-behind commo capabilities, and ran agents in place. One team that had deployed black into the area—in other words, entered the country completely illegally and with the understanding if caught, U.S. government knowledge of them would be denied—was conducting a recon mission on the Iraq-Kuwait border at the time of the Iraqi invasion of Kuwait. The team took cover in the flood of refugees moving toward Baghdad. Trapped in Iraq, their lives were at risk if discovered by Iraqi intelligence. The CIA chief in Baghdad had a similar problem. He went to ground to save his skin and the secrets of the CIA. Memories of William Buckley were still fresh.

According to press reports, they spent hair-raising weeks evading detection until an exfiltration plan was put together. The end of the Cold War had created new opportunities, and the CIA called upon Polish intelligence for assistance. The Poles had capabilities in place in Iraq as a large number of Polish workers were employed on construction projects, not only in Baghdad but in the countryside. Polish intelligence officers who infiltrated into Iraq pulled off a daring escape plan into Turkey, disguising the CIA officers as drunken Eastern Europeans.[2]

Meanwhile, the CIA officers assigned to Kuwait took refuge in the U.S. embassy with members of the diplomatic mission. The chief there, whose identity was known to Iraqi intelligence, was in a perilous situation. There were grave doubts that Saddam Hussein would honor the Geneva Conventions, especially once Hussein ordered the closures of diplomatic missions and revocation of diplomatic immunities held by diplomats accredited to Kuwait, in contravention of international law. The CIA maintained a twenty-four-hour open connection by secure communications with the Kuwait office, monitoring the deteriorating situation.

In the tense days that followed, the mission officers lived on stored canned food and drank the swimming pool to survive, reporting nonstop on the situation on the ground. In the early days of the crisis, I pulled midnight duty to man the Langley side of the phone connection, because I was the junior officer for the Arabian Peninsula. While it was midnight in Washington, it was 3:00 P.M. in the Gulf—prime reporting time. I was amazed and proud to be given such responsibility so early in my career. My job was to report up my chain of command the intelligence and needs of those left in country. It was my first real exposure to a crisis and to senior management. I prepared spot reports of rapidly evolving events and briefed the Seventh Floor (CIA senior management) on operational details. It was pretty heady stuff, and I knew I was living history in the making. Of course, the operational aspects of that history remain hidden in the dusty files of the CIA. However, the CIA has permitted me to tell one of the more personal stories of those trapped in Kuwait at that time.

Safe passage out of Kuwait for most of the assembled group was eventually negotiated. On August 24, 1990, the majority of the U.S. mission personnel, officers, and families, drove in convoy with Iraqi military escorts (guards) from Kuwait City to Baghdad, where they were held under guard. His own situation grave, the chief did not neglect the concerns of the rest of the mission officers. Evacuating a location is personally difficult, as one must leave all possessions behind with the odds of never retrieving them. It was not as if the U.S. government would assume responsibility for your personal property. The government insurance policy would compensate at the rate of sixty cents per pound—that would mean three dollars for your lost television.

Many mission officers had pets they did not want to abandon to the desert, or to starving Iraqi soldiers. It was a well-founded fear. Iraqi soldiers looted Kuwait City, including the homes of the American diplomats. While some raided the pantries for food, others raided the zoo, eating the large animals. The chief bent regulations, requisitioned a bus, and piled all the pets on the bus, which joined the convoy to Baghdad.

U.S. Ambassador Nathaniel Howell, his deputy Barbara Bodine, and three "essential officers" remained in the mission keeping it open in name, as the United States refused to recognize the Iraqi seizure of Kuwait. They lived without electricity, surrounded by hostile troops until being evacuated four months later, just prior to the U.S. counteroffensive liberating Kuwait.[3]

U.S. military commanders waged a war far different from those previously fought. Technology had delivered new capabilities to the warriors. However, the technological edge was not even. Although satellites provided vast new amounts of intelligence on the battleground, commanders could not get the intelligence in their hands as fast as they wanted. CIA and military systems were not interoperable, which led to delays and disputes. Analytical methods were also different, which led to yet more disputes. Commanders complained about mushy intelligence that did not meet their tactical needs. The military vocalized its complaints to the media. As usual, the CIA had "no comment" for the public. The CIA was comfortable with keeping knowledge of its field successes limited to those with a need-to-know. We felt we were above having to play the spin game for the U.S. public.

While Americans cheered Allied troops during the prime-time war, boasting about the surgical strikes with smart bombs that targeted military sites and spared civilians, the Arab world looked on in horror. The fabled army of Saddam, hardened by years of war with Iran, was squashed like a pesky fly. Gone was the bravado; in its place came conspiracy theories. The United States had tricked Saddam into invading in order to give the United States a pretext to occupy Arab land, steal Arab oil, kill Arab children, and defile Islam.

SEVENTH FLOOR, LANGLEY, VIRGINIA, 1991: The CIA's failure to predict the collapse of the Soviet Union and the Iraqi invasion of Kuwait had eroded presidential support for Webster. President Bush (Sr.), who had inherited Webster from the Reagan administration, thought he was too timid in his approach. Congress continued to laud his ethics, praising him for doing an exceptionally straightforward, conscientious, honest job. However, the loss in confidence in his ability to lead the intelligence community effectively was a silent testimony to the reality that the good guy didn't have the mettle to do the job. On May 8, Webster announced his intention to resign.

The Directorate of Operations was relieved when Webster made his announcement. Webster's legalistic approach put a real damper on operations. Webster's intent was to reel in the cowboys. This he did. But he also squashed the desire of the field operatives to take aggressive and creative actions against national security threats. It felt as if the lawyers, who now proliferated at all levels of the Agency, were running the show. For example, by the end of Webster's tenure, the hostage crisis had largely unwound as the change in the geopolitical situation caused Iran and Hizballah to modify their activities. However, those *responsible* for the kidnappings remained at large. They ran free in countries outside the reach of U.S. law. If they were to be caught and made to pay for their terror activities, the CIA could not play by gentlemen's rules. When the operations officers proposed kidnapping Hizballah leaders,

the extralegal aspects were just too much for Judge Webster to accept—
or approve.

While many in operations thought the Israelis had the right
approach of hunting down and assassinating terrorists, Webster would
authorize only a law enforcement approach, characterized by a slow
but methodical collection of evidence, followed by arrest, and capped
by trial in a court of law. The Agency could not even ask the Israelis to
do the dirty work for them, which they were more than willing to do
when it came to Middle Eastern terrorists. As a judge, Webster would
not and could not approve the use of unsavory means to accomplish
the desired end. The Agency's preferred way might be quicker, but it
was wrong, Webster deemed. Webster had made a career of upholding and enforcing the law; by charter, the CIA operations division was
a lawbreaking organization. It was an irreconcilable relationship from
the beginning.

From inside the Agency, we viewed Webster more as a Band-Aid, a
needed protection from external infection. Webster was not there to
change us, but to placate Congress and public opinion, giving the
Agency time and room to heal. Once removed from the Seventh Floor,
the Band-Aid was not missed. All was as it had been before. All was well.
The culture of the Agency remained intact. To the Directorate of
Operations, the world was still made of many shades of gray, truth was
relative, and Congress was dangerous and best avoided. With Webster
gone, field officers hoped they could return to using traditional methods to get the job done. Sitting and watching terrorists was no way to
do business.

★ ★ ★ ★

Webster arrived at the CIA at a very troubled time. The Iran-Contra scandal damaged the credibility of the institution. Webster attempted to set a new
moral compass for the CIA, cleaning house, rewriting regulations and
introducing a legalistic approach to intelligence. Standard operational
methods, the book of dirty tricks, were replaced with less controversial
tools. Although he made some notable changes within the structure and
bureaucratic processes of the Agency, such as the creation of the
Counterintelligence Center, the proliferation of special assistants and
lawyers, and standardized memo formats and covert action approval procedures, Webster would go down in the collective memory of the Agency
of having served, without grand distinction, from May 1987 to August 1991.

62 •   MELISSA BOYLE MAHLE

Webster led the Agency at the time when the most significant change in the world power structure occurred. Instead of capitalizing on this great success and laying out a new strategic vision, Webster and the CIA became bogged down in internal disputes and intelligence community turf battles. At a time when the CIA needed to demonstrate its core capabilities in collection and analysis, to show Americans its continuing relevance in the post–Cold War period, the CIA gave a mixed performance during the Gulf War. The secret successes were quickly forgotten in the wake of the public admonition for the jobs not so well done. The widening Iran-Contra investigation took a toll on officer morale as well. The decade was off to a shaky start.

New to the Agency, I was in training during this period. I lacked the experience or perspective to judge the magnitude of the events swirling around me. While I heard a lot of grumbling from my seniors about Iran-Contra, I also saw people working very hard to capitalize upon the new opportunities after the fall of the Berlin Wall and to confront the new threats coming out of Iraq and Eastern Europe. I felt proud to be part of an elite organization whose sole purpose was to serve the intelligence needs of the president and keep the nation safe.

PART

3

THE GATES YEARS
(NOVEMBER 6, 1991–JANUARY 20, 1993)

"Change is inevitable. It must come and come quickly. It must be constructive and informed by broadly agreed missions and priorities for U.S. Intelligence."

ROBERT GATES
Confirmation hearing, 1991

5
Confirmation of an Insider

CAPITOL HILL, WASHINGTON, D.C., 1991: In November, Robert Gates returned to the CIA as DCI after a long and hard-fought battle. The elevation of Gates to the position of DCI was notable. He was a career CIA officer, not an outsider like Webster. Very few DCIs had ever come from within the CIA. Furthermore, he was a foreign affairs junkie and a substantive expert. Gates grew up in the Directorate of Intelligence, working Soviet issues. A wunderkind, he caught the eye of senior management early in his career and was promoted quickly. He moved back and forth between the CIA and the National Security Council and was praised widely as a brilliant analyst. He served as Deputy Director of Intelligence for a year and then headed up the National Intelligence Council. In 1986, he was selected to become DDCI, serving under Bill Casey and then acting DCI after Casey's death.

Casey had been grooming Gates to take his place, but the Iran-Contra scandal swirled too fiercely and scuttled any chance of a successful confirmation. In 1987, Gates withdrew his nomination as DCI. Instead, in March 1989, he left the Agency after working for Webster for several years and worked at the National Security Council as Brent Scowcroft's deputy for national security affairs. It is a testimony to Gates's political savvy and intellectual prowess that he was able to return to the fray and win confirmation after Webster's retirement. That said, the confirmation process reopened many old wounds within the Agency, and gave fodder to the ongoing public debate on Iran-Contra and CIA credibility.

Gates was the ultimate insider. He had a history, both good and bad. This history was seized upon by Congress during debate on his suitability and capability to serve as DCI. While the public thought the main issue of the confirmation hearings would be Iran-Contra, Gates sensed through the detailed prequestioning and sworn testimony that his views on the Soviet Union would be the tricky part.

On support to the Contras, Gates maintained he was kept largely out of the loop. He was not read in to the operation until after the story hit the press and then only on a very limited basis. Independent Counsel Lawrence Walsh suspected otherwise, but was unable to prove that Gates misstated the facts to cover up earlier and greater knowledge. Renowned for his retention of the smallest of details, Gates claimed a memory gap during congressional testimony, sounding more like a Directorate of Operations officer than a Directorate of Intelligence officer.

Gates's performance raised the issue of candor among those asking the questions. If the DCI is candor-challenged, will the CIA return to its bad behavior under Casey? The issue of Gates's suitability was fiercely debated on the Senate floor. Gates sought to balance out these doubts by reminding Congress of the role he had played in the post-Casey days, rebuilding the relationship between the CIA and its oversight committees. Gates had demonstrated his personal commitment to full cooperation and his willingness to drag the Directorate of Operations along, despite its kicking and screaming. He also tried to convince Congress that he had learned important lessons as a result of working with Casey and that he (Gates) had matured as a leader.

Gates was a hard-liner when it came to the Soviet Union. He was accused of exaggerating the Soviet threat in the first half of the 1980s, exaggerations that encouraged a costly arms race. Some in Congress planned on skewering him with his past dire assessments on the evils of the Evil Empire. It was payback time, and the congressional doves were lining up.

History has a weird way of happening. The Soviet Union had dissolved just prior to the confirmation hearings. Rather than being the burning issue of the day, the Soviet Union was seen as old news, old debates, and irrelevant to the future challenges of the CIA. The congressional debate quickly fell into the familiar fight over what the essence of the Soviet Union was and how the U.S. government should have dealt with it, all with hindsight and a lack of enthusiasm.

As it turned out, the major challenge to Gates did not come from ideological antagonists within Congress but from the worker bees inside the CIA. Former and current CIA analysts accused Gates of the most damning of charges, cooking intelligence and stifling dissent. Gates tried to minimize the damage, characterizing it as an intellectual food fight, not a subversion of the analytical system. He noted that those who leveled the accusations came from a small stratum of the analysts, from one particular office within Soviet analysis. He countered their specific examples of politicization and suppression of reports with reams of disseminated reports that expressed assessments counter to what the politicos wanted to hear. He buried them and Congress in paper.

NEW HEADQUARTERS BUILDING, LANGLEY, VIRGINIA, 1991: The decision of CIA analysts to come forward in a culture that demands loyalty and punishes disloyalty was remarkable. While Gates was successful in easing the mind of Congress, by offering guarantees and reform initiatives to ensure rigorous debate, CIA Headquarters was experiencing an open revolt. We in the Directorate of Operations were more than a bit amazed by the vocal opposition coming from the Directorate of Intelligence. We assumed that our directorate was Gates's target and enemy, based on memories of Gates's actions and attitudes when he was DDCI and Deputy Director of Intelligence. In his memoirs, Gates even writes about his uneasy relationship with the Directorate of Operations, noting it was fraught with suspicion (not his, but the operations officers, he insisted).

Although only a few analysts had the personal courage to speak up at the hearings—and thereby commit career suicide—the corridors were filled with stories of Gates' imperious management style, disdain for opinions in conflict with his own, and his huge ambition to make his mark. The criticism was not limited to Soviet analysts; my analyst friends in the Near East and Latin American branches voiced similar concerns. Many years later, a respected intellectual who taught generations of CIA analysts tools of analytical prediction would talk about Gates—albeit not by name when speaking outside the CIA—and tell about one of his more memorable run-ins with him. After giving a seminar on predictive analytical tradecraft—in which the intellectual concluded the Soviet Union was on the verge of collapse—Gates literally cornered him, jabbing him with his forefinger, saying, "Soviet Union will never fall. Not in your lifetime or in mine!"

Analysts were anxious about Gates's plans to reorganize the intelligence community and reduce the number of analysts as a cost-cutting measure. Morale was so low and anxiety so high during the confirmation hearings that then–Deputy Director of Intelligence John Helgerson gave a pep talk to his troops assembled in "the Bubble," broadcast across the Agency TV net, promising them all would be well. Dissent would be "tolerated," and there would be no major reorganization of the directorate. My analytical colleagues left, wondering why dissent would be only tolerated and not encouraged, and what constituted major versus minor reorganization.

The greatest fear that permeated the Agency was generated by rumors of impending RIFs, reductions in force. Those who had been around for a while had personal memories of the last great RIF, known as the Halloween Massacre, under DCI Stansfield Turner. Those who were new, like me, heard the stories of the dreaded pink slips that appeared from nowhere, telling seasoned and loyal officers that their services were no longer needed. Blood flowed in the corridors of the Directorate of Operations, an organization viewed by Turner as over-rated and therefore overstaffed. Vietnam was over, and it was time to clean house.

Operations officers were certain they would be the primary target of the RIF, citing Gates's disdain for Directorate of Operations elitism and covert action, calling him a Turner reincarnation. Analysts were equally certain they would take the biggest hit. The Directorate of Administration officers knew that any reduction anywhere would include a reduction of support personnel.

Indeed, Gates was on the record from when he was DDCI for criticizing the bureaucratic encrustation in both the operations and intelligence directorates. He felt that those coming from the ranks lacked sufficient creativity and imagination thanks to the stifling effect of senior officers. Frustrated by the bureaucracy, Casey had decided to bypass it, creating an agency within an agency, something that brought him only grief. Gates had set his sights upon tearing it down by getting rid of the old boys, moving in younger officers that he could mold in his own image.

It was a time of uncertainty at Langley, and the rumor mill was running at full pace. Those of us in the field were kept up to date by colleagues visiting our field stations who would feed us the latest RUMINT. This was long before the days of secure e-mail. Being a junior officer, I felt the insecurity of the time. Given the "last in, first out" rule of RIFs, my continued employment was anything but secure. I could only hope to distinguish myself through exceptional performance and as a representative of a new genre of field operatives.

CAPITOL HILL, WASHINGTON, D.C., 1991: Gates convinced congressional leaders that he was the right man for the job. One of the deciding factors was the experience he had under his belt that would allow him to move rapidly to make sweeping changes in the intelligence community. Congress was in a hurry; it did not want to wait two to three years while a new DCI learned the current programs before thinking about how to change them. Congress wanted a DCI who could and would work with them to develop new structures and budget priorities and who had the respect and confidence of the president. In Oklahoma Senator David Boren's words, they wanted a DCI who could hit the ground running.

The congressional relationship with the CIA was changing. In the early years of the CIA, the relationship had been informal and controlled by a few of the old guard in both houses. Congress seldom asked for or received intelligence briefings. For example, in 1968, the CIA briefed "its committees" eight times. In the 1970s, the relationship began to change, with both the Senate and the House demanding broader accountability for intelligence activities. Permanent oversight committees were set up in the Senate and the House. The resolution establishing these committees contained a nonbinding requirement that the oversight committees should be kept "fully and currently informed with respect to intelligence activities." In addition to operational briefings, the CIA expanded its substantive briefings to the oversight committees and committees involved in foreign policy, such as the Senate Foreign Relations Committee. The committees received finished intelligence, but no raw reporting or the special report for the president, the *President's Daily Brief.*

The Intelligence Oversight Act of 1980 made the "fully and currently informed" language a legal obligation for the intelligence community. It also was widely interpreted to require the CIA to furnish intelligence reports to Congress. Congress increasingly began investigating intelligence community performance, demanding access to substantial amounts of analysis and information on collection capabilities. By the late 1980s, Congress had become a major consumer of intelligence and had won access to information of unprecedented scope and sensitivity.[1]

The general relationship of trust between the CIA and the oversight committees broke down during Casey's tenure. Casey assigned an operations officer as the chief congressional liaison officer, and— surprise!—congressional members and staff found him less than forthcoming. Congress continued to push for more sensitive intelligence, including raw reporting, National Intelligence Estimates, and on occasion, the names of sources. Casey pushed back and began withholding intelligence activity details.

In the aftermath of Iran-Contra, the oversight committees conducted deep investigations and were given access to very sensitive information, some showing CIA wrongdoing. In his position as acting DCI and DDCI under Webster, Gates earned congressional respect because he consistently supported forward-leaning disclosure to the oversight committees. Accordingly, Gates was deemed trustworthy by the majority of Congress. This more than anything else allowed Congress to put aside Gates's other baggage—that he politicized intelligence on the Soviet Union, stifled analytical debate, and lied about his knowledge on Iran-Contra. Because he had proved himself willing to work with Congress, Congress gave him its vote of approval.

After six months of hostile confirmation hearings that included four full days of open- and closed-session testimony from Gates responding to almost nine hundred questions, committee review of thousands of documents, and interview of hundreds of witnesses, Gates was sworn in as the twelfth DCI on November 6.

6
A New Vision

SEVENTH FLOOR, LANGLEY, VIRGINIA, 1991: In his first address to CIA officers, Gates talked about boldly moving forward to address the challenges of tomorrow. It was the same speech that he had delivered to Congress. He emphasized the need to make the threat posed by proliferation of chemical, nuclear, and biological weapons his first priority. He saw economic intelligence as something the CIA must do better in the future. The Directorate of Operations needed to obtain better human sources intelligence about the intentions of potential adversaries to provide earlier warning in an era when fewer American forces were forward positioned around the world. National collection capabilities needed to be better integrated to support the military. Intelligence needed to get to policymakers faster to a make a difference. He also supported the call for new educational programs to create a larger pool of expertise in foreign language and area studies. He also predicted budget reductions.

In practice, Gates moved at a measured pace and opted for an evolutionary approach. But he had vision. He knew where he wanted to take the Agency, but was prudent about his timing and the path he took. He accurately sensed that the troops feared the worst and would resist bold moves. He first needed to win the support of Agency officers. There is no doubt that he thought he would have all the time in the world to make his mark on the Agency, that his president would be reelected and continue to give him strong support.

Gates started off the 1990s reform movement. He convened fourteen task forces to study different aspects of the intelligence business, both to guide him in remaking the CIA and intelligence community for the post–Cold War period, and to build internal support for the changes. The task forces were wide-ranging and were charged with a comprehensive reexamination of the post–Cold War intelligence community:

- One persistent problem with which successive DCIs grappled was how to manage a very unwieldy intelligence community. The DCI's command-and-control levers were very weak, as they were purposely designed to be from the first days of the CIA. The new staff was charged with reducing duplication of effort, identifying cost-cutting areas, and evaluating competing proposals for funds.
- One task force looked at CIA classification and declassification standards, with the goal of making the CIA more open to the public. The group assigned to study the issue submitted a fifteen-page report, "Task Force Report on Greater CIA Openness," in December 1991. The report was classified "secret." The "secret" classification is formally reserved for information "the unauthorized disclosure of which reasonably could be expected to cause serious damage to the national security." After a public brouhaha, Gates declassified the report, which, in fact, had nothing in it of a sensitive nature. It was a reflection of the culture. If drafted by an Agency officer, it must, by extension, be secret. The internal reaction was the complete opposite. With typical paranoia, officers accused Gates of wanting to open the doors to journalists and other story seekers, threatening to expose sensitive sources and methods. The debate seems silly now, but there was the idea that if you opened the door a crack, it would be forced completely open in no time and the CIA's capabilities would be destroyed.
- Gates was concerned about the quality of CIA analysis and put together a task force to forward recommendations on improving quality and responsiveness to policymakers. The CIA had failed to predict the fall of the Soviet Union and Iraq's invasion of Iran. Gates promised aggressive promotion of competing "Red Team–Blue Team" studies to avoid analytical failures due to conventional wisdom. Gates did not deliver on this promise, nor did subsequent DCIs. One can only imagine what the difference would have been if alternative analysis teams had been institutionalized and productive in the run-up to the 2003 Iraq war.
- Upon recommendations of another task force, Gates created a National Human Intelligence Tasking Center to develop requirements for collection. Field officers use requirements—specific or

general questions—to focus their collection efforts. Requirements were typically generated in Washington, but not by policymakers or those interacting directly with them. The goal was to tighten the relationship between consumers (policymakers and analysts) and collectors. As the two groups were not allowed to mix, because of the security firewall, there needed to be an intermediary group that could translate intelligence gaps—what the policymakers did not know and wanted to know—into requirements, prioritize them, and provide feedback as necessary.

- One task force examined ways to improve the coordination of imagery collection and to establish uniform standards for interpretation and dissemination of imagery to the field. Based on recommendations, Gates decided to create a new Central Imagery Office, but did not endorse the merging of independent efforts of the CIA's National Photographic Interpretation Center and the military's exploitation offices into a national imagery agency. This decision would mark the kickoff of a long struggle within the intelligence community for centralized control of imagery capabilities.

- One task force on training examined the overall effectiveness, cost, and quality of the many training activities being conducted or sponsored throughout the intelligence community.

- Improving intelligence support to military operations was the focus of another task force. The Pentagon was dissatisfied with the level of tactical and strategic intelligence support it received in the first Gulf War. The Pentagon wanted more intelligence and wanted it integrated into commands differently. Gates established the Office of Military Affairs in order to address support and coordination weaknesses with the military. It established a central point for contact through which all matters dealing with the military had to pass.

- A task force examined options for increasing exploitation of open-source information and disseminating it to consumers. The World Wide Web had led to an explosion through the information superhighway. Although still in the early days, it was already apparent the Web offered tremendous opportunities to access and disseminate information of interest to U.S. policymakers. The question was how to exploit it without being overwhelmed by it.

- A task force looked at electronic dissemination capabilities in order to get intelligence to consumers rapidly in a secure computer network. Intelligence reports at the beginning of the decade were hand-delivered; by the end of the decade, almost all products were disseminated electronically.

- A task force on wrongdoing looked at ways to strengthen reporting to the Justice Department on criminal activity discovered in the course of intelligence collection. This initiative was part of the fallout of the BCCI (Bank of Credit & Commerce International) scandal. Congressional hearings on BCCI—called by many the Bank of Crooks and Criminals—were being held at the time of Gates's confirmation hearing. According to the Senate report, the CIA had been collecting intelligence on BCCI since 1971. In the course of targeting BCCI for laundering drug money, the CIA learned of BCCI's involvement in manipulating certain financial markets, in arms trafficking, and in supporting international terrorism, including handling the finances of Sabri al-Banna, aka Abu Nidal, and his terrorist organization.

The Senate investigation found that in 1985 the CIA learned BCCI had illegally obtained the controlling shares of First American Bank, a prominent bank in the Washington area. The CIA reported the information to Treasury and the Office of the Comptroller of the Currency. The CIA did not provide the intelligence to the Federal Reserve or the Justice Department (DOJ) in the form of a crimes report. There was speculation that the CIA purposely cut out DOJ because the CIA wanted to cover up its own operational use of the bank.

The CIA provoked congressional ire when it was slow in responding to the requests of the subcommittee conducting the investigation. CIA reluctance to cooperate with the subcommittee reinforced suspicion of a cover-up. After Senator John Kerry advised the CIA that the nomination of Gates would be delayed until the CIA provided such testimony, acting DCI Kerr provided a limited amount of information. Needless to say, the controversy attracted Gates's attention. Once confirmed, Gates initiated new procedures within the CIA to ensure that intelligence on potential criminal activity in the United States or by U.S. citizens was passed to DOJ in a timely manner.[1]

While Gates's task forces were at work, the House and Senate intelligence committees introduced draft legislation to restructure the intelligence community. The Boren-McCurdy legislation called for the creation of a Director of National Intelligence with authority over the intelligence budget as well as authority to transfer personnel temporarily from one intelligence agency to another.

Under the draft legislation, the CIA would be broken up, with the analytical elements placed under the direct control of the Director of

National Intelligence. The DCI would remain wearing only one hat—that of the director of the CIA. The draft legislation also proposed a National Imagery Agency to coordinate imagery tasking, collection, processing, and dissemination.

The legislation stirred up a hornet's nest. Fears of having an excessively strong intelligence community—a Gestapo complex—resurfaced. Bureaucratic turf battles raged, with the CIA being seen as the big loser of turf and the military the big winner. Adamantly opposed to the draft legislation, Gates countered the initiative effectively by arguing that his fourteen task forces were already at work realigning the intelligence community. He argued that legislating change in a turbulent time would make the CIA *less* flexible and *less* effective.

Faced with opposition from all sides, legislators switched tactics and instead codified and clarified the existing statutory framework for the intelligence community. The Intelligence Organization Act of 1992 outlined the structure and lines of authority within the intelligence community, and the relationship and responsibilities of the DCI and Secretary of Defense.[2]

The rejection of the original Boren-McCurdy legislation to reform the intelligence community represented the first post–Cold War missed opportunity to restructure the intelligence community. The compelling need to fix major structural problems of command and control just were not compelling enough in 1992.

Nonetheless, in the year-plus that Gates was DCI, he started the wheels of reform moving. Speaking at a university forum in 1993, Gates stated that at the time of his confirmation, 60 percent of the CIA budget was devoted to Soviet issues. By the time he left, Russian issues accounted for only 13 percent of the budget.[3]

When money moves, people move. Soviet specialists were forced to move on to other accounts or leave the Agency. But now that the Cold War mission had been removed, what was the CIA to do? What was its mission? Every day, when CIA officers got up and went to work, whether in the antiseptic offices at Langley or in the backwaters of the Middle East and the states of the former Soviet Union, they asked this million-dollar question: What is the mission? What am I supposed to do today, tomorrow, for the duration of this assignment? And does anybody out there really care? For me, on my first overseas assignment, I just did not understand the larger picture. What I saw was an absence of response from Headquarters when I proposed operational initiatives, whether against nationals of the former Soviet Union, or Arabs. I ended up doing what I thought was important, hoping at promotion

time that my judgment would be in line with management. What did
I think was important in 1991? The implosion of the former Soviet
Union, proliferation of weapons of mass destruction, terrorism, the
Arab-Israeli conflict, Iran, Libya, China, and the political stability of
Arab regimes. As it turned out, I was not too far off from the strategists
of Washington.

In 1991, when strategic thinkers sat down to consider the national
security challenges and opportunities in the post–Cold War period,
there was little consensus on what the decade would bring. There were
those who felt the splintering of the Soviet Union posed a greater
threat than a unified but weak Soviet Union. Ethnic, religious, and
nationalist conflicts in the states of the former Soviet Union were desta-
bilizing the region, and there were grave concerns about control of
weapons of mass destruction. There were those who were concerned
about a military countercoup in Russia, which would take the United
States into a hot war. There were concerns about other growing transnational threats, such as international terrorism, narco-terrorism, international organized crime, and proliferation of chemical, biological,
radiological, and nuclear weapons and technology (CBRN). These
strategists saw a dangerous new world order.

Others saw opportunities with the collapse of the Soviet Union. The
postwar period offered global business opportunities previously blocked
by the Soviet sphere of influence. With global stability, the United
States could spread democracy, and American businesses would prosper. Global health and environmental issues could be given greater priority in a world that no longer was under threat of nuclear annihilation.
In their view, the new world order was a new Camelot.

In the early 1990s, the CIA toyed with—but did not fundamentally
change—its collection priorities. There was a lot more reporting on
"targets of opportunities"—in otherwords, stuff that fell across the lap
that may or may not be of interest to policymakers. Some of the new
reporting was well received because policymakers were not getting it
from anywhere else. There was a lot of trial and error as we tried to
make ourselves more relevant to post–Cold War policymakers.

Gates called upon us to "do more with less." New requirements actually were added, but none were removed. A government-wide review on
intelligence needs for the future produced 176 topics and no suggestions for areas of cutbacks.[4] The CIA began expanding the number of
topics it covered, to include economic reporting and global health and
environmental issues like AIDS. Gates knew this was a problem, but a

problem that could go on his to-do list of reform as his next major initiative, along with the RIF.

Gates saw the writing on the wall and anticipated that intelligence budgets were certain to decrease as part of the peace dividend. The rumblings for cuts to the intelligence and national security communities had already begun. The United States was no longer at war, congressional appropriators were saying. Peacetime budgets look different than wartime budgets. Changes were on their way. Congress expected Gates to be cooperative by cutting back the intelligence community programs and cutting back its budgets. "Demobilization" was the correct term, although no one used it in the intelligence context.

As part of the realignment of government spending, the intelligence community would be asked to pare down its employment force. Gates saw downsizing as an opportunity to remake the Agency consistent with his vision of the new requirements. He wanted to strengthen what he viewed as the core capabilities of intelligence collection and analysis. He wanted out of the business of covert wars. Most of all, he wanted to get beyond the scandals that were still plaguing the Agency.

WASHINGTON, D.C., 1991: Independent Counsel Lawrence Walsh announced a new round of indictments of CIA officials in the fall. An earlier indictment was cause for concern by CIA officers, despite the fact that it was ultimately dismissed. Former CIA Costa Rica chief Joseph Fernandez had been indicted in April 1989 for making false statements to the CIA Inspector General and Congress. Rather than assist Fernandez, the CIA conducted damage control by firing him, just short of his retirement eligibility. The CIA also declined to provide any legal assistance to him. This did not go over well inside the Agency.

Fernandez was on his own when it came to justifying his activities in helping construct a secret airstrip in Costa Rica for use in resupplying the Contras. His case was dismissed seven months later, when the administration refused to declassify information pertaining to the charges. Outsiders viewed the refusal to declassify documents as a CIA attempt to protect Fernandez. Insiders knew better: the CIA was interested only in protecting its own organizational equities.

The September and November indictments were different and more alarming. Alan Fiers, the former chief of the Central American Task Force, had been under tremendous pressure by the independent counsel for his role in illegally supporting the Contras. He was in trouble and he knew it. From the moment of the Hasenfus shoot-down, he began lying about his and the CIA's knowledge of the North operation. Congress and the independent counsel could not get to their real targets—the U.S. president and vice president, or the primary lawbreakers—because of already-granted immunities, so they went after who they could get.

Alan Fiers broke ranks in order to save himself and decided to cooperate with the independent counsel. He cut a deal, pleading guilty to two misdemeanor counts of withholding information from Congress in exchange for providing information that would implicate CIA officers up the chain of command, namely former Deputy Director for Operations Clair George and former Chief of European Division Duane Clarridge. In July 1992, six years after the initial operational compromises—and in the intervening years the Berlin Wall fell and the Soviet Union disintegrated, spelling an end to the Cold War—Clair George went on trial, and Alan Fiers was the star prosecution witness. Clarridge's trial date was set for March 1993. The charges were not selling arms illegally or arming the Contras illegally, but felony charges of lying to Congress and obstructing justice.

CIA officers were horrified by the exposé factor of the 1992 trial, but were torn by the dilemma of duty to protect mission, organization, and commander in chief and duty to respect the Constitution and uphold the law. Clair George and Alan Fiers were honorable men. They had devoted their careers to serving their country, at times putting their lives and livelihood on the line. They made extraordinary sacrifices, not to win a good wage or to seek the limelight, but to keep America safe from external threats to its security. They operated in a secret world, using tools of deceit and manipulation to achieve their mission. They excelled at their craft, winning the highest awards from the CIA.

CIA officers were not taught to subvert the Constitution, but to serve the president. They were not taught to lie to Congress, and yet they existed in a culture that had a disdain for Congress and a flexible definition of truth. We asked how could the CIA permit this situation to occur, to allow conflict of duties to result in the public exposure and humiliation of two of their best and brightest? Where was the CIA support for these men in their time of need? Instead, both officers were forced out and advised to seek their own legal counsel. They were being called bad Americans because they lost sight of what democracy is all about while waging the Cold War. These were not rich men who amassed vast fortunes as a result of their career dedication, but middle-class civil servants with small nest eggs for their retirement. Although exiled from the Agency, they were not alone. CIA friends gathered together to set up a legal defense fund. The brotherhood would band together and provide the safety net.

The brotherhood did not want to accept that times had changed. The Cold War was over and there was no need for cold warriors, or so they were told. Furthermore, the warriors remaining on the books needed to be taught a lesson. The new CIA leadership set out new rules of behavior. In the New CIA, there would be no tolerance for skirting the law, let alone breaking it, even upon the instructions of a sitting president. Congressional policy and national policy must be respected. The United States is a government of checks and balances designed to prevent corruption of the system by one branch or another. The end does not justify all the means. Congress was serious about oversight and reporting obligations. These were powerful messages to all employees of the CIA and to the Directorate of Operations in particular.

We were not listening. Operations officers felt they had been made the scapegoat of a failed White House policy. Lives and careers were ruined, unfairly, operations officers argued. We did not hear the call to do its business in a new way, in a way that would be more attuned to the attitudes of the post–Cold War 1990s. We demeaned Gates as *merely* an analyst—what did he know about running operations? Congress had never before been serious about its intelligence oversight responsibilities, especially in regard to the Clandestine Service, so why should it be now? Directorate of Operations officers put the whole affair down as being a "one-off," an abnormality as a result of leadership betrayal, not a sign of changing times.

Perhaps it was not that we were not listening, but that we were reading conflicting signals. Suddenly the old system began to work again. President Bush pardoned Clarridge, Fiers, and George on December 24, 1992, three months before Clarridge's scheduled trial was to begin. Covert action had always been dangerous, politically and physically. That is why there were unspoken rules to the game.

7

Rethinking Covert Action

WASHINGTON, D.C., 1992: The mere mention of covert action attracts attention. It is a secretive art connected to a secretive policy implemented by secretive operatives. Images of operatives dressed in ninja suits sneaking into secret nuclear facilities, emplacing sophisticated miniature bombs with complicated booby traps for overattentive guards and then slipping away into the night gets the juices boiling and begs for attention. Perhaps that is why President Truman did not use the term when delineating the mission of the CIA in the National Security Act of 1947.

The words "covert action" are not mentioned in the text, but the authorizing language has been interpreted to be in the dull phrase "other functions and duties related to intelligence affecting the national security as the National Security Council may from time to time direct."[1] There has been on-and-off debate whether the National Security Act of 1947 really authorized the CIA to engage in covert action. President Truman and the National Security Council apparently thought so, as indicated by their tasking the CIA in the very first meeting of the National Security Council to conduct psychological operations in Eastern Europe.[2]

The tradition of covert action stems from World War II and the Office of Strategic Services, when officers fought on the front lines, conducting black operations in support of the Allied effort. Many members of the former Office of Strategic Services joined the CIA at its creation.

In the post–World War II period—that is, the Cold War—covert action was seen as an inexpensive third way to achieve U.S. foreign policy goals that required more muscle than diplomacy but fell short of military action. Public opinion on CIA covert action operations throughout the years has swung on a pendulum of vocal strong support, to quiet support, to vocal condemnation. Public opinion did not balance so much on specific CIA activities but on the political environment of the moment. The CIA's reputation, on the whole, and standing in the government, tended to swing on the same pendulum.

The extent and nature of covert action operations in the 1990s was defined largely by the fallout of Iran-Contra, the distaste that Gates had for all covert action and then later the administration of President Clinton, who would, to put it crudely, rather make love than war.

Up until the 1980s, covert action programs were designed to be secret and to give the executive branch "plausible deniability" should the operations be exposed and result in negative political fallout. Successive presidents set up special secret boards to approve and oversee CIA covert action programs and to function as the "circuit breaker" between the president and the CIA. These boards were never advertised, and their membership was cloaked in the best of fashion—seemingly boring administrative boards. Yawn. Under President Eisenhower, it was called the 5412 Committee, and Nixon set up the Forty Committee. Ford established the Operations Advisory Group, and Clinton, who did not have that secrecy thing quite down, the Covert Action Interagency Working Group.

CIA leadership and officers embraced covert action and plausible deniability, even at the risk of being called rogue elephants. Ultimately, as a presidential arm for action, they knew the president would protect the CIA. For example, after the shoot-down over the USSR of the U-2 piloted by Francis Gary Powers in 1960, the State Department, conducting damage control, invoked the circuit-breaker mechanism by announcing that President Eisenhower did not authorize specific U-2 missions. The blame was placed on the CIA. DCI Allen Dulles stepped up to the plate and offered his resignation, which Eisenhower did not accept. It was a well-scripted system, and everyone knew the game.

CIA directors and senior staff were expected to serve as the scapegoats when the flames became too hot. After the Bay of Pigs fiasco in 1961, DCI Dulles, Deputy Director of Central Intelligence Charles Cabell, and Deputy Director for Plans Richard Bissel were initially protected from the political fallout, but eventually were asked to resign by President Kennedy. Kennedy reportedly told Bissel, whom Kennedy liked and respected, "If this were the British government, I would resign, and you, being a senior civil servant, would remain. But it isn't. In our government, you and Allen have to go, and I have to remain."[3]

This is the way the system worked. That is why CIA officers were so appalled by how Iran-Contra played out. There were not supposed to be public trials or personal accountability. The president was supposed to protect the CIA and its clandestine capabilities. It has always been understood at the outset that the capabilities were worth protecting.

The decision to maintain covert action as a policy tool has periodically been reconsidered, notably by Congress, but it has always been upheld as a valid instrument of foreign policy. Every president since Truman has utilized covert action and has protected the presidential option to authorize it, lie about it, and scapegoat it, despite the foreign policy flaps resulting from it.

Part of the CIA's new problems resulted from the Reagan approach to covert action. Under President Reagan, the U.S. government began the practice of publicly justifying covert-action policy by announcing covert action programs in support of specific political policies. This solved the sticky political problem that covert action could pose to the executive branch—that is, after exposure, having to justify publicly what one publicly denied doing.

The CIA entered into a new phase of "overt covert action," a marvelous oxymoron that should join the ranks of "jumbo shrimp" and "military intelligence," with more than a bit of trepidation. To put it mildly, the CIA is publicity shy. For the CIA, the overt covert action caused continuous security problems requiring damage control, as foreign governments, Congress, and the press sought more specific information that exposed actual operational activity. The initial CIA aid to Nicaraguan rebels (the Contras) and Afghan fighters against the Soviet invasion are good examples of overt covert action.*

As Congress and the public later learned, not all covert action in the 1980s was overt. The Iran-Contra affair would reopen the wounds of the 1960s and 1970s. Congress, in particular, felt as though it had been duped by the CIA, and that the CIA had resorted to the "dirty tricks" of decades past. Congress, through the legislative investigations, new laws, and intelligence oversight committees, coupled with

---

* Until recently, the 1980s Afghan covert action program had been considered a success by Agency insiders and outsiders. In the 1990s, it was not discussed too much by insiders, other than vague mentions as a success story, because the concept of covert wars had been so sullied by the Nicaraguan experience.

new restrictive executive orders (E.O. 12333), thought the CIA had been "reined in" permanently.

The Iran-Contra affair was a seminal event for the CIA in terms of how covert action operations would be approached in the 1990s. A friend of mine, a Latin American field officer deeply involved in the resupply effort to the Contras, aptly summed up the political storm brewing, telling his station officers, "Pay attention; this is the end of an era." Indeed, the political fallout of Iran-Contra spelled an end to the large paramilitary operations, at least through the 1990s.

Beginning under Gates, covert action programs began to evolve and shift away from the traditional programs that had so inflamed the 1970s and 1980s. There was a sense that influencing foreign governments and international opinion could be done better by open activities of U.S. scholarship, travel programs, and national endowments run by the Republican and Democratic parties and financed openly by the U.S. government. In the new age of a single superpower, there was no need for the hidden hand of power.

The large paramilitary branch within the Directorate of Operations was pared down, with contract officers dismissed, staff paramilitary officers assigned to other duties, and proprietary companies sold off. The paramilitary officer, known affectionately as a knuckle-dragger, became an endangered species in the 1990s. Staff paramilitary officers who remained in Special Activities Division were engaged in assignments training foreign military and intelligence officers or supporting U.S. military actions in Iraq, Somalia, Haiti, and the former Yugoslavia. Gone were the days of large counterinsurgency operations, such as the Philippines (1950–54), Guatemala (1954), Cuba (1961), Laos (1963–69), Cambodia (1970–71), and Angola (1975), which had become the hallmark of CIA covert actions.[4]

Operations to influence the outcome of elections had come to a halt. Past practices of funding opposition political parties, labor organizations, and radio stations, with the explicit intent of overthrowing a current "socialist" leader or ensuring the defeat of a "leftist" challenger, were viewed as no longer politically correct, and undemocratic. In the 1990s there was little room for large-scale operations to overthrow democratically elected governments like those that took place in Iran (1953), Ecuador (1963), British Guiana (1963), Chile (1964–73), and Australia (1972). As the policy on Iraq in the 1990s reflects, the politicos were uncomfortable with the business of overthrowing governments.

By the mid-1990s, the propaganda branch, located within Special Activities Division, virtually ceased to exist. The large media projects, geared to counter anti-Americanism, such as Radio Free Europe, Radio Liberty, *Encounter, Preuves, Tempo Presente, Forum, Hiwar, Cuadenos,* and *Chinese Quarterly,* had long been ended.[5] Because of political and operational security sensitivities, CIA field officers gave wide berth to the press, both domestic and foreign.

Sending miniature Bibles and banned literary works by refuseniks to Moscow came to an end when the opposition presses were shut down and the operators told to return to their homes, which were now liberated. Agents hired to place pro-U.S. articles in foreign newspapers were terminated. When the CIA wanted to influence opinion in support of military operations, it resorted to dropping leaflets from military planes. This is hardly covert.

Then there was the issue of assassination. The question of whether or not the CIA should engage in assassination operations is one that has been hotly debated both within and outside the CIA, before and after Gates. Up until the mid-1960s, assassination was an accepted—albeit closely held—covert action practice and was sanctioned at the highest levels of the U.S. government. The written record of political authorization is murky—not surprising given the practice of maintaining plausible deniability for covert action. Whether the CIA actually assassinated foreign leaders is debatable, but it certainly tried.

In 1975, the Church Commission investigated the Agency's involvement in lethal operations and the murky political authorizations, exposing the CIA to public censure. The congressional hearings took place in a highly charged political environment. The general public was skeptical of the official results of the investigation into President Kennedy's assassination. Conspiracy theories abounded (and are still debated) on CIA direct involvement in the assassination. Others charged that Fidel Castro had ordered the assassination in revenge for the CIA attempts against his life.

The Church Commission was breathing fire and the CIA seemed about to be incinerated. President Ford decided to take preemptive action in order to curb congressional legislative initiatives that would cripple the CIA's ability to function. Ford issued Executive Order (E.O.) 11905 in 1976, which detailed a number of reforms, including an explicit prohibition against assassination. President Reagan issued E.O. 12333 in 1981, which superseded E.O. 11905, which states: "No person employed by or acting on behalf of the United States Government shall engage in, or conspire to engage in, assassination."

Gates was on the Seventh Floor when the "assassination manuals" scandal hit the press. In October 1984, Associated Press stringer Robert

Parry wrote that the Contras were using a CIA-produced manual, *Human Resources Exploitation Training Manual,** which "advocated selective use of violence to neutralize civilian opponents and arranging other deaths for political advantage." Coupled with other press reports the following year, stating that Latin American security forces were using a revised version of the manual, which still contained language on coercive interrogation techniques—which in some corners was interpreted to condone torture at a minimum and to instruct how to do so at a maximum—the CIA faced a major public relations problem, to put it mildly.

Gates was determined no similar scandal would occur during his time as director. He made sure that E.O. 12333 was the mantra all Agency officers recited as the regulations that guide intelligence activities, and every Agency officer was aware of the language banning assassination. If you asked a CIA officer if the Agency conducted assassination operations, to an officer, all would cite the regulation banning the practice. To make sure, Gates directed the Agency lawyers to be ever vigilant.

The lawyers interpreted the ban broadly. Operations would come to a screaming halt if the lawyers caught a whiff of anything that could be interpreted on the most liberal basis of practicing assassination, condoning assassination, or assisting indirectly in assassination. The CIA determined it had a "duty to warn" individuals who were targets of assassination so that the CIA could not be charged with complicity. Absurd situations arose with the CIA warning its own enemies of threats, terminating agents who were hired by the CIA to support regime change operations or to stop terrorists, but then actually put together plans to do so, crossing the lawyers' red lines.

During my first tour overseas, I had one of those situations come up that make operations officers very nervous. I was handling an agent whom I'll call Ahmed. Ahmed hated his boss, and this hatred was one of the reasons that Ahmed cooperated with the CIA. One night at a meeting in a safe house, Ahmed was beyond his normal range of hostility and was ranting and raving that his boss was ruining his life. He begged me to give him a gun so he could just shoot the bastard and solve all of his problems at once.

I declined, telling Ahmed that while killing the boss might make him feel better for an instant, it would cause him all kinds of other troubles,

---

* The *Human Resources Exploitation Training Manual–1983* and its earlier version, *KUBARK Counterintelligence Interrogation–July 1963*, were declassified in January 1997.

not the least of which would be getting caught and being sent to prison or worse. I implored him to be calm and seek revenge by helping me. Ahmed was not convinced and stormed out, saying he would get his own gun.

The next morning I went to my chief to tell him what happened. He told me not to report it and not to worry about it, as Ahmed was known for his emotional outbursts. But I *did* worry about it, because he seemed so set on his boss's removal. I had images of going to the safe house only to find a pool of blood and a body in the middle of the sitting room.

When I went to our next meeting, I had a knot in the bottom of my stomach as I unlocked the safe house door. Much to my relief, I found no macabre scene, but Ahmed in much-improved spirits. If this incident had occurred just a few years later, all reporting discretion would have been removed. I would have sent a cable without even asking my boss out of fear of becoming complicit in an assassination attempt. The legal eagles would have reviewed the case and made a determination on whether there was a duty to warn. The agent would have been put on ice, if not fired ("terminated" in spook-speak) and there would have been a human rights/suitability review. It would have been a big bureaucratic deal rather than a few nights of lost sleep.

Gates's views on covert action and his dismantling of CIA paramilitary and other covert action capabilities would have tremendous impact on the Agency in terms of its ability to conduct a war on terrorism. Paramilitary officers, with their distinctive skill sets, left in droves because their services were no longer required. Later in the decade, when the CIA looked at its options for countering the threat posed by a new breed of terrorists, the paramilitary option was not a consideration. Not only did the CIA no longer have a real capability to wage a secret war, it no longer thought in those terms. The vast majority of CIA officers had neither military experience nor military inclinations. Insiders viewed the loss of covert action capabilities with concern; the impact would not be noticed outside the organization until after September 11, 2001.

And then it was too late.

8
The Directorate of Intelligence

NEW HEADQUARTERS BUILDING, LANGLEY, VIRGINIA, 1991: When Gates arrived as DCI, he found the Directorate of Intelligence largely unchanged from the time he left in 1989. The analysts in the directorate also found Gates unchanged. He was still very smart and convinced that he had all the right answers. Analysts either loved him or hated him. There was not much in between. Gates had big plans for remaking the directorate. He had the benefit of knowing it well, perhaps too well.

The Directorate of Intelligence is the analytical arm of the CIA. As a brain trust, the directorate has incredible and diverse intellectual capabilities to throw at issues of interest to U.S. policymakers. Unlike many intellectuals in the ivory tower, directorate analysts are firmly rooted in what is relevant to policymakers, today and in the near future. The analysts are the most visible of Agency employees, as they regularly participate in interagency committees, some public-sector contact groups, and university/scholarly groups. They typically are overt employees—that is, they acknowledge their Agency affiliation.

As with the rest of the Agency, the end of the Cold War brought many changes to the Directorate of Intelligence. The extensive resources devoted to Soviet analysis had to be retooled. Many senior analysts were retired "in place," and few new analysts were hired. Junior analysts were worked to the bone, and many left out of sheer exhaustion or lack of promotion opportunities. Analysts were often criticized in the 1990s for poor performance. However, it took several dramatic intelligence failures before the CIA could convince policymakers that resource outlays were insufficient to maintain a world-class analytical capability—but this would come after Gates's tenure.

The mission of the Directorate of Intelligence is to develop and provide finished intelligence to U.S. policymakers who decide matters of national security and foreign policy. They do this by conducting integrated, multidisciplinary analysis on key foreign countries, regional conflicts, and issues that transcend national boundaries, such as terrorism, weapons proliferation, and narcotics trafficking.

Analysts produce finished intelligence reports, drawing upon raw intelligence from the Agency and other members of the U.S. intelligence community, open source information, and analytical and informational pieces from the U.S. agencies. The product can be in the form of written assessments or oral briefings. The directorate produces a variety of different products, including briefings, quick-reaction papers, and in-depth analysis. Most of these respond to specific requests by intelligence consumers. Analysts also provide support to diplomatic negotiations and military operations. The Directorate of Intelligence does not make foreign policy, but provides the intelligence assessments upon which policymakers make decisions. Finally, the intelligence is supposed to be timely, accurate, unbiased, nonpartisan, and nondepartmental.

The "raw intelligence" the analysts draw upon comes from the human intelligence (HUMINT) reporting from the Directorate of Operations and the Defense Intelligence Agency, as well as intelligence collected through technical means, such as signals intelligence (SIGINT), measurement and signature intelligence (MASINT), communications intelligence (COMINT), and satellite imagery (IMINT). The State Department provides valuable diplomatic and atmospheric reporting.

In the 1990s, sources of information exploded with the advent of the information highway and the proliferation of small commercial news stations and papers. The Foreign Broadcast Information Service captures and translates the most important of these. In other words, the directorate has no shortage of data, not all of the same reliability or usefulness.

The analyst's challenge is to winnow out the chaff and assess the remainder to come up with accurate, timely, and useful assessments. While describing a current situation accurately is helpful to policymakers, accurately predicting what will happen is what separates the mediocre from the competent.

The directorate's customers are U.S. foreign policy and national security officials. The most important is the U.S. president, who receives a daily briefing by a designated directorate analyst. Not all presidents like their intelligence briefing in the same format, and therefore the briefing is tailored to the individual. Some past presidents preferred to read the briefing book and ask the briefer questions. Other presidents preferred to be briefed by their own national security advisor, with the CIA briefer sitting outside but available to answer questions. Other presidents wanted the DCI present for the briefing. As a former DCI, President George Bush Sr. was a voracious consumer of intelligence and liked to have his briefing from the experts. According to Bush, "The PDB, the President's Daily Brief, was the first order of business on my calendar. I made it a point from day one to read the PDB in the presence of the CIA officer and either Brent [National Security Advisor Scowcroft], or sometimes his deputy. This way I could ask the briefers for more information on matters of critical interest, and consult with Brent on matters affecting policy."[1]

The directorate delivers "finished intelligence" information and analysis in a variety of forms to U.S. policymakers, law enforcement, and military officials. In addition to the daily reporting—called "current intelligence"—the directorate produces classified serial publications, situation reports, and medium- and long-term intelligence research papers.

The Directorate of Intelligence went through significant reorganization during the 1980s and 1990s as it first worked to integrate analytical disciplines and then to flatten the management structure. The directorate was battling structural problems that had led to analytical failures of one sort or another. Prior to 1981, the directorate was organized primarily by discipline, with political, economic, military, and leadership offices each subdivided by geography. For example, there was the Office of Leadership Analysis. Within this office, different analysts monitored Arab leaders, Asian leaders, European leaders, and so on, developing psychological profiles and decision-making style analysis. The analysts used models specific to leadership analysis (rational decision-making model, for example) to determine how, for example, Pakistan's Zia al-Haq would respond to a U.S. covert war against the Soviets in Afghanistan—would he support the U.S. policy or not? The leadership analysts worked largely in isolation from those monitoring political, economic, and social issues for the country of the particular leader—factors that, for example, were shaping the Pakistani premier's decisions.

In 1981, a reorganization created regional offices, which combined political, economic, military, and other types of research into cross-disciplinary units. The reorganization had the benefit of grouping analysts into country teams, making possible more detailed analytic research. Analysts within country teams focusing on their own discipline coordinated their work with the others to produce a corporate product reflecting the expertise of the group. By working within a geographical group, the analysts were expected to gain additional insight into cultural and social issues that impact their discipline study. Past intelligence failures had been attributed to an inadequate understanding of these dynamics.

With the breakup of the Soviet Union, transnational threats proliferated, leading Gates to reorganize the directorate, creating new offices that were issue oriented. The new issues, such as weapons proliferation, counternarcotics, counterterrorism, global organized crime, and environment, did not fit neatly into existing groups and required substantive knowledge on global trends versus regional or country-specific issues. At a time when budgets were decreasing, the directorate found it difficult to support these new requirements while doing business as usual in the geographical offices.

During the same period, layers of management multiplied because the path to promotion was through the management track, and the best and most ambitious analysts demanded management positions as the cost of retaining their expertise. More analysts focused upon managing other analysts as well as the intelligence process. Fewer experts were devoted to the core work of analysis. With the increased layers of management, coordination became cumbersome. In order to get a piece out the door, analysts would have to make analytical compromises—too many, sometimes—leading to "groupthink." It was this groupthink to which new intelligence failures were attributed.

Starting under Gates, the Directorate of Intelligence went through tremendous downsizing, cutting the analytical service to the bone. While the directorate significantly reduced new hiring, it also lost many analysts through resignations. The idea of spending a full career at the CIA became less attractive. More than half of the analysts from my Career Trainee class had left within five years. Junior analysts left for a variety of reasons and returned to academia, either to teach or to finish a dissertation. The directorate also had problems retaining experienced analysts. Senior analysts left for many of the same reasons operations officers left: budget problems slowing down promotions, confusion in mission, burdensome workloads, discontent with management, and lack of opportunity to conduct long-term research.

Many of the slots in the Senior Intelligence Service (SIS) traditionally filled by senior analysts had been cut in the early 1990s, which provided little opportunity for analysts to move into senior management positions within the CIA and the intelligence community. Demands for briefings from Congress as well as current intelligence requirements expanded exponentially in the 1990s, leaving analysts with little time to do the long-term research that is intellectually fulfilling. The practice of giving analysts two- to three-year assignments on accounts made them more broad-based, but with little depth. Intellectually, this was found less than satisfactory.

Analysts took issue with the concept that coverage would be good enough if "it was an inch deep and a mile wide, with the ability to go a mile deep on any given issue" as proposed by reform-minded congressional intelligence oversight committees.[2] Good analysis depends upon a deep understanding of nuances of a situation, people and historical development, coupled with critical thinking and analytical rigor. The analysts were right to be concerned about quality.

The Directorate of Intelligence, as well as the rest of the analytical units within the intelligence community, came under fire for poor performance. The directorate failed to predict the imminent implosion of the Soviet economy—although its weakness was noted by the CIA as early as 1987 with the assessment of a growing likelihood of the collapse of the old order—and the fall of the Berlin Wall. The demise of the Soviet Union was the most important event affecting the 1990s. The directorate failed to accurately assess the intentions of Saddam Hussein prior to Iraq's invasion of Kuwait in 1990, assessing he was bluffing to extract concessions from the Kuwaiti government. Military commanders during the Gulf War criticized CIA analysis as mush, with rounded corners and with "safe" conclusion.

Those who grumbled about Gates focused on his impact on the coordination process. He berated his analysts for "analysis that was irrelevant or untimely or unfocused or all three." At the same time, if he did not agree with the analysis, he would sit on the report. As a micromanager, it could take months before he would sign off on finished pieces, ensuring that the work was untimely. For those who offered up analysis that did not fit with his views, they were continually fearful of being removed from their managerial positions. When existing institutions would not do what he wanted, he supported the creation of new offices within the intelligence directorate, new managerial levels within existing offices, and new centers to focus on topics of particular concern. The overall impact was that dissidence was stifled.[3]

One of the misperceptions of the CIA is that it is monolithic. There are internal differences among the analysts, but they are encouraged to reach a consensus assessment. The Agency strives to speak to policymakers with "one voice"—that is, to keep its internal debate in-house and present the consensus assessment. The problems arise when a consensus cannot be found, or when the debate is stifled. It is in these circumstances that press leaks start to reveal gripes from unhappy analysts. In Gates's time, the dissent came from the Soviet analysts. In 2003, the gripes came from Middle Eastern and counterterrorism analysts who took issue with the rationale for going to war with Iraq.

Supporters of Gates argued that the culture of the Directorate of Intelligence, with thousands of voices of independent thinkers, ensured that Gates could not stifle debate and politicize intelligence, even if he wanted to do so. Given that the culture is characterized by intellectual diversity, there is a certain truth to this viewpoint.

When asked, analysts have difficulty in describing the "Directorate of Intelligence culture" because they see more diversity than uniformity. This certainly is true upon examination of the wide breadth of substantive and academic backgrounds. The directorate is peopled with experts in every conceivable field who have come from a wide variety of universities across the United States. Directorate offices select their own new-hires, using different criteria, hence ensuring diversity of characteristics.

However, in comparing the Directorate of Intelligence with the Directorate of Operations, the Directorate of Intelligence has more officers with advanced degrees, frequently at the PhD level, or ABDs (all but dissertation). They are book smart, rather than street smart. There is a sense of intellectual arrogance within the directorate, with academic credentials being an important union card.

The culture of the directorate is overwhelmingly scholarly, but more like academia on steroids. There is a sense of urgency that drives the directorate. The urgency is part a function of the nature of the work and part self-imposed. The directorate uses an analytical model that is event driven. That is, each morning, the first actions that analysts take are reviews of new intelligence reports and open-source information (newspapers, journals, etc.) that arrived overnight. They will read the information, identifying what is new and noteworthy, and put this information aside for "current intelligence" reports.

Current intelligence is produced on a daily basis, and there are production schedules to be met. As analysts assess trends in order to forecast future developments, other nuggets of information are set aside for more in-depth analysis, once the current intelligence products are out of the way. The self-imposed urgency is caused by the directorate's drive to be "relevant" to U.S. policymakers.

Gates pushed the directorate to be more relevant to policymakers. When he was at the National Security Council, he was a consumer of intelligence. He saw firsthand the disconnect that can happen when intelligence does not address the questions or interests of the consumer. During Gates's tenure, more analysts would be seconded to work inside policymaking offices in order to provide direct intelligence support.

The unintended consequence of the push for relevance through the decade was that the directorate has increasingly gotten into the business of answering questions from policymakers rather than telling policymakers what they think they should know. Looking forward to the war on terrorism, policymakers (notably those in the Pentagon) ask a list of daily questions, expecting a response within twenty-four hours. While the directorate must be responsive to the policymakers' needs, merely responding to questions allows the policymakers to frame the debate and removes the independent input of issues of relevancy that all-source analysis should provide. Even before the war on terrorism, analysts were hard pressed to complete production requirements for current intelligence and intelligence memorandums. Because of more immediate requirements, long-term research papers and strategic analysis have now all but fallen off the table.

Gates also was the first DCI to chisel away at the stovepipe culture that dominates the Agency. He encouraged greater interaction between analysts and collectors. Despite great resistance, Gates promoted the assignment of analysts to positions with the Directorate of Operations, both in Headquarters and overseas. Analysts received assignments as chief of field offices, positions traditionally held by senior operations officers. Analysts were assigned to provide close analytical support in some larger field offices as well.

The cultural divide between analysts and field officers is vast. The Directorate of Intelligence is a more open organization and views the secretiveness of the Directorate of Operations as excessive. Analysts often complain that they do not have access to key raw intelligence reports from the Directorate of Operations, reports to which they need access if they are to fulfill their missions. It is not unusual for the most sensitive raw intelligence reports to be so restricted in dissemination that only those above the group-chief level will be authorized access, and not the analysts who routinely follow the issue. Sometimes the most sensitive raw reports can be the most authoritative reporting.

Operations officers are fiercely protective of their sources and do not want anyone outside of Operations to know more than necessary about them. Past improper handling of intelligence by analysts was the reason that field officers demanded limited access across the board. If there is to be continuing access to the stream of intelligence, the Directorate of Operations must protect sources and methods.

Rather than viewing each other as players on the same team, the relationship was often contentious and laced with suspicion. When analysts would ask for more information about sources in order to assess the authoritativeness of the information, operations officers would suspect they were trying to outspook the spooks and figure out the identity of the source. I remember the first time I was asked to meet with analysts to brief them on issues related to terrorism. My branch chief insisted that his deputy accompany me to the meeting "in order to keep the analysts in line." My thought at the time was that the chief was worried that I would tell the analysts too much, and the deputy was there as my minder. I always resisted this organizational paranoia, and as a result, through the years, I developed excellent working and personal relationships with CIA analysts. My calculation was simple: I wanted the smartest people on my team, and I knew I would have to give in order to get.

By institutionalizing direct contact between analysts and operations officers, Gates hoped to build new lines of communication and new relationships. This would be a slow process. Gates started the ball rolling, despite opposition from both directorates. The next DCI would take the initiative a step further.

9
Post–Cold War Convulsions

THE THIRD WORLD, 1991–93: While the collapse of the Soviet Union had immediate impact in most of the states of Eastern Europe, it took a bit longer for the convulsions to reach the Middle East and Africa. When it did, suddenly the borders established in the immediate aftermath of World War II were challenged. The Iraqi invasion of Kuwait and the U.S. intervention that reimposed the status quo in the Gulf was just one example.

With the exit of the Soviet Union, the context of proxy wars in both the Middle East and Africa suddenly changed. The Arab-Israeli conflict, where Washington and Moscow backed competing players, became less central to U.S. strategic interests once the Russians were out of the game.

A weakened Palestine Liberation Organization chairman Yasir Arafat had jeopardized Gulf Arab financial backing for the Palestinian cause when he chose to tailgate Palestinian popular opinion and support the Iraqi position during the Gulf War. The Gulf War removed a significant threat to the Israelis and made them more confident in the willingness of the United States to protect friends. The dynamics were enough to convince all parties to participate in a new round of regional talks. The Madrid Peace Conference convened in October 1991, signaling a willingness to discuss new relationships between Israel and its Arab neighbors.

These same dynamics that produced a change for the better in the Levant led to a breakdown in stability in Africa. Events started in the Horn of Africa but spread through the sub-Saharan region over the next few years as ethnic and tribal groups sought to remake borders and change governments along sectarian lines. In May 1991, Ethiopian President Mengistu Haile Mariam was overthrown by rebel troops. Ethiopia was being split apart by various separatists' movements, many of which were Muslim dominated. The United States intervened to maintain the territorial integrity of Ethiopia, forging a compromise solution that permitted a coalition of Ethiopian rebel groups led by Meles Zenawi to take charge. Islamic leaders became convinced that the United States had assumed an anti-Islamic position for Africa. Ultimately, the U.S. effort to maintain status quo borders would fail, when predominantly Christian Eritrea split off from the rest of Ethiopia.

SUDAN, 1992: Sudan had been unstable for decades, plagued with an unending civil war, famines, and a dictator who could not decide whether he was a Marxist or an Islamist. In 1989, Sudan took a turn for the worse. General Omar Hasan al-Bashir led a military coup against Sudanese strongman Ga'afar Muhammad Nimeiri and established an Islamic state. He selected Hasan al-Turabi as Sudan's spiritual leader. Bashir's and Turabi's policies set Sudan on a collision course with the United States.

Under Turabi's influence and direction, the Sudanese government embarked on an extensive program to turn Sudan into a base of operations to spread a militant pan-Islamic ideology. The goals were to reshape the Middle East, Africa, and Central and Southeast Asia into an Islamic community ('umma) based upon Islamic law (Sharia) and to dismantle the existing nation-state structure through armed struggle. The collapse of the Soviet Union proved the failure of the Communist Doctrine. Arab nationalism was discredited many years previously, with the failed policies of Egypt's Gamal Nasser. American democracy was viewed as a front to westernize and oppress the Muslim world by destroying the Muslim culture. The American war on Iraq was proof of the evil intentions against Islamic people. Islamic thinkers converging in Sudan felt that only Islam could save the Muslim world from oppression.

In a show of Islamic solidarity Sudan changed its visa laws in 1991, allowing any Muslim into the country without a visa. Turabi forged ties with Iran, Afghan Arabs', (Arabs who had trained and fought in the Afghan-Soviet war), and other established Islamic extremist groups in order to unite these disparate entities into a coordinated global *jihad* against apostate Arab regimes and their Western backers—the United States, France, and Britain.

To this end, Turabi created an umbrella organization for adherents to this militant ideology, the Armed Islamic Movement. He organized a number of Islamic conferences, under the name of Popular Arab and Islamic Conference, as an overt activity bringing together *jihadis* for clandestine meetings to create and execute an action plan for armed struggle throughout the region. Important *jihadis* assembled in Sudan and participated in the Armed Islamic Movement program to varying degrees. Turabi founded a number of training camps for extremists and provided funding, direction, and direct support for terrorist operations. The CIA watched with concern as various *jihadi* groups set up shop in Sudan: Gama'at al-Islamiya, Egyptian Islamic Jihad, Hizballah, Hamas, Palestinian Islamic Jihad, various Palestinian rejectionist groups, Yemeni radicals, Iranian and Iraqi intelligence officials, and an odd Saudi figure, Usama bin Ladin.

Bin Ladin first appeared on the CIA's scopes during the Afghan-Soviet war, but the Agency did not task its field stations to collect on bin Ladin until 1992 when he appeared in Sudan. At that time, CIA interest in bin Ladin was tangential to its investigation of state-sponsored terrorism by Sudan. Bin Ladin appeared to be a moneyman and logistics expert, creating financial networks for moving money and extremists in the Middle East. He appeared to be working at the behest of Turabi, the primary focus of U.S. attention, and in concert with other dangerous extremists who were being given safe haven and support by Turabi and the Sudanese government.

The CIA began watching bin Ladin, trying to figure out who he was and what he was doing. His name and face kept popping up in association with some serious bad guys. The CIA assessment of bin Ladin changed over time, as did the amount of resources deployed against him and al-Qa'ida, as the CIA realized that he was not just the administrative assistant to evil, but the chairman of the board. But in 1992, bin Ladin was just a face in the crowd.

The CIA window into bin Ladin's activities was limited. Some activities were easily observed. Bin Ladin continued the practice, which he began in Afghanistan during the Afghan-Soviet war, of bringing together like-minded Sunni Muslims who believed in the establishment of an Islamic state through armed struggle against unbelievers. Bin Ladin funded their training in Sudan at military training bases he established under the aegis of the Sudanese government. Building upon ties established in the international training camps in Afghanistan, and the contacts of Turabi, bin Ladin spent his years in the Sudan establishing a loose network of Sunni and Shia militants.

What the CIA did not see, or only saw in isolated bits and pieces, was that bin Ladin was becoming a significant player. While in Sudan, bin

Ladin cemented international credibility among *jihadis* through effective operational support, unwavering commitment to the cause, and
strong support from a state sponsor (Sudan), effectively consolidating
the reputation that he established in Afghanistan. He increased his
efforts to spread his ideology by giving speeches at mosques and nightly
gatherings and by granting press interviews. Through Turabi, bin Ladin
developed a crucial relationship with Ayman al-Zawahiri, one of the
leaders of Egyptian Islamic Jihad. Bin Ladin began to support Egyptian
Islamic Jihad operations.

Sudan was quickly evolving into a terrorist state. The CIA found
strong links of official Sudanese support to Muslim armed factions in
Somalia and Eritrea that were engaged in a vicious civil war using
famine as a weapon. There were also links to Islamists in other countries in the Horn of Africa. Muslims from Ethiopia, Somalia, Eritrea,
Kenya, and Uganda were training in Sudanese camps.[1] The CIA had
multisourced information that Sudan directly supported the Egyptian
Islamic Jihad operations to overthrow the Egyptian government.

Given the important relationship between Egypt and the United
States, the CIA deployed extensive resources against the Egyptian
Islamic Jihad wherever it was present in an attempt to neutralize this
threat to Egyptian stability. There was a large concentration of
Egyptian Islamic Jihad members in Sudan, and there was extensive
evidence that they were using Sudan as a staging point for cross-bor-
der operations into Egypt to destabilize the Mubarak regime. The last
thing the U.S. government wanted to see was Mubarak assassinated
and an extremist Islamic government led by Egyptian Islamic Jihad
seize control. The fear was not unfounded; only a decade before,
Egyptian extremists assassinated Mubarak's predecessor, Anwar Sadat.
The United States decided to thump Sudan to get it to change its
behavior—to stop hosting terrorists and supporting their destructive
ideologies. In 1993, the State Department placed Sudan on its list of
states sponsoring terrorism. It was a good move, but it did not stop the
forces that were already in play.

SOMALIA, 1992: The borders of the entire Horn of Africa were
suddenly being challenged by internal ethnic and religious separatist
movements. Somalia in particular was imploding. Armed bands ter-
rorized the streets after General Mohammed Farah Aideed overthrew
the U.S.-backed autocrat Siad Barre. While Aideed controlled
Mogadishu, other clans challenged his authority in the country.
Warlords reigned supreme as they carved out their turf and annihilated

those who stood in their way, each outdoing the other in terms of brutality. The humanitarian crisis had reached shocking proportions. Scenes of starving Somali children flashed across the television screens of America. Somalia was putting additional pressure on the surrounding states, especially Kenya and Ethiopia, with hundreds of thousands of refugees moving across their borders.

The United Nations decided that the situation could not be ignored. With U.S. support, UN peacekeeping forces entered Somalia in late summer with a humanitarian mission—feed the starving people of Somalia. When the UN personnel and other relief workers met warlord opposition to getting food and medicine to the people, the United States decided to send in troops.

For the CIA, Somalia was a nightmare scenario from the very beginning. The CIA had closed its field office in Mogadishu a year earlier, because the U.S. government decided it was not interested in things Somali. The operational environment was dangerous and the mission—force protection—seemed more appropriate for military intelligence officers. Pentagon sniping at the CIA after the Gulf War had eroded any goodwill at the top. Somalia was a humanitarian military effort destined to be a mess; let the military and NGO types work it out.

Then–Deputy Director of Operations Tom Twetten tried to keep the CIA out of the UN humanitarian initiative in Somalia. Twetten's reluctance was met by a direct order from the National Security Council to field a team to secure the airport and assess the conditions on the ground before U.S. troops arrived. In late 1992, the CIA sent a team of paramilitary officers, who quickly determined that Somalia was a war zone, where the good guys and the bad guys all looked the same.

The team was on the ground for less than a month when disaster struck. On a recon mission in the Bardera area on December 23, 1992, four members of the team were in a vehicle that struck a land mine, killing one CIA officer and wounding three others. The tragic loss did not spell an end to the mission, but was rather a bloody prelude to more death and destruction.[2]

LANGLEY, VIRGINIA, 1993: On January 25, during the morning commute, chaos broke out in front of the gates of CIA Headquarters. Lansing Bennett and Frank Darling were murdered as they sat at the traffic light, waiting to turn into the restricted drive leading into the CIA compound. A lone gunman stepped out of his car, walked between the two left-turn lanes, and sprayed bullets to the left and the right. Despite the posting of CIA security officers only a hundred yards away, the shooter made a clean getaway.

CIA officers already in the Langley compound learned of the attack from local news programs, then CNN and word of mouth. Shocked at the carnage at their doorstep, officers throughout the Agency delayed mourning their dead and immediately went to work to identify the terrorist. I was assigned to a North African post at the time, chasing terrorists. (I would love to say more on the nature of my work in counterterrorism, but CIA censors will not permit this. However, to put some perspective on the issue, in 1993 I had never heard of bin Ladin, but was well aware of Egyptian Gama'at al-Islamiya, Egyptian Islamic Jihad, and Abu Nidal Organization.) After reading the cable advising the field stations of the attack, besides shock and anger, I had an odd feeling. I had automatically assumed that we field officers on the front lines were most at risk, not my colleagues at home. From that day forward, I never let my guard down and watched my back wherever I was. I used the front entrance to Headquarters only when I absolutely had to do so. I internalized the fact that terrorism knew no boundaries.

While the FBI took the lead in the criminal investigation, the CIA Counterterrorism Center focused on pulling together a list of terrorist groups that had the capability and the interest in attacking U.S. intelligence on U.S. soil. The list was long and thought to be comprehensive. But al-Qa'ida was nowhere on the list.

Less than one month later, the FBI identified the prime suspect for the shooting. Responding to a missing persons report, the FBI searched a Reston, Virginia, apartment and found the weapon used in the attack. The missing person was Mir Aimal Kansi. He disappeared on the day of the shooting. There was no derogatory intelligence information on Kansi—no information linking him to a terrorist group. Further investigation by the FBI found that Kansi had left the United States for Pakistan the day after the attacks. The international manhunt began. We were focused on Pakistan and Afghanistan. We were not paying attention to the larger context of growing anti-Americanism and resurgent political Islam throughout the region. We simply did not see the links between events in Sudan, Somalia, Lebanon, Pakistan, and the United States.

WASHINGTON, D.C., 1992: The convolutions of the end of the Cold War would impact the United States as well as the Third World, especially because it was an election year. President Bush was riding high in the public opinion polls following the Gulf War. Great things had happened on his watch. Bush led his country to victory against the main enemy and a regional Middle Eastern bully. Diplomatic efforts had brought all the parties of the Arab-Israeli conflict to the table, and for once, the prospects for Middle Eastern peace were looking up. There was no doubt in his mind and in the mind of administration officials that his reelection was a foregone conclusion.

While Bush was solving the problems of the world, the American people were thinking about their pocketbooks. They appreciated that they were no longer under threat of a nuclear holocaust. However, the removal of this threat permitted Americans to revert to their traditional isolation. Bush just did not seem to understand what was important to average Americans. Presidential candidate William Jefferson Clinton focused his energies on telling Americans how he planned to turn around the economy, reform Social Security, make health-care coverage more affordable, and make all Americans prosper. Americans liked what they heard, and on November 4, 1992, voted in Mr. Clinton.

★ ★ ★ ★

Gates tendered his resignation upon hearing of Bush's electoral defeat. Gates never had time to implement his full vision. While his reforms met some resistance, he made a good effort to reach down through the organizations to collect ideas and to build support. The initial fears about drastic changes were largely assuaged, and the bulk of the organization was moving with Gates rather than undermining his efforts at the working level. But the dreaded major reform shoe would not fall. The RIF would not come to pass. In the short year-plus with Gates as DCI, new threats emanating from the Second and Third Worlds moved to center stage. Sudan had emerged as a state sponsor of a new kind of international terrorism—one that encouraged the coalescence of groups and individuals of different nationality and Islamic beliefs to wage an international *jihad.* Failing and weak states in the Balkans and Africa led to humanitarian and political crises, provoking U.S. military intervention.

Yet the CIA met these and many other new requirements by shifting resources away from the former Soviet Union. The Agency tried to do everything in order to please all consumers rather than refocus or redefine a strategic mission. Instead of change, evolutionary or revolutionary, the Agency was left with drift—mission drift, leadership drift, and reform drift.

PART 4

THE WOOLSEY YEARS
(FEBRUARY 5, 1993–JANUARY 10, 1995)

"We now live in a jungle filled with a bewildering variety of poisonous snakes, and in many ways the dragon was easier to keep track of."

JIM WOOLSEY
Confirmation hearing, 1993

10

The Technocrat and the New World Order

SEVENTH FLOOR, LANGLEY, VIRGINIA, 1993: R. James Woolsey became DCI in February, appointed by a new president, William Jefferson Clinton. It was a very quick transition; the big DCI desk was empty for only sixteen days. Unlike Gates, the CIA did not know a lot about the new DCI, so there was an air of pleasant anticipation. With a new president and a new DCI, perhaps there would be a new sense of mission to guide the Agency. Perhaps the dire messages of drastic budget cuts, personnel cuts, and organizational cuts would go away, or at least be moderated. Some might have called the feeling "blind optimism."

The Woolsey-Clinton relationship was the exact opposite of the Casey-Reagan and the Gates-Bush relationships. Woolsey was not personally or professionally close to Clinton or any of his main team members. He was not involved in Clinton's campaign. Although a Washington lawyer with a good reputation, Woolsey was not a big-time player. He had served under both political parties as a technocrat. Perhaps that is why Clinton selected him and Congress confirmed him with ease. He was not threatening and indeed seemed a predictable, safe choice. Clinton was simply uninterested in foreign policy and intelligence during his first term and did not want activists leading foreign affairs agencies. Woolsey was a nice guy. He liked to solve problems and broker solutions, working out of the limelight. He had few enemies, because he was a consensus builder. Woolsey had many great attributes. He was smart, knew the intelligence business, and was well-connected to the traditional Washington power centers.

Woolsey did not turn out to be the Woolsey as expected. Clinton wanted Woolsey to manage the CIA quietly, keep it out of trouble and out of Clinton's in-box. Congress wanted Woolsey to be predictable and build consensus with Congress—that is, to follow Congress' lead and continue to reform the intelligence community. The CIA wanted a strong leader who would keep it relevant in the post–Cold War age and restore its sagging morale. World events would keep the CIA in business, but accompanying turf conflicts, poor performance, and uninspired leadership would dog the CIA.

NEW YORK CITY, NEW YORK, 1993: The explosion that ripped through the basement of the World Trade Center building would kill six New Yorkers, wound more than one thousand, cause millions of dollars in damage to one of the premier buildings in the city, and leave law enforcement and intelligence officers puzzling for years. Immediate confusion about whether it was an accident or a criminal act was settled when FBI investigators found explosive residue. Then the hunt for the perpetrators began. A lot of theories circulated, attributing the attack to Serbians, Iraqis, and radical Palestinian groups—in other words, the usual suspects.

There was no question that the FBI should take the lead in the investigation. The attack happened inside the United States, putting it squarely within the jurisdiction of the FBI. Luckily, the bombers left a string of clues behind, permitting the FBI to close in quickly on the operational cell. The FBI traced the van that carried the improvised explosive device to a rental company, who identified Mohammad Salameh as the person who leased the vehicle. The FBI arrested Salameh, an illegal immigrant of Palestinian-Jordanian background, when he returned to pick up his deposit for the van—he needed the money to pay for an airline ticket to escape from the United States. The FBI then raided the apartment listed on the vehicle rental agreement.

The New Jersey apartment was a forensic treasure trove. One would expect bomb makers to be very neat and careful in their art, if only to not blow themselves up in the process. This group was not. Harsh chemical fumes from mixing urea in water and nitric acid permeated the walls, changing their color from white to blue. The doorknobs and door hinges were corroded from the chemical compounds. Urea nitrate was splattered on the walls and ceiling and spilled on the floor. Nitroglycerin, too, had been spilled on the floor and on the bomb-makers' clothing.

Through physical evidence at the apartment and telephone toll records, the FBI found evidence linking Salameh to Ramzi Yousef, a Palestinian-Pakistani who had entered the United States in 1992 and filed for refugee status; Nidal Ayyad, a chemist; Mahmud Abouhalima, a taxi driver of Egyptian origin; and Ahmad Ajaj, a Palestinian who had earlier been arrested at JFK Airport trying to enter on a forged passport and with bomb-making manuals in his luggage. Yousef, Abouhalima, and two other suspects, Abdul Yasin and Eyad Ismoil, escaped FBI arrest by leaving the country shortly after the bombing. The FBI soon discerned a pattern that all the suspects had connections to Afghanistan and to a radical Islamic leader Shaykh Omar Abdal Rahman.[1]

COUNTERTERRORISM CENTER, LANGLEY, VIRGINIA, 1993: Upon notification from the FBI that the explosion at the World Trade Center (WTC) was the result of a bomb, the Counterterrorism Center set up a new group to support the FBI investigation. The group would quickly outgrow the few cubicles assigned to it and move to larger quarters elsewhere in the building. The group's mission was to follow up leads overseas. And there were many.

Before the WTC bombing, Ramzi Yousef was unknown to the CIA. He disappeared in Pakistan after the bombing. While not sure what his role in the bombing was, the CIA started work on collecting intelligence on his background and connections, with the goal of capturing him. It was slow going, with the major break not coming until 1995. Meanwhile, the FBI identified Yousef as being the mastermind behind the WTC bombing. Mahmud Abouhalima was easier to find; Egyptian intelligence arrested and interrogated him before the CIA arranged a handover to the FBI in March 1993. Abouhalima's confession would greatly aid the effort to link the plotters together. It would take a little longer to find Eyad Ismoil, but with Jordanian assistance, he was arrested and interrogated before being handed over to the FBI in Jordan in August 1995. Yasin disappeared into Iraq and remained at large.*

---

* Yasin's Iraqi identity fueled speculation on Iraqi government involvement in the first World Trade Center attack, which would resurface after the September 11 attacks. Fringe "counterterrorism experts" argued Iraqi complicity in both attacks, while the intelligence community dismissed the linkage as being devoid of evidence. Nonetheless, the idea of Iraqi involvement gained traction with neoconservative policymakers, some members of Congress, and the American public in general, adding to the confusion over the policy rationale of the preemptive war against Iraq in 2003.

Shaykh Omar Abdal Rahman was well known to those who followed Egyptian extremism in the Counterterrorism Center. Shaykh Rahman, or the Blind Shaykh, was an Egyptian with a sordid past. He had issued a *fatwa*, a religious ruling that called Egyptian President Anwar Sadat an infidel for making peace with Israel. Sadat was later assassinated by members of Gama'at al-Islamiya, an Egyptian terror group. Although the Egyptian courts acquitted the sheikh after the assassination, Egyptian intelligence considered Shaykh Omar Abdal Rahman to be the spiritual advisor for Egyptian terrorists.

Shaykh Omar Abdal Rahman had received a U.S. tourist visa in Khartoum, Sudan. All roads seemed to lead back to Sudan and Egyptian terrorists. This link, more so than the many others, occupied CIA counterterrorist officers. However, Yousef was the odd piece. He did not fit easily into the Sudan picture.

There was also the problem of how Shaykh Rahman received a visa. He was on the State Department's terrorist list, and therefore his application should have been flagged, if not outright denied. In the end, it was determined to be an honest mistake. False allegations that the CIA had an operational relationship with the Blind Shaykh would sully public opinion toward the Agency and fuel conspiracy theories in the alternative press that the CIA or the FBI/CIA was somehow behind the bombing.

The FBI/CIA relationship during the WTC investigation was typical: there were moments of good cooperation and many more moments when turf battles gained the upper hand. Allegations that the CIA was totally cut out are wrong. The CIA was not kept informed in detail about the progress of the FBI criminal investigation. The FBI was on receive mode; it wanted information from the CIA, but gave little feedback when it was obtained. In many ways, this permitted the CIA to have a more free-ranging investigation, because it was not limited or guided by the assumptions of the FBI. The CIA investigated tangents that became relevant only years later. But it also meant that the CIA did not learn about important details until after cases went to trial—in other words, years too late.

The tension between the CIA and the FBI on division of responsibilities and authorities was there from the beginning and would fester. The problem was drawing the line between domestic and foreign and between criminal and intelligence investigations. Clinton would try to clarify responsibilities with a Presidential Decision Directive, PDD-39, which he signed in June 1995. PDD-39 declared that the United States saw "terrorism as a potential threat to national security as well as a criminal act and will apply all appropriate means to combat it. In doing so, the United States shall pursue vigorously efforts to deter and preempt, apprehend and prosecute, or assist other governments to prosecute, individuals who perpetrate or plan to perpetrate such attacks." In essence, PDD-39 enshrined a law enforcement approach to terrorism, giving diplomacy and intelligence supporting roles.

NEW YORK CITY, NEW YORK, 1993: The FBI was not really interested in the many tangents that the CIA was pursuing, or in considering a wider conspiracy—they just needed evidence to convict the operational cell that committed the crime. In June, the FBI uncovered another plot to terrorize the commercial capital of America. The FBI arrested a group of Muslims, all linked to the Blind Shaykh, who were plotting to blow up the Lincoln and Holland tunnels, the FBI's New York headquarters, and the United Nations. The FBI would find evidence to link many of these suspects to the first World Trade Center conspiracy. But their trial would come later; the first matter at hand was to convict those arrested immediately after the bombing.

In September, the first WTC bombing trial opened, with all four defendants—Salameh, Ayyad, Abouhalima, and Ajaj—being convicted on all charges in March 1994. The government's case was that Ajaj was the advisor for the bomb making. Ayyad procured the chemicals and assisted Ramzi Yousef (who was still a fugitive) in making the bomb. Salameh assisted in the bomb making and transporting the bomb to the basement parking garage of the World Trade Center, along with Ramzi Yousef. Abouhalima drove the getaway car. The government's case did not make any attempt to connect the bombing to a larger conspiracy.

The bomb-making manuals that Ajaj had in his possession when he was detained at JFK Airport saw the light of day only when portions of them were introduced into evidence during the trial. The court was presented with sections of the manuals, translated into English from Arabic, with the heading reading "The Base." While this is an accurate translation, more bells would have rung in the ears of intelligence officials if the heading had been only transliterated—versus translated—and read instead "al-Qa'ida." Additionally, if all six manuals had been made available in the original Arabic, the intelligence community would have been able to make connections to a similar bomb-making manual on CD-ROM obtained by Belgian investigations in 1995. This version included a dedication to bin Ladin.[2]

WHITE HOUSE LAWN, WASHINGTON, D.C., 1993: The September 13 signing of the Oslo Accords signaled a new chapter of Middle Eastern relations. Over the preceding months, Palestine Liberation Organization Chairman Yasir Arafat had reached the accord with the Israeli government in great secrecy. Arafat renounced terrorism and committed the Palestinians to seek a negotiated peace with Israel, under the principle of land-for-peace. Israeli Prime Minister Yitzhak Rabin, although reluctant to press the flesh with Arafat, did so in order to pursue his vision of a lasting peace for the people of Israel.

The Oslo Accords offered new hope for the region. If a solution—final, fair, and lasting—could be reached, the roots of terrorism might be removed. The Arab-Israeli conflict had bred three wars and innumerable other acts of violence and terrorism. Much of the regional instability could be traced directly or indirectly to the conflict. Now was a chance to end all of that.

I watched the ceremony with interest, but had no idea that I would become deeply involved in the so-called Middle East Peace Process in a few short years. I remember thinking as I watched that the historical handshake made peacemaking look so simple—too simple. I would find it anything but simple. But I am getting ahead of myself.

President Clinton was clearly basking in the new image of peacemaker. No doubt he was thinking there might be some benefits to being the leader of the new world order. However, once the delegations went away, he turned his thoughts and energies to the topics that consumed him. He was the Domestic President, elected on a domestic platform. Foreign policy was quickly delegated to others. The lack of presidential attention would have immediate impact halfway around the world.

MOGADISHU, SOMALIA, 1993: The death of the CIA paramilitary officers did not end the CIA's force protection mission. A cable went out to the field asking all officers with Somali experience or Italian language capabilities to cable back with a volunteer message. I assessed that my limited Italian, gleaned from menus and the occasional Italian opera, would be of no interest. I stayed where I was in Arabic-language immersion training. Meanwhile, the CIA, in surge mode, began deploying officers for short rotations with the assignment to reestablish contact with former agents and develop new surveillance networks. Before the arrival of U.S. troops, CIA field officers moved in and set up an office in the former U.S. embassy in Mogadishu, which had been taken over by the United Nations.

While the initial tasking was to develop intelligence on potential threats to U.S. forces, the mission evolved into a manhunt. The CIA was tasked to provide tactical intelligence on the movement and location of General Mohammed Farah Aideed and his key lieutenants. Aideed led the Somali National Alliance and was the dominant force in Mogadishu. The United Nations had launched the humanitarian program named Restore Hope with the limited goal of feeding the starving masses. Once the edges of famine were relieved, the program quickly turned into a peacekeeping and nation-building effort. In the process, Aideed and other warlords came to view the United Nations as a threat to their political agendas. Aideed in particular began to wage war against UN forces, which included a contingent of U.S. soldiers.

The U.S. senior representative in Somalia, U.S. Navy Admiral (Ret.) Jonathan Howe decided that Aideed represented a clear and present danger to UN troops. Howe issued an arrest warrant for Aideed and offered a $25,000 reward for his capture. Howe requested CIA intelligence support in tracking Aideed. As is typical with operational planning, events never proceed with the degree of control that one would wish. In an amazing act of stupidity and bravado, the primary agent in the tracking operation killed himself playing Russian roulette before delivering a CIA-fiddled walking stick to Aideed. The ultimate game of risk—one round in the cylinder—was the bet that the trigger, once pulled, would connect with the empty chamber rather than the one live round. With a bullet in his temple, the agent was no longer in the game. The walking stick would later be used to track one of Aideed's aides, his moneyman Osman Atto. The main target—Aideed—remained elusive.[3]

Meanwhile, U.S. Delta Force arrived with the explicit mission of catching Aideed and, failing that, taking down his organization, lieutenant by lieutenant. Delta Force launched six operations in six weeks before embarking on the assault of the Olympic Hotel, memorialized in Mark Bowden's book *Black Hawk Down*, which was subsequently filmed. Delta Force had two sources of intelligence: human intelligence from the CIA and signals and imagery intelligence from Orion spy planes overhead.

The quality of the human intelligence was inconsistent. In some operations, the reporting did not mesh with images from the spy plane or developments on the ground. The surveillance network had been put together on the quick. There had been no time to follow normal procedures, including vetting and training. The field office was in

surge mode, and everything was being done under the guidelines of
field expediency. The networks were comprised of Somalis who were
willing, as opposed to Somalis who were proven capable. However, all
the field office needed was to get one spy with communication capabilities in the right place at the right time. Pressure from Washington
for results was intense; the field felt compelled to provide results, even
if reliability suffered.

Conditions in Mogadishu were deteriorating. The embassy compound was being shelled by RPGs on a nightly basis. The streets of
Mogadishu were unsafe. All movements required extensive preplan-
ning. The CIA officers were armed and had a special security group,
then called POCs—bodyguards by another name—providing inner-
ring security. While Congress was pressing to withdraw U.S. forces from
Somalia, the new Clinton administration wanted immediate and positive
results—that is, the capture of Aideed. CIA officers began taking more
risks to recruit better sources and expand surveillance capabilities.

In September 1993, the CIA deputy chief, John Spinelli, was seriously
wounded during a vehicular movement through Mogadishu. His
armored vehicle came under attack when it entered the kill zone of an
ambush set up for somebody else. It was the field officer's nightmare;
being in the wrong place at the wrong time, despite extensive planning.
A round hit Spinelli in the back of the neck, a spot unprotected by a
gap in his flak jacket. The team was en route to meet with potential new
sources, two Aideed bodyguards, who volunteered to give up Aideed's
location in exchange for the $25,000 reward.[4]

In the post-incident investigation, Spinelli's protective detail lodged
charges that the operational environment was too dangerous to support
the kinds of risks that Spinelli was taking in his frequent movements
through Mogadishu. Some of the protective officers felt Spinelli was
playing fast and loose with his and their lives. Their complaints were
used by CIA management to demonstrate that the CIA was pushing the
envelope, countering military complaints that the CIA was not doing
enough to support the manhunt.

The POCs were used to taking risks. I later had an opportunity to
work with some of the POCs from the Somali team when they were
assigned to protect me in a different high-risk zone (You must use your
imagination since the CIA will not permit me to say exactly where, but
one hint is that I spent my entire career in the Middle East.) It was an
odd experience for all of us. They had never protected a woman, and
I had never been protected. I was used to blending into my environment by donning a head scarf and the local version of the black tent

dress worn by many Muslim matrons. There was no blending in with four burly guys surrounding me. I quickly learned to operate within their security-risk perimeters and grew to respect their judgment. At times I pushed their envelope in order to meet my mission requirements. Several times we were trapped in a hostile area, with live fire and violent demonstrations shutting down all possible exit routes. On one of the occasions, we took cover in an all-but-empty hotel located on high ground, giving us a view of the armed clashes below. The only remaining employee of the hotel served us Arabic coffee, and a tape of Whitney Houston was playing in the background. It was the soundtrack from *The Bodyguard*. We all had a quiet chuckle, but only for a moment, before we had to beat feet out of the hotel as the neighborhood suddenly erupted in gunfire. It was a delicate balance—one I sought to maintain out of my own personal interests of staying alive.

The POCs told me their side of the story about Somalia. They did not appreciate being exposed to death on the whims of an officer who just wanted to get out of the secured zone, to scope out the town or spend some time (drink some wine) with other Westerners deployed to the peacekeeping effort; it was easy for me to see both sides of the argument. At the end of the day, however, the fact that there was an incident meant that, at a minimum, one too many risks had been taken.

The CIA worked closely with Delta Force in Somalia. There was a CIA liaison officer colocated with Delta Force command at the airport to provide close intelligence support. When the field office developed intelligence on a National Alliance meeting at the Olympic Hotel on October 3, 1993, the intelligence was briefed immediately to Delta Force. The intelligence was partly collaborated by overhead, when an Aideed lieutenant was observed entering the hotel. It was not known if Aideed would also attend the meeting, but it was considered a possibility.

Howe made the fateful decision for a takedown. Although the initial stage of the operation went according to plan, things quickly deteriorated as the assault team attempted to exit with the captured National Alliance members. The force came under heavy fire. The battle raged overnight, with the Somalis bringing down two Black Hawk helicopters and killing eighteen American soldiers. It was called the worst defeat of American forces since Vietnam.[5]

LANGLEY, VIRGINIA, 1993: The Somalia operation fell under the authority of the Directorate of Operations Africa Division. Analytical support in the Intelligence directorate came from Somali experts,

African hands. These experts knew all about the Somali clans, Somali tribal conflicts, Somali warlords. They were steeped in the history of Somali colonial developments, its independence as a state, and its role as a proxy player in the Cold War. The CIA's assessment was that the political fragility of Somalia was not conducive to external nation-building efforts. The assessment was based on things Somali, not on the regional spread of extremist Islamic ideology hostile to U.S. presence in Muslim countries. The analysts and operations officers were thinking about force protection and support to military operations, not about dissecting the ideology being espoused by the warring clans. They were not counterterrorism experts. Nor was the Counterterrorism Center encouraged to play a role.

The vertical stovepipes between divisions and directorates, between operations officers and analysts, between analysts working terrorism and analysts working Somalia ensured no one was asking questions at the strategic level about the source of the anti-American, extremist Islamic rage that flowed through the streets of Mogadishu. When bin Ladin did claim credit, the CIA initially dismissed the claim as opportunism. It would be years before the CIA would discover that bin Ladin was the unseen hand.

The fires were not even out before accusations were launched that the CIA had led the force into an ambush. The White House moved to cover itself by suggesting that there had been an intelligence failure, not a policy failure. An immediate investigation found otherwise, but a stink lingered over the quality of intelligence support the CIA provided to the military. In retrospect, the knowledge that battle-hardened *jihadis* were on the ground, teaching the Somalis the lessons they had learned in bringing down enemy helicopters in Afghanistan would have been significant tactical intelligence for the U.S. military. Would the U.S. Special Forces have changed their tactics in light of such intelligence is an entirely different question. The fact that military leaders accused the CIA of leading the forces into an ambush with faulty intelligence indicates the level of skepticism with which the military viewed CIA-offered intelligence.

WHITE HOUSE, WASHINGTON, D.C., 1993: During his first term, Clinton was completely uninterested in foreign affairs and intelligence. At first Woolsey tried to see the president and focus his attention on important matters, but Clinton was like the Cheshire cat, ever disappearing when Woolsey appeared. Woolsey had such limited access to the president that he became the butt of Washington jokes. He was viewed as the ultimate lightweight, but a desperate one at that. When a small plane crash-landed on the lawn of the White House, Washington insiders quipped that it was Woolsey trying to get in to see the president.

Inside the CIA, Woolsey's lack of access to the president was noticed, and it eroded respect for his leadership capabilities. Presidential access would become an issue in intelligence-reform debate, with some suggesting that the DCI must hold cabinet rank to ensure proximity to—if not influence—the U.S. president.

Clinton inherited a number of foreign policy initiatives from the former administration that could not be ignored, although he tried his best to do so. Somalia fell into that category. President George Bush had authorized sending U.S. troops to Somalia as part of a UN force with the noble—but limited—goal of feeding the starving Somalis. Under Clinton, the mission quickly grew to a nation-building program to restore stability and democracy to war-torn Somalia. It is a classic example of mission creep, which occurred under the inattentive eyes of a new and inexperienced administration.

The downing of U.S. Black Hawks and death of U.S. soldiers got the president's attention. So did the negative public reaction to the loss of servicemen. Clinton's reaction was immediate; within a few days after the losses, Clinton announced that U.S. participation in the Somali campaign would end by March 31, 1994.[6] It was the story of Beirut Barracks all over again: a noble deployment of U.S. forces to a country being torn apart by civil war; a devastating loss of American life; and a quick exit of U.S. troops following the tactical defeat. While the Clinton administration was trying to pull out of this fire in a way that did not look like an American defeat, another U.S.-backed peacekeeping mission was about to implode.

WHITE HOUSE, WASHINGTON, D.C., 1994: While campaigning in 1992, Clinton seized upon the plight of the Haitian boat people, who were fleeing the dictatorship that had overthrown the democratically elected government of Jean-Bertrand Aristide. Clinton made a commitment that he would pursue a more humanitarian foreign policy. However, once in office, the CIA presented Clinton with compelling evidence that his campaign statements had created a new wave of Haitian immigration, as Haitians were hoping to take advantage of a new, kinder immigration policy. Faced with the prospect of a possible two hundred thousand new Haitian refugees, Clinton backed off his campaign pledge. The Clinton administration was divided on what to do, but Clinton felt compelled to do *something*. The administration

started with economic sanctions to pressure Haiti's military strongman, Lieutenant General Raoul Cedras, to reinstate Aristide. Senior
Pentagon officials continued to oppose a peacekeeping mission.

The entire policy initiative ended extremely embarrassingly for the
White House. Through the United Nations, the Clinton administration
orchestrated a nation-building program, sending two hundred
American soldiers to prepare the way for the return of Aristide. On
October 11, 1993, the USS *Harlan County* attempted to dock and off-
load soldiers, but a mob of jeering Haitians, many armed, blocked their
way. The mob shouted anti-American slogans, including "Somalia!
Somalia!" rubbing in the painful and tragic events of Mogadishu that
had transpired just one week earlier. The USS *Harlan County* turned
around, and the White House officials looked like a bunch of naïve ama-
teurs.[7] Clinton blamed the National Security Council and the CIA for
putting him in a no-win situation.

After Haiti, the Clinton administration became very cautious on
foreign policy issues. Such issues were tricky, with greater possibility
for negatives than positives. Little good could come from foreign policy adventurism. The administration's caution was evident in the
types of activities that the National Security Council Covert Action
Working Group and the so-called White House Small Group would
authorize.

Covert action programs have to be authorized by the National
Security Council, and they are usually paid for by fenced National
Security Council funds. Individual operations that are consistent with
the language of the approved covert action program do not normally
require additional National Security Council approval. However, if the
operation is deemed risky, with potential political blowback, the CIA will
seek National Security Council approval for individual operations. The
rationale for this is to keep the administration informed and in control,
and to avoid unpleasant surprises. From the CIA management perspective, it also spreads responsibility for risk taking

During the remaining years of the Clinton administration, propor-
tionally more operational initiatives were submitted to the National
Security Council for approval; fewer approvals were given.

BUENOS AIRES, ARGENTINA, 1994: A car bomb, carrying
hundreds of kilograms of explosives, decimated the Jewish Community
Center (AMIA) on July 18. The blast caused serious damage to adjoin-
ing buildings and killed 86 people and injured another 250. This was
not the first bomb to have shattered the Argentine Jewish community.

Two years earlier, another car bomb destroyed the Israeli embassy in Buenos Aires, killing 29 people and wounding 220. What had brought terrorism to South America? Was it simply anti-Semitic violence, or were the bombings connected to other acts of terrorism in the United States or in the Middle East?

The initial investigation of the two attacks was such a disaster that it became the focus of an investigation into corruption and complicity. Witnesses disappeared, crucial evidence was lost, and taped interviews with witnesses were stolen from police safes. Once the Argentine government regrouped—a number of years later—the hand of Hizballah and Iran was revealed.

In September 1999, Argentina's Supreme Court issued an arrest warrant for Imad Mughniyah—the same terrorist believed responsible for the kidnapping of William Buckley—for ordering the 1992 bombing of the Israeli embassy. This was based on, among other pieces of evidence, information from an Iranian defector. In 1998, Iranian defector Abdolghasem Mesbahi gave a sworn statement to an Argentine judge that Iran's supreme religious leader, Ayatollah Ali Khomeini, ordered the AMIA bombing. He described how Hizballah carried out the bombing. Mesbahi was viewed as a credible witness; he had been the third-ranking officer in VEVAK, the Iranian internal security service, until he defected in 1996.[8]

Although the details did not come out until later, early intelligence focused on Hizballah. Hizballah had long had a presence in the Tri-border area of South America—the border area where Argentina, Brazil, and Paraguay meet. Arabs, especially Lebanese and Palestinians, had settled in the area starting after World War II. This presence gave Hizballah a natural recruiting ground to build support and military sleeper cells. What better indicator of a global capability than to be able to launch two successful operations thousands of miles away from their base at a time of Hizballah's choosing? What better advertising could international terrorism seek? While Hizballah and Iran blazed the trail, al-Qa'ida watched. And learned.

SEVENTH FLOOR, LANGLEY, VIRGINIA, 1994: Woolsey's honeymoon as DCI was short. Less than a year into his tenure as DCI, Woolsey would find himself on the defensive, all around. Woolsey found he was on a team of one. Clinton undercut him by not giving him the time of day, a deathblow in an environment where perceived influence with the president is currency around town—and around the globe, for that matter. Congress worked against him by not listening to his needs and adopting a vocal, hostile stance against him when he refused to quietly accept their policies that would decimate the capabilities of the intelligence community. The CIA failed him the most, by putting in his lap one scandal after another, despite Woolsey's efforts to be the CIA's best and most vocal champion.

11
New Directions

LANGLEY, VIRGINIA, 1992: Woolsey was the Agency's advocate and not afraid to say so. His legacy should be that he was the first prime-time DCI. He spoke publicly about the Agency, in positive terms, on popular television shows, such as *Nightline* and *Larry King Live*. For a DCI—the chief spook of the nation—he was surprisingly oriented to the public. He worked hard to put past Agency scandals behind by focusing public attention on what the CIA was doing of a substantive nature "here and now."

Woolsey must have carefully read the recommendations from the Task Force Report on Greater CIA Openness, requested by Gates when he sat at the big desk. The task force recommended that whatever the new program was, the CIA should first get its employees on board, be consistent, be excellent, be credible—admit when the CIA is wrong, personalize the Agency, and preserve the mystique. The report stated that the CIA had an important story to tell. Many Americans did not understand the role of intelligence in national security policymaking and held romanticized or erroneous views of intelligence from movies, TV, books, and newspapers. These views often damaged the CIA's reputation and made it harder for the CIA to fulfill its mission.

The report recommended that Agency briefing programs to new members of Congress, key congressional staffers and Congressional Research Service should expand. To reach the public directly, the CIA should accept that television has become the primary conveyor of information to most Americans.[1] Up until Woolsey's time, the CIA avoided television, preferring to speak on background to a few choice reporters. Before he announced his retirement, Judge Webster appeared on television only three times.

Woolsey took up the latter recommendation with gusto and did the "talking heads" rounds with confidence. He defended past actions; but, more importantly, he talked about CIA contributions to current requirements, such as the collection of economic intelligence, counternarcotics, organized crime, and arms proliferation. He publicly defended CIA and intelligence community budget requests, provoking ire in Congress.

The report also recommended that the CIA declassify and release records that describe the CIA's history and activities. Testifying before Congress in September 1993, Woolsey stated he had directed for review the declassification of significant Cold War covert actions more than three years old. These included activities in support of democracy in France and Italy in the 1940s and 1950s, support to anti-Sukarno rebels in Indonesia in 1958, support to Tibetan guerrillas in the 1950s and early 1960s, operations against North Korea during the Korean War, and operations in Laos in the 1960s. Woolsey announced that he was lifting the veil on a broad range of Cold War secrets as part of an effort to open the spy Agency, "warts and all," to public scrutiny.[2]

However, Woolsey was not a Gates reincarnation. He stopped many of the reforms Gates set in motion. Recommendations from the fourteen task forces would gather dust in a safe, out of sight, out of mind. Woolsey was not averse to making changes, such as doing more economic counterintelligence reporting and perhaps sharing the reporting with Corporate America, or permitting satellite imagery to be sold on a commercial basis. He just did not share Gates's vision that fundamental and drastic changes were necessary. He focused his reform efforts on management and personnel issues, not on remaking the CIA.

Woolsey won initial favor with the Agency because he clearly stated that an RIF—a formalized reduction in force through the distribution of pink slips all at one time or in a planned series like the "Halloween Massacre" under DCI Turner—would not happen on his watch. Woolsey knew morale was low, and he did not want to exacerbate it by taking drastic measures to change the workforce. He recognized that one of the real strengths of the CIA was the people who work there. The officers were carefully recruited from candidates who had demonstrated records of success. They were smart and not satisfied with the status quo. They shared a common bond of dedication to mission and a willingness to make personal sacrifices to achieve that mission.

Nonetheless, he had to face the reality that the "peace dividend" meant that the CIA had to scale down the number of employees on the books. Woolsey reached an agreement with Congress to cut the CIA by roughly 22 percent. According to a speech Woolsey delivered in July 1994, he planned on cutting 700 people from the Directorate of Operations by 1997, plus 1,000 analysts and 1,700 administrative support officers. He planned on drawing down 26 percent of the personnel in the Directorate of Science and Technology.[3]

Woolsey announced that downsizing would take place through normal attrition and voluntary early-out retirement packages. He would continue the virtual freeze on new-hires started under Gates. It might have seemed more humane to not let the blood flow on the floor all at once, and let those who wanted to leave depart. Everyone would make their own choices, and all would be well. The unintended consequence of Woolsey's good intentions, however, was that it was a messy and protracted downsizing, for those who stayed rather than for those who left.

Mid-level officers who opted to resign were not replaced, thinning out the ranks in the middle. Little new blood came in to keep a healthy junior rank alive—and as everyone in government knows, it is the junior officers who do the heavy lifting when it comes to workloads. Initially, the Directorate of Operations was largely excluded from eligibility for early retirement, because the Agency did not want to lose the seasoned officers. When management wanted to clean house, the old hands wouldn't leave. Officers who were eligible to retire delayed their retirement because of an expected pay increase in the Senior Intelligence Service, that would greatly augment their retirement annuities. Because of lack of movement at the top, the Directorate of Operations suffered from headroom problems (ability to promote upward), creating a personnel bulge at the GS-14 and GS-15 levels.*

The Directorate of Operations managed the bulge poorly, allowing it to reach crisis proportions, so that promotions slowed down to the GS-11 level. Seeing no opportunity for promotion, mid-level officers bailed out. This was compounded by a change in the career development program, whereby promotions of junior officers were made virtually automatic. Junior officers now reached mid-level status with less time in grade. When the headroom stoppage at the top finally cleared (once the pay raise came through and there was a relaxing of the

---

* The majority of CIA employees are paid on the U.S. Government General Services (GS) pay scale.

eligibility requirements for the early-out program), everyone who remained standing moved up. The senior officers, newly promoted, retired at the higher grade.

The promotion backlog persisted into 2000 and was the topic of much grumbling and a few jokes. I remember when I was serving as a chief of base in the late 1990s, my newly arrived boss, Jeff, came to visit my operation and meet my staff. After giving him the "tour," we went to lunch at the neighborhood Arabic restaurant. Apparently, Jeff ate something that did not agree with him and was ill the next few days. Thereafter, when Jeff introduced me, he would say, "This is Melissa, my deputy who tried to poison me in order to create some promotion headroom."

By the late 1990s, the personnel profile was very lean, but also skewed. There was little new talent coming in at entry level, and the workforce was overwhelmingly mature. There was also not the right mix of subject expertise. The Directorate of Operations faced a new problem; insufficient mid-level full performance officers with significant field experience to manage operations and intelligence

Not only did Woolsey have to deal with changing numbers, but he also faced the changing nature of the workforce. By Woolsey's time, the Agency was already a diverse organization. The Directorate of Operations, however, was—and is—much less diverse than the rest of the Agency. That is not to say we did not have ethnic minorities—especially native speakers of foreign languages—but we had far fewer than we should have, given its overseas mission of collecting foreign intelligence and recruiting spies. In Woolsey's time, this was not the main issue when discussing diversity. The issue was the status of women in the workforce.

The Directorate of Operations in particular has had a poor performance record in creating equal opportunity for women. A major element of the Directorate of Operations culture was that it was a brotherhood. Traditionally, women have been welcome in the directorate, but only in support positions. The Directorate of Operations was (and is) run by men, and men have controlled the assignment process and the promotion boards since the days of the Office of Strategic Services. In the 1980s some of the assignment barriers began to break down. A handful of female officers were cross-trained as operations officers and assigned overseas. By the mid-1980s, the CIA was actively recruiting female operations officers, and some of them were forging positive hall reputations as recruiters. In the 1990s, women pushed hard to break down the remaining barriers, with imperfect results, and at significant career costs.

In 1992, the CIA conducted a still-classified "Glass Ceiling" study in response to growing complaints that women in the Agency were not treated equally, in comparison to male colleagues, when it came to assignments and promotions. The study found that women's achievements were not recognized by the Directorate of Operations at the same pace or to the same degree as men. Women spent longer time in grade at the higher levels and received proportionately fewer awards. Men were traditionally given the choice assignments—that is, assignments with opportunities for high-impact operations that could lead to assignments of greater authority and prestige.

As of 1991, the study found that women made up 40 percent of the workforce in the CIA, but held only 9 percent of the Senior Intelligence Service positions. Women made up 17 percent of the operations officers, less than 1 percent had made the rank of Senior Intelligence Service. Half of Directorate of Operations white female operations officers reported experiencing sexual harassment, and more than half of black respondents reported racial harassment.[4]

CIA management took some action after the study, but found strong resistance by the old boys in the Directorate of Operations. There was a strong belief that women could not recruit agents, the core job requirement of the directorate. When female officers were assigned to European and East Bloc stations and proved the critics wrong, the argument was refined. Women could not recruit Arabs because of the low standing women have in Arab culture. Women could not recruit Latinos, because Latin men would never accept female authority in a macho culture. A few token women were assigned as operations officers to the Latin America and Near East Divisions. Women were placed in assignments destined to be failures because of lack of management and peer support and lack of operational assignments once in the field. Many women tried, but after a field assignment or two, assessed the career as a losing battle and moved elsewhere within the CIA or left the organization. Some women survived, but none really thrived.

When I decided to join the Near East Division, many of my classmates were aghast, given its poor reputation for creating equal opportunity for women. There was still a pervasive belief that women could not recruit Arab men, and therefore female operations officers were not really welcome in the division. I had confidence that I would be able to overcome the doubts, because I was familiar with the Arab world and knowledgeable about the culture. Indeed, I turned out to be a successful recruiter and came to be held up as a model by division management. But the path from rookie to full performance—that is, a seasoned officer—was hard. Recruiting the Arab male was actually easier than winning the support of management. Frankly, I always found Arab men easy to manipulate. They loved the attention of an attractive Western woman. Once I made it clear that I was not interested in making whoopee, they were normally completely disarmed—if it is not sex, what else could it possibly be? They were on totally new terrain with me, giving me the control and influence I needed to convince them to betray confidences and commit treason. An agent-handler relationship is a very powerful one in terms of the emotional interplay—perhaps more powerful than the trysts of lovers—because the stakes of getting caught are so high. No, I found the Arab male infinitely more predictable and manageable than Near East Division management. With the latter, I always felt as if I were walking on eggs. I sensed that at the first mistake my career would be ended, because I did not have protectors in the old-boy system. My fears proved true.

In December 1992, one mid-level female officer began a class action lawsuit, which would eventually include 250 female operations officers. The CIA initially fought the suit's organizers, penalizing them with marginal assignments and harassing them. Women operations officers were discouraged from participating, with management not so subtly reminding them about what happens to officers who grieve the system. As the Glass Ceiling report documented, female officers tended to tolerate harassment by male colleagues "in order to be accepted." There was widespread belief that those who complained about unequal treatment or harassment would create career advancement problems for themselves. Women officers were split on the best path to take. They knew they could not force themselves into an exclusive club and then truly be considered equals in the club.

There were many women who felt they could play the game and recruit the recruiters, wining acceptance. They wanted to work the issue in an evolutionary way inside the Agency, or at least behind closed doors within the intelligence community. Those male colleagues with "dinosaur brains" could be worked around, won over, or would eventually die out. The complaints were referred to the in-house Equal Employment Opportunity office, the inspector general, and congressional oversight committees, none of whom were very sympathetic. Congressman Larry Combest, then-chairman of the House Permanent Select Committee on Intelligence, said in 1995 that he was aware of female military and intelligence officers who had done great jobs, but cautioned, "I think we had better be very careful not to use [the intelligence agencies] as areas of social experimentation. That should not be the goal."[5] Clearly, dinosaur brains were not exclusive to the CIA.

Under threat of a lawsuit that would expose embarrassing aspects of its human resources policies, the CIA opted to negotiate after one year when it became clear that the women would not back down. Separately, another female operations officer, "Jane Doe Thompson," filed a sexual discrimination lawsuit after she was made a target of official retribution.* Her crime was reprimanding a male subordinate for beating his wife. At the time, "Thompson" was the field chief in Jamaica. She was subsequently investigated by the inspector general, denied promotions, and assigned to non-career-enhancing positions. Her character and integrity were challenged in very petty and ugly ways, from suggestions of inappropriate sexual behavior to abuse of position. The CIA decided to settle the suit without admitting wrongdoing. Knowing that she had no career to return to, "Thompson" retired and accepted monetary compensation. She went on to become a lawyer whose specialty is litigating cases against the CIA.

Before 1995, I was not aware of the Glass Ceiling report, the class action lawsuit, or "Thompson's" lawsuit. I was in the field, focusing on proving myself worthy of the operations officer career track. If there had been cable traffic on these at the time, I must have missed them. However, I am certain that these issues were not raised directly with me by management. I was the only female operations officer at my post. I was aware of the challenges of being one of the few female operations officers in the Near East Division. The presumption in management was that I would fail or at least be marginal and would not be around long. It was a constant struggle in the early part of my career. I had to fight for each opportunity: field assignments, agent-handling assignments, language training.

For example, toward the end of my first assignment, I asked for additional Arabic-language training. My field chief supported my request because I had performed well. Headquarters management declined my request. My chief, Mike, was a cynical, hard-hitting old boy who taught me more about operations and making it inside the organization than any other boss I had. It was baptism by fire with him, and I have the

---

* The CIA will not permit Agency officers to confirm leaked classified information, no matter how many times the information appears in public sources of information. Accordingly, the CIA has requested that I call this individual by the pseudonym she used in her court case against the CIA.

deepest respect and appreciation for his mentoring. He went to bat for me and arranged for me to have a meeting with the Chief for Arab Operations. In this meeting, I personally presented my case, showing exceptional training reports and performance appraisals. I already spoke some Arabic, but lacked the needed fluency to debrief effectively.

I was informed that I was a little old to be put in the program, given the investment of resources required. I was also grilled on my child-rearing plans, as women with babies tend to drop out of the career track as their priorities change. I was caught in the classic discrimination quandary: Do I make an issue of fairness, or do I put all my efforts into getting what I want? I elected to do the latter (in the two seconds I had to think about it) and insisted that I had no babies in my future and as a more mature student of thirty-two years of age, I would get more out of the program. I ended up getting the language training, but I never felt comfortable with the way I handled the situation.

Meanwhile negotiations on the class action suit moved slowly. In June 1995, the CIA settled with the class, giving female case officers back pay totaling nearly $1 million, twenty-five retroactive promotions, and promising to give twenty "stretch" and career-enhancing assignments to mid-level officers. As an automatic member of the class, I received a settlement check out of the blue for $1,000. Only when I received the check did I learn the details of the lawsuit. According to the notification, in addition to the financial settlement, fifteen female officers who transferred to other career categories were allowed to return to the operations officer track. The CIA promised to open positions that previously were offered exclusively to male operations officers. The judge who approved the settlement also approved a measure that required the CIA to report back on remedial efforts for a five-year period.

The settlement brought short-term benefits, but few long-term changes. After the settlement, division chiefs made the rounds of all field and Headquarters offices, reading the riot act to officers that sexual harassment would no longer be tolerated in the workplace. Chiefs of station and office managers were required to sign documentation that they had read the new sexual harassment guidelines and that they were responsible for reporting up all incidences of harassment known to them, removing any line-management discretion. Managers who failed to do so would be held personally accountable. Sexual harassment and diversity training was required for all officers.

Male officers knew the rules had changed, but there was great uncertainty on what was and was not permissible in terms of conduct when interacting with female officers. They felt vulnerable, and there was underlying frustration and hostility. Working relationships in close office environments were upset because of uncertainty of the new rules. I felt this acutely because I served in a small-sized field station. I was no longer "one of the boys," but someone potentially threatening. Over time, the undercurrents of fear, misunderstanding, and anger disappeared and "normal" male-female professional relationships materialized.

The real benefit of the class action lawsuit was that women were empowered to stop harassment themselves by the mere threat of filing a formal complaint. When the harassment did not stop, more women elected to use formal channels to address their complaints. In the years immediately after implementation of the new guidelines, the number of sexual harassment and discrimination grievances filed through Equal Employment Opportunity office rose to 65–75 cases per year, versus the 10–15 cases per year presettlement. The new harassment guidelines have been one of the few lasting benefits of the class action suit.

In accordance with the negotiated settlement, the assignment process was realigned in order to promote transparency, and the Directorate of Operations was required to augment its minority and female recruitment program. Under the new system, all job openings were advertised internally, and any officer could bid on any position within the Agency. The bid had to be evaluated and the individual interviewed, regardless of the individual's qualifications for the position. The new system was resisted, with the old boys citing that it was cumbersome (which it was).

Division chiefs learned to work around it by invoking "needs of the service," which gave them the authority to place a specific officer in a specific job, omitting the requirement to compete. There are a few women who are outstanding officers who have made their way through the system and are now senior officers, at the GS-15 or Senior Intelligence Service level. They are to be commended for their perseverance and their skills. Many more remain stuck at mid-levels because of blemishes on their record. While male officers can frequently overcome an operational failure or two, female officers have more difficulty and are quickly labeled "marginal."

Many female officers believe that when it comes to promotions and job assignments, women continue to be disadvantaged. Men's perceptions differ. Some male officers are very supportive of the diversity program and make a point of mentoring female officers under their command. Some feel the emphasis on diversity hiring and the catch-up promotions of women destined the white male operations officer to become a minority. There is a perception among some male officers that the CIA now uses a quota system for assignments and promotions, a perception that is probably true. Some feel that women are being favored on the basis of gender, versus performance. When a woman was appointed deputy chief for the Near East Division in 2000, her credentials were an issue. Critics pointed out that she had never run an agent, questioned her substantive experience in the Middle East, and so forth. The assignment was short-lived.

As important as perceptions are, the statistics reflect the fact that the Directorate of Operations continues to fall behind on diversity issues. For example, as late as 2002, there are no female operations officers home-based in the Near East Division who are currently serving as chiefs of station in the division. Why? Few female operations officers choose to join the Near East Division because of its reputation as biased against women. I elected to take my chances because I wished to utilize my university education—an advanced degree in Middle East Studies and years of language study—and I was passionate about the region.

The women who are home-based in the division are seldom put into Arabic or Farsi language programs. Arabic or Farsi fluency is a required ticket for officers to become "players" in the division and, as already explained, I had to fight to realize the opportunity. The handful who have done so over the past ten years have fallen victim to an unfriendly system and have left by choice or by force.

The rest of the organization—that is, directorates other than the Directorate of Operations—demonstrated more equitable statistics on diversity. There is almost an equal split between the percentage of male and female officers in the Directorate of Intelligence, for example, showing that improvement was achieved during the 1990s.

Challenging the system has its costs. The female operations officer who started the class action suit remains employed by the Agency. After wining compensation and a promotion, her career has been altered dramatically. Subsequent to the suit, she left the Directorate of Operations, knowing the suit was in reality a divorce, with reconciliation impossible. She has started a new career in the Directorate of Intelligence, which she has found to welcome her talents and support her courage for taking on the all-powerful Directorate of Operations. While she is content, the fact remains that her options became limited when she decided to fight back. The other female officers who were given promotions as part of the settlement did not see follow-on promotions for an extraordinary period of time. These women paid the price of making the CIA a more equitable and diverse workplace.

Years have passed since the class action settlement, and it still remains controversial inside the CIA, especially among female officers. Whether a supporter or critic of the class action route, most women were in agreement that Woolsey and his senior staff handled the complaints poorly. They were not taken seriously, judged by the low priority with which Woolsey and the senior staff dealt with them. The results of the Glass Ceiling study, which was very damning, was limited in dissemination, with many women learning about it only after the class action lawsuit was filed. Rather than dealing with the issue in an open, transparent manner, senior staff attempted to marginalize complainers and complaints.

As to why the issue came to a head in the early 1990s, the overall downsizing pressures, with the slowing down in promotions, made everybody grumpy. The feast of the Casey days—when there was enough cream to keep most happy—was over. Those who elected to remain in the service found that they had to fight to get the good jobs—the jobs that led to promotions—or else they might find themselves walking the halls with no assignment in hand. As the Agency convulsed, everyone reverted to survival mode. And after the Ames scandal broke, it *was* an issue of survival.

12
Aldrich Ames

LANGLEY, VIRGINIA, 1994: Stories of spies are always packed with intrigue, betrayal, death, destruction, and acute fascination with all of the above—the story of Aldrich Ames more so than most. It is hard to say what was worse; the damage Ames did by spying for the Soviets or the damage the CIA did to itself in how it handled the affair.

In February 1994, CIA operations officer Aldrich H. Ames was arrested for selling secrets to the Russians. The timing could not have been worse. The CIA was reeling from mission loss and budget and personnel cuts. Morale was low. Iran-Contra and CIA wrongdoing had just disappeared from the front pages, but not from the memories of CIA officials. Public and congressional criticism of CIA still rang high.

The reaction inside the Agency was one of shock. The arrest shattered the myth that the Directorate of Operations was impenetrable and different (better) from all other intelligence organizations. Until Ames, the CIA was able to delude itself into believing that CIA traitor Edward Lee Howard was an anomaly, not a symptom of a larger ill. The treachery by Ames exposed a CIA "blind spot," a firmly held assumption that no serving operations officer would ever sell out, particularly one in Soviet Operations, the inner sanctum.

The Agency's counterintelligence and security measures had been woefully lax, it was judged in subsequent internal and external investigations. We felt the fallout throughout the CIA. Reforms were instituted, and the Office of Security was given license to take whatever measures were needed to keep out suspected bad apples and to get rid of anyone who could possibly become a problem. Security staff went from lax to paranoid, taking extreme positions. Careers of loyal officers have been destroyed on the basis of suspicions versus facts, assumptions versus proof. A zero-risk-tolerance attitude developed in Security, and no one in the rest of the Agency dared challenge it, because the memory of Ames was too recent and too awful.

Ames was a twenty-seven-year veteran of the Directorate of Operations who for nine years led a double life as a mole for the Soviet KGB (and later the Russian SVR). Ames was not always a terrible employee, as some would like to characterize him. Ames's problem was that he was not a great operations officer, a fact he had difficulty squaring with his own high opinion of himself. A great operations officer is one who has a proven track record of significant agent recruitments. Ames showed in his first overseas assignment that he did not have what it takes to be a good recruiter and received a harsh performance appraisal documenting this assessment.

Ames was an "okay" handler and debriefer, and he did well on desk work (akin to staff work in the military). In his early years, he received solid marks on his performance for handling Soviet agents while assigned to New York with the Foreign Resources Division.* Within the Directorate of Operations culture, being designated as a "good handler" rates a place on the "B team."

Handling agents is a very important part of the recruitment cycle, because in the handling stage, the operations officer is debriefing the agent and obtaining intelligence. Handling tends to be routine and not as exciting as the hunting stage—in other words, developing and recruiting. Culturally, the Directorate of Operations places a premium on recruiting, as it is deemed the most difficult and risky part of the job. There is a false—but predominant—belief that "anyone can handle." Recruiting and handling take two different kinds of skills. Many intelligence services separate the careers, in recognition that different kinds of people excel in the two activities.

When I was in training, I was challenged to demonstrate that I had the "killer instinct" to recruit. There are many hard parts to being a spy; recruiting is one of the hardest. First you must get close to your target—find him and cut him out of the crowd. This can be difficult if the target has orders to not meet with Americans, or if he is afraid to be seen with you. After forming a relationship of trust and figuring out what makes the guy tick, which takes time, you go for the soft

---

* The Foreign Resources Division was merged with the National Collection Division to form the current National Resources Division.

spots, manipulating him down the path of your choosing. Eventually, you pop the question: Will you spy for me? It is a question that is of monumental risk. Creating the timing and emotional play are everything. Those case officers who wait for the right moment, fearing the accusations of betrayal and the resounding "no," will always be waiting and never close the deal. Ultimately, it comes down to the love of the hunt, instincts, and fearlessness.

The presumption was that most people—especially women—do not have the instincts and the mettle to close the deal. My management made it quite clear to me during my first overseas tour that it was either "do or die"—make several solid recruitments or move to a different career track as a reports officer or staff operations officer. The pressure to prove myself was incredible. The last thing I wanted was to be designated "a good handler"—in other words, a failed recruiter.

After his first assignment in Turkey, Ames gravitated to positions where he was not expected to recruit and therefore did not have to compete on a daily basis against "full performance" operations officers. Counterintelligence work, which was considered a dumping ground for marginal operations officers, suited his personality. Counterintelligence is the ultimate chess game and does not often require aggressive interpersonal skills. However, at performance review time, Ames was rated against all his fellow operations officers—not just counterintelligence officers—and his slow rate of promotion ate at his self-esteem.

Ames's good performance traits gradually dissolved as he became increasingly unhappy with his personal and professional life, to the point where the CIA Inspector General came to describe him as having "little focus, few recruitments, no enthusiasm, little regard for the rules and requirements, little self-discipline, little security consciousness, little respect for management or the mission, few good work habits, few friends and a bad reputation in terms of integrity, dependability and discretion."[1]

When I read the inspector general's report, at first I wondered why in the world the CIA continued to employ Ames, given the above description. The answer came quickly: it was easier to keep him on than to go through the bureaucratic process of shoving him out the door. So on he stayed to do unbelievable damage.

Suffering from personal and psychological problems, such as alcohol abuse, divorce, financial pressures, an expensive girlfriend, and low self-esteem, Ames became disillusioned with the CIA and the incestuous nature of the spy versus spy counterintelligence game. Having convinced himself the CIA was engaged in activities that were self-propitiating and unrelated to national security, Ames became a disbeliever, an angry disbeliever. In April 1985, he volunteered his services to the Soviet KGB.

For nine years Ames sold everything he could get his hands on to the Russians. His treachery caused the deaths of at least ten Soviet agents. He compromised a significant number of Soviet agents who were able to escape execution either by defection, fast talking, or gulag sentence. A handful of agents were doubled back against the CIA in an elaborate double-cross disinformation campaign. He compromised technical and human operations around the globe, exposing CIA operational sources and methods. He gave away the identities of CIA officers. He left a huge wake of destruction behind him everywhere he went.

For nine years, the CIA knew there was something significantly wrong in Soviet operations. Rather than shine daylight on the problem to flesh out the source, the CIA compartmentalized the compromises to minimize knowledge of the problem and the investigation.*

In 1985, when Ames started working for the Soviets, there were a series of agent wrap-ups, which alone should have started a full-fledged counterespionage investigation. The Agency's blind spot—that the sources of the compromises could not be an operations officer—crippled the investigation from the very beginning. At first the CIA assumed that the source of the compromise was a technical penetration. After facilities and communication systems were checked and found secure, the CIA tried to explain away the wrap-ups by attributing them to Edward Lee Howard. Howard had access or potential access to some, but not all of the cases that were blown in 1985.

The chief of Soviet and Eastern Europe Division held the Moscow chief in low regard and suspected he was running a loose operation with poor operational tradecraft. He concluded that sloppy tradecraft was the problem. A 1986 memo prepared by John Stein, a former CIA Inspector General, substantiated the idea that operational tradecraft was the problem, saying each compromised case contained "seeds of its own destruction."[2]

In 1986, the Counterintelligence staff formed a small group—an ultrasecret special task force—to look into the possibility that there was a mole among the two hundred officers in the Soviet Division. In its early days, the Counterespionage group never really had a chance for

---

* The practice of compartmentalizing problem cases is not an isolated one. A proven bureaucratic move to silence criticism on a case is to remove the critic's access to the case by placing the case in a special compartment to which the critic is denied access.

success because of its lack of resources and counterespionage expertise and its low level of priority in terms of management interest.

The mole hunters toiled in darkness, lost in a wilderness of mirrors because they were operating on the assumption that there was only one mole. They were trying to match up the compromises with individuals who had or could have had access to all the cases. As it turned out, the CIA mole hunters were confused by compromises made by moles outside their purview. The conundrum would be clarified only years after Ames's exposure, with the arrests of FBI agents Earl E. Pitts and Robert P. Hanssen, in 1996 and 2001, respectively.

In 1991, a CIA source provided intelligence that led to the identification of Ames as the probable mole. Only at this point did the CIA bring the FBI fully into the hunt. With a finger pointed directly at Ames, it took four additional months of investigation before the FBI was certain that Ames was the mole. The FBI started to build a case against him. Ames was exhibiting classic signs of criminal behavior: living beyond his means, breaking CIA regulations on foreign travel, and disregarding other CIA reporting regulations. Ames was arrested on February 21, 1994, the day before he was scheduled to fly to Moscow on official CIA business. Although the FBI preferred to catch him in the act of loading a dead drop, they were unwilling to take a chance of letting Ames escape to Moscow, as Howard had done.

The depth of the betrayal cut to the bone of the organization. Almost everyone in the Directorate of Operations had a personal story about the negative fallout from the spy scandal. First, there was the tragic loss of life of clandestine reporting sources. Second, there was the often-painful and protracted damage assessment process, identifying the extent of the compromises and why they happened in the first place. Third, there were careers marred by the operational compromises. Fourth, there was the growing counterintelligence paranoia and concomitant overreaction of Security and Counterintelligence staffs. Fifth, there was the dysfunctional accountability process that operates without rhyme or reason. From the insider's viewpoint, it all added up to low officer morale and bureaucratic paralysis. Seen from the outside, critics and supporters alike saw mission failure, incompetence, an inability to self-police, and lack of accountability.

Directorate of Operations officers are inculcated from the moment of their swearing-in on their primary duty, the protection of sources, their lives, and their well-being. When you take on a case, especially when the other side plays for keeps, you never stop thinking about the risks of getting caught. Sure, you might end up spending some time in a foreign jail, get roughed up a bit, and declared *persona non grata*, but your agent faces loss of life or livelihood. The agent's family will be persecuted, the subject of equally horrific retribution as the agent.

Before you recruit an agent from a country whose penalty for treason is death—there are still many in the world today, not just Russia, but China, North Korea, and many Arab countries—you weigh carefully the potential intelligence gains against the risks. You use your best tradecraft in handling these sources, and when it is time for you to turn the case over to other officers, you trust in your heart that they will do the same, and protect your agent. Even though you may never see the agent again, or hear news on the case after your involvement ends, that agent is always *your agent.* It is a very personal bond. So, when an agent is compromised, all the officers involved in the case feel a personal loss. When the compromise is due to a betrayal by a fellow officer, the betrayal is personal.

The Directorate of Operations is viewed by insiders as a very elite club. Only the best and the brightest can run the gantlet and gain entry to the secret society. Once in, the training regimen reinforces the concepts of elitism, fidelity to the system, and personal sacrifice to the system. The shroud of secrecy further bonds together those on the inside, separating Directorate of Operations officers from the outside world.

When I assessed another operations officer, I would query the person's "hallway reputation." My questions would focus on tradecraft and team skills. Does the officer have a successful track record? Does she cut tradecraft corners? Does he accurately report what happened, whether positive or negative? Is she out only to climb the ladder and is she a backstabber? Can I depend on him in a danger zone to be on the green line on time for the pickup to get you to safety? I did not ask about the officer's loyalty to the institution or the U.S. government; it was assumed.

Because we trust nobody on the outside and we must trust somebody if anything is to get done, fellow officers are the most likely candidates. They went through the same screening process that you did. Their loyalty has to be assumed unless there is undeniable proof to the contrary. It is a band of brothers and sisters. Furthermore, to question loyalty is to question the system, which is an act of disloyalty in itself. This is the mind-set of the Directorate of Operations, for better or worse. This is the mind-set that blinded us to the existence of moles in our midst. Because betrayal is an unthinkable concept, Directorate of Operations officers will consider every other possibility to account for operational failures.

When denial is no longer possible, and betrayal by a fellow officer is inescapable, Directorate of Operations officers respond with anger and shock, pointing fingers at everyone but themselves. How could *Security* miss the bad apple? *Everyone* knew the individual was a *10 percenter* (in the lowest 10 percent in performance ranking). Why did *Management* shuffle the problem to other divisions rather than shuffle the employee out the door? And yet, because of the bond of the elite club, no one feels that it is his or her duty to regularly report *unconfirmed* suspicions of fellow officers.

During the periodic security reinvestigation process, there is a time and place to comment on fellow employees. Investigators ask for personal assessments of the employee's performance, security practices, personal behavior, and financial affairs. Investigators inquire discreetly about the individual's suitability for continued access to classified information. Unlike the agent validation process, there is no direct, routine questioning on the possibility of the individual working for a foreign government, and assuming the possibility for the sake of argument, for which government(s). It is the duty of Security, Counterintelligence, and management staffs to take action. No one will step up to the plate and accept responsibility because the CIA culture does not reward those who voluntarily admit to making mistakes.

Counterespionage work has a bad name in the Directorate of Operations. There is a belief that it takes a special breed to work counterespionage for a career. Many attribute this attitude to the heavy-handed ways of James J. Angleton, the legendary CIA counterintelligence chief who ruined careers of Agency officers and paralyzed the Directorate of Operations in search for a "mole" he believed to exist in the old Soviet and East European Division in the 1960s and 1970s. Perhaps, but there are few officers remaining who date to Angleton's era, and his memory no longer provokes the same level of fear and hostility that it once did. Counterespionage work has a bad reputation for the same reason that the internal affairs offices within law enforcement have bad reputations: nobody likes an entity whose sole reason for existence is to question the loyalty, integrity, and honesty of the workforce.

Counterespionage staffs are housed in the Counterintelligence Center. Counterintelligence and counterespionage are different but related activities, with counterespionage being a subset of counterintelligence. Counterintelligence is focused upon exposing the activities of foreign governments and entities to penetrate the U.S. government and steal national security secrets (spy versus spy). Counterespionage is focused internally to identify sources of leaks and compromises inside the U.S. government (spy versus moles). All Directorate of Operations officers work counterintelligence issues as a necessary part of their duties; few chose to work in the Counterintelligence Center, or to work counterespionage issues, which are not considered career enhancing. In every operational assignment I had, I worked on counterintelligence issues. Only in two instances did I become involved in counterespionage investigations—once as an investigator and once as the one being investigated.

Once Ames was exposed, counterintelligence and counterespionage officers were unleashed to do damage control. Damage assessments are painstaking reviews to identify the full extent of the operational and intelligence losses. Debriefing the captured mole is one part of the process. The U.S. government has pursued a policy of making deals with moles on sentencing in exchange for cooperative debriefings. The CIA took the lead on the debriefings of Aldrich Ames, and attempted to walk him through his career as a double agent, day by day, to flesh out which documents he had passed, which agents he had exposed, which operations he had compromised. Ames passed volumes of extraordinarily sensitive documents, including numerous National Intelligence Estimates, over a nine-year period and claimed he could no longer remember exactly what he passed. He explained his poor memory as resulting from a drunken haze. The CIA deemed Ames as sufficiently cooperative, which, for Ames, meant a lighter sentence for his wife.

As part of the damage assessment, the CIA conducted a computer audit to obtain a list of all documents the mole accessed or could have accessed. The audit capability was established in the 1980s as an espionage countermeasure. Ames was warned in a 1989 letter from his Soviet handlers to take care with using Agency computers.[3] Apparently, he did not heed the warning. Why should he? He had complete disdain for the capabilities of the CIA to uncover him.

Coworkers and colleagues were questioned about violations of the need to know rule in their discussions with the mole. Directorate of Operations officers are known to frequently violate the need to know rule by telling "war stories." Apart from bragging, war stories are useful ways of passing along operational know-how, but they usually omit key bits of information on the source, target or the location. In some cases, an offhand comment that so-and-so recruited a Russian while serving in Africa is enough information to compromise the case, especially if told to a Russian mole.

Many of the sources who Ames compromised were executed, but not all; some were doubled back and fed the United States "controlled materials." The Russians and East Germans, by feeding the CIA controlled information, were in a position of leading the mole hunters as well as policymakers down the wrong track. In order to make the information credible, it is a standard procedure in double-agent operations to mix significant amounts of true information, which often is partially verifiable, with disinformation. Even when it is known the agent is a double, it is extremely difficult to determine what portion of the "intelligence" provided by the double is true and what is not, making the whole of the agent's reporting suspect. The CIA suspected some of these sources may have been bad, but disseminated their reporting. The political fallout from this would come after Woolsey's tenure, a good indication of how long the damage assessment process took.

The betrayals by Ames damaged the careers of many Directorate of Operations officers. My classmates who went to the Soviet Division—now renamed Central Eurasian Division—had been burned. Ames passed the Russians the names of Non-Official Cover officers (NOCs). These officers could no longer serve in this capacity. The risk became too high. Typically, NOCs handle the most sensitive cases because they are the most difficult for foreign intelligence services to identify due to their deep cover. Unlike officially covered officers, NOCs cannot expect to receive immunity from prosecution if arrested for espionage in a foreign country.

The exposed NOCs had to be brought "inside" and integrated into the Directorate of Operations. It was a hard transition for many of the NOCs, because what made them good NOCs made them poor inside officers. NOCs are used to almost complete freedom of action, and they are stifled by bureaucratic regimens Their teamwork skills had not been developed. Because they did not go up through the ranks on the inside, they never learned the basics of how to survive and thrive in the world of internal politics. At the mid to senior levels, the old-boy network controlled the assignment process. As outsiders, it was hard for the former NOCs to break into the network, because they did not have the contacts, and by personality they did not have the desire to play the bureaucratic games.

After Ames's arrest in 1994 and the realization he had operated for nine years with few suspicions, the CIA began to tighten up security and counterintelligence practices. Some measures it took were by its own volition; others were imposed. The Counterintelligence Center created by Webster was supposed to foster greater cooperation between the FBI and the CIA. As the Ames scandal proved, the administrative reorganization did not achieve the desired impact. The CIA purposely did not advise the FBI on the magnitude of the 1985 losses and did not give the

FBI access to CIA files. Policymakers were unimpressed by the CIA's ability to police its officers. In May 1995, President Clinton signed Presidential Decision Directive-24, establishing a National Counter Intelligence Center under a senior FBI officer on rotation to the CIA. Per the Intelligence Authorization Act for Fiscal Year 1995, the CIA is now required by law to notify the FBI immediately when it learns that an intelligence source has been compromised.

The CIA adopted some, but not all, of the recommendations offered by the Senate Select Committee on Intelligence from its investigation into the Ames case.[4] The CIA strengthened counterintelligence capabilities by requiring Directorate of Operations officers to serve in a counterintelligence or counterintelligence-related position (a position with substantive counterintelligence responsibilities) as a requirement for promotion into managerial positions.* Additionally, counterintelligence was added to the Operating Directive of every station and base, thus requiring each to account yearly upon activities on the counterintelligence front.† Directorate of Operations officers' performance evaluations included a new section on counterintelligence and security.

The Performance Appraisal Reporting System (PARS) was modified to institute a system that reflected job performance more accurately. The 1 to 5 number rating system was abandoned because the criteria had been so inflated over the years that the number ranking had become meaningless. Everyone rated either fours or fives, regardless of performance. Although the PARS format has been modified several times since Ames, there remains a persistent problem of "dishonest PARS"—in other words, reports that omit criticisms of performance, but "damn the employee by faint praise." Because of the inadequacy of official reports, "hallway reputation" is extremely important in the CIA. Difficult or poor-performing employees are frequently shuffled to other divisions in order to get rid of the problem. The receiving division takes the employee on the basis of the official record, without checking out the hall reputation first. Ames was shuffled about in this manner, from Soviet Division, to Latin America Division, back to Soviet

---

* This requirement was quietly dropped in the late 1990s, as it had become a box-checking requirement and was frequently waved when senior management wanted to promote one of their own protégés.

† The Operating Directive (OD) is a prioritized list of reporting requirements for CIA stations and bases. Typically, there are no more than five general requirements, such as counterterrorism, counterproliferation, on each OD. Station OD requirements are directly linked to CIA collection requirements, such as those defined by PDD-35.

Division, then to Europe Division, Counterintelligence Center, and finally to Counternarcotics Center, without sufficient assessment of his suitability, per the inspector general report.

The CIA revised policies and procedures governing operational activities, increasing the level of scrutiny of field officer activity. Officers had been required to write contact reports following all operational meetings, a requirement that was often overlooked. Report writing was enforced more stringently after Ames, to the great benefit of operational review. By documenting case development and management, officers had to rely less on institutional knowledge. Directorate of Operations officers, especially those who had been around for a while, fought the requirement, complaining they had to spend more time writing up their meetings than actually conducting them. The CIA also instituted an annual financial disclosure requirement for all CIA employees and tightened up the reporting requirements for foreign contacts and foreign travel. These were recommendations from a 1986 Senate Select Committee on Intelligence report following the betrayal by Howard that had never been implemented systematically.

According to security procedures in place prior to 1994, all Agency officers require reinvestigation every five years in order to maintain a top-secret security clearance. Before 1994, this was honored more in the breach than in the observance. Office of Security had insufficient resources, and the backlog of reinvestigation was such that some officers went as many as fifteen years between polygraphs. Starting in 1995, the Agency provided more resources to Security, and the office was instructed to work through the backlog quickly. Having been censored and embarrassed by the Ames treachery, Security was determined to rout out any remaining moles. The whole Agency was "boxed" for good measure.

The value of the polygraph is controversial inside and outside the Agency. In principle, Agency officers support the continued use of the polygraph as a personnel vetting procedure. They feel that no employee of the Agency should be exempt from the polygraph, an issue that came up when Webster and Woolsey refused to undergo the exam as part of their screening to become DCI.* Many Agency officers are also critical of the FBI and Defense Intelligence Agency selective polygraph policy of its personnel. That said, many Agency officers question the reliability

_____

* Webster agreed to take a reinvestigation polygraph shortly after becoming DCI. Woolsey agreed to do so after the arrest of Ames and the press exposure on Ames's polygraph results.

of the polygraph. This distrust comes from their own personal experiences with the polygraph and the knowledge that the polygraph has yet to catch a spy. There is an old saying in the Directorate of Operations among operations officers: If you don't like a case, for whatever reason, but do not have a good reason to terminate it, polygraph the agent. The test can be engineered to ensure that the agent fails.

CIA Security and Counterintelligence staffs have used the polygraph to support preconceived notions. If there are no preexisting suspicions and the subject passes the test, then the subject will be cleared. If a subject passes a polygraph, and there are preexisting concerns, then the test must not be accurate. If a subject fails a polygraph, and there are no preexisting concerns, then the subject is likely to be cleared if upon reexamination there is nothing else in the case history that indicates a security problem. If there is the least bit of an indication of problems, such as a poor performance report or workplace issues, the test must be working and there *is* a problem. The case will be referred to the FBI, which will decide whether or not to investigate. If the case involves a clearance for a potential new-hire and the results are not absolutely clear and negative, the clearance will not be granted.

Polygraph sessions are structured with an interview between the subject and the examiner in the polygraph room before the subject is hooked up to the polygraph machine. The subject has the opportunity to raise any concerns before the start of the test. Once the test begins, the examiner establishes levels for normal physiological responses. As the examiner asks security and counterintelligence questions, the examiner looks for significant fluctuations from the "normal" level. If a normal level cannot be established, there is no basis for a comparison. If there are significant responses, the CIA normally provides three testing sessions to resolve the issues. If the issues are not resolved after three sessions, the subject is considered to have failed the polygraph. For a routine polygraph, the atmosphere is designed to be stressful but nonconfrontational.

Officers will never forget their first post-Ames polygraph. One of the findings of a post-Ames polygraph study was that Ames was able to pass two polygraph exams after he started spying for the Russians, because the polygraph examiners failed to establish the required psychological atmosphere of fear and intimidation. Polygraph examiners overcompensated, making examinations hostile polygraphs, intimidating, threatening, and accusing loyal officers of all kinds of misdeeds and crimes. Gone was the collegial relationship between examiner and examinee where "concerns" were discussed, with the examiner saying, "Gee, you are showing discomfort on that question . . . can you tell me why?" The post-Ames approach was "You are lying. I know you are lying. The machine shows you are lying. Admit your guilt now or your career is over." One colleague of mine was so traumatized by the experience that she became completely incapable of undergoing future tests.

One senior Directorate of Operations officer who was serving overseas as a chief of station was recalled on a pretext of Headquarters consultations. As he came down in the elevator in a Tysons Corner hotel, he was met in the lobby by CIA security officers, who escorted him back upstairs for hostile interrogation and polygraphs, during which he was accused of being a mole. The interrogations lasted several days, and the officer was not permitted to return to his assignment. Even though he passed the polygraph, he was stuck in career limbo, walking the halls without an assignment, because Security would not clear him. Security turned a great field officer into a cynical and bitter individual. Although he went on to serve overseas years later, his career was negatively impacted because he was no longer on the track for promotion into the Senior Intelligence Service.

As part of the post-Ames reforms, the Agency was required to send to the FBI all cases of CIA employees who fail the polygraph. There were approximately four hundred cases of Agency officers who "failed" in the several years after the Ames reforms. These officers went into career limbo while the CIA and FBI tried to work out a method of dealing with them. At first, the FBI asserted all cases had to be investigated—a process that could take years. Meanwhile, the officers were either placed on administrative leave with their security clearances revoked, or they were allowed to remain in the workforce, but they were not allowed to take assignments overseas. Some maintained their access to classified information but were placed in "less sensitive" positions, per the recommendation of the Ames inspector general report.

It was a mess, and officers were angry about arbitrary and unjust treatment. A handful of CIA employees sought legal counsel. But suing the Agency is extremely difficult, because the DCI can invoke national security protections and have the case thrown out, regardless of its legal merits. Eventually, a compromise was worked out, whereby a failed polygraph was not the sole criterion for the FBI decision to open an investigation. The FBI would decide whether or not to investigate the cases, but the CIA is required to refer all cases of failed polygraphs, regardless of exculpatory information.

Given the bad blood between the FBI and CIA institutionally, CIA officers could not expect gentle treatment if thrown to the FBI for investigation. Indeed, there was an element of overzealousness—or some might say vindictiveness—to the FBI's unrelenting hunt for CIA wrongdoing. Tensions could not help spilling over into all areas where the CIA and the FBI had to work together, including the investigation into the World Trade Center bombing.

13
Doing Less with Less

LANGLEY, VIRGINIA, 1993–95: The organization was in tremendous flux under Woolsey. Many of the reforms introduced by Gates were shelved—the recommendations of the task forces placed in safes only to gather dust—creating reform whiplash. It was not that Woolsey was against reform, he just did not share Gates's vision on what the New CIA should look like. However, some of the changes Woolsey made would have far-reaching consequences. One of Woolsey's biggest challenges was deciding how to spread the CIA's dwindling resources around competing priorities. The other was to prove to the White House, Congress, the American people, and officers of the CIA that the Agency was relevant to the post–Cold War national security needs.

A review of the early 1990s public debate reveals the depth of the challenge to the CIA to reform or perish. Bold headlines labeled the CIA a dinosaur and Cold War relic. The continued requirement for a civilian intelligence organization was questioned; in 1994, Senator Daniel Patrick Moynihan called publicly for the dissolution of the CIA.[1] "Abolish the CIA!" read the bumper stickers and the picket signs. Some argued for the organization to be disbanded and its various functions divvied up among the Department of Defense, Department of State, Department of Commerce, Department of Agriculture, and the FBI.

While the political fringe favored the extreme, the vast majority argued that if the CIA remained, it had to be reformed. The CIA needed a new mission and a new way of thinking about national security. In mid-1994, the National Security Council started a review of how to redefine the roles of the U.S. intelligence community. In 1995, a congressionally mandated presidential commission was formed to study the post–Cold War roles and missions of the intelligence community, starting from the basics on whether the CIA should live or die. Two congressional committees also studied how to reform the intelligence community. The results of these studies would come in after Woolsey's departure. Nonetheless, the hearings, investigations, and interviews were conducted under Woolsey's watchful eyes, a constant reminder to him that if he did not make changes, outsiders would try to do so.

The sense was that the intelligence community was too big and too duplicative for the needs of the twenty-first century. There was no question that the Agency had grown rapidly in the 1980s, by about 33 percent, and had become top-heavy with multiple layers of management. But cutting back the workforce meant there had to be cuts in the amount of work done. The external calls for reform pressured the CIA to embark on changes, but without a strategic vision of where the Agency was going. This was no more apparent than in rewriting collection priorities and the assignation of collection authorities.

Under Gates, the CIA cut a little here and a little there to adjust for the budget shortfalls. Woolsey decided that cutting entire programs was a more efficient way to align operational budgets. The CIA henceforth would do "less with less." Woolsey started closing stations and bases, both overseas and domestically. As the CIA abandoned its position as a "worldwide" intelligence organization, it had to build a new mechanism to respond to rapidly developing situations that required intelligence-reporting capabilities in areas in which it either no longer had a presence or had its presence greatly diminished. Paralleling the military "global reach" concept, the CIA developed a "surge" doctrine as a way to convince policymakers that the Agency would retain worldwide capabilities, if not presence.

The CIA closed large numbers of stations and bases. Large stations were reduced in size by over 60 percent. The number of deployed, officially covered case officers declined at an average rate of almost 10 percent a year.[2] Africa Division was the hardest hit, with Europe and East Asia following close behind.

The CIA was not the only government agency to downsize. The State Department took major cuts in both budget and personnel throughout the 1990s. Ambassadors were told to reduce the size of the diplomatic missions as part of the budget realignment. The cut in overseas slots included slots filled by Agency officers under the cover of other agencies. Some of the lost slots were easily folded into the CIA's own plan for downsizing. However, sometimes the requirements of an ambassador did not dovetail with the requirements of the CIA, and problems arose on how to keep officers deployed to the field.

I remember an intense argument that broke out between my chief and the ambassador. The ambassador wanted the office to cut one slot. The chief resisted because the operation was already small. When the chief offered up the slot that was under official cover—with the officer spending 50 percent of his time doing diplomatic work—the chief thought that the ambassador would reconsider. After all, it would mean that the ambassador would lose half a person doing diplomatic work, for free. Much to the chief's chagrin, the ambassador said yes.

The CIA had to think about doing its business differently. Moving outside of ████████ (official U.S. installations) was not necessarily a negative result of downsizing. Transnational issues posed a different kind of collection challenge for the Directorate of Operations. Terrorists, Russian Mafia, and nuclear scientists are not the kind of folks one typically finds on the diplomatic circuit, the traditional hunting ground for Cold War targets. Too bad. Just envision the business card:

USAMA BIN LADIN
MASTER TERRORIST

CORPORATE HEADQUARTERS: Afghanistan
BRANCH OFFICES: The World

(Don't call us, we'll call you.)

The CIA looked to ████████████ platforms to meet these needs. The CIA augmented the Non-Official Cover (NOC) program as a way of keeping officers overseas utilizing cover identities not associated with the U.S. government. Moving away from positions with diplomatic immunity meant more risk and up-front capital. The NOC program, always small, has suffered from weak management and ossified vision. Although attempts to reform the program and increase its productivity and flexibility were made, the program remained troubled. There are some legendary NOCs in the Agency. Many of these ran afoul of Security, which took issue with their fast and loose operating style.

NOCs are truly operating out in the cold and are not cut from the same cloth as an inside officer. They require more support than inside operations officers and have different kinds of problems that need solving. NOC operations are the most difficult and costly clandestine human operation to support and the most dangerous, because the penalty of being caught can mean jail or death in certain countries. Furthermore, because of the high risks involved, the types of activities in which they are involved are more limited. Given the choice between having a full-service operations officer or a supersecret NOC with a limited playbook, Directorate of Operations division mangers too frequently chose the easy path. The end result was a lot of underutilized and unhappy NOCs.

To be relevant to the new intelligence needs of the post–Cold War period, the CIA expanded collection to nontraditional topics. We added economic espionage to our priority list. There was a heated debate on whether the CIA should collect only defensive economic intelligence to protect American companies and/or collect economic secrets from foreign companies. We felt strongly that economic intelligence collection should be limited to key economies such as Russia, China, Eastern Europe, and large emerging markets; intelligence support for bilateral and multilateral negotiations; monitoring of foreign compliance with economic sanctions against Iraq and Libya; and information on unfair trade practices, such as bribery and corruption. We viewed industrial espionage as being outside the mission of the CIA.

The CIA also began collecting environmental intelligence and established the DCI Environmental Center. We increased collection on illegal drugs and started programs against international organized crime, establishing the DCI Crime and Narcotics Center in the Directorate of Intelligence in 1994. As the CIA expanded the topics that it collected, other members of the intelligence community accused the CIA of encroaching on their turf.

The feeling inside the CIA was that these new collection priorities were largely soft topics and not appropriate for clandestine collection. We prided ourselves on collecting intelligence that could not be collected by any other means. Human intelligence was the collection means of last resort. If you could not suck it out of the airwaves, spy on it from the sky, read it in a paper, or get it off the diplomatic circuit, then and only then did you call upon the services of the Directorate of Operations.

The intelligence on the soft topics was often not well received, because there frequently was no value added to what was already being collected and analyzed by other members of the intelligence community. For Directorate of Operations officers, it was one thing to risk your life or your career for national security; it was quite another thing to do so for the benefit of Corporate America or foreign rain forests. If this was the wave of the future, there would not be a future for the CIA. Morale was low, and a wave of resignations from entry- and mid-level officers began.

While the CIA was being called upon to cut back, turf wars with the FBI and the Pentagon erupted as these agencies expanded their presence overseas. CIA insiders feared that the Agency was losing power and turf to other members of the intelligence community under the guise of reform.

The CIA felt the most vulnerable to an expansionist FBI. Responsibility for counterintelligence was one of the contentious issues, and the Ames spy scandal brought the conflict out in the wide open. The post-Ames investigation was scathing of the CIA's handling of counterintelligence. Policymakers found that the CIA's performance was proof positive that it could not police itself. The investigation revealed the CIA failed to inform the FBI of information it had relating to as many as a dozen counterintelligence cases. Policymakers were also critical of the FBI's performance, but at least the FBI apprehended Ames. FBI Director Louis Freeh went on the offensive, lobbying policymakers to give the FBI clear-cut authority on counterintelligence issues, taking away the CIA's in-house counterespionage responsibilities. Discussion on transferring all overseas intelligence-related activities to the FBI began in Congress.

Many in the CIA felt the FBI made a big show of rubbing the CIA's face in the dirt, portraying CIA incompetence while highlighting FBI professionalism. Building upon the momentum of this bureaucratic success, Freeh sought and received congressional authorization to expand FBI operations overseas. The FBI embarked on an ambitious program to set up offices and establish liaison relationships with foreign police and intelligence agencies, many of which had established relationships with the CIA. Naturally, giving the FBI more authority did not solve the problem of interagency cooperation.

As a result of a U.S. court ruling that suspects can be arrested abroad and brought back to the United States for trial, the FBI has had a handful of legal attachés assigned overseas for a number of years before the push by Freeh. The FBI had limited its role to law enforcement issues, such as drugs, money laundering, and hiding of assets. As international organized crime—especially that emanating from the states of the former Soviet Union—became a growing domestic problem, Freeh forged contacts with Russian and Eastern European governments, offering training to their police forces. Freeh had plans to expand the FBI presence rapidly, proposing opening ten new offices in 1996. He was also the driving force behind the creation of an international law enforcement academy in Budapest, Hungary, to offer training and promote global networking.

The FBI gained congressional support to expand its overseas operations because of the belief that national security threats in the post–Cold War world would be primarily law enforcement issues, such as organized crime and drug trafficking. Some influential members of Congress were concerned that the FBI was moving too quickly and put the brakes on Freeh, slowing the expansion while the FBI developed short- and long-term expansion plans.[3] However, the balance of power had shifted, evidenced by the fact that while the FBI was expanding overseas, the CIA was closing down stations and bases.

The infighting within the intelligence community over mission and turf during the governmentwide downsizing initiative was sufficient to gain the attention of Vice President Al Gore, who was shepherding a "Re-creating Government" program. He ordered a National Performance Review (NPR) of the intelligence community in 1993. NPR found the main ill was that the intelligence community failed to work as a team, and called upon the community to finds ways to share resources, be more efficient and effective, and reduce overhead. Without changing to a team focus, the community would not be able to respond to the speed of change and, with shrinking budgets, to intelligent downsizing. The message to Woolsey was that the intelligence community needed to consolidate for more efficiency and better service.

NPR noted that the intelligence community and the Defense Department have different budget systems, processes, and schedules and, as a consequence, different approaches to strategic planning, programming, and budgeting. NPR did not recommend centralization, but rather the creation of common frameworks in which the elements of the intelligence community could pursue their departmental and national intelligence roles.

NPR also recommended integration in the following areas and relationships: producer-consumer relationship (focusing collection efforts on actionable intelligence the consumer wants and expanding support to nontraditional consumers), support to military operations, personnel and training, infrastructure, resource management (establishing a common set of definitions, procedures, and schedules for planning, programming, and budgeting processes), classification and declassification standards, and information management systems.

With greater integration, intelligence officers would see their particular mission within the framework of an integrated community and therefore would draw upon team capabilities rather than competing frameworks that lead to turf battles and "stovepipes." Indeed, the issue of integration would be a major theme of the NPR and all subsequent intelligence reform initiatives in the mid-1990s.

While not interested in major restructuring of the intelligence community, Woolsey did endorse the concept of integration. He was well aware of the stovepipes within the CIA that served as barriers to communication, collection, and analysis. In 1994, Woolsey informed the Directorate of Operations and Directorate of Intelligence that it was time to break down the stovepipes separating these two arms of the Agency. Named the DO/DI Partnership program, Woolsey started an experiment in the Africa Division. Using the smallest division as a proving ground, the plan was to test the impact of colocation and integration of analysts and operational personnel. The goal was to improve both collection and analysis by directly linking producers and consumers. If the experiment was judged successful, the model would be applied to the other regional divisions.

Representatives of the directorates began to attend each others' morning meetings and pass along pertinent information. In certain cases, analysts were allowed to read operational cable traffic, learn the identities of sources, and be informed about specific operations. Proponents of the partnership program felt there were significant advantages. Analysts helped operations officers better target their recruitments and exploit their sources. The analysts gained a better understanding of the access and reporting of clandestine sources and therefore were better able to assess the value of the information provided. Being closer to those in the field, the analysts also gained a better understanding of the ground truth. Critics of the program felt that it led to analytical bias, putting too much emphasis on human intelligence (HUMINT) rather than balancing open source, foreign service reporting, and intelligence collected by other means.

The chief of Africa Division for the Directorate of Operations assessed that the program was successful and recommended other geographical divisions follow suit. The Near East Division (Operations) and Near East and South Asian Affairs (Intelligence) were slated to colocate next. It never happened. The colocation program did not expand because of excuses related to logistical relocation problems and the press of other business. The truth is that the two directorates embraced the partnership program with something less than enthusiasm because of issues of turf and control as well as a clash of cultures. Once again, the culture proved resistant to reform.

14
Woolsey's Undoing

SEVENTH FLOOR, LANGLEY, VIRGINIA, 1994: After the Ames story broke, Woolsey was never able to get ahead of the curve. Indeed, he made a conscious decision not to be proactive. While the CIA was being battered by public opinion and Washington power, Woolsey insisted on waiting to see the results of the internal review. The internal review was rightfully scathing, indicting the Directorate of Operations, Counterintelligence Center, Office of Security, and most senior management of dereliction of duty and gross mismanagement. Because the wrongdoing was so widespread, CIA culture—and especially that of the Directorate of Operations—was found to be the greatest enabler of the organizational failure.

Woolsey wanted to be fair. Woolsey wanted to do the right thing. So many of those most responsible for the failure to fully investigate the initial loss of Soviet sources were beyond his reach, having already retired in glory from the service. How could he punish only those remaining? How could he not?

Woolsey chose the middle ground, reprimanding five active and six retired senior Agency officers. Reprimands for naughty boys, it seemed. The major blame was placed on the CIA culture, that intangible . . . thing. No one was fired or demoted. For this he was roundly criticized by outsiders, and by some insiders.

CAPITOL HILL, WASHINGTON, D.C., 1994: For Congress, Woolsey's performance in managing the Ames investigation was the final straw. The heat index on Capitol Hill was so high, the dome glowed. Culture does not bleed, and Congress wanted blood. Culture does not have a face that can be held up before the nation to accept accountability, and Congress wanted accountability. Culture cannot be changed overnight, and Congress wanted change yesterday.

The CIA was engaged in some highly public turf battles within the intelligence community. Given the perceived poor performance of the CIA on traditional issues, Congress was in the mood for more cuts in CIA responsibilities, such as removing all counterintelligence responsibilities from the CIA and giving them to the FBI. With no natural constituency to rally behind the CIA, and with weak, reactive leadership at the top, the CIA entered a downward spiral. The nadir was when Congress decided maybe Senator Daniel Moynihan's then-three-year-old proposal to eliminate the CIA was not so crazy after all.

Discontent with Woolsey had been growing for months. Congress expected Woolsey to play ball on the intelligence community budget and reform. But as far as Woolsey was concerned, discussions on major reform would not be on the table, which generated more sighs of relief within the Agency and shocked anger in Congress. Not only did he believe that business as usual was the appropriate course, he wanted *more* of the usual business. He fought Congress over a budget increase for the intelligence community. Congress wanted deeper cuts in the budget, not increases. The budget battle was fierce and planted the seeds of congressional ill will toward Woolsey, who they felt was not attuned to the needs of the nation. Congress found him combative and inflexible. Congress did not like it when Woolsey came to the Hill with a briefing package illustrating how budget cuts were destroying CIA and intelligence community capabilities. He was willing to fall on his sword to protect what he felt was to the best interests of the United States. He would not play the lightweight and roll over before congressional pressure.

WHITE HOUSE, WASHINGTON, DC, 1994: The normal DCI defensive tactic when Congress starts feeling its oats is to take cover at the White House. A phone call from the president to a key senator or representative usually does the trick. But Woolsey did not have a key to the White House. Clinton's benign neglect had turned into something less than benign. The CIA only caused him problems. The administration was still sore about Haiti, with the CIA being accused of undercutting Clinton's policy for reinstating Haitian president Aristide.

Clinton was unwilling to expend any political capital on an organization that brought him no domestic benefits. Clinton read the newspapers, watched the popular talking heads on TV; he knew what the public was hearing and saying. The public opinion president did not like what he heard and saw. He certainly did not want to be marred by it.

There was a popular notion that something was rotten inside the CIA. The notion was fed by CIA officers who were jumping ship and giving exit interviews to the press. There was no sense of mission, they complained. Budget cuts were destroying CIA capabilities and morale. Africa Division was all but shut down. CIA personnel practices toward women and minorities—important groups of voters for Clinton—were unfair. Because Woolsey opted to indict CIA culture, public opinion decided to indict the whole organization, not seeing the difference between the two.

LANGLEY, VIRGINIA, 1994: Internal support for Woolsey had been eroding for months as well. It did not go unnoticed that Woolsey—and therefore the Agency—had no clout with the White House. The president could talk endlessly about what was going on in Middle America but did not know a thing about threats in the Middle East, because the one paper he did not read was the *Presidential Daily Brief*—the highly classified publication prepared exclusively for him by the CIA.

Insiders faulted Woolsey's leadership skills. We felt the drift in acute ways. Low morale, ongoing turf battles, and personnel crises all showed an organization lacking strong leadership. Woolsey's handling of the Ames investigation divided the organization. While the old boys applauded Woolsey for protecting them in the face of congressional wrath, many at the working level—me included—had a different view, wondering how management could not be held accountable for not taking earlier action against Ames. The old boys were let off with only a slap on the wrist. Woolsey had been recruited by the recruiters, his vision fogged, and, as a member of the brotherhood, he could not accept the findings of the CIA inspector general report: "the effort [on Ames] was plagued after 1987 by senior management inattention and failure to apply an appropriate level of resources to the effort until 1991."[1]

Having "stood up to Congress," Woolsey was not repaid with loyalty. Just one day after announcing the Ames reprimands, the chief of Near East Division, with the approval of the Assistant Deputy Director of Operations, gave a plaque of appreciation to one of the sanctioned officers, in a special awards ceremony, on the eve of that officer's retirement. Enraged at the act of insubordination, Woolsey reprimanded and demoted the two officers pushing the award. The officers, with their peers' support, argued that the retiring officer had served his country honorably, and his whole career should not be judge on the basis of one failure. Besides, "the award was not official," they countered in the best Directorate of Operations tradition of exploiting the gray zones. They resigned as old-boy martyrs to an unfair accountability process.

In the minds of directorate officers, there was no question who was right and who was wrong. In the "us" and "them" mentality, Woolsey just became a "them." Near East Division, in particular, was in an uproar because the chief had been respected, right down through the ranks. The revolt of the Directorate of Operations was the final straw. Woolsey—who had fought to retain the old system, and who honored those who had served the country with such dedication by being balanced and fair by looking at their whole record rather than one incident in a career—understood that it was over.

No one was listening to him. No one believed in him. Not Clinton. Not Congress. Not the CIA. The only blood that would be let was Woolsey's. The only one held accountable would be Woolsey. The only change that would occur would be Woolsey. Woolsey tendered his resignation in December 1994 to a surprised president, who, as usual, had not been paying attention to matters on the other side of the river.

LANGLEY, VIRGINIA, 1995: Woolsey's send-off at the CIA was a sad affair. There was too much anger, resentment and disappointment floating through the corridors for there to be any sense of levity or willingness to let bygones be bygones. There was no appreciation for the reality that Woolsey had fallen on his sword to save the CIA from those who wanted to destroy it, by cutting responsibilities, budget, personnel, and mission. For those who wished to be civil and thank Woolsey for the contributions he made in his twenty-two months as DCI, they would be hard-pressed to come up with anything concrete that he achieved. It was more what he did *not* do that the Agency appreciated, such as not caving into Congress and not instituting an RIF or a new round of major reforms. Instead, he was thanked for introducing casual-dress day on Fridays.

There is nothing worse than being damned by faint praise.

MANILA, PHILIPPINES, 1995: While CIA Headquarters was in total disarray, others were focused on terrorizing the West. On January 6, a small fire in the kitchen of a Manila apartment broke out. The occupants fled. A police officer decided to inspect the apartment, where she found a bomb factory, packed with all the paraphernalia to wreak havoc and destruction. A laptop computer that contained very incriminating evidence was also recovered. When the apartment occupants returned, one was immediately captured: Abdul Hakim Murad. Under intense interrogation, Murad began to talk.

The cell had planned to assassinate Pope John Paul II, who was due to arrive in Manila the following week, with the procession passing along the street of the apartment building. As if this were not enough, the cell had also been well into the advanced planning stage of a multiple bombing attack against international airlines. Named "Project Bojinka," the cell planned to simultaneously blow up twelve airplanes as they flew across the Atlantic. According to information retrieved from the laptop computer, the cell was also discussing other potential plots, such as crashing airplanes into government buildings and nuclear facilities. Murad was a pilot. He told his Philippine interrogators that he had suggested hijacking an American commercial aircraft and diving it into the CIA Headquarters—a suicide mission he was willing to execute.

Murad also talked about his associates (after giving them enough time to flee), who included none other than Ramzi Yousef, the fugitive from the World Trade Center bombing. Their association went back to their childhood, when they lived in the same Palestinian expatriate neighborhood in Kuwait. Yousef had been in the apartment at the time of the fire, but had eluded capture. Philippine security determined that Yousef had fled to Pakistan the day after the fire.

Murad identified two other co-conspirators: Wali Khan Amin Shah and Khalid Shaykh Muhammad. Shah was arrested immediately, but then escaped from custody one week later. On December 11, he was arrested in Malaysia and turned over to the FBI. He became a cooperative witness for the FBI in exchange for leniency. Murad said Khalid Shaykh Muhammad was someone who helped Yousef finance and develop the Manila plot. He was also identified as a relative of Yousef. Khalid Shaykh Muhammad would remain a shadowy figure for some time.[2]

I read the cable traffic as the operation against Murad, Shah, and Yousef unfolded. It was complicated, with the pieces coming in a bit at a time, in the most confusing of patterns. Khalid Shaykh Muhammad was just a blip on the screen. He would later become a major target on my screen.

RAWALPINDI, PAKISTAN, 1995: Pakistan was a good place to go to ground. The Pakistani government did not even dare send government troops into parts of the country because of tribal opposition.

Perhaps if Yousef had gone to Peshawar, he would have eluded his hunters. Instead, he chose to hide in the moderate comfort of Rawalpindi, located on the outskirts of Islamabad, the new Pakistani capital. In a television interview with *60 Minutes*, FBI Special Agent Brad Garrett described the rendition of Ramzi Yousef. According to Garrett, a team of Pakistani military officers in civilian clothes, FBI agents, "a couple of State Department agents," and a DEA agent captured Yousef in a guesthouse in Pakistan, took him to a secure location, and finger-printed him to confirm his identity. On February 7, the FBI got their man. Garrett's description made it sound easy, because it eliminated all of the heavy lifting that the CIA field officers had done just to find Yousef—a story that still remains classified.

NEW YORK CITY, NEW YORK, 1995: Meanwhile, the second World Trade Center trial was getting under way. Shaykh Omar Abdel Rahman (the Blind Shaykh) and eight other conspirators, were charged with a wide-ranging plot to terrorize New York City, including render-ing assistance to those who bombed the World Trade Center, planning to bomb bridges and tunnels in New York City, assassinating Rabbi Meir Kahane, head of the militant Jewish Defense League, and planning to assassinate the president of Egypt, Hosni Mubarak.

The Blind Shaykh was identified in the government's case as the leader of the seditious conspiracy, the purpose of which was to wage a *jihad* against the "enemies of God." His speeches and writings were used as evidence. In these, the Blind Shaykh identified the United States as the primary oppressor of Muslims worldwide, active in assisting Israel to gain power in the Middle East. He also labeled Mubarak's secular Egyptian government as oppressive and as a supporter of Israel.

Evidence seized from the home of another defendant, El Sayyid Nosair, included a notebook in which Nosair wrote about the need to attack American landmarks. He stated that in order to establish a Muslim state in the Muslim holy lands it would be necessary to "break and destroy" the morale of the enemies of God and the structure of their civilized pillar, such as the tourist infrastructure, "high world buildings," and "buildings in which they gather their leadership."

The trial, which started on January 9, 1995, ended ten months later, with the defendants being found guilty on most charges. Security around the courthouse building made the place look like a U.S. base in a war zone. The FBI was on alert for possible new terror attacks or attempts to free the accused. The closest similarity the American pub-lic had ever seen in recent memory was security measures during the civil rights movement more than thirty years earlier.

During the trial, there were numerous mentions of links to Pakistan, Sudan, Egypt, and Afghanistan. The majority of the defendants were of Egyptian origin. One was Sudanese and another Palestinian. The Sudanese-Egyptian link was the one that gathered the most attention. There was no mention of al-Qa'ida or bin Ladin.[3]

On February 21, a New York grand jury indicted Yousef, Murad, and Shah for various crimes relating to their conspiracy to bomb U.S. airliners in Southeast Asia in 1994 and 1995. When Yousef was being brought back to the United States by the FBI, he made incriminating comments while bragging about his role in the World Trade Center bombing. Murad, who was turned over to the FBI on April 12, also talked to the FBI about his role in the airline bombing plot, as well as giving a confession to Philippine authorities, to which the FBI had access.

Why did Murad, Yousef, and Shah want to create chaos in the international airways and attack American institutions? A letter recovered from the laptop computer captured their feelings of anger against the United States and their desire to make Americans pay for pro-Israeli policies against the Palestinians. In the U.S. government's case against the three, the letter, translated from Arabic, was entered as trial evidence showing the group's motivations:

> We, the Fifth Division of the Liberation Army under the command of Staff Lieutenant General Abu Bakr al-Makki, declare our responsibility for striking at some American targets in the near future in retaliation for the financial, political, and military support extended by the American government to the Jewish State, which occupies the land of Palestine. While the government of America is donating military planes to the Jewish State, the Jewish State continues its massacres in south Lebanon and is killing, torturing, and detaining our Palestinian brothers with American money, weapons, and ammunition, in addition to the support and blessing [to Israel] given by the U.S. Congress. The American people are quite aware of all of this. [Therefore], we will consider all American nationals as part of our legitimate targets because they are responsible for the behavior of their government and its foreign policies, for the policy of the government represents the will of the people. . . .
>
> Again, we warn the American government that if it does not stop its aid to Israel, then our retaliatory operations will

continue, inside and outside America. Some of our operations will include attacks against American nuclear targets. We consider the America government an accomplice of Israel in the occupation of the land of Palestine and the aggression against its people.

Allah is Great and victory for the believers.[4]

As with the Blind Shaykh's trial, there was no mention of al-Qa'ida. The government's case included no role for bin Ladin either. This was because the connection had not been made. Yousef and Murad were of Palestinian origin, not Filipinos or Egyptians. The only "Sudan link" was through the Blind Shaykh to Yousef. The Yousef Manila cell was thought to be either independent, or perhaps to have loose links to Abu Sayyaf, a Philippine Muslim separatist group. The airline bombing case was open and shut quickly. The trial began on May 29 and ended on September 5, 1996. Yousef, Murad, and Shah were convicted on all accounts.[5]

★ ★ ★ ★

When Woolsey testified at his confirmation hearing, he described the new world order as a jungle filled with a bewildering variety of poisonous snakes. It was an apt metaphor of the new problems emerging as the convulsions of the imploding states of the former Soviet Union worked their way around the globe. It was also an apt description of Washington and the powers that be. The CIA had few friends in Washington, with the new president ignoring Woolsey and Congress practicing its knife-throwing skills, particularly after the Ames exposure. Budget and personnel cuts put the CIA in retreat. It was no longer a worldwide intelligence service, but a smaller, leaner organization with many blind spots around the world.

Internally, the CIA suffered from reform whiplash, hemorrhage of personnel, and low morale. The downsizing brought personnel management disputes to the forefront, exposing discriminatory practices against women and minorities. The Ames scandal devastated the Clandestine Service, as its culture was held accountable for the mother of all breaches. The failure to hold anyone accountable for Ames's long spying career destroyed Woolsey's standing and left an open wound to fester for the rest of the decade. Security and Counterintelligence staffs were given a free rein to root out potential bad apples, giving rise to a new kind of bureaucratic security paranoia not seen since the bad old days of Angleton. The CIA needed new accountability procedures; instead, it opted for witch hunts.

I remained overseas, keeping my head low and my nose to the grindstone. I finished my Arabic language training, obtaining the fluency I needed to succeed both in the back alleys of the Middle East and in the corridors of power in the Near East Division. I did my utmost to avoid returning to Headquarters, where morale was low and political infighting high. Instead, I won a follow-on field assignment that took me to the Persian Gulf.

While CIA Headquarters was in total disarray, a very lethal snake showed its fangs in New York and then Manila. The Egyptian origin of many of the terrorists involved in the New York plots fed CIA assumptions that the groups were linked to Egyptian terrorist groups of the traditional model. The FBI wanted to keep the investigation simple and did its best to ignore links to a global conspiracy. The Somali attacks, the Argentine car bombings, Bojinka project, and World Trade Center bombings were all viewed as separate and unrelated events. CIA stovepipes kept operations officers and analysts from looking at events within an integrated matrix. Turf battles reduced the intelligence community's ability to fuse capabilities.

Woolsey appeared to be bewildered by how best to lead the community, let alone how to counter these emerging threats. Lacking a strategic vision, reforms continued to be ad hoc, without a sense of direction or urgency. CIA officers plugged along. We did the best we could, setting our own priorities while wondering if anyone really cared. We knew that senior management was really just on automatic pilot.

PART

5

THE DEUTCH YEARS
(MAY 10, 1995–DECEMBER 15, 1996)

"Finally, my first and most important challenge will be to improve the management and thereby the morale of the dedicated men and women who make up the intelligence community. . . . I am certain . . . the intelligence function, like all other functions of government, can be managed with a system of accountability at all levels so as to meet standards of propriety and legality."

JOHN DEUTCH
Confirmation hearing, 1995

15
The Reluctant Spy

SEVENTH FLOOR, LANGLEY, VIRGINIA, 1995: John Deutch did not want to be DCI. When Clinton first approached him for the job, Deutch deflected deftly and offered to find a "better" candidate. Retired Air Force General Michael P. C. Carns seemed an ideal candidate. Congress wanted a uniformed director, believing what the Agency really needed was discipline. Carns, although interested, proved unwilling to subject himself and his family to an ugly confirmation process. He withdrew his nomination, leaving Deutch, then–Deputy Secretary of Defense, holding the bag. Clinton directed Deutch to take the job, telling Deutch he would have no chance at the position he really wanted—Secretary of Defense—if he failed to meet the current needs of the president. Deutch, the good soldier, did so, but made no bones about showing his displeasure.

Once given the job, Deutch set about leading the Agency forcefully. Deutch understood what Woolsey did not. With the change in the world power structure, the CIA had to change drastically in order to remain relevant. He also understood that while the CIA wanted to be relevant, it did not want to change. Congressional intelligence committees and a presidential commission were reevaluating the intelligence community and the CIA, starting with a "blank page." If the CIA did not prove itself capable of change and capable of responding to the new needs and vision of the nation, it would be eliminated from the future organizational chart of the intelligence community. Espionage responsibilities would be assigned to other organizations, who were more than willing to pick up the mantle.

Deutch put no credence in this culture thing. *People* were deficient, not culture. People and rules drove organizations, not culture. Deutch would change the attitudes, practices, and habits and remake the CIA into an organization that had the wherewithal to perform vital missions.

Deutch also understood he had to be empowered to make changes. One important element was support from Clinton. He had to be on the team, be visible with the president, and be a force. He needed a role in setting national security policy. Deutch demanded and received cabinet status. This was controversial at the time because of lingering bad memories of the last DCI who held cabinet status—Casey, alleged lawbreaker, the subverter of the president, Congress, and the Constitution. There were also the more recent memories of what happens when the CIA director is excluded from the president's inner circle.

Deutch realized that having Clinton's support was not enough. He needed the support of Congress. Historically, officers of the CIA had viewed their role as serving the president, the executive arm of the government. The CIA provided the president, first, and then "other policymakers"—all lumped together in a secondary status—with intelligence on threats to national security. The CIA undertook covert action at the request of the president, not "other policymakers." Congress was a consumer and had new and expanding oversight responsibilities, but Congress was not the CIA's boss and most important customer.

During his confirmation hearings, Deutch stated that he considered Congress to be his board of directors.[1] With this simple statement, Deutch signaled his inclination to change the very nature of the CIA's relationship with Congress and, by extension, its relationship to the president. Bill Casey must have turned over in his grave. Shock waves went through the intelligence community. We in the Directorate of Operations knew that our new director had caved in to power-hungry congressional leaders before even setting one foot down in Langley.

In order to lead the intelligence community and the CIA, Deutch needed capable aides who shared his vision and would execute it. CIA officers had already proved their inability and unwillingness to rise to the occasion. Deutch had judged us, and we showed poorly, an opinion Deutch did not mind sharing with the world. His assessment was on a par with that held by those less informed. At Deutch's confirmation hearing, he advised Congress of his intention to bring in new people to fill upper-management positions.

The CIA needed to go to boot camp, Deutch decided. With the right sergeants, Deutch could break down the bunch of sniveling, undisciplined, and unethical kids and make them into real men, a fighting force, capable, honorable and responsive to authority. Deutch selected his leadership team almost exclusively from the military. He empowered them to make decisions and to act upon those decisions. His chief executor for the CIA was Nora Slatkin, whom he also brought over from the Pentagon. At first she was the troubleshooter, sent out to walk the halls and figure out exactly what was broken. She quickly assumed the position of Executive Director, and would grow into the day-to-day manager of the CIA.

The feelings were mutual. From the outset, the CIA did not like Deutch and his cabal. The Directorate of Operations loathed them. Deutch was taking aim at the old-boy system. The old-boy system defined the Directorate of Operations. He stated his intention to change the senior management before he was even confirmed, before he had even met them. In his first speech to the CIA after confirmation, tellingly called a Town Meeting—Town Meetings are held in government only when things are seriously amiss—Deutch would not commit to selecting a Deputy Director of Operations from within the directorate.

Indeed, he did not. He selected David Cohen, a brilliant CIA analyst who had few operational credentials. The message to the Directorate of Operations was as clear as a two-by-four to the head: anyone can run operations except operations officers. Cohen would not get very much respect—let alone cooperation—from the Directorate of Operations. From the directorate's perspective, we needed a strong advocate interacting with Deutch and Slatkin, someone who understood the difficulties and the risks of collecting secrets and running operations in difficult environments. Cohen was not up to the job. He was a poor advocate for the directorate, just as Deutch was a poor advocate for the CIA.

The Directorate of Operations' real wrath was reserved for Nora Slatkin, who was denigrated behind her back. She was an easy target, a woman in a man's world, and an outsider. The senior operations officers knew she knew nothing about intelligence or about the Directorate of Operations. In her misguided opinion, the directorate was broken, and Nora Slatkin thought she would fix it. Finding fault charged her batteries. She was not interested in hearing the facts, nor the pseudo-facts.

The truth was that Slatkin had the power, the authority, and the will to make changes. When she walked the halls, the Directorate of Operations alarm bells rang. People turned over the papers on their desk, put the screen savers on their computers, and hid. She would target the lowly desk officer, trying to get around the obfuscation she invariably received from managers. The directorate was always collecting intelligence on what she was doing, her newest targets, in order to prepare and "manage" her. No one was exempt from her assaults. One deputy director of operations tasked a classmate of mine who was one of his special assistants with the sole responsibility of keeping Nora Slatkin off his back.

Deutch promised there would be reforms, evolutionary—not draconian—reforms within the CIA. He promised it would take time for the reforms to be implemented and to take hold. Deutch delivered what he promised, on both accounts. He removed from the safe the dusty recommendations of the task forces of the Gates's era and reopened the review process. He expanded other initiatives started under Woolsey, such as the agent scrub. He changed the system by which the CIA reported to Congress, increasing the structure to make sure failures and triumphs were reported upward.

Deutch dismantled and inspected all of the processes the CIA used to conduct its business. Everything was open to review and reform. He encouraged participation in the process at all levels. Rather than announcing a new way of business to the workforce—that is, change from the top—he set up process action teams. The CIA became totally focused upon its own innards. It was the rise of the committee, the anointing of the bureaucracy, and the crowning of process.

The field became irrelevant. No one was interested in conducting operations. Operations were risky. I wanted to run operations, recruit agents, steal secrets. My operational proposals to infiltrate terrorist camps were too risky. Someone might get killed, or worse—caught and interrogated, revealing the hand of the CIA. My ideas to recruit mosque watchers were dismissed as too labor intensive with low impact. That was State Department work, not something valuable spies should be spending their time monitoring. My cables to Headquarters went unanswered. I did not immediately understand the politics, but I did grasp the reality. Stand down until further notified.

The worldview had changed. Operations could lead to failures, losses, and embarrassments. All operational initiatives had to be reviewed by Headquarters teams who would vet them carefully for risk. Field officers did not like their new standing. We were used to running the operational show. Now we were being told we did not have the judgment to make operational calls. Our knowledge of intelligence requirements, operations, and the operational environment was not the right basis for making operational decisions. The

knowledge of Washington and Seventh Floor politics was more important. Washington was risk averse, something the field did not seem to
appreciate. Therefore, calls had to be made by those in Headquarters,
not the field. The Deputy Director of Operations could not be
expected to weigh in on the side of operations officers—asserting that
operations were worth running, and that failure must be an acceptable part of the process—because he did not know operations.

While Deutch was so intent upon breaking down the CIA piece by
piece, the world did not accommodate him by providing quiet and stability. Indeed, important events were unwinding around the globe, far
away in the Middle East, Africa, and Southeast Asia, and close to home.
As the CIA watched these events and responded with some tactical steps,
the level of distraction inside the Agency, coupled with reduced capabilities, meant that the CIA failed to get out in front of what would
become the greatest threat to U.S. national security in the post–Cold
War world. Of course, hindsight permits such conclusions. The conclusions at the time, by CIA officers, were that internal developments
were impacting our ability and will to survive in an organization going
through epileptic fits, let alone meeting shifting mission requirements.

16
Politically Correct Espionage

OLD HEADQUARTERS BUILDING, LANGLEY, VIRGINIA, 1996: During Deutch's tenure, "risk management" was the new theme. There was the notion that risk could be spread upward, downward, and laterally, which would somehow make risk a tangible substance that could be anticipated, measured, minimized, and allotted in a politically acceptable manner. Officers of the Directorate of Operations had a hard time getting their minds around this alien perspective on risk. For us, risk taking was inseparable from the job at hand: nothing ventured, nothing gained. It was part of the challenge of the job, the thrill of doing something dangerous, risky, and illegal to collect intelligence and to counter threats to U.S. national security.

But by the mid-1990s, the consequences of taking risks had changed, forcing us to view risk taking in negative rather than positive terms. After what came to be known as the Guatemala Affair and the Paris Flap, a sense of uneasiness began to permeate the Directorate of Operations. As risk was being "managed out," operational proposals were being rejected. Most operations officers had more than a few personal examples of operations they tried to initiate but failed to get approved. Furthermore, most seasoned field officers who had worked on threshold-pushing operations had new concerns about future accountability. The thought of the phone call convoking them to testify before Congress was enough to sends chills down the spines of hardened foot soldiers.

For an agency that has a reputation for taking risks, and being a rogue elephant, how did the CIA became risk averse in the 1990s? The answer is simple to the insider: CIA management failed to be consistent in rewarding risk taking, and worse, CIA management left officers out in the cold when the going got tough. Traditional CIA methods were deemed to be too messy, too dirty for the decade of political correctness. The CIA was asked to clean up its behavior, just as the 1990s James Bond of filmdom was scripted to give up sexism, brute force, and that *je ne sais quoi* that made Bond an icon that was "shaken, not stirred."

It started in Guatemala.

GUATEMALA, 1992: The CIA station was fully engaged in the war against drugs. It was working closely with the Guatemalan internal security service and military. At the same time, the Guatemalan government was combating an internal insurgency, a dirty war utilizing right-wing death squads as action arms. The U.S. government supported in principle the Guatemalan government's effort against the insurgency since it was viewed as being supported by Communists trying to bring down a democratically elected government. However, U.S. policy did not support the tactics used by the Guatemalan government, and one policy objective was to promote greater respect for human rights.

Because the CIA viewed its mission in Guatemala as primarily counternarcotics and counter Communist insurgency, the human rights objective was given less weight (read, no weight) in the risk-versus-gain criteria for conducting operations. Consequently, the CIA became embroiled in a human rights controversy because some of its paid agents for the counternarcotics program were connected to the death squads and linked to human rights abuse.

The chain of events started with the disappearance of Efraim "Bamaca" Velasquez in 1992. He was a senior Mayan resistance leader, also known as Comandante Evarardo. He disappeared during a skirmish with the Guatemalan army, which reported that he had died. He was married to U.S. citizen Jennifer Harbury, who learned from an eyewitness that Bamaca had been captured alive and was being tortured at a Guatemalan military base. In the CIA's view, Bamaca was a terrorist, and no tears were shed at his disappearance.

Harbury approached the State Department, along with other international organizations, and began a long campaign to force an investigation into his disappearance and to force the U.S. government to share with her the results of that investigation. Highly visible hunger strikes by Harbury, and exhumation of the purported remains of Bamaca, whose dental records did not match, brought the issue to the attention of the senior-most levels in the U.S. government. The State

Department stuck to its initial story that there was no information on Bamaca, other than the Guatemalan government's statement that he had been killed, but promised to continue to follow up with the Guatemalan government on the issue.[1]

The subsequent internal investigations and public exposés revealed the CIA had sent in a report six days after Bamaca's disappearance, stating that he had been captured alive and the army would probably fake his death to better take advantage of intelligence obtained from him. The U.S. government did not share this intelligence with Harbury. A second issue, which eventually converged with the first, was that among the CIA's Guatemala station's stable of reporting assets were individuals alleged to have committed human rights abuses. This became a political hot potato when it was alleged that Guatemalan Colonel Alpirez was present at the killing of Bamaca and another U.S. citizen, Michael DeVine; Alpirez was also alleged to be a former CIA asset.[2] Leaks to the press ignited a firestorm, with the CIA being accused of human rights abuse, supporting human rights abusers and covering up illegal activities. Once again, the Latin America Division was under public scrutiny.

WASHINGTON, DC, 1995: For three years, the controversy engulfed the CIA. An internal CIA investigation failed to put the matter to rest to the satisfaction of the public and Congress. Finally, President Clinton's Intelligence Oversight Board issued a report in June 1995 on its investigation. The board reviewed a number of aspects of the controversy and exonerated the CIA of most of the allegations. The report concluded that the "CIA station was not operating as a 'rogue' station, independent of control by its headquarters," and the derogatory information about Colonel Alpirez was based upon "information that was unreliable and was contradicted by other evidence." The board uncovered "no indication that U.S. government officials were involved in or had prior knowledge of the death, torture or disappearance of U.S. or Guatemalan citizens."

However, the board did not exonerate all of the CIA's conduct. It found "credible allegations of serious human rights abuse against several then-active CIA assets," and criticized the CIA for not informing ambassadors and other policymakers before late 1994 of allegations of human rights abuse by Guatemalan assets. Finally, the board concluded while there were no grounds for criminal liability concerning CIA actions, "the CIA leadership violated its statutory obligation to keep the Congressional oversight committees 'fully and currently informed.' "

The board determined that the CIA's asset validation system did not pay sufficient attention to human rights abuse and recommended that the CIA pay closer attention to the potential costs of establishing or continuing relationships with foreign intelligence assets with suspect human rights records. It identified those costs as "their moral implications, the damage to U.S. objectives in promoting greater respect for human rights, the loss of confidence in the intelligence community among members of the Congress, and the public, and the effect of such relationships on the ethical climate within U.S. intelligence agencies."[3]

LANGLEY, VIRGINIA, 1995: Deutch arrived at the CIA one month before the report came out. During his confirmation hearing, Deutch went on record promising that he would introduce more accountability into the CIA. All officers would be held to standards. When they performed below expectation, their feet would be held to the fire. He named names he would have fired for the Ames scandal if he had been in charge. These are easy words to say when somebody else is in charge, insiders criticized. If there was any question on whether he would be a man of his word, the Directorate of Operations found out quickly.

The allegations that CIA participated in or directed the murder of a Guatemalan revolutionary-cum-U.S. citizen would be Deutch's first test case for accountability. Before the results of the investigation were in, Deutch promised he would take swift action to prevent further abuses—the assumption was that there had been abuses. Deutch was caught in a leadership vise. He had to make the decision in a highly charged political atmosphere, and whatever decision he took had to demonstrate that he was attuned to the congressional displeasure of how his predecessor, DCI Woolsey, handled accountability for the Ames scandal.

Congress was quite clear during Deutch's confirmation hearing. They wanted a strong leader at the CIA, and Deutch had responded in very forceful statements that he would take strong action. Deutch stated he would fire CIA officers peremptorily if they did not meet his standards. Deutch could not afford to look as if he, too, was sweeping CIA wrongdoing under the carpet. He had to act decisively. Plus, he wanted to clean house.

While the investigation of the Presidential Intelligence Oversight Board determined that all the major allegations of CIA wrongdoing were false, Deutch deemed the behavior of those involved to have been below his standards. Deutch fired two senior officers and reprimanded seven station officers. The grounds for firing two senior officers was "lack of candor," the useful catchall phrase CIA management utilizes when it has nothing really concrete as a basis to dismiss or punish someone. John Deutch remains the most widely disparaged DCI of recent history by the Directorate of Operations because of this and some other actions he took.

Some officers thought Deutch acted fairly; the vast majority of the Directorate of Operations did not. The day the two officers were fired, the Directorate of Operations literally rose in defiance. Officers lined the halls, waiting to shake the hands of the departing officers, praising their commitment to the mission of the CIA. Our view was these officers were fired for doing their job, as defined by the mission that had been placed before them by senior management. Deutch's orders for dispersal were ignored, and after four hours of working their way through only part of the farewell line, the officers were escorted out, long after the regular close of business hours.

Years later, I had the opportunity to work with one of these officers. As an example of commitment to mission, he had returned to work for the Directorate of Operations as a contract employee just prior to September 11, 2001. Although he continued to feel that he had been treated unfairly, he felt it important to put aside his own personal feelings and respond positively when the Directorate of Operations came knocking, citing the "needs of the service." Besides his loyalty and dedication, I was impressed by his professionalism, honesty, and perspective. It truly was the CIA that lost by the decision to scapegoat him.

Deutch was heckled when he addressed the organization in "the Bubble" (a secure auditorium), explaining his decision to assign accountability at the working levels. Deutch, who was personally uncomfortable with the messiness of human operations, directed the Directorate of Operations to change its practices. Stringent human-rights restrictions were placed upon the Directorate of Operations, limiting its ability to recruit agents or deal with foreign liaison officers with murky human rights records. Even more fundamental, Deutch accelerated the process of transferring authority from officers in the field to the bureaucrats in Headquarters in order to control field operations more tightly.

In retrospect, it is apparent that senior CIA leadership badly mismanaged the entire Guatemala affair, giving Congress the impression that the CIA was hiding incriminating information and covering up greater misdeeds intentionally. Briefing material was prepared for senior CIA officials on the Seventh Floor for briefing Congress, but for reasons still unclear, the briefing never took place.[4] Operational rules were changing and were being applied retroactively. By the time all the dust settled, the lessons to the working level were clear: senior management is neither trustworthy nor loyal to the troops, and dealing with less-than-savory individuals to accomplish the mission is too risky. Iran-Contra was not an abnormality, but rather a gauntlet. Congress was serious about being kept "fully and currently" informed. Oversight was here to stay. The rules of conduct for "honorable espionage" would henceforth be defined by Congress, not by the practicality of what worked.

Recruiting murderers, rapists, drug runners, wife beaters, swindlers, and thieves—the "bottom feeders" of the world—in order to support national security requirements did not meet the congressional definition of a proper ethical profile for agents. In the real world of espionage, vetting on the basis of ethical profiles would become a showstopper, because agent candidates tend to come from the dark underbelly, not the upstanding-citizen side of the world. After all, agents are asked to break the laws of their own countries. Getting dirty was a job requirement—both for the agent and the handling officer. Now we were charged with weighing the "moral implications" of our actions and contacts. From the CIA's viewpoint, morality, like truth, has many different layers. In a world of shadows, there are few absolutes. So much is situational, especially such issues as what is acceptable and what is not in terms of human rights abuse.

For example, the Israeli external intelligence service attempted to assassinate a Hamas leader in Jordan in 1997. The leader, Khalid Mishal, was living in Amman, Jordan, and was [is] a spokesman for the military wing of a Palestinian Islamic group that is engaged in a struggle against Israeli occupation of Palestinian lands. Like Bamaca, Mishal was a freedom fighter or terrorist, depending upon one's political viewpoint. Continuing a long practice of extrajudicial killing of those opposed to the Israeli state, the Israeli government sent a team of undercover Mossad officers to Amman, traveling as Canadian tourists. In broad daylight, the team tried to execute a "wet job" reminiscent of the Bulgarian assassins during the Cold War. The Mossad agents, armed with a lethal syringe, attempted to poison Mishal as he walked down a busy Amman street. The operation was botched, the team arrested, and the press briefed.

I immediately saw the similarity to Guatemala and worried about the political implications. Like the Bamaca case, the killing was sanctioned by a legitimate government that is an ally of the United States. Unlike the Bamaca case, there was neither U.S. public outcry against human rights practices of Israel, nor congressional investigation into the relationship between the U.S. government and Israel, nor did allegations spread that the United States assisted or condoned the operation. I was not asked to testify before Congress or grilled by the CIA inspector general. It was the luck of the political draw. Nonetheless, at the time, I was concerned that I would be drawn into an investigation years after the fact for an operation that I knew nothing about in advance, but would be considered dirty by the mere fact that I was in Israel at the time.

The personal political risk was a sensitive issue for all of my colleagues in the field office. The Halloween after the assassination attempt, two of my colleagues came to the office party dressed in black, with the wraparound sunglasses preferred by Israeli security officials. They wore mocked-up Canadian passports suspended around their necks and carried a large syringe. Half of us could laugh about it by that time; our boss was not amused. However, it was tough to take him seriously as he was wearing a superhero costume (male bosses should never wear tights to office parties), with the logo SSMEC across his chest—Secret Special Middle East Coordinator. But that is another story.

Operations officers learned to read political tea leaves. We understood that if things went wrong (or right), we were on our own. We had to decide whether or not to take a risk. In the 1990s, we were encouraged to take out our own personal liability insurance to help cover legal fees if we became caught in a difficult situation. Officers elected to do so because we knew we could no longer depend upon support from the CIA. Inspector general investigations after flaps became the norm, and finger-pointing was a defensive survival tactic. Increasingly, in the Directorate of Operations, officers decided to not play the game, because the personal risks outweighed the gains.

WESTERN EUROPE, 1995: Politically correct espionage also came to mean espionage activity that did not offend allies or cause negative political blowback. This would spell disaster for the New CIA and further reduce its capabilities, especially in Western Europe. While still reeling from the Guatemala accountability decision, the CIA would see Deutch's next ax fall on the Paris office. Their crime was operational failure leading to embarrassment of the Clinton administration. The punishment was forced retirement, reprimands, and a shutdown of operations in Europe.

Western Europe has always been the spy's playground. It was a favored location as a "benign" venue to conduct agent meetings, switch identities for onward travel under an alias, or conduct other operational activities that were not "safe" in the agent's country of residence. Europe is ethnically diverse, which allows CIA officers and their agents to blend into the masses. Between business activity and tourism, there were plenty of reasons for foreigners to visit Europe and move from country to country, providing a wide variety of potential covers for action.

Europe was my favorite operational ground. I could become anybody—a high roller, a budget tourist, a businesswoman, a student. I could blend in and disappear in a sea of faces. In the Middle East, I was always concerned that as a tall, blond Western woman I stood out in a crowd. The challenge for me was to distinguish between the men scoping me out for visual entertainment from those monitoring my movements for more sinister reasons. When I was operational, I often switched to local clothes, including a veil. Culturally, it is rude for a male to stare at a veiled woman, or to try to make eye contact. I sought anonymity by slipping behind the protective veil that hides the forbidden sex. Despite the light disguise, I preferred an empty Middle Eastern street to flesh out surveillance. In Europe, I had so much more latitude and found the crowds to be my ally. I could sit on a bench or in an outdoor café, stroll alone through a park or down a street late at night, without the locals thinking me odd, or my presence an invitation for a romantic interlude. In addition, there were myriad bars and nightspots, isolated forests, winding backstreets, and shopping venues perfect for clandestine meetings, brief encounters, and dead drops. Europe was the well suited operational environment. For the same reasons, it was a favorite location for the Russians as well.

The United States had benefited from being relatively low on the collection priority list for most European countries. This came to a screeching halt in the mid-1990s. Suddenly, the CIA itself became a collection target. Europe became less benign for U.S. intelligence because of several factors. The public debate on whether the CIA should collect economic intelligence on allies was not missed by European intelligence services. It was predictable these intelligence services would devote more resources to monitoring American activities as part of their counterintelligence posture.

The issue came to a head and splashed across front-page news headlines in February 1995, with the so-called "Paris Flap." The French government publicly announced that it had asked Washington to recall five U.S. citizens, including four diplomats, for conducting business and trade espionage against France. The flap led the Senate Select Committee on Intelligence to conduct a review covering a wide range of issues related to counterintelligence and economic intelligence. As part of the review, the committee requested that the CIA inspector general conduct an investigation into the Paris Flap and to provide recommendations for corrective measures.[5]

According to the committee report, Deutch accepted the recommendations of the CIA inspector general's report and took disciplinary action against the CIA officials involved and formulated new guidelines for economic intelligence collection. After the Paris Flap, the Europe Division became so risk averse that internal operational activity slowed down to a near standstill. The office joke, which was too close to the truth, was all European Division officers did was frequent fine restaurants.

Pressures to downsize, operational flaps, and growing risk aversion led to the implosion of European stations. It became easier to do nothing rather than justify taking risks. It is no wonder that the CIA did not have a better understanding of the Islamic extremist threat emanating from Europe in the late 1990s. CIA eyes in the European capitals had been blinded, because the risks of offending our European allies were judged too great.

OLD HEADQUARTERS BUILDING, LANGLEY, VIRGINIA, 1996: The CIA used to brag it was the least bureaucratic agency in Washington. This changed under Deutch. Suddenly, the bureaucrats reigned supreme. This was an interesting phenomenon, given that the Directorate of Operations was run by operations officers who, by nature, hate bureaucracy. The personality type of most operations officers was a strong, independent worker, who, if forced to work on a team, wanted to be boss. We did not like to be told how to do our jobs, and personal control was very important. Bureaucratic requirements (someone else's control mechanism) were viewed as obstacles to overcome.

To combat bureaucracy, there was a strong tendency to create empires, with the senior officer putting his people in key positions to make sure the job got done to his liking. Under Deutch, this structure morphed into a proliferation of "managerial" positions that became filters rather than enablers. Each manager had to add his mark of approval or disapproval to activities within his sphere of interest or responsibility. Whether operational proposals, authorizations, or simply comments, all paperwork must travel up the bureaucratic chain of command for coordination, authentication, and release. The more layers of bureaucracy, the longer the process takes. It could take days, weeks, and even years, given the priority, complexity, and controversial nature of the matter.

An example of the new bureaucratic dross was the infamous letter-head incident. There was a rapidly evolving situation requiring notification of the Seventh Floor (in other words, DCI-level notification) of a development on a Russian operation. Russia House required Deputy Director of Operations and DCI approvals to proceed with an operational act. Time was of the essence. In order to speed up the process, the office chief personally walked the memo through the various chains of command for the necessary approvals, only to have the memo rejected summarily by the Deputy Director of Operations' secretary. The memo was printed on CIA stationery. Unfortunately, it was printed on the reverse side, on the ass of the eagle. The secretary felt the Deputy Director of Operations should not be subjected to such slipshod workmanship and refused to send the insulting memo forward.

When in the field, the junior officer learned that to be promoted and to make a name, he or she must demonstrate an ability to recruit agents and collect intelligence on the highest—and presumably the hardest—priorities. Once the officer was seasoned, and had proven himself, he was offered a position as a manager-in-training-wheels. This could be in the field, but more often than not it was in Headquarters. Traditionally, the purpose of Headquarters mid-level management was to support the field, which typically meant deferring to the field in decision making while providing the goods and services the field requested.

As the field-Headquarters relationship shifted in the mid-1990s, the mid-level Headquarters manager became empowered at the expense of field managers. The new Headquarters perspective was radically different from that of the field, and junior managers learn quickly to "manage risk." Rather than focusing their efforts on *how* to support the field, the idea was for Headquarters to focus on *how best* to meet the field's mission. In other words, Headquarters management evolved into a weeding-out element, a second-guesser, a "naysayer."

Knowledge of the operational environment of the field became secondary to knowledge of the Washington environment. Previously, the field would decide what constituted a risk worth taking, based on field-operational and political equities (i.e., assessment of the impact of negative blowback on the field). As the Clinton White House and the Seventh Floor became more risk averse in the 1990s, the Washington risk threshold was significantly lower than that in the field. Operations that made sense in the field—that is, where the potential gain outweighed the risk—did not make sense in the Washington environment. Headquarters came to have the first and final say on operations.

Technology was the enabler for this fundamental change in the field-Headquarters relationship, although most people did not recognize it at the time. With the introduction of advance information technology, many of the barriers that restricted communication within the directorate, and between the field and Headquarters, began to break down, strengthening the command-and-control capabilities of Headquarters. The culture that promoted independence of the field and to operations in general developed in the early days of the CIA. Before the electronic age, communication between the field and Headquarters was the old snail-mail system. (*For some inexplicable reason, the CIA has decided to censor my description of the old communication system that has not been in use for at least the last forty years.*) The time lag necessitated that the field have the authority to run its own operations.

Early in my career, I handled a longtime agent who was old—I mean, really old. He had been recruited during World War II. I always feared that he would drop dead of a heart attack during a meeting, given all the adrenaline that clandestine encounters caused. What would I do with his body? Leave him on the side of the road or to rot in a safe house? I don't think so! I was very fond of the old gent, and to do so would have been disrespectful. Thank goodness, he never presented me with the situation. In any case, before I picked up the assignment, I read the gentleman's file—all twenty volumes. The early volumes were a hoot, not only for the flowery writing style, but for the painstaking effort that went into piecing together (*censored by the CIA*)—remember, Scotch tape had yet to be invented! Most of the messages originated from the field, with only a few from Headquarters giving general guidance. There was no question who was running the show—the field officer and the agent!

In the late 1980s, the CIA still worked with paper. I would type my reports in the field and then send them up the chain of management for coordination. If changes were made, the document was sent back to me to be edited and retyped in its entirety. It was not infrequent for this to happen multiple times, depending on the layers of management. After the chief read and made final changes, the secretary would retype the document in the exact format required for the communications officer to copy and transmit it electronically. In some places, the communications officer had to retype the document; some places were on the "cutting edge" of technology (at least for the U.S. government) and had optical readers. It could take days for messages to go out; the typewriter was the bottleneck.

Once in Headquarters, the document was received, printed, and sent to the appropriate division registry. The office secretary would pick up piles of printed cables throughout the day and distribute the carbon copies as required. Administrative personnel would "walk" cables with "pink devils" attached through Headquarters. The pink routing slips guided the paper through the review and coordination process, with the slips eventually returning to the originating offices, full of signatures and scribbled notes. There was an elaborate system of pneumatic tubes so that messages could be placed in a capsule and shot through the walls and floors, managed by invisible hands that transferred them from one route to another, eventually arriving at the correct office. Again, it took days for cables to be read, discussed, responses drafted, coordinated, and released. With the time lags, it was impossible to manage operations and field personnel from Headquarters. Authority to make large and small decisions continued to rest with the chiefs in the field.

With the arrival of instant secure communications from the desktop, Headquarters officers for the first time were in the know in real time, with the information always at their fingertips. As a consequence, throughout the 1990s there was a gradual shift away from "inform Headquarters" on what you did (after the fact) to "request Head-quarters' concurrence" for permission to do. Gradually, the chief in the field lost authority and initiative and Washington-based bureaucrats were empowered. The attitudes in Washington at the time accelerated the shift of power. Perceptions that the Directorate of Operations was out of control and needed reining in—evidenced by the scandals of Iran-Contra, Guatemala, the Paris Flap, and Ames's treachery—were met with new regulations restricting the independence and authority of Directorate of Operations officers.

Under the newly evolving system, as operational proposals made their way up the chain of command in Headquarters, each manager managed out the "unnecessary risk" by either not concurring, or worse, sending it up another level of command for further review. Decisions that should have been made at lower operational levels were pushed upward, timelines lengthened, and operational momentum lost.

Senior management was not unaware of this problem. In the late 1990s, Deputy Director of Operations Jim Pavitt initiated a review of management authorities and pushed down the decision-making author-ity for a variety of operational and administrative issues. Unfortunately, Pavitt treated the symptom, not the disease. Decisions were being pushed upward not because managers did not *have* the authority, but because they were afraid to *exercise* their authority. Managers were afraid to authorize risky operations, because they did not want to be held personally accountable if the operation went sideways. We had an old saying in the Directorate of Operations: there are old officers and bold officers, but there are no old, bold officers.

Despite the premium placed on "managing risk," operations did get authorized, and there are many successes in the secret files of the Agency. The CIA did some incredibly risky things when there was an *overwhelming* belief that the gains outweighed the risks. For the truly exceptional, officers were given medals, which, after the festivities, are packed away in dusty safes for posterity. For the merely amazing, officers received a performance award, a slap on the back, and a nod of respect from their peers. Officers who participated in risky operations held their collective breaths during the operation. Officers make hundreds of decisions on the fly, adapt to and optimize fluid situations, and utilize the best tradecraft possible in the given situation, because operations are more art than science.

and we arranged and oversaw the removal and safe disposal of the ▬▬▬▬▬▬ we stopped for the day and went to dinner at my favorite haunt, the American Colony in East Jerusalem.

Sitting in the garden patio, surrounded by bougainvilleas, flowering roses, and the trickling noise of the fountain, Roger explained to us that the friction of opening the bag—let alone a bit of ash from the cigarette, or an accumulation of fumes—could have initiated an explosion that would have leveled the police station and all the surrounding buildings, including the Church of the Nativity. We fell silent as the magnitude of the danger sunk in and the reality that we had saved a Christian holy site from destruction. (In fact, Tenet brags about this one operation as the one in which he saved Christianity!)

I was also thinking about the fact that I was five months pregnant at the time. It is one thing to put yourself at risk, another to risk your child. But I did not have much of a choice if I wanted to keep my assignment—the CIA does not have a maternity program. Sure, we could have left the explosives in place, but that would have been morally irresponsible, knowingly endangering the civilian population, not to mention Christian pilgrims and religious shrines. ▬▬▬▬▬ ▬▬▬▬▬▬▬▬▬▬▬▬▬▬▬▬▬▬▬▬ ▬▬▬▬▬▬▬▬▬▬▬▬▬▬▬▬▬▬▬▬▬▬ I could just imagine them throwing the bags in the back of a truck, driving to the local garbage dump, and tossing in a match. Instead, we did the needful and reported back ▬▬▬▬▬▬▬▬▬▬▬▬▬▬▬▬▬ ▬▬▬▬▬▬▬▬▬▬▬▬▬▬▬▬▬▬▬▬▬▬▬▬ ▬▬▬▬▬▬▬▬▬▬▬

WASHINGTON, D.C., 1996: While senior CIA managers denied a problem of growing risk aversion, others in government were less afraid to speak honestly. As early as 1996, experts outside the CIA were concerned about risk taking. A panel from the Council on Foreign Relations in 1996 made a series of recommendations in a report that addressed increased covert action flexibility. The panel found covert action was "an important national security tool, one that can provide policymakers a valuable alternative or complement to their policies, including diplomacy, sanctions and military intervention." The panel expressed concerns about degraded capabilities within the Clandestine Service, citing "a lack of initiative brought about by a fear of retroactive discipline and a lack of high-level support." The panel recommended a fresh look at some of the legal and policy constraints on the CIA, limiting the kind of nonofficial covers Directorate of Operations officers can use and "the rules that can prohibit preemptive attacks on terrorists or support for individuals hoping to bring about a regime change in a hostile country."[6] The panel recommendations were dismissed because CIA management was in denial.

Denial would persist until September 11, 2001.

17
Al-Qa'ida Dawns

SUDAN, 1995: Putting Sudan on the State Department's list of states sponsoring terrorism in 1993 did not result in an immediate change of Sudanese policies. Khartoum continued to be a magnet for Sunni and Shia extremists, along with secular nationalistic groups, such as the Palestinian rejectionist parties. Sudanese denials of fostering terrorists were interpreted as proof positive that Sudanese officials lacked credibility; therefore, all Sudanese promises were suspect.

Directly menacing to the United States, the Sudanese government also appeared to be pursuing a chemical weapons program. The CIA had sensitive reporting on a request by Usama bin Ladin to Sudanese officials to help him obtain chemical weapons that could be used against U.S. installations. The CIA began monitoring Sudanese procurement of dual-use equipment and raw materials. Suspected bin Ladin front companies managed large parts of the procurement chain. The United States was also concerned about Sudanese contacts with Iraqi scientists who had past involvement in chemical weapons development. Chemical weapons in the hands of terrorists were a threat the CIA could not ignore. More than any other activity, it was the chemical weapons threat that raised bin Ladin's profile with the CIA.

The United States did not know about the activist role bin Ladin was playing in waging *jihad* from Sudan. At the time, there was fragmented intelligence on his activities supporting other militants, but the CIA placed him in the category of a financier, not a leader, not a military planner, and certainly not the creative mind behind a new ideological movement. He was seen as a cog in the wheel of state-sponsored terrorism.

ADDIS ABABA, ETHIOPIA, 1995: Egyptian disorganization kept Egyptian President Hosni Mubarak waiting at the airport long after his motorcade was supposed to depart for town for the Organization of African Unity annual conference. Ethiopian police lined the motorcade route, providing security for the numerous high-profile VIP visitors. When the motorcade launched, more than a half-hour late, sluggishness had already set in from the hot June sun. The motorcade traveled along the secured route, exiting the airport and headed toward town. Suddenly small-arms fire pierced the air; the Ethiopian-provided limousine came under attack. A bomb-laden truck broke into the lineup next to the limousine, cutting the motorcade into two segments, separating the VIP limousine from the motorcade to its rear.

As shooting erupted from all quarters, Mubarak escaped the assassination attempt, with his driver conducting a reverse-180 defensive maneuver, retreating away from the kill zone back to the airport. At the last moment, Egyptian security had insisted that Mubarak bring along his own armored Mercedes, which had caused the initial disruption at the airport. Not only was it a snub to the Ethiopians, but the motorcade order had to be reworked. The last-minute change of putting Mubarak in his own car toward the end of the motorcade saved his life. The attackers were working with then-outdated intelligence and focused the attack on the wrong vehicle.

Gama'at al-Islamiya claimed responsibility for the attack. This was the same group that killed Egyptian President Anwar Sadat; its spiritual leader Shaykh Omar Abdal Rahman, was currently on trial for, among other activities, plotting to kill Mubarak. Egyptian and Ethiopian security officers tracked down cell members in Ethiopia. Links to Egyptian extremists in the Sudan were many; the Egyptian government suspected that Sudanese officials had also assisted in the attack.

RIYADH, SAUDI ARABIA, 1995: Five months later, on November 13, a 220-pound car bomb exploded outside the Riyadh headquarters of the Office of the Program Manager/Saudi Arabian National Guard (OPM/SANG). The blast shattered windows and destroyed one side of the building. The timing coincided with the noon prayer, a time when observant Muslims would be on the other side of the compound at the mosque. Seven people died in the blast, five of whom were U.S. citizens, and forty-two were injured. At least three groups claimed responsibility for the attack, including the Islamic Movement for Change, the Tigers of the Gulf, and the Combatant Partisans of God.[1]

Saudi Arabia had been considered a restrictive country—but not a dangerous one—for U.S. citizens and soldiers. The bombing shook this sense of security. Little was known about any of the groups that claimed responsibility. The State Department and Defense Department conducted an Accountability Review Board investigation and an Antiterrorism Senior Assessment, respectively, which acknowledged a growing terrorism threat in the country. Despite these assessments, the prevailing view was that the violence was isolated and targeted primarily against the government of Saudi Arabia. Americans were few in number at the building, and it was assumed that the National Guard—an important instrument of the Saudi ruling family's control—was the intended target. Nonetheless, force protection could use some augmentation.

On April 22, 1996, Saudi authorities televised the confessions of four Sunni Saudi nationals who admitted to planning and conducting the bombing. Three were veterans of the conflicts in Afghanistan, Bosnia, and Chechnya. Despite repeated requests from the U.S. government, the FBI was denied access to interview the accused. The four were executed on May 31, 1996. Case closed. It was an internal Saudi problem.

WASHINGTON, D.C., 1996: The United States increased pressure on Sudan, implementing economic and political sanctions, demanding, among other things, the deportation of terrorists and closing of terrorist training camps. Again, the focus was on shutting down Sudan's program of state-sponsored terrorism and export of terrorism. Bin Ladin was not the biggest fish that the United States wanted to fry—that honor went to the Egyptian extremists. He was just one of many non-Sudanese extremists operating from Sudan. The belief at the time was that by denying the extremists a base of operation, the United States could disrupt the organizations' ability to plan, train for, and execute terror operations.

The relationship between Washington and Khartoum deteriorated rapidly. The United States had information that extremists in Khartoum were targeting U.S. official personnel. In the U.S. view, Sudanese officials were not cooperative in countering the threats. Not willing to risk personnel on the ground, the U.S. government decided to "vacate" the embassy in Khartoum in February 1996. In doing so, the U.S. government closed one of its few windows into what was transpiring inside Sudan.

Post–September 11, 2001, much has been made of the failure by the United States to capture bin Ladin while he was in the Sudan. Press reports stated that the United States declined to accept a handover of bin Ladin from the Sudanese. Lacking from the post-September 11 debate is the context of 1996. The United States had decided that Sudan totally lacked credibility and was not interested in being caught up by more lies and distractions. Furthermore, bin Ladin and al-Qa'ida had yet to assume a position of center stage for the United States. He had yet to arise as a new leader of a specifically anti-American *jihadi* group. He had yet to merge al-Qa'ida with Ayman al-Zawahiri's Egyptian Islamic Jihad. He had yet to declare war on the United States.

A telling indication of how low a priority terrorism and bin Ladin were for the United States is found in the Worldwide Threat Assessment briefing that Deutch delivered to the Senate Select Committee on Intelligence in February 1996. Terrorism was so far down the list of threats that only drug trafficking, organized crime, economic security, security of information systems, and the environment came after it. In the section on terrorism, Lebanese Hizballah, Egyptian al-Gama'at al-Islamiya, Philippine Abu Sayyaf Group, the Kurdistan Workers' Party, Japanese cult Aum Shinrikyo, Chechen rebels, Iranian and Sudanese state-sponsored terrorism all merited mention. There is no mention of bin Ladin or al-Qa'ida.[2] When President Clinton signed Executive Order 12947 on January 23, 1995, which designated foreign terrorist organizations as threatening to U.S. national security and imposed economic, immigration, and criminal penalties against the named individuals and groups, bin Ladin and al-Qa'ida were not on the list. Hizballah, Egyptian Gama'at al-Islamiya, and Egyptian Islamic Jihad were included.

The United States did not request extradition of bin Ladin, because the United States did not have an indictment against him and no immediate prospects for getting one. Extralegal options, such as assassination, were not even considered, because the New CIA did not do such things, in accordance with Executive Order 12333. Nor could the New CIA ask another intelligence service to do the dirty work. It was 1996; these kinds of ideas were not even on the table. The law enforcement approach was the only approach, as decreed by President Clinton in PDD-39.

There were discussions among allies as to where bin Ladin could be extradited. The Egyptians had other priorities—in particular, members of the Egyptian Islamic Jihad and al-Gama'at al-Islamiyya, those groups committed to overthrowing the Egyptian government. The Saudis did not want bin Ladin, because he would cause more of an internal stability problem for the House of Saud if he were in their kingdom. Bin Ladin had considerable support within the Sunni majority for his opposition to the Soviet presence in Afghanistan and Western presence in the Gulf. The Saudi government assessed that bin Ladin posed less of a threat exiled from the kingdom. They did not want him to become a cause célèbre as a result of imprisonment there. Additionally, given the relationship between Turabi and bin Ladin, it is highly unlikely that Sudan would have cooperated with any handover. Nonetheless, the CIA was working the issue, but the effort was overtaken by events when bin Ladin left Sudan of his own accord.[3]

SUDAN, 1996: The tide was turning, slowly. Bashir asked bin Ladin to consider the intense pressure Sudan was under, an indirect and very Arab way of requesting his departure. Calculating his options, bin Ladin decided to leave on his own terms, preserving his relationship with the Sudanese, and not risking the chance that Bashir would make the "un-Islamic" choice. Sudan was heating up for bin Ladin. He had been the target of an assassination attempt. It was time to go. Bashir, no doubt relieved by bin Ladin's flexibly, facilitated his clandestine flight from the country. Denied his Sudanese safe haven, bin Ladin disappeared from the radar screen for a bit, but then resurfaced in Afghanistan in June 1996.

DHAHRAN, SAUDI ARABIA, 1996: The U.S. Air Force deployment in Dhahran was part of Operation Southern Watch, the coalition air operation over Iraq enforcing the no-fly zones. The U.S. military had arrived in Saudi Arabia in 1990 to fight the Gulf War. Although the war was long over, the military operation had never come to an end. Saddam Hussein, still in power, defied the United States and the international community whenever the opportunity presented itself. While the Iraqi people suffered from a stiff UN sanctions regime, Saddam Hussein lived high on the hog, rebuilt his military capabilities, and occasionally took potshots at Allied aircraft patrolling the skies. Far from a satisfactory political situation, the U.S. military accommodated itself to a long stay in the Gulf, building bases on Saudi sand and re-creating the creature comforts of home in this alien land.

Many Saudis watched with horror as the infidel Americans soiled their sacred land. In a country that permits only Muslims to worship in public or in private, Americans did not hide their religious activities. Men and women solders mixed freely. Women drove vehicles and went about uncovered, in complete disregard for Saudi laws. Conservative Saudis were offended; extremists were enraged. Year after year, the anti-American rage built, until it exploded on June 28.

The truck was stopped outside the northern perimeter of Khobar Towers, the housing facility for the U.S. Air Force. Denied entry, the drivers parked the truck against a concrete wall, approximately 100 feet away from the apartment complex. When the truck occupants ran away to a waiting escape vehicle, security attempted to sound the alarm. There was no time. The force of the explosion sheared the face off of the apartment tower, collapsing floors, flinging deadly debris in all directions. The blast created a crater 54 feet across and 40 feet deep. Nineteen solders were killed and approximately another 500 were wounded as a result of the attack. Military investigators estimated that the truck bomb contained between 3,000 and 8,000 pounds of explosives, with a blast force equivalent to 30,000 pounds of TNT.

As a result of increased force-protection measures following the OPM/SANG bombing, the Khobar Towers facility had upgraded security practices and infrastructure. The upgrades certainly saved lives. If the truck had cleared the perimeter and gained access to the inner compound, the force of the blast would have brought down the entire building, killing most of the occupants as they slept.

Who did it? Uncertainty persists eight years later. Immediately after the bombing, three groups claimed responsibility: Hizballah-Gulf, Legion of the Martyr Abdullah al-Huzaifi, and the Islamic Movement for Change.[4] It could have been homegrown groups, Saudis angry at the continued presence of Americans on holy land. They could have had external help. Evidence led investigators in different directions, showing possible links to Syria and Iran.

Louis Freeh, who was the FBI director at the time of the attack, blamed Iran. Testifying in U.S. court in December 2003, Freeh gave his own knowledgeable thoughts on the topic, saying the attack was planned, funded, and sponsored by the senior leadership of the government of Iran. He based his opinion on interviews of six men detained by the Saudi government. They admitted that they were members of Saudi Hizballah and had worked in coordination with Lebanese Hizballah, which obtained funding, other support, and orders from Iran.[5]

COUNTERTERRORISM CENTER, LANGLEY, VIRGINIA, 1996: The CIA had long been concerned about Iran and its support for terrorism. In the February Worldwide Threat Assessment Brief to the Senate Select Committee on Intelligence, Deutch testified that Iran continued to divert scarce economic resources to its military buildup and to flout acceptable standards of international behavior. Tehran

actively supported terrorism and political violence, opposed the Middle East peace process, and abused the human rights of its citizens. According to Deutch, Iran provided up to $100 million annually to Lebanese Hizballah—a group responsible for killing over 250 Americans.[6]

The United States knew a lot about Iranian support to terrorism, but the details were tightly compartmentalized in top-secret dossiers. The United States knew that Iran funded, provided arms and explosives, trained, and exercised operational control over Hizballah through the Iranian Ministry of Information and Security (MOIS), the Iranian external intelligence service. The United States knew, for example, that the MOIS had ordered the attack on the U.S. Marine barracks in 1983. In late September 1983, the United States had intercepted a message from the MOIS to Ali Akbar Mohtashemi, the Iranian ambassador to Syria. The Iranian ambassador was directed to contact the Lebanese terrorist group Islamic Amal—at that time, Hizballah was an extremist faction within Amal—and to instruct them to "take a spectacular action against the United States Marines." From a source who was a member of Hizballah and a member of the cell that carried out the attacks, the CIA later learned that Ambassador Mohtashemi contacted a member of the Iranian Revolutionary Guard Corps (IRGC) and set the plan in motion.

The IRGC officer met with the senior leadership of Hizballah and devised a plan to attack the American and French barracks. They put together an operational plan—one that would be copied and executed with similar lethal results against other U.S. and Israeli targets in the decades to come. Hizballah operatives modified a truck to conceal a large improvised explosive device. The truck resembled a water delivery truck that routinely arrived at the Beirut International Airport, where the Marine barracks were located.

On the morning of October 23, 1983, Hizballah operatives ambushed the real water delivery truck before it arrived at the barracks. The substitute truck, driven by Ismalal Ascari, an Iranian, proceeded to a large parking lot behind the barracks. The pedal floored, the truck rammed through the concertina-wire barrier and a wall of sandbags, breaching the security perimeter. When the truck reached the center of the barracks, the bomb detonated as the Marines lay sleeping. The explosion reduced to rubble the four-story Marine barracks, shattered the windows of the control tower located over half a mile away, and dug a crater over eight feet deep. Two hundred forty-one Marines died.

Eight minutes later, a driver of a second vehicle attempted to breach the perimeter of the French barracks. Alert guards shot and killed the driver before the vehicle could enter the barracks. However, the improvised explosive device was detonated by remote control, killing fifty-six French soldiers.[7]

Thirteen years had passed since the bombing of the Marine barracks. For thirteen years, the United States had proof positive of Iranian responsibility. For thirteen years, the United States never retaliated against Iran, although individual officials in the United States government wanted to. For example, Richard Armitage regretted that the United States had not "put a cruise missile through the window of the Iranian Ambassador to Syria."[8] There were lots of reasons arguing against military action in the 1980s, such as the fate of the American hostages held in Lebanon. But at the end of the day, it meant that Iran got away scot-free and was emboldened to act again. The United States withdrew its forces from Lebanon. Only the CIA stayed, attempting to piece together the plot, find the hostages, and capture those responsible for terrorizing America.

In the intervening years, Hizballah broke off from the more moderate Amal and, with Iranian backing, unleashed terrorism on a global scale. Hizballah members participated in the international gatherings and planning sessions for terrorists in Sudan and trained *jihadis* at their bases in the Baqaa Valley. Hizballah, with Iranian backing, blew up the Israeli embassy and AIMA building in Argentina. Now, Hizballah fingerprints were all over the Khobar Towers.

After the Khobar bombing, the CIA hardened its language against Iran. In the annual threat assessment for 1997, the CIA assessed that Iran sought to undermine the U.S. position by improving their military capabilities relative to their neighbors and by using asymmetric means—ranging from the increased use of terrorism to developing weapons of mass destruction—in order to subvert or intimidate U.S. allies, undermine the confidence of U.S. friends and allies in the U.S. military presence, and eventually expel the United States from the region.[9]

According to Richard Clarke, the former National Security Council "Counterterrorism Czar" under Clinton, the United States considered a military response against Iran after the Khobar bombing. The option was dismissed out of concern that it would develop into a "tit-for-tat" escalation, drawing the entire Persian Gulf into a regional conflict (threatening the supply of oil). Clarke writes in his memoir, *Against All Enemies*, that the United States instead chose an intelligence-operation option to drive in a stark private-channel threat to the Iranians. It took "months to put CIA assets in place and to choreograph a more or less simultaneous series of intelligence actions around the world." The purpose was to send a powerful message through the shadowy spy versus spy world. The message to the Iranians was: "We have just demonstrated what we can do to hurt you. If your agents continue to engage in terrorism against us, we will hurt you in ways that will severely undermine your regime."[10]

Did it work? Iran watchers noted a change in Iranian aggressive behavior in the Persian Gulf after 1997. Some attributed it to a change in government in Iran, with the election of Mohammad Khatami, an Iranian reformer who supports improving relations with the West. Others cite a secret deal between Iran and Saudi Arabia to ensure each other's security. I would argue that Iran did not abandon terrorism as a foreign policy tool, it just altered its MO to better hide its hand. Iran became more adept at hiding behind its surrogates—especially Hizballah—when doing dirty work. Every so often, however, Iran would be caught red-handed in supporting terrorism, such as shipping two tons of high explosives, long-range katyusha rockets, and other instruments of death to the Palestinians in 2002.

AFGHANISTAN, 1996: Bin Ladin wasted no time in setting up shop. He immediately began to build a sanctuary for Islamic extremists who shared his ideology. What he did on a small scale in the Sudan, he began to build on a large scale in Afghanistan. Afghanistan was an ideal haven for him, as the Taliban supported his ideology and his goals. At the time, Afghanistan was regarded by U.S. intelligence as a "denied area"—in other words, a location that access to and movement within was extremely limited. By 1996, the regime was largely hostile to the United States, and there was no official U.S. presence. Bin Ladin had moved outside our easy reach.

COUNTERTERRORISM CENTER, LANGLEY, VIRGINIA, 1996: In July 1995, the intelligence community produced *The Foreign Terrorist Threat in the United States,* a National Intelligence Estimate (NIE). The NIE drew attention to a new kind of terrorist danger, one emerging from transient terrorist groupings that were more fluid and multinational than the older organizations and state-sponsored surrogates. This new terrorist phenomenon was made up of a loose affiliation of Islamic extremists angry at the United States. They obtain weapons, money, and support from an assortment of governments, factions, and individual benefactors. Growing international support networks were enhancing their ability to operate in any region of the world. The NIE was not written specifically about bin Ladin or al-Qa'ida, but about the phenomenon the CIA witnessed in Sudan and New York City.[11]

In January 1996, the CIA began to focus specifically on bin Ladin and his role in this international conglomeration. The CIA created a new focal point and operational element, called the Usama bin Ladin issue group, within the Counterterrorism Center at the urging of National Security Advisor Tony Lake. The initial mission was modest: tracking the financial flows from bin Ladin to terrorists and the flows to bin Ladin from ideological supporters of *jihad*.

Once ensconced in Afghanistan, the CIA began to modify its assessment of bin Ladin, from terrorist financier and logistician to mastermind of an international terrorist conglomeration. It was a gradual change rather than something that happened overnight. George Tenet liked to describe bin Ladin as having moved from a state sponsoring terrorism to having become a terrorist sponsoring a state. The changed assessment demanded that the CIA deploy more intelligence resources against bin Ladin and al-Qa'ida. However, because the CIA continued to focus on bin Ladin the man, it failed to understand the significance of the al-Qa'ida ideology.

The mission of the issue station evolved as the assessment of bin Ladin changed from terrorist financier to mastermind. The new mission was to bring down bin Ladin. The CIA threw tradition to the wind in order to centralize intelligence on bin Ladin and al-Qa'ida and to run operations against the organization. One office targeted against one guy—it had never been done before. This action was unprecedented within the CIA. Neither the threats posed by Abu Nidal nor those of Imad Mughniyah, the most lethal and infamous terrorists of the 1970s–1980s, precipitated the creation of a single-issue group within the Counterterrorism Center. There had never been a Carlos the Jackal issue group or a George Habash issue group. But then again, the CIA had a poor batting average of bringing big-name terrorists to justice or judgment. A new modus operandi was in order.

Why did the CIA change its assessment of bin Ladin? It was a combination of factors. An important element was new intelligence of reliability that became available to the CIA in 1996, according to the 9/11 Commission. Jamal al-Fadl, an al-Qa'ida fighter and moneyman—again, according to the 9/11 Commission—walked into a U.S. embassy in June 1996. (The CIA will not permit the release of the exact location, as it would reveal sources and methods.) The al-Qa'ida defector was an extremely important source, because he gave his handlers one of the first insider accounts of how al-Qa'ida was formed, information on key al-Qa'ida personalities and responsibilities, operational methods, and its dirty laundry. In 2001 he would be a key government witness in *U.S. v. Usama bin Ladin*, the trial of the East African embassy bombings. In his court testimony, he described the birth of al-Qa'ida, its ideology, and the range of activities it undertook in its *jihad* against the United States. Al-Fadl was the perfect intelligence source. He was an al-Qa'ida paymaster and, as such, his breadth of knowledge was wide. He filled in the holes—"gave texture," in CIA jargon—showing the United States that even by the early 1990s, al-Qa'ida was a worldwide organization plotting on a grand scale.[12]

Al-Fadl was at the first meeting of al-Qa'ida, before the organization-cum-movement had even decided on its name. He described how bin Ladin's first organization—Maktab al-khidemat—recruited Muslims (*jihadis*) to fight in Afghanistan. Fadl worked for a branch of Maktab al-khidemat at the Farouq Mosque in Brooklyn—the same mosque at which the 1993 World Trade bombers worshiped and with which the Blind Shaykh was associated. He described how the newly recruited *jihadis* (himself included) were brought to Pakistan and then to Afghanistan for training. The training included religious indoctrination, weapons and military tactics training, and explosives training and terrorist tactics. Then they were sent to the front to practice their newly acquired skills.

As the Afghan war wound down, bin Ladin split from Abdullah Azzam (cofounder of Maktab al-khidemat) and set up his own organization in 1989. The agenda of the organization—alternatively called Islamic Army and al-Qa'ida—was to set up an Islamic government for the whole of the Islamic world through waging *jihad* against enemies of Islam. At first the front was Afghanistan, but later the front moved to Bosnia, Chechnya, Somalia, the Philippines, Tajikistan, Sudan, Lebanon, Kenya, and the United States. Al-Qa'ida relocated to Sudan in 1990 at the invitation of the National Islamic Front. Once there, al-Qa'ida established military training camps and business enterprises. Al-Qa'ida also attempted to develop chemical weapons, working with the National Islamic Front, as well as to purchase uranium.

Fadl named names and described his personal relationship with al-Qa'ida leadership. The diverse national makeup of the first several levels of leadership was striking. While Egyptians were the most numerous, there were Saudis, Sudanese, Libyans, Lebanese, Syrians, Palestinians, Jordanians, Algerians, Pakistanis, Iraqis, and Yemenis. He described how al-Qa'ida was organized, with a *Shura* Council to provide policy guidance, a military committee to organize and direct *jihadi* activities, a business and money committee to generate income and distribute it to al-Qa'ida members, a *fatwa* committee to provide religious edicts, an Islamic-study committee for indoctrination, and a media and newspaper committee to disseminate al-Qa'ida ideology and news. Fadl was a walking dictionary and historian.

Some *jihadis* waged war with guns—in Bosnia, Chechnya, and Somalia, for example. According to Fadl, in accordance with the Islamic principle of *jihad fardh al-ein*, Muslims are obliged to assist other Muslims in expelling armies of nonbelievers waging war against Muslim people. Fadl told how al-Qa'ida sent *jihadis* to Somalia in 1993 to fight against U.S. troops there. Bin Ladin personally called upon al-Qa'ida members "to stop the head of the [US] snake." These same *jihadis* would train Somalis in the art of warfare, especially how to shoot down enemy helicopters. Al-Qa'ida formed associations with Shia and Sunni Islamic groups, including Hizballah, the Sudanese National Islamic Front, Egyptian Islamic Jihad, Egyptian Gama'at al-Islamiya, the Algerian Armed Islamic Group, the Libyan Fighting Group, Yemeni Islamic Group, Syrian Islamic Group, the Abu Ali Group, which operated in Jordan and the Palestinian territories, the Eritrea Jihad Group, the Philippines Moro Islamic Liberation Front, the Tajik Hizb al-Nahda, and others.

Also according to Fadl, other *jihadis* supported the war effort by building infrastructure for self-financing, recruiting, training, and media relations. These cells were spread throughout the world. In London, the Advice and Call Society was set up to manage internal Saudi affairs. In Sudan, an extensive network of businesses was established to fund *jihad* operations. There were al-Qa'ida front companies in Cyprus and East Africa. Al-Qa'ida collected charitable donations from Islamic charities, like the Qatari Charitable Association. Fadl was a rich source of information—it took two days of testimony just to outline the most immediately relevant of his knowledge on al-Qa'ida. But his testimony made it clear: al-Qa'ida was an army at war with the West.

Al-Qa'ida may have been born in 1989, but its birth notice was not read in the West until 1996. Once the CIA focused collection on bin Ladin and developed new collection capabilities, the extent of his global *jihad* activities began to be revealed, notably in Africa, Asia, Europe, the Gulf, and East Asia. Bin Ladin links to Kashmir, Albania, Kosovo, Chechnya, the Philippines, Mauritania, Bangladesh, Jordan, and Kuwait were uncovered.[13]

The second factor to cause the CIA to take note was that bin Ladin began to switch his focus from a global *jihad* to an America-first *jihad*. By focusing on the United States, bin Ladin hoped to unite his allies, notably militants in the Egyptian Islamic Jihad and Gama'at al-Islamiya, in a common cause and minimize ideological differences.[14] Fadl testified about ideological discussions between Sunni and Shia religious leaders while he was in Sudan. Bin Ladin gave numerous sermons, calling upon all Muslims to focus on their common enemy: the Christian and Jewish West.

In addition to being single-issue focused, the bin Ladin issue group broke with tradition in other ways. The station ran a worldwide operation, tasking operational elements overseas to develop operations, follow up on leads, and otherwise report on anything and everything related to bin Ladin. Contrary to traditional practices, Directorate of Intelligence analysts shared offices with Directorate of Operations officers in the Counterterrorism Center in order to fuse their efforts. Operations officers and analysts had the same access to the hundreds of messages that poured into the Counterterrorism Center from the field on a daily basis. Standard security practice throughout the Agency is to build a wall between operations and analysis to keep knowledge of operations strictly compartmentalized, creating vertical stovepipes within the analytical and operational worlds.

The direct give-and-take between analysts and operations officers was designed to facilitate targeting and development of reporting requirements. The analysts would comb the information, assessing each fragment of intelligence in order to gauge where it fit in the puzzle. To further complicate matters, there was not one puzzle, but hundreds, with no straight edges, few perfect fits, and many extraneous pieces. Their job was to figure out the nature of al-Qa'ida, its plans and intentions, and its leadership, operational, and support structure and to feed requirements back to the operations officers. The task was enormous.

The operations officers would look at the same information, but from a different perspective. The Directorate of Operations' job was to take the organization down, piece by piece, so that the organization would lose its command-and-control capability and become unable to reconstitute itself.

The Counterterrorism Center conceptualized a plan that applied the same methodology that was used to take down the Cali drug cartel in the 1980s–1990s. The Agency wanted to go after the operational elements and the support cells, degrading al-Qa'ida's ability to engage in terrorism, bringing operatives to justice, and disrupting al-Qa'ida finances.

Penetrating operational terrorist cells is difficult, to put it mildly. Ideologically, most of the members were anti-American. They lived strict Islamic lifestyles, eschewing exploitable vulnerabilities of alcohol and drug abuse, greed, and materialism. They maintained close-knit relationships, usually through kinship. To join the group, recruits had to show credentials—in other words, participation in military or terror operations. Because penetration of the small cells and collecting intelligence clandestinely were so difficult, it was judged more effective to disrupt cells and gather intelligence through interrogation. That does not mean that the CIA did not try to recruit sources inside al-Qa'ida.

As an outgrowth of the ban on assassinations, the CIA expanded its practice of rendition, one of the "new tools" of covert action. Rendition operations involve snatching or receiving an individual in one country and transporting the person to another country more often than not, using extrajudicial methods—in other words, working outside of the law. If there is an indictment in the United States, we will coordinate the rendition operation with the FBI, arranging for the FBI to take custody of the individual in a foreign country. If there is no warrant in the United States, but in another country with which the United States has mutual interests, we hand over custody of the individual to officials of that country. Sometimes the handover takes place in a third country; sometimes the CIA will transport the individual directly to the country with the warrant. We are very careful in how we orchestrate the handover so that our role remains hidden and not subject to legal discovery during the judicial process.

The CIA will resort to snatch operations when the targeted individual is located in a country that would not cooperate with an unofficial (or official) handover. Ronald Kessler's book, *Inside the CIA*, described a risky snatch operation. According to Kessler, the CIA and FBI conducted a joint operation to snatch Fawaz Younis, by luring him out of Lebanon onto a yacht in international waters. Younis, a terrorist involved in the 1985 hijacking of a Royal Jordanian airplane at Beirut Airport, thought he would be meeting a drug dealer and having some fun in the sun with several bikini-clad bimbos on deck. Instead, the ladies and the drug dealer turned out to be FBI agents who arrested him and brought him back to the United States for prosecution.[15] Although the excitement factor of such operations is high, the CIA prefers to work with foreign liaison services that cooperate willingly with the hunt and a quiet, informal handover. It is simply less risky on the high-risk scale.

When I worked in the Counterterrorism Center in the late 1980s, the Younis rendition was the favorite "war story" told. It was one of the few examples where the CIA was able to do more than just watch a terrorist. It was judged so successful that renditions became a standard counterterrorism tool.

In the 1990s we conducted numerous rendition operations against terrorists, drug traffickers, and the occasional fugitive foreign government official. Not all operations were successful; there were many more aborted operations than successful renditions. We would gear up an operation the instant we obtained tactical intelligence on the specific location or planned travel route of an individual previously identified as a rendition target. Frequently, the initial intelligence was not validated, and there would be an operational stand-down. Understandably, there is a premium on getting the right guy.

These operations can get very complex. I remember one time when I spent two days and nights continuously in my field office with phones stuck to my ear, coordinating the movements of various *national capabilities*—a nice vague term to indicate that I can't be more specific on operational and collection resources. When we actually eyeballed the target, we realized we had the wrong guy. The description "disappointed" hardly captures the feeling, particularly since the target was one of the worst of the bad guys.

The CIA rendered a number of operatives belonging to al-Qa'ida and other terrorist organizations loosely linked to al-Qa'ida during the 1990s, according to the testimony of senior CIA officials before Congress.[16] A number of terrorism specialists and journalists have done extensive research, exposing a pattern of arrests and handovers of extremists, especially to Egypt, Jordan, and Morocco. The benefits of rendering terrorists to third countries are multiple. In some cases, the United States had insufficient evidence or evidence that could not be used to convict the individual in a U.S. court of law. Sometimes there was no U.S. warrant, because the crimes were not committed against U.S. citizens or property.

Legal codes and practices of some foreign intelligence services permit these organizations to suppress detention information to the public. From an intelligence perspective, there is a tactical advantage to making a terrorist "disappear." Upon news of an arrest, fellow cell members and whole networks go underground quickly, reducing the ability of law enforcement to act upon any information obtained from the individual in custody. Additionally, interrogators who have a cultural affinity with captives can utilize subtle techniques—such as invoking shame on the reputation of the captive's family—as a mechanism to get the captive talking.

Some foreign intelligence services utilize interrogation techniques that are effective, but illegal in the United States. Many intelligence services torture their prisoners in order to extract information, such as Israel and Egypt, to name just two. Before September 11, internal regulations generally proscribed CIA officers from conducting joint interrogations with foreign intelligence services in non-CIA-controlled facilities in order to protect officers from becoming involved in interrogations where torture was used. Joint interrogations occurred, but we were neither physically present in the room nor did we observe the interrogations remotely. Since the imposition of abuse of human rights reporting requirements, CIA officers are required to report any knowledge that they have on abuses and abusers, including torture.

Exploiting the gray area, if torture was not witnessed but merely alleged, the CIA was not put in the position of imposing sanctions or ending otherwise productive relationships because of proven human rights abuse. Instead, to shield them from direct knowledge of—or involvement in—human rights abuse, we would receive the intelligence take and provide debriefing questions at a separate location. Reportedly, the rules have been loosened up after September 11, permitting CIA officers to observe interrogations through one-way mirrors and to conduct interrogations directly. It is unclear how the change will impact human rights reporting requirements and "weighing the moral implications." Because of this murkiness, the CIA preferred to conduct rendition operations quietly, so as to achieve maximum operational benefit, while reducing public scrutiny and criticism of the less savory aspects of the effort to neutralize the national security threat.[17]

According to press reports, an early operation of this type with the Egyptians was the "disappearance" of Fuad Tala'at Qassim in August 1995. *Newsday* reported that Qassim, a refugee in Denmark, was the spokesman for Gama'at al-Islamiyya, the Egyptian Islamic extremist group whose spiritual leader, Shaykh Omar Abdal Rahman, was convicted in the United States for his involvement in the first World Trade Center bombing. Overtly, Qassim was using Denmark as a distribution base for Islamic literature and pamphlets, disseminating the militant ideology of al-Gama'at al-Islamiyya. He was suspected of clandestine activities in support of terrorist operations, especially the first bombing of the World Trade Center. Qassim was also one of Egypt's most wanted militants.

According to a *Newsday* interview of Montasser El-Zayyat, an Egyptian lawyer who has defended many Islamists, Qassim met his destiny when he disappeared on his way to Bosnia. In a joint operation, he was arrested by Croatian intelligence agents and handed over to the CIA. After interrogation, he was turned over to Egyptian authorities. His exact fate was unknown to fellow extremists for years before information on his arrest leaked out. Qassim is believed to have been executed by Egyptian authorities implementing a death sentence issued in absentia by a military court in 1992.[18]

KHURASAN, AFGHANISTAN, 1996: It is unclear how long bin Ladin had been working on the 11,500 word *fatwa*, but it certainly framed the main tenets of the ideology that he would promote over the next half decade. On August 23, he delivered the *fatwa* to his supporters in Afghanistan. In the months that followed, Muslims around the globe would learn about the *fatwa*, either through its publication in the Movement for Islamic Reform in Saudi Arabia's newsletter *Islah*, or by listening to tapes of bin Ladin reading it.

A close reading of the *fatwa* should have made alarm bells go off in the West—correction—a mere reading of the *title* should have created a five-alarm alert: "Declaration of War against the Americans Occupying the Land of the Two Holy Places." Few took note of it. Those who did relegated it to a strictly anti-Saudi context. Indeed, much of the *fatwa* was specific to Saudi Arabia, with accusations of poor governance, persecution, and un-Islamic practices. However, a significant portion was directed against the United States and Israel.

The *fatwa* was a clear declaration of war, enumerating the crimes committed by the United States against the Muslim people. It explained and justified to Muslims their obligation to put aside their differences and to undertake a defensive *jihad* against the United States and its supporters. The U.S. presence in Saudi Arabia after the end of the first Gulf War offensive was termed an occupation of the Holy Lands. Bin Ladin accused the United States of evil intentions and deeds, subjugation and humiliation of the Muslims, theft of their natural resources, destruction of their culture, and massacre of their people. Bin Ladin called the United States a paper tiger, evidenced by its cowardly withdrawal after being attacked by Islamic fighters. Bin Ladin did not mince his words, but painted a vivid picture of the United States as the new Crusader state, drawing upon cultural and historical references and Islamic symbols that struck deep resonance in the Muslim world:

It should not be hidden from you [believers] that the people of Islam have suffered from aggression, inequity and injustice imposed on them by the Zionist Crusader alliance and their collaborators; to the extent that Muslim blood became the cheapest and their wealth loot in the hands of the enemies. Their blood was spilled in Palestine and Iraq. The horrifying pictures of the massacre of Qana, in Lebanon, are still fresh in our memory. Massacres in Tajikistan, Burma, Kashmir, Assam, Philippines, Pattani, Ogadin, Somalia, Eritrea, Chechnya and in Bosnia/Herzegovina took place, massacres that send shivers in the body and shake the conscience. All of this while the world watched; not only did it not respond to these atrocities, but [it engaged] in a clear conspiracy between the United States and its allies and under the cover of the unfair United Nations, while denying the dispossessed people from obtaining arms to defend themselves. . . .

If there is more than one duty to be carried out, then the most important one should receive priority. After belief, there is no duty more important than pushing the American enemy out of the Holy Land. . . .

Utmost effort should be made to prepare and instigate the community of believers against the enemy, the American and Israeli alliance occupying the country of the two Holy Places and the route of the Messenger [Muhammad] to al-Aqsa Mosque. . . .

The [Saudi] regime is fully responsible for what has been incurred by the country and the nation; however, the occupying American enemy is the principal and the main cause of the situation. Therefore, efforts should be concentrated on destroying, fighting and killing the enemy until, by the Grace of Allah, it is completely defeated. . . .

We say to the [U.S.] Secretary of Defense . . . where was this false courage of yours when the explosion of Beirut took place in 1983? You were turned into scattered pits and pieces at that time; 241 marines were killed. And where was this courage of yours when two explosions made you leave Aden in less than twenty-four hours! But your most disgraceful case was in Somalia; where after vigorous propaganda about the power of the United States and its post–Cold War leadership of the new world order you moved tens of thousands of international forces, including twenty-eight thousand American solders into Somalia. However, when tens of your solders were killed in minor battles and one pilot was dragged in the streets of Mogadishu, you left the area carrying disappointment, humiliation, defeat and your dead with you. Clinton appeared in front of the whole world threatening and promising revenge, but these threats were merely a preparation for withdrawal. . . . It was a pleasure for the heart of every Muslim to see you defeated in the three Islamic cities of Beirut, Aden and Mogadishu. . . .

Terrorizing you, while you are carrying arms in our land is a legitimate and morally demanded duty. . . .[19]

18
Mission Alignment

OLD HEADQUARTERS BUILDING, LANGLEY, VIRGINIA, 1995: In March, President Clinton signed the still-classified Presidential Decision Directive 35 (PDD-35), which set out the administration's collection priorities. During Deutch's confirmation hearings, he noted the new priorities had yet to be implemented by the intelligence community, and he intended to do so immediately once confirmed. The change did not occur overnight; there was lingering lack of clarity over the next several years on what the field should and should not be doing. Additionally, the collection capabilities had to be realigned to meet the new collection priorities.

Under the new system, collection priorities were designated in tiers 00 to 04. Tier 00 represented crisis requirements, open to change as crises erupted and were resolved. The remaining tiers provided long-term priorities. No longer was everything Moscow-related, but there was a more complicated set of targets. Effectively, the CIA broke the collection requirements down into three primary categories: support to military operations, geographical strategic threats (rogue nations), and transnational threats. According to DDCI Admiral Wiliam O. Studeman in a speech at Marquette University, the priorities include states that represent a strategic threat to the United States, such as Cuba and North Korea, regional, ethnic, tribal conflicts, and transnational threats like terrorism, narcotics, proliferation, and international organized crime.

With budget and personnel resources declining as a consequence of demobilization, only the top priorities received consistent attention.

Tier 04 countries were those of virtually no interest to the United States, with PDD-35 specifically designating them as targets against which the CIA would not collect. The Agency consciously began doing "less with less." This trend was reinforced when officer performance became rated by the impact of the officer's activities on top-tier targets. For example, an operations officer who recruited a North Korean sea captain might have good promotion potential; an operations officer who recruited three Saudi mosque watchers might not. Political Islam was not a collection priority.

With a new set of collection priorities, the asset base had to be realigned. Latin American and African issues were so low on the priority list that these divisions were unable to win resources in the bureaucratic fight for people and budget; there was no choice but to terminate—in the sense of ending relationships, not lives—large numbers of reporting and support assets. They were no longer relevant to the mission of the CIA as defined by PDD-35.

Europe, Asia, and Near East Divisions also cleaned house. In the "asset scrub" of 1995 and 1996, agents were terminated because they were irrelevant to the new collection priorities, poor performers, and/or they had "unwanted baggage"—in other words, histories of human-rights abuse or criminal activity. For example—a theoretical one—a lowly immigration officer in a backwater of South East Asia, who used to report on Soviet travels, would become irrelevant and untouchable because he also facilitated the trafficking of prostitutes and children. Having eyes at airports would not seem worth the risk or money given the new restrictions.

As part of Deutch's efforts to clean the Directorate of Operations shop, he ordered a comprehensive "asset scrub," a bottom-up review of all agents on the books. The asset scrub had started under Webster as part of the new asset validation system, but had yet to be implemented throughout the Directorate of Operations. The review had both positive and negative impact. By conducting a detailed reevaluation of all cases, the directorate was able to separate the solid performers from the marginal ones and to get rid of the latter. This, in turn, reduced the caseload of operations officers, to the benefit of security. Tradecraft practices were suffering, because officers were expected to handle an unrealistic number of cases. The reduction of operations officers deployed to field stations compounded an already bad situation. The mantra became "quality over quantity."

The negative impact was the new criteria for what made an "acceptable" agent. Agents with unsavory pasts were terminated. The administrative goal was to weigh the reporting value (the gain) of the agent against the negatives of past misdeeds (the risks)—and if the gains were not assessed to be greater, the relationship was terminated. While this sounds logical in theory, in practice the risk threshold was low and kept creeping lower through the 1990s as the tolerance for flaps dropped. Recruiting and running agents has been, and will always be, messy and unpredictable, and therefore did not mesh well with the prevailing interests of the 1990s.

In addition to loss of reporting breadth, a long-term negative impact of the asset scrub was the creation of a rigid asset validation system that encouraged a box-checking environment. Agent categories were defined in a way that allowed little variation for reality. Operations officers frequently had to deal with agents or agent candidates who did not fit neatly into the defined categories. The layers of bureaucratic process and review grew, stifling operational initiative and momentum. The trend of shifting operational authority from the field to Headquarters to manage risk accelerated. Headquarters bureaucracy grew while the numbers in the field diminished, changing the tooth-to-tail ratio rapidly. Furthermore, the ability of the field to respond quickly to new requirements was diminished by reduced agent recruiting flexibility. The past practice of having an "agent in the pocket"—that is, a developed relationship without formalities, ready to be pulled out and deployed when needed—was no longer possible.

Access agents, useful in meeting people or providing operational support, became something of the past as well. The Agency went from having far too many access agents to having none—an overcompensation of the worst kind. Every meeting had to have a formal purpose. Every agent had to have a current requirement. All expenditures had to be pegged to a specific program. While administrative control is desirable for focusing mission and maintaining accountability, the system in the Directorate of Operations became so rigid and bureaucratic that field officers spent more time meeting bureaucratic requirements than on trolling, recruiting, and handling agents.

As the CIA abandoned its position as a "worldwide" intelligence organization, it had to build a new mechanism to respond to rapidly developing situations that required intelligence reporting capabilities in areas where it either no longer had a presence or had its presence greatly diminished. Paralleling the military "global reach" concept, the CIA developed a "surge" doctrine as a way to convince policymakers that the Agency would retain worldwide capabilities, if not presence. Surge requirements would fall into Tier 00 priority and include support to military operations (SMO) and support to policymakers. In theory, the Agency planned to draw officers from other requirements to meet surge requirements through short-term assignments ranging from thirty days to six months.

Realizing that reduced staffing levels would make meeting surge requirements more difficult, the CIA envisioned the creation of a surge or reserve cadre composed of former Agency officers and civilian specialists who could function much like the military reserves. This idea never really got off the drawing board until after September 11, 2001. Meanwhile, the CIA robbed Peter to pay Paul to meet surge requirements, creating problems of lack of continuity, consistency, and quality. It also meant that intelligence support to nondefense policymakers suffered.

Surging CIA officers to a location is one thing; surging reporting if there are no agents on the ground is another. Recruiting new agents does not happen overnight. It takes months—if not years—to develop quality reporting sources. When the U.S. military went into Somalia for Operation Restore Hope, there were no eyes on the ground to provide the mission with a body of intelligence on the operating environment. The CIA had closed its field office in Mogadishu a year earlier because the U.S. government decided it was not interested in things Somali. The CIA surged to Somalia to meet the new requirement, but there was negative operational impact by not having a previously established presence with vetted reporting sources.

CIA officers did not like the surge doctrine, because it was inefficient and ineffective. The concept that the most important issues could be covered through permanent reporting infrastructure and the unanticipated requirements met through ad hoc measures did not fit well with the realities of the 1990s. The decade was a period of instability as post–Cold War convulsions worked their way around the globe. From the inside, in the 1990s it felt as if the Agency was constantly in surge mode, from Haiti, to Bosnia, to Somalia, to Kosovo, and to the mother of all surges, the Counterterrorism Division following September 11.

We had no choice but to surge. I joined the surge ranks and understood what it felt to be behind the curve, trying to learn the lay of the land in two days rather than two years. We took pride in our ability to be flexible, quick learners and fast producers. We were lying to ourselves when we said it was good enough to have global reach rather than global presence.

SEVENTH FLOOR, LANGLEY, VIRGINIA, 1995: Deutch knew he had a personnel problem. He had too many senior officers who were part of the old CIA, cold warriors who had no place in the New CIA. They represented old thinking and ossification. They were clogging up the promotion ladder and teaching the younger officers bad habits (dirty tricks). Overall, the CIA and the intelligence community were too big for the needs of the post–Cold War period.

Deutch was determined to clean house. The ad hoc dismissals were not Deutch's preference, but his other initiatives for a wider housecleaning had been foiled. Deutch looked around at the tools available to him to reduce staffing. The voluntary buyouts for early retirements were not working. The senior CIA officers were not leaving. Why should they? They were at the pinnacle of their careers, at the summit of their power and influence within the CIA. They could stay on, doing a job they love, and make even more money as they moved up the Senior Intelligence Service ladder. If they stayed thirty years, their pensions might be sufficient for a comfortable retirement. If they left, what would they do? Retire to a life of leisure? Sell insurance? These were hardly tempting options to those who had lived lives of intrigue and action in the distant corners of the world. Furthermore, their skill sets and résumés full of blanks made transition to the private sector difficult. There was no incentive to leave.

Deutch could institute an RIF, but federal rules required reductions to be based on seniority; last in, first out. The entry-level and mid-level officers were not the problem. They were leaving on their own accord, given the hard times at the Agency and lack of promotion opportunity. Recruiting new people was hard. The CIA was not welcome on most campuses, its reputation in tatters and pay rate abysmal. What to do?

Even before Deutch arrived at the CIA, he had been working on the issue and quietly supported a new initiative: "directed retirements." In the national security world, directed—as in directed assignments—was code for action forced from above. Targets of the directed retirement program would be GS-13 officers and above who had reached twenty years of service with the government, regardless of age. The forced retirements would be at the discretion of senior management, so they could pick and choose who stayed and went. It was a creative way to get rid of the old boys, those who were resistant to change, and those who carried baggage from failed operations or failed management of operations.

With a stroke of his pen, Deutch could send out pink slips saying "Your services are no longer necessary" to those implicated in the Ames or the Iran-Contra scandals. There would be no internal appeals

board and no right to recourse to any other government board. Age discrimination legislation would be exempted. It was a perfect solution.
Deutch could clean house, right-size the workforce, skills mix, and
quality. Headroom would be cleared, and Deutch could promote those
down in the ranks who fit his vision of the New CIA.

CIA officers, as well as the rest of the civil service, screamed "Foul!"
Under the Civil Service Retirement System, which covered most senior
and mid-career intelligence and civil service personnel, employees
were entitled to retire at the age of fifty-five years after thirty years of
service. Pensions were based on salary and service. The typical federal
worker retired at age sixty-one and received a pension equal to 55 percent of salary, assuming thirty years of service. Employees did not pay
into Social Security and therefore could not receive benefits upon
retirement. Pensions were reduced 2 percent for each year that the
retiree was under the age of fifty-five. As salary levels were low to begin
with in comparison to the private sector, forced early retirement would
be financially devastating for many mid- to senior-level officers.[1]

Deutch sent the forced retirement proposal to Congress one week
after being confirmed as DCI. It was sent quietly, to the House
Permanent Select Committee on Intelligence, bypassing normal channels. It was sent without clearances from the Office of Management and
Budget (OMB), which usually approves or rejects proposed major legislation. OMB did not like being cut out. The intelligence community was
quietly told that operating outside usual channels may be normal for
intelligence work, but not government bureaucracy issues. The proposal died an equally quiet death. The powerful OMB had spoken.[2]

NORTHERN IRAQ, 1995: Covert action had not come to an end
in the New CIA; it had just become so restricted that covert operators
could do little more than talk. It was hard to talk up a storm of sufficient
strength to blow Saddam Hussein out of the picture, so the CIA and the
world would discover. Theoretically, Iraq was a priority because it had
been designated one of those "rogue nations." While critics of the CIA
attributed the failure to CIA incompetence, insiders understandably
had a different view.

The U.S. press aptly laid out the opposing views. According to Randy
Stearns of *ABC News*, the Clinton administration never formulated a
cohesive policy, nor supported its stated policy consistently.[3] Inside the
administration, there was considerable disagreement on what the policy toward Iraq should be. Tim Weiner at the *New York Times* reported
that when the CIA submitted a draft covert action plan, dissenters

would derail the review process, and the plan would hang in limbo.[4] Furthermore, some administration officials used tactical leaks to the press to ensure that a plan would not be approved.[5]

Policy problems, coupled with a general unwillingness by the administration (and the Agency's management) to take risks, led to low morale in the Iraqi task force. By the mid to late 1990s the reputation of the task force was very low, and good officers did their best to avoid assignments there. No one wanted to work on a program that was designed to go nowhere.

As described by Stearns in an *ABC News* report, starting immediately after the end of the first Gulf War the Bush administration ordered the CIA to find a covert means to bring down the Iraqi dictator. The CIA spent roughly $20 million on anti-Saddam propaganda and at least $11 million in aid to various Iraqi opposition groups in London and Kurdistan (northern Iraq). The CIA supported the Iraqi National Congress, an umbrella organization for Kurdish and Iraqi opposition groups. According to Stearns, by late 1994, the CIA had set up a base in the northern Iraqi city of Salahuddin to assist and to keep an eye on opposition activities.[6]

Infighting within the Iraqi National Congress significantly reduced the effectiveness of the organization. Fighting between groups, particularly between Jalal Talabani, head of the Patriotic Union of Kurdistan and Masud Barzani, head of the Kurdistan Democratic Party, paralyzed the organization, as these two opposition groups spent more effort fighting each other for supremacy than overthrowing Saddam Hussein. The ultimate goal of the Kurdish groups was to establish an independent Kurdistan, which the United States did not support. This was one of the reasons Washington consistently declined to provide heavy weaponry to the Kurdish groups to engage Iraqi forces. This difference created tension between the Kurds, the Iraqi National Congress, and the U.S. government, and was a huge distraction to the job at hand.

In 1995, at the same time as a military offensive by the Iraqi National Congress, the CIA became embroiled in the infighting and competing political agendas of Iraqi National Congress members. The leader of the Iraqi National Congress, Ahmed Chalabi, reportedly told two Iranian intelligence officers that the U.S. government had finally decided to get rid of Saddam Hussein and asked Chalabi to contact the Iranians to gain their support. Chalabi reportedly showed the Iranians a letter on National Security Council stationery, asking Chalabi to provide to the National Security Council team leader, Robert Pope, "all assistance requested for his mission." There was no Robert Pope; the CIA team leader was Bob Baer, who was operating in true name.

When the story got back to National Security Advisor Tony Lake, the assumption was that it was true. Lake ordered the CIA team to advise the Iraqi opposition groups that the U.S. government would not support the military offensive that had just gotten under way. So much for keeping the eye on the ball—regime change. Furthermore, Lake ordered an investigation, and the Northern Iraq Liaison Element team was called back, interviewed by the FBI, and polygraphed. They were accused of running a rogue operation and soliciting the assassination of Saddam Hussein, in violation of Executive Order 12333.

Baer pleaded innocence, called the letter a fake, and tried to explain the context of the situation, a likely attempt by Chalabi to gain one-up on his rivals by getting Iranian support based upon his (false) credentials with the National Security Council. During the investigation, the team was placed in administrative limbo and never did return to northern Iraq. Eventually, the FBI dropped the investigation. Nonetheless, the careers of these officers were damaged as doubts lingered as to what really had happened. Their risk taking—trying to make regime change happen—was penalized.

The coup attempt failed, and the Iraqi opposition felt that the United States abandoned it in midstream. When a new team was inserted, it was led by a more senior officer, but the mood was cautious, with no one wanting to get burned by the Kurdish infighting or be accused of exceeding authorities. Mission achievement suffered.

Baer was later forced out of the CIA. He was the last of the cowboys; there was no room for people like him in the New CIA. In his memoir, *See No Evil*, Baer wrote about the brouhaha over the letter. Whether Baer did or did not write it, and whether or not there was approval to assassinate Saddam, how the incident was handled on the political level shows just how afraid Washington was of doing anything that could smack of impropriety. In the political environment of 1995, the risk of removing a designated enemy of the U.S. by lethal force was just too much for the White House to accept. In the political environment of 2003, we would see a radically different environment emerge, with the Bush White House neoconservatives calculating the threat of doing nothing was higher than the threat of loosing U.S. servicemen in what turned out to be a costly war of urban warfare and occupation.

Chalabi also burned some bridges. When Chalabi emerged as a Pentagon favorite in the 2003 "liberation of Iraq," the CIA/Chalabi bad blood resurfaced with a vengeance across the front pages of the political debate. Once unreliable, always unreliable in the CIA book.

The *New York Times* and the *Washington Post* reported on a new initiative in 1995, funding a group of Iraqi military officers who had defected and were living in Jordan. This group, the Iraqi National Accord, was more cohesive and was thought to have greater potential to achieve the mission. The press reported that through this group the CIA established a network of agents inside the Iraqi military that, according to the plan, would instigate a palace coup. The Iraqi National Accord also ran a radio transmitter that beamed anti-Saddam messages into Iraq. The National Accord had previously set up a radio station, Voice of Free Iraq, in Saudi Arabia.[7]

Tim Weiner reported in the *New York Times* that in January 1996, the CIA stepped up action, with a new finding signed by President Clinton that authorized providing weapons, training, and intelligence-gathering technical equipment. The new program was to prepare the Kurds for a military offensive inside Iraq. The CIA continued to collect intelligence, conducted propaganda operations, and debriefed Iraqi defectors. The CIA had not given up on a palace coup, but wanted to add more mettle to the operation by training and arming opposition forces.[8]

In the summer of 1996, Saddam Hussein wrapped up the network that the Iraqi National Accord was running inside Iraq and launched a major offensive into the Kurdish zone. The Saddam regime was aided by the tactical switching of sides by Kurdistan Democratic Party leader Masud Barzani as part of a power move against his Patriotic Union of Kurdistan rival. The Iraqi army briefly occupied Irbil, arresting Kurdish opposition supporters and seizing Iraqi National Accord records and equipment. The Iraqi army shut down the opposition radio station run by the Iraqi National Accord. The Iraqi National Accord claimed that fifteen hundred opposition figures were imprisoned by the Iraqi army, a figure that is exaggerated. Nonetheless, there were significant human losses. The offensive shut down the Northern Iraq Liaison Element operation for the remainder of the 1990s.

The CIA has requested that I redact several paragraphs that discussed a lack of accountability for Iraq operations.

NEW HEADQUARTERS BUILDING, LANGLEY, VIRGINIA, 1995: Not all was well in the Directorate of Intelligence or the Directorate of Science and Technology. With constricted budgets and lean staff, the directorates had to adjust the way they did business. In the Intelligence directorate, it became a luxury to have more than one analyst on an account. In the post–Cold War world, analytical redundancy, once viewed as a strength for keeping a vibrant community challenging each other's assumptions and assessments, increasingly became viewed as wasteful. The Directorate of Intelligence began to cede military analysis to the Defense Intelligence Agency. Independent imagery analysis disappeared with the establishment of the National Imagery and Mapping Agency under Department of Defense control. Increasingly, the Directorate of Intelligence focused its analysis on the core national security issues, giving only light coverage to a range of other regional issues of less immediate interest.

Like the rest of the Agency, the Directorate of Intelligence management assumed it could surge to meet new and special requirements, reassigning analysts as needed, with little negative impact upon mission. The problem is that even the best analytical mind needs to have subject expertise for maximum effect. By surging to meet new requirements and by moving Directorate of Intelligence analysts around, the analysts were being deprived of the opportunity to develop substantive knowledge on their accounts. *Real* substantive knowledge comes after years of working on an issue. The analyst then has the experience to draw upon within the context of the issue and can develop the framework and intuition needed to accurately assess events and predict future behavior using a variety of analytical models.

Consumers and oversight committees identified problems in quality. A House Permanent Select Committee on Intelligence report criticized the analytical depth, breadth, and expertise of the CIA on critical countries and issues. It also criticized the intelligence community's shift to short-term, event-driven analysis at the cost of critical long-term/strategic analysis.[9] Because the Directorate of Intelligence had been cut so slim and surge and current intelligence requirements occupied the vast majority of analysts' time, the Directorate of Intelligence had difficulty covering all of their accounts to the required depth. For example, there frequently would be only one analyst per account. Moving the analyst to meet a surge requirement would leave that account vacant. The demands on the analysts were very high, as is apparent by the attrition rate of junior analysts.

Congressional oversight committees and outside review committees made a number of recommendations for reform to correct the perceived ills of the directorate, including hiring more analysts, improving their training, increasing contact with outside experts to challenge conventional wisdom, and reducing the gap between analysts and policymakers to increase the relevance of intelligence. Deutch found willingness inside the directorate to consider outside recommendations and to undertake a comprehensive review of business practices and goals.

As a result, in 1996 the directorate produced its first strategic plan. In the plan, management recognized that the directorate was losing good talent and had to work to improve retention by enhancing career development opportunities through training, rotational assignments, and a more open assignments process, establishing clear performance management standards, developing nonfinancial awards systems that focus on performance excellence, and balancing professional and personal needs through flexible schedules.

The strategic plan also identified a need to sharpen the analytical skills of its officers through more rigorous training on analytical methodologies. Training of analysts had been limited, especially after the directorate opted out of the Agency Career Training program in the early 1990s. Training was expensive and, frankly, training historically has been a low priority—not just with the Directorate of Intelligence, but throughout the Agency. A person who can be spared for training is a person who can be spared—or so the thinking went. So when budgets were cut, training was the first to go. The CIA only gave analysts a couple of weeks of training, more focused on Agency issues (security, information systems, and other specifics.).

The CIA expected analysts to learn analytical tradecraft on the job. When the directorate was organized along disciplinary expertise lines (political, economic, military analysts), mentoring new analysts in the discipline methodology was part and parcel of the tradecraft training learned on the job. Under geographical-based organization, analysts learned the tradecraft through mentoring, but the indoctrination of disciplinary expertise in the theory and practice that underlies the individual analytical occupations suffered by the dispersal of occupations. Analysts had to rely upon their prior formal education in methodology to get through the initial trial period of sink or swim.

In 1996, through the CIA Office of Training and Education, the Directorate of Intelligence began experimenting with substantive analytical training for new analysts. A month-long survey course for new analysts developed into a twenty-two-week curriculum that covered the full range of tradecraft and disciplinary expertise issues new analysts need to master. While this was a good step, it fell short of the past practice of a year-plus training for incoming analysts as part of the Career Training (CT) program. My CT class was one of the last classes that had participation from all directorates. Not only did new recruits learn their trade, they also were familiarized with the work of the other directorates. Even more important, CTs established relationships with their peers that were invaluable in forming a corporate mind-set that is required for those destined for senior management. However, in 1996, the cost factor of putting analysts in the CT program was just too much for the directorate to consider.

The directorate developed the analyst expert track to address dissatisfaction with the established career progression of analysts. In the old system, in order for an analyst to continue to be promoted and work on challenging accounts, he or she had to become a manager. Not all analysts wanted to manage people and resources, and some had no capacity to do so, but were excellent analysts. In order to keep strong analysts on board doing the kind of work they were hired to do, the directorate created the expert track. Reducing the sheer number of managers by transferring them to the expert track allowed management to reorganize the directorate into fewer offices and flatten out management. The creation of the Senior Analytic Service, the career track for analytical experts versus analytical managers, created a niche for world-class experts inside the directorate.[10] The goal was to increase the number of experts in-house, or within close reach through established outreach programs, so that having the recognized expert immediately available becomes the norm rather than the exception.

The elimination of many mid-level management positions permitted an increase in the number of senior, nonmanagerial positions for substantive experts. Ultimately, the reform created more promotion headroom at the top, but slower promotions for mid-level officers. However, the benefit was that analysts were able to choose which track they preferred—expert analyst or management—and there were fewer levels of review, returning analysts to the primary responsibility of analysis rather than management of analysis.

The Directorate of Intelligence increased the number of rotational assignments available to mid-level officers. By providing mid-level analysts greater opportunity to serve overseas and in policymaking institutions, the directorate moved analysts closer to issues and requirements. Policymakers had complained that analysis often failed to meet their needs by being too late or too unfocused, or by adding little to what they already knew. The lower-level policymaker frequently has lived in the country where he or she is engaged, has daily contact with his or her counterparts from there, and with substantive experts in the United States, and reads the current literature. It was difficult for the analyst who has not "been there and done that" to provide fresh insight to the policymaker. By expanding the range of opportunities and experiences of the mid-level analyst, their assessments had more weight with the policymakers.

It would take several years and a large infusion of funding before the benefits of the plan would be felt. In the beginning, analysts just felt the pain of a seemingly unending process of reorganization and reform. The directorate continued to hemorrhage. Between 1992 and 1998, 40 percent of newly hired analysts resigned with less than five years in service.

Deutch was a man of technology. Long before he came to the CIA, he had been involved in cutting-edge initiatives for technical collection and remote reconnaissance platforms. As a prominent professor of chemistry at Massachusetts Institute of Technology, he was often the go-to guy for the government for next-generation thinking. In addition to serving as the Undersecretary of Defense for Acquisitions and Technology just prior to coming to the Agency, he had also worked at the Department of Energy on energy research and technology and served on the president's Nuclear Safety Oversight Committee and the White House Science Council. He was far more comfortable with widgets and engineers than agents and handlers. One would have expected the Directorate of Science and Technology would have flourished under Deutch. But it didn't.

For a directorate known for making quantum leaps in technology and planning for needs decades far into the future, the directorate somehow got lost in the immediate post–Cold War period. It was slow to transition from Soviet-focused programs. Although the scientists in the directorate understood far better than most Agency employees the implications of the information revolution, the directorate failed to harness emerging technologies and adapt them for intelligence work.

There was also a fundamental change in the thinking of senior CIA management concerning the role of technology in general and the directorate specifically in the field of intelligence. DCIs of the 1990s saw the directorate as a support office for analysis and operations, not a scientific powerhouse driving new generations of collection methods. This vision change was best illustrated by the appointment of a non-scientist to head the Directorate of Science and Technology. The scientists and techies did not much like this "support" designation, since they saw themselves as creators, not as mechanics. They wanted to make cool gizmos that could see through walls; unimaginative management wanted them to fiddle and tune others' creations to make life easier for the more important stealers of secrets and crystal-ball readers.

If this was not bad enough, the cultural divide that separated the scientists and engineers from the rest of the Agency was one the size of the

Grand Canyon. Their idea of a quick turnaround from research and development to production and installation was measured in decades. They were geeks, or nerds in the jargon of the time. They were used to keeping apart in their own specialized cocoons of secrecy. Only a small portion of the directorate officers were accustomed to interacting with operational and analytical personnel and were intimately knowledgeable about their mission and needs. The directorate was simply not suitably staffed to identify support requirements and harness technological capabilities to isolate acceptable solutions in a timely fashion. The fault was not just with the scientists and engineers, but also with the operations personnel and analysts, who did not understand technology enough to articulate their needs in a meaningful manner. To the scientist, the demands were ever-shifting and had unreasonably short delivery timelines. Satellites were not built overnight; new exploitation tools should not be either.

Computer and Internet exploitation was a perfect example of the opportunities and the challenges for the Directorate of Science and Technology. Operations officers saw great operational opportunities with the global spread of Internet and World Wide Web usage. We wanted to exploit the Internet for clandestine-agent communications because of the security advantages. Agents would no longer need to be issued "spy gear" that was difficult (or impossible) to explain away if discovered in their possession. Agents instead could purchase a computer in the local economy and use the computer for overt purposes, as well as covert communications. The most sophisticated and secure agent communication systems were closely protected, and the vast majority of agents working for the CIA could not meet the counterintelligence vetting requirements necessary to qualify for receiving this spy gear. We were frequently trapped in a vicious circle, needing to improve the security of operations by the issuance of impersonal communication systems, but not being able to get the equipment because the operation was not sufficiently secure.

The Internet and World Wide Web promised tremendous variety and agility that could be exploited with different levels of security firewalls. Through the Internet or the World Wide Web, we could keep in contact with Headquarters handlers and have no need to operate out of ███████ or official U.S. installations for secure communications. The Directorate of Science and Technology studied the requirements and began researching possible solutions. However, rather than generating a solution that could be deployed quickly to the field, quasi-solutions remained stuck on the drawing board or in security never-never land.

We were bombarded with new security requirements, emphasizing the threats posed by the Internet and World Wide Web.

Foreign governments, as well as nontraditional targets, such as terrorists and scientists, used computers to store data and to communicate, offering new collection opportunities. Electronic paper trails are difficult for the layman to obscure, providing good evidentiary details that could be used in establishing relationships and documenting illegal activities in courts of law. Field operations increasingly resulted in the acquisition of electronic media or hardware containing information of potential intelligence value. We would send the material to Headquarters for exploitation by the Directorate of Science and Technology. In the 1990s, the CIA did not have the capability to exploit the submissions in a timely manner. Information of potential intelligence value would sit for months, if not years, before being assessed. Intelligence has a shelf life. What is of value today is quickly considered overtaken by events (OBE) as history happens.

The Directorate of Intelligence was being overwhelmed by information and needed new tools to organize and fuse different kinds of data into agile databases. Furthermore, it needed far more powerful search engines than those available on the commercial market. Given the vast amount of information, the analysts needed tools that would perform complex analytical functions at high speeds. An example of system overload: Around the time of the fall of the Berlin Wall, the CIA gained access to the ███████████ more than 320,000 documents that the East German internal intelligence organization maintained on its foreign operations. Buried in the millions of entries of mundane and aged operational details were nuggets of counterintelligence details of current interest to the CIA. It took years for CIA officers to read through all the documentation. Because of the time lag, compromises continued and opportunities were lost.

Deutch embraced the concept of integrating technology into all aspects of the CIA mission. He brought in new leadership in order to shake up the directorate from head to tail. Ruth David, the new deputy director, introduced the concept of "agile intelligence" as a new strategy to meet rapidly shifting priorities of the 1990s. David placed major emphasis on exploiting advanced information technology as she assessed that developments in this area were driving changes in the behavior of adversaries, and information technology would be the key enabler for the intelligence business of the future.

With resources very tight, David proposed cutting entire programs linked to technical collection and analysis in order to distribute the budget to technical support–related programs and offices. When large portions of the Foreign Broadcast Information Service were put on the chopping block in 1996 to free up funding, customers screamed, Congress asked uncomfortable questions, and the program remained largely untouched. Viewed as a relic and out of date given the development of sophisticated computer imaging, the modeling office was not so fortunate. Perhaps the last battle of the Cold War, it finally closed in 1996 and only after its longtime chief retired. In 1996, the National Photographic Interpretation Center, the directorate office responsible for analyzing spy satellite imagery, was transferred to the newly created National Imagery and Mapping Agency

The reforms were slow to take root, and morale remained low during Deutch's tenure. Officers were drawn off to other agencies conducting research into new fields and technologies. The New Economy was flowering, and scientists and engineers were in demand in private industry. The opportunity to break new scientific thresholds and make big bucks drew away some of the best brains of the organization.

19
Unethical Spies

LANGLEY, VIRGINIA, 1996: It is impossible to overstate just how low morale had fallen by the mid-1990s. The worst part was that everything Deutch did seemed to make life inside the CIA more difficult rather than less. Morale in the Directorate of Operations was especially low, which led to a disproportionate number of resignations. The CIA inspector general studied the rate of attrition in the Directorate of Operations for the period of 1994–96. The study found that high-quality officers were leaving, people the Agency could not afford to lose. Many pointed to dissatisfaction with Agency management including their own supervisors as well as the lack of clarity about the current mission. Heavy-handed bureaucracy made it hard for collectors to take risks and achieve mission. The Ames spy scandal had tarnished the reputation of the Directorate of Operations.

Deutch was no beacon of light for the Operations folks. He held us in such disdain he had no compunction against criticizing us publicly. The directorate, which had always been considered the darling of the Agency, received poor marks from Deutch. In comparing Directorate of Operations officers to military officers, he said, "They certainly are not as competent, or as understanding of what their relative role is and what their responsibilities are."[1]

The malaise ran deep. No one in Headquarters wanted to run real operations. "Avoid risk" became the watchword. False allegations that the CIA introduced crack cocaine into black communities in the 1980s as part of a plan to raise money for the Contras astounded CIA officers. I was speechless that anyone could believe stories that painted my colleagues and me in such poor light.

The truth was the reputation of the CIA was so low that there were some Americans who would believe anything of us. And then there was Deutch, who also believed the worst about us. We wondered why we should stay. We were overworked, underpaid, and accused of horrible crimes against the very people we swore to serve and protect. The Cold War was over. There was no clarity of mission. There was no good reason to put up with the manure being piled upon us. Underpaid, overworked, not respected, not wanted—it was not too tough a decision to vote with our feet. The CIA hemorrhaged personnel. Deutch knew he should do something about the morale problem.

It was Nora Slatkin's brainchild, and it was ill conceived from the get-go. The program was called Quality of Life. Rather than address the core problems within the organization, the lack of mission, operational inactivity, the never-ending reforms and process reviews, the Quality of Life program tried to make life inside the Agency more warm and fuzzy. Field officers wondered why no one was answering the mail, operational proposals ignored, requests for help unanswered. Headquarters was now focused on how to make working in Headquarters bearable.

Headquarters officers were equally upset. They did not want a dry-cleaning service, but secretarial support—or at least computers that worked. Proposals for a new $10 million CIA field house and other facility improvements became the priority. While Slatkin was overseeing her new design for a fishpond to spruce up the landscaping around the Bubble, al-Qa'ida executed the Khobar Towers bombing, killing nineteen American solders, wounding 500 others, and planning the future attacks on American embassies in Africa that would kill more than 220 people and wounding 4,000 others. The Quality of Life program would have been a laughingstock if we were in any mood to laugh, which we were not. Instead, in utter disbelief, we were watching Deutch destroy the Agency piece by piece.

CAPITOL HILL, WASHINGTON, D.C., 1995–96: Recalling intelligence reports is a nightmare because it cast doubt on the credibility of all Agency reporting. However, in this instance, the CIA had no choice; the overall stakes were just too big. The CIA disclosed to Congress that it had provided U.S. policymakers tainted intelligence on the Soviet Union. The Ames damage assessment, a long and painful review exposing the depth of Ames's treachery, revealed that Moscow used information from Ames to set up a disinformation campaign to feed tainted intelligence to the CIA. The tainted intelligence presented a view that exaggerated the strength of the economy and military might of the Soviet Union. The disinformation skewed the CIA's understanding of internal Soviet developments to an extent the CIA did not forecast the collapse of the Soviet Union and the Warsaw Pact.

It is one thing to be fooled. It is another to knowingly be fooled. The CIA suspected some of its Soviet sources were controlled—that is, they said they were working for the CIA but in fact were loyal to the Soviets. In the very confusing world of double agents and triple agents, establishing the degree of agent reliability is hard. If there is any serious doubt about an agent, the whole of the agent's reporting becomes suspect. One tried-and-true method of confusing and misleading the opposition is to feed it bad information along with true stuff, making the reporting partially verifiable. The Russians and East Germans were pros at this. The Ames damage assessment revealed the Soviets were playing a grand game of disinformation, partly to mislead the mole hunters and to protect Ames and partly to mislead the policymakers.

Even when it is known the agent is a double, it is extremely difficult to determine what portion of the "intelligence" provided by the double is true and what is not. Providing questionable intelligence from a known double agent to policymakers is problematic. If the CIA dubs the source unreliable, even the most generous of critics would wonder why the report was being disseminated. If the source is identified as a fabricator, and this juicy tidbit is leaked, the Soviets could learn that their game had been exposed. If the CIA disseminates the information without any special caveats, it abrogates its mission of providing accurate and timely intelligence to consumers. Not knowing that the sourcing was a problem, policymakers would have no reason to give the intelligence less weight in decision-making factoring. And yet, this is what the CIA opted to do. It violated the basic rules of intelligence collection and dissemination.

In presenting the CIA's findings, Deutch expressed concerns that foreign policy and military procurement decisions had been influenced adversely by the tainted intelligence. Subsequent review by the Pentagon found that while the tainted intelligence had a substantial role in framing the debate on U.S. military strategy, it had a limited impact on the decision making, with the exception of several specific cases. Correctly, Deutch admitted that the intelligence reports should never have been disseminated, even if the information was believed to be true, on the sole basis of the lack of credibility of the sources.

To restore credibility with Congress, Deutch promised he would hold accountable those who provided the tainted intelligence, and he would provide U.S. policymakers with the names of operational sources. While the first part was anticipated, the second part was beyond the pale. Operations officers threatened to walk out the door rather than risk the lives of their agents to the whims of politicians. Thankfully, Deutch recognized that a mutiny was afoot and backtracked before Congress.

As with Guatemala, Deutch opted to spread accountability downward, exclusively. He exempted the Office of the DCI of the responsibility to keep policymakers informed when he stopped short of holding three former DCIs accountable. Senator Bob Kerrey, then–vice chairman of the Select Senate Committee for Intelligence, echoed the feelings of the working level when he commented that he did not believe morale at the CIA was improved when the people at the top are not held to the same level of accountability as those below.[2] The message received was "Do as I say, not as I do."

DULLES AIRPORT, VIRGINIA, 1996: The FBI arrested CIA officer Harold J. Nicholson on November 16, 1996, to the complete surprise of fellow Counterterrorism Center officers who were accompanying Nicholson overseas on official business. Nicholson had started spying for Moscow in the same year Ames was arrested. Although Nicholson spied for a shorter period before being caught, it proved Ames was not unique, an abnormality, and that the CIA had a lot more work to do on the counterintelligence front.

Unlike Ames, Nicholson was a strong performing operations officer and was on the management track. At the time of his arrest, he was a sixteen-year veteran, a former chief of station, generally well-respected by his peers, although considered a bit eccentric. But something had gone wrong in his career, evidenced by the fact he had been shipped down to "the Farm" to teach. In 1994, the Farm was still the place with a reputation—deserved or not—for drying out drunks and sidelining otherwise troublesome officers. It is also a location at which officers have limited access to sensitive classified information. Like Ames, Nicholson had personal difficulties, including a recent divorce, a new girlfriend with expensive tastes, and a limited government salary. Nicholson started selling information to the Russians probably in 1994 while still assigned as deputy chief in Kuala Lumpur, Malaysia.

Like Ames, Nicholson used sloppy tradecraft, took frequent foreign trips, and had too much unexplainabe cash in his wallet. Neither officer seemed very concerned about the prospect of getting caught. The CIA learned hard lessons from the Ames fiasco and called in the FBI when

Nicholson registered significant deception on the polygraph. The CIA Counterespionage staff had been looking at Nicholson before his polygraph because of his unusual behavior and other intelligence. The mole hunters knew there was another bad apple, somewhere. They had already determined Ames could not have known about some of the operations compromised in the late 1980s and early 1990s.

Nicholson also passed along the names of new officers in training. The Agency's primary offsite training facility, the Farm, maintained class lists in true name for years. Nicholson compromised a decade of class lists, exposing baby spies before they had even hit the streets. By knowing the CIA officers, the Soviets (now the Russians) were able to concentrate their counterintelligence activities worldwide. By knowing the operational methods, the Russians could identify when an officer was going operational.

For the more experienced officers, compromise to the Soviets was less complicated because there was relatively little hardship in adjusting assignments to declared positions working in liaison operations. My identity was compromised to the Russians by Nicholson. While the compromise did not negatively impact my upward advancement, knowledge of the compromise shed light on some operational oddities that transpired when working against the Russians. It explained why, for example, when I went hunting for Russians, the only ones willing to spend time with me were the known or suspected spies; the Foreign Ministry types would disappear into thin air. At the time, this did not bother me because there was no greater achievement than recruiting a Russian intelligence officer—a KGB scalp. Unless you could find them, spend time and money on them, drink vodka into the wee hours with them, and spar over the meaning of life, you had no chance of landing one. I had no problems finding and spending time with them; recruiting one always remained elusive. In the "Wilderness of Mirrors" in the spy versus spy game, knowing the true identity of the players from the beginning changes the game, especially if one side is operating from wrong assumptions. The Russians had one up on me, and I did not know it.

For the new officers, exposure meant they would be denied unilateral positions under deeper cover, which typically are the most challenging and exciting. New officers cut their operational teeth in unilateral positions and make names for themselves. Their careers were stunted before they even went operational.

Nicholson's exposure further bolstered the call for change. The fact that Nicholson began his treachery immediately on the heels of

Ames's exposure indicated that the CIA counterintelligence policies were not sufficient to deter further spying. To counter any perception of inattention, the CIA moved from a dangerously relaxed posture to a dangerously rigid one. The thinking evolved from the presumption that there could not possibly be a human penetration inside the CIA to a belief that there most certainly *were* current moles as well as those who would metamorphose into moles if preemptive action were not taken. There evolved a zero-tolerance factor when suspicions arose. There was no incentive to give the benefit of the doubt, to accept exculpatory evidence, or to balance security concerns with other organizational needs. There was no incentive for officers to speak up and offer dissent once Security named someone as suspect. It was like a huge, rolling boulder; not worth trying to stop because you would get crushed in the process. Post–Ames and Nicholson, Security had the final say. This state of affairs would hamstring the Agency, from recruiting new personnel to retaining seasoned officers.

OLD HEADQUARTERS BUILDING, LANGLEY, VIRGINIA, 1996: Assaults upon CIA professionalism and ethics would not stop. Just as the light was beginning to show at the end of the tunnel, with discussion of Ames dropping off, a new traitor was found in our midst. Why did Nicholson do it? Why does anyone betray his country? It was not low morale or job dissatisfaction. At his sentencing, Nicholson stated that he committed espionage for the money, to provide for his children and make up for the long hours at work and for failing to keep his marriage together.[3] There was probably a motivational element of adventure and risk taking as well—as if being a CIA field operative was not exciting enough. Not ideology. Not revenge. Not blackmail. For the idealistic public servants, there was nothing lower than grubbing for money. Something was rotten.

An internal debate opened on what was wrong inside the Agency, specifically inside the Directorate of Operations. There was a growing understanding that the organization was suffering from dishonesty within the ranks. Not dishonesty toward agents, but toward colleagues and CIA management. The source of the dishonesty was disputed. Some said it was the nature of the job that takes honest people and teaches them to lie and manipulate expertly. At some point, they start using these same skills inside the organization in order to get promoted, gain influence, to win scarce resources, or to protect the organization. In a world where so much is ambiguous and situational, they justify their actions with perverse logic only an insider can understand. Over time, they simply lose their moral and ethical footings.

Others said the source of the dishonesty was in the agent recruitment "numbers game." In the late 1970s, the basis upon which an operations officer (then called a case officer) was promoted changed. Objective criteria were introduced into the performance appraisal system, tracking with the then-current business management philosophy of management by objective. Operations officers were rated on the basis of the number of agent recruitments and intelligence reports. Using the new objective criteria, promotion panels met and determined who would be promoted.

This was seen as an improvement to the system of patronage (old-boy network) that had been in place since the days of the Office of Strategic Services. While certainly more "fair" than the old system, it had unintended consequences. Operations officers went out and recruited to their hearts' content, racking up the numbers so they looked like superheroes. There was little quality control on either the agents recruited or the intelligence produced. The officer who recruited one prized KGB officer would be disadvantaged at the time of promotion, when compared to an officer in Latin America who recruited ten access agents during the same period. Many marginal agents were recruited at this time, and more than a few phantom agents, who existed only in the minds of operations officers and on paper. Most seasoned operations officers have had that unsettling experience of going to a "cold turnover," only to find out the "agent" did not know he had been recruited, or simply did not exist.

Whatever the root cause, the directorate realized even before the Ames scandal broke out that it had slipped into a system that tolerated dishonesty and promoted it unintentionally. In 1991, the directorate introduced the "Asset Validation System" (AVS) as a means of systematically assessing foreign agents and the tradecraft utilized by their handlers. The new system was promoted as an integrated method to ensure that double agents were not recruited and run for long periods of time. That had happened with Cuban agents in the 1980s, the vast majority of whom had just been judged to have been doubles. In reality, AVS had a second purpose: instilling accountability into handling.

Under Deutch's process reviews and reform, the AVS program—which up until then was being treated as a paper exercise and ignored by many of the seasoned officers—received new emphasis. It began to take hold once AVS implementation became one of the criteria for promotion. AVS evolved into an effective assessment tool that brought accountability to field officers. Because of its integrated nature, incidents of falsification, or just poor tradecraft, became apparent far more quickly. Headquarters officers reviewed AVS documentation routinely and put into writing reporting inadequacies, omissions, and contradictions. It became far more difficult to create agents and reports from whole cloth. Headquarters now expected and demanded a level of detail in reporting that even the most creative of integrity-challenged officers would find difficult to meet. Directorate of Operations management had always sent its officers out to the field with a pat on the back, telling them that they were trusted to do the right thing. Now management had a tool that allowed them to trust, but verify.

Coupled with a change in the promotion criteria for operations officers, the AVS system has gone a long way in bringing more honesty into the system. Operations officers are rated upon the impact of their achievements, not on the number of agents recruited. One solid recruitment in an assignment is considered good; two is considered excellent, assuming they both are reporting high-quality intelligence on topics of high priority for the directorate. The "asset scrub" of the early 1990s got rid of most of the marginal agents, and the AVS system put quality checks on new recruiting. Operations officers have more time to spend on each case, which theoretically should enhance case security. The numbers game came to an end and recruitment expectations became reasonable. Incidents of falsification still occurred, but they were isolated.

But what about when rules and regulations were broken, performance deemed substandard, and ethical standards ignored? The CIA had long demonstrated an inability to deal with these problems in a fair and equal way. Simply put, the accountability system at the CIA was broken. Unlike the system of the military services, accountability practices within the CIA had never been standardized. Inconsistent accountability practices have been one of the most criticized problems by CIA officers. Nothing destroys faith in management more than to see one person penalized severely for doing something that another colleague did with impunity.

Deutch, who found CIA accountability practices woefully lacking, was the driving force behind increased accountability, especially in the Directorate of Operations. Accountability boards with set review procedures were established only in the 1990s, as part of the reforms following the Ames scandal. Deutch certainly beat the accountability drum, but his efforts were dismissed when he proved to be as reactive and selective as previous directors.

Why is one chief of station forced to retire when officers under his control practice poor tradecraft, resulting in the exposure of a non official cover (NOC) officer, expulsion of four CIA officers from a European country, and a political flap with an important ally? Why does another chief of station walk away with no censure after officers under his control practice poor tradecraft in a Middle Eastern country and more than a handful of agents are exposed, resulting in their arrest and execution?

Why are staff officers who use unauthorized chat rooms in the Agency internal computer system to criticize management practices and personalities fired and their security clearances pulled? Why are contractors who do the same retained on contract and their security clearances left untouched?

Why is a male operations officer not censured for having a personal relationship with an agent, and a female operations officer is fired for doing the same?

Why was nobody held personally accountable for the Ames fiasco, but the system indicted instead? Why was Deutch unwilling to hold three previous DCIs accountable for knowingly providing policymakers with tainted intelligence on the Soviet Union, but willing to reprimand officers at the working level?

Congress was also unimpressed with CIA accountability. A House Permanent Select Committee on Intelligence review found post-Ames a proliferation of systems meant to ensure the accountability of Directorate of Operations personnel for their professional judgments. There were internal Directorate of Operations accountability boards, CIA-wide review boards, counterintelligence reviews, and the CIA inspector general.

The committee wrote:

> The processes are frequently redundant in their charters, inconsistent in the qualifications of the participants, and take upwards of a year to reach their conclusions. In an organization that demands its officers take risks, involves the use of highly specialized skills, and by definition will have numerous false starts and failures for each major success, it is essential to have a single independent, authoritative, professionally competent, and timely system of reviewing questions of professional judgment. None of the current systems meets all these criteria.[4]

Because of the unpredictability of the accountability process, CIA officers were less willing to admit mistakes or wrongdoing. There evolved the belief that if you deny everything and make counteraccusations, you will have a greater chance to survive the system. For those who took integrity seriously, and were honest about their failings, the system did not reward that honesty. Since ethical or unethical behavior often reflects an organization's operating culture, it made insiders worry that the organizational ethics of the CIA had begun to erode.

LANGLEY, VIRGINIA, MID-1990S: The issue of organizational ethics is one that has not received much senior-level attention in the CIA. This is surprising, given the popular view of the CIA as being either an unethical organization from its very essence, or an organization that at times uses unethical means to achieve its mission. Furthermore, public tolerance for unethical business and government behavior during the 1990s and into the 2000s dropped. Management's approach to organizational ethics was that the practice of good ethics happens automatically because management screens new-hires for strong ethical foundations. Starting off with "good stock" and subjecting the stock to annual ethics briefings in the Bubble would guarantee that the workforce would operate ethically. Those who breach the "code of ethics" were abnormalities and were treated as such. However, this ethics "inoculation approach" has been demonstrated in the private sector to have only marginal effectiveness for attaining the desired results. So, too, in the Agency.

The CIA code of ethics is not explicit, varies by directorate, and tends to be legalistic in nature. A review of the CIA treatment of organizational ethics as represented through its official Web site is instructive; there is no mention of a code of ethics. On the Web page titled "CIA Vision, Mission and Values," the CIA merely states under "How we do our work" that it is done with "personal and organization integrity," in one organizational bullet. The bullet is given the same emphasis as "teamwork throughout the Agency and the Intelligence Community" and "innovating and taking risks to get the job done." Inside the CIA, one does not talk so much about ethics, but integrity. Integrity denotes commitment to deeply held priorities and values, even if it goes against one's self-interest.

In the mid-1990s, Kent Pekel, a White House Fellow assigned to the CIA for one year, conducted a study of CIA organizational ethics as part of a program to develop and improve ethics education within the CIA. Pekel's study was right on the mark when it came to its conclusions, a remarkable achievement showing that Pekel, as an outsider, was able to penetrate the Agency's culture of secrecy. Pekel interviewed fifty Agency employees who were selected as a rough cross-section of the employee population.

According to Pekel, Agency employees identified four core challenges to integrity in the CIA in the 1990s. There was "a sense that the Agency's guiding values have been clouded in the aftermath of the Cold War"; a belief that "open discussion and dissent" were "discouraged," "making it less likely that people will speak out about ethical problems"; "an unwillingness to acknowledge failure as an acceptable outcome," which led officers to "cover up mistakes and avoid risk"; and a "belief that promotions and performance appraisals regularly reward those who acted without integrity."[5]

During the Cold War, there was a broad consensus among Americans that Communism was a threat to the American way of life, and there was a moral dimension exalting the work of those engaged in the anti-Soviet struggle. The conduct of espionage, which in and of itself lacked moral underpinnings, was viewed as having moral force within the context of the Cold War. Once that context changed, the very requirement of maintaining an espionage capability came into question by the public and by Congress. Those engaged in espionage—those who had the personal interest in maintaining their jobs—had to find a new context that would give their activities moral force.

The idea that CIA officers were there to promote and protect the interests of the U.S. government was not sufficiently universal, since there was no broad consensus of what constitutes U.S. interests—and the priority of those interests—in the post–Cold War environment. What was more important: protection of human rights or stopping the illegal drug flow into the United States? Condemning assassination or supporting a regional ally? Lack of national consensus created situational responses that were inconsistent from a policy point of view, if not an ethical one. Asked to navigate these waters, the CIA went with the drift of the moment, and officers suffered from the lack of clarity.

Demands for institutional loyalty challenged the individual's ability to offer dissent. This was particularly troublesome in the Directorate of Intelligence, where it could stifle analytical debate. The past practice of the use of footnotes to document dissent virtually disappeared. The Directorate of Intelligence's drive to "speak with one voice" in order to present a corporate view discouraged the new analyst from develping his or her own voice within the group. Intelligence failures as a result of "groupthink" were the extreme result.

Demands to "please the customer" placed pressure upon analysts and senior managers to politicize the product. Politicization of intelligence was (is) an extremely sensitive issue within the Directorate of Intelligence, and a pledge to not do so was part of the Directorate of Intelligence ethics. The issue was far more complicated than just willfully skewing intelligence to tell policymakers what they want to hear. It also included providing answers only to questions the policymaker asked when knowing the unasked questions and unoffered answers politicized the intelligence as well. This problem has flared in the post–September 11 environment on intelligence related to Iraq, al-Qa'ida, and weapons of mass destruction.

Within the Directorate of Operations, institutional loyalty has led to the entrenchment of a culture that promotes cronyism and cover-ups, and a system that provides little room for dissent. In their decision to lie to Congress, Clair George and Alan Fiers clearly showed the strength of institutional loyalty. They saw their actions as protecting the CIA and the president, not as a corrupt act. After the fact, Alan Fiers stated he did not have the courage to be the first to speak the truth, even though he saw pending personal destruction.[6] When he did break ranks and testify against Clair George, Fiers was branded a traitor and became unwelcome in the Directorate of Operations brotherhood. George, who stayed loyal, took the rap, was pardoned by the president, and became an icon in Directorate of Operations culture. Fiers is known as the directorate's first Judas.

Communication from a station to Headquarters was controlled by the chief of station, who had the authority and the Directorate of Operations cultural mores to support a tradition of keeping unwelcome or damning information from dissemination. Chiefs of station quickly learned what can go into cable traffic and what best remained unreported. If a station officer decided to do an end run utilizing unofficial channels of communication to report something, the officer would be judged disloyal and insubordinate by the more senior management. The officer's career was effectively over.

Within the Agency at large, dissent or criticism of a policy could be judged as disloyalty to the government, making the individual a security risk. The DCI is not required to prove that an individual breached laws as grounds for revoking a security clearance; the mere statement questioning loyalty is sufficient grounds to consider someone a security risk. Stifling of dissent allowed discriminatory personnel practices to persist, questionable operations to go unsupervised, and abuse of power in the name of national security and secrecy to go unchecked. Congress condones this when they exempt the CIA from controls governing other government agencies, such as the exemption of CIA employees from protection under the "whistle-blower" laws and civil service employee rights laws.

Fear of failure threatened to paralyze the Agency and to erode organizational ethics probably more than any other element within the Agency. Whether the failure was analytical, operational, technical, or administrative, the Agency had developed an organizational mind-set that failure was not acceptable. This led to operational and analytical risk aversion. If failure happened, for whatever reason, it was not to be admitted. It was better to lie or cover up the failure in the cloak of secrecy. If failure was admitted, the person making the admission was certainly not to be rewarded. For perverse reasons, admission of one failure was suspected to be a cover for additional unadmitted failures. An admitted failure must be punished; a cloaked or unreported failure never happened.

Agency officers talked frequently about integrity issues, but usually over lunch with friends, not in the office in the context of best-practices discussions. Organizational ethics discussions were rare. Individuals were promoted on the basis of mission achievement, not on mission achievement within an ethical framework. There was no formalized process to recognize or promote individuals whose actions were always guided by ethical behavior. Indeed, people were frequently promoted despite their ethics. It was not uncommon to hear about a "great operations officer" who also had a reputation for "creative report writing," or a "great manager" who also had a reputation for intimidating dissenters. By promoting the great officer with questionable integrity, management sent a clear message as to what was more important.

Risk taking, accountability, and ethics are very important elements in the field of espionage. Without taking risks, the mission cannot be achieved; nothing ventured, nothing gained. Without acknowledgment that the CIA must use methods that do not easily fit with societal norms or trends, CIA capabilities will be diminished. Without adhering to firmly established corporate ethics, the CIA and its officers are institutionally weakened by scandals and cover-ups, and mission achievement suffers. During the 1990s, the CIA suffered on all accounts as methods were challenged, a cycle of wrongdoing was met by dysfunctional accountability practices and corporate ethics that then fostered risk aversion. At a time when we should have focused aggressively on rising threats to national security, we were fractured, afraid to move boldly, and ultimately ineffective when it came to winning the war on terrorism in the 1990s.

20
Turf and Policy Battles

LANGLEY, VIRGINIA, 1995: In the 1990s, the Agency frequently came into conflict with other members of the intelligence community. In the view of intelligence community members, the CIA began collecting intelligence on nontraditional topics, topics that fell more naturally within the purview of other agencies. To CIA insiders, there was a general perception that the CIA was in decline, and certain government agencies sought to regain lost turf or expand into areas traditionally monopolized by the CIA. Old turf wars resurfaced, especially during the Deutch years. The real driver for the turf battles was not Deutch, but the reform debate.

In the first half of the1990s, there were multiple initiatives within government and private think tanks that studied various aspects of the intelligence community in the post–Cold War world, with an eye on how to make it meet the needs of the new era. The problem was that while the reformers understood the old world order left behind, they had not yet begun to reach a consensus on the character of the new world order. Indeed, they did not even have a name for it, a term to aptly sum up the essence of a new age of international relations. By the year 2000, eleven years after the fall of the Berlin Wall, the decade was simply called the post–Cold War period. Rather than describe the period for what it was, they simply called it for what it was not. The challenge for the reformers, a challenge to which they aspired—but failed to meet—was to redefine the intelligence community in an undefined period.

The impetus for change was not only the fall of the Soviet Union, but the sense that the intelligence community was somehow broken,

240 •   MELISSA BOYLE MAHLE

dysfunctional, and long overdue for remaking. The intelligence community had been created in bits and pieces, with no overall strategy. Successive DCIs complained they did not have the right tools to manage the intelligence community. Their management capabilities were hampered by the intentional and unintentional limitations to DCI authorities contained within the National Security Act of 1947. Intelligence community missions were simultaneously ill-defined and overlapping. Memories were fresh with too many lackluster or downright poor performances.

The left hand and the right hand of the national security establishment could not work together in providing timely battlefield intelligence to the commanders of the greatest army on earth during the first Gulf War. The interplay between the FBI and the CIA resembled more of a sandbox war than an integrated effort to counter threats to national security. The Ames spy scandal revealed just how rotten things were in the state of Denmark. When looked at on the whole, one saw not a community but a quagmire, and it was not unreasonable to question whether it would not just be better to start from scratch. The timing, it seemed, was perfect. A new age requires a new strategy that could capitalize on the innovations and the opportunities presented. It was the moment to take action: out with the old and in with the new.

Rationalization within the intelligence community was the stated goal. There was too much duplication of activities, unacceptable in the eyes of efficiency-minded reformers. With efficiency at the top of the agenda, no less than twenty-two groups—one presidential commission, one vice presidential review, a House committee, and fifteen task forces, umpteen investigations, and various draft legislation proposals—were founded by the reformers; an irony lost on few. While the scope of each differed in varying degrees, all were well-intentioned efforts to understand what existed, what was wrong and right with it, and to fix what should be fixed. These studies ultimately reached the same conclusions on the ills of the community.

The DCI could not manage his intelligence community effectively, because he could not move people or money to meet strategic goals, and his job—as structured—was too large for one man to do well. Those doing related tasks did not work together, share information, or challenge each other's assumptions. Personnel management practices across the intelligence community accentuated and reinforced stovepipes within agencies and disciplines, not only forbidding people to work and share, but making them not want to do so. While the reviews agreed on the problems, they did not agree on the solutions.

No consensus could be found. Because of this, the bold intentions to remake the community dwindled to relatively minor adjustments. The status quo was largely endorsed. The sense was that while the existing system was not perfect, the alternatives were not much better, and anyway, the performance of the intelligence community was not really *that* bad. The more dramatic changes in structure recommended in the studies would not be implemented. Redesigning the community would open bureaucratic internecine warfare, and the end results would not justify the blood on the ground. By the time the various groups passed their judgments, life moved on and the terrible failures and scandals of the 1980s and early 1990s had been reduced to history, losing the impact of their broad emotional appeal for radical change. Interests of the politicians and the bureaucrats would be better served by letting major reform initiatives pass away quietly—or so it was judged by Congress and the administration.

At the CIA, this meant that we would not be forced to address the core structural problems that made us dysfunctional. We contented ourselves with superficial reform, all process oriented, some useful, some debilitating—best called "bureaucratic tinkering." Meanwhile, reformers in Congress switched their focus to policy. How should the CIA spy? Should the CIA recruit agents with unsavory pasts? Should the CIA use U.S. journalist cover? Should the CIA conduct economic espionage? Should the CIA spy on its allies? If yes, under which conditions? Should the CIA be assigned in-house counterintelligence responsibilities? How should problem employees be identified and handled? Should the intelligence budget remain classified? The CIA wrote new guidelines (established new processes) for reporting to Congress, agent handling and reporting requirements, asset validation, human rights abuse review, sexual discrimination, Freedom of Information requests, and other issues, and set up new systems to implement the guidance.

Reforming the intelligence community was a priority for Deutch— at least at first. After seven months as DCI, he asked Congress for new powers. He wanted to be able to control people and resources within the community, not just inside the CIA. Deutch assessed that the intelligence community budget was wasteful and duplicative. The DCI has statutory authority to put together the National Foreign Intelligence Program, but has no say about the larger Tactical and Related Activities Program or the Joint Military Intelligence Program. Deutch wanted all three budgets to be under the control of the CIA director, so that if there was reprogramming of people and dollars after congressional approval, the DCI would also have a yea or nay. The proposed reforms would strengthen the DCI significantly, giving him control rather than mere "responsibility" over the intelligence community. Deutch later backed away from his proposals. Although he was strongly pro-military, future DCIs might not share the same interests, and the military might suffer a loss of power within the intelligence community as a result.

Deutch's past and his passion suited him to focus on intelligence community issues rather than managing the CIA. For Deutch, it meant focusing on rationalizing intelligence support to military operations and building dominant battlefield awareness through the provision of fused intelligence to military field commanders. Under Deutch, support to military operations would become a key intelligence requirement within the intelligence community to the extent that it became the CIA's highest priority for intelligence collection. Directorate of Operations engaged in major commitments in Bosnia, Kosovo, and elsewhere. In this quest, Deutch championed the creation of the National Imagery and Mapping Agency and placed it under the control of the Pentagon. He also supported a transition to smaller satellite systems, putting the nail in the coffin of Directorate of Science and Technology's role in satellite development, and making satellite R&D a complete National Reconnaissance Office road show.

Deutch changed the way intelligence support was provided to the military by the CIA by creating a new organizational element on the DCI staff. Deutch created the position of Associate Director of Central Intelligence for Military Support (ADCI/MS) and appointed a military officer to the position. When the military moved to expand human intelligence (HUMINT) operations overseas, Deutch championed the initiative rather than defend CIA turf. Through the Office of Military Affairs, the CIA played a role in refining the concept of National Intelligence Support Teams (NIST) as a new mechanism to provide intelligence support to U.S. forces deployed overseas. A National Intelligence Support Team is typically composed of personnel from the Defense Intelligence Agency, National Security Agency, National Imagery and Mapping Agency, and the CIA to provide a flow of timely all-sourced intelligence between a Joint Task Force in Washington and the battlefield during crises or contingency operations.

Despite Deutch's efforts, the intelligence community resisted greater DCI control because of the tradition of bureaucratic independence. The White House's lack of interest in the CIA and traditional intelligence issues further undercut CIA standing. In terms of budget and personnel cuts, the Agency was taking big hits, while other agencies, such as the FBI and the Defense Department, were on the ascendancy, their missions deemed more relevant. This was lost on few people.

ARLINGTON, VIRGINIA, 1995: The Pentagon grumbled loudly about the level of intelligence support it received during the 1991 Gulf War. The core issues were that imagery intelligence was not provided to the battlefield commanders in a timely fashion, and there was insufficient human intelligence reporting on what was happening on the ground. In assessing the post–Cold War national security requirements, one view was that the strategic threat from the Soviet Union would be supplanted by regional conflicts requiring U.S. military intervention in unstable areas around the globe. The Pentagon, a main proponent of this view, engaged in an effective bureaucratic initiative to gain more resources and capabilities in support of military operations. Weakened from the Ames scandal, budget cuts, and mission loss, the CIA opted to follow rather than challenge the Pentagon's lead.

To address the issue of insufficient human intelligence (HUMINT) reporting, in the early 1990s, the Pentagon put together a new program called the Defense HUMINT Service (DHS) to run covert intelligence operations overseas. The DHS program brought together the individual military services programs of Army, Navy, Air Force, and Marines into one central organization in the Defense Intelligence Agency. In 1995, Congress authorized the DHS to carry on commercial activities as cover for intelligence collection operations overseas, threatening to permit DHS to morph from a strictly military profile to one more like the CIA. Critics of the DHS program questioned the need for two clandestine human intelligence services, especially in the time of shrinking national security budgets. Many inside the CIA viewed the program as another potential deathblow to the Agency and a power move by the Defense Department to diminish the influence the CIA had on intelligence issues.

The CIA did put up a fight to maintain its role as the premier human intelligence agency. As the DCI's representative overseas, the chief of station is responsible for the conduct and coordination of all U.S. government intelligence and liaison activities relating in any way to espionage. After an intense bureaucratic struggle, the CIA maintained overall control by requiring military officers, when sent overseas as covert collectors, to report to the CIA chief of station, who has the authority to approve or disapprove all intelligence operations. Nationally, the CIA's deputy director of operations headed up the interagency group coordinating human intelligence activities, thus providing a modicum of control at the policy level.

As the program has developed, the collection priorities of DHS have been military-specific, complementing, for the most part, rather than duplicating CIA collection efforts. DHS officers have a difficult existence because they are stepchildren of two agencies. DHS is struggling inside the Defense Department to be recognized as a meritorious career track and thus lacks the attention, resources, and career development incentives to make it a truly capable clandestine human-collection enterprise. DHS officers deployed overseas must report through two different chains of command; one that controls their resources but is essentially disinterested in their mission (Defense Attaché) and one that is intensely interested in their activities but has no control of their resources (CIA).

An important element in the shift of power to the Defense Department was Deutch's leadership. Deutch had come to the CIA directly from the Pentagon, and he brought his inner circle with him. When Deutch was offered the DCI position, he accepted it only after President Clinton made it clear that he would not be offered the job as Secretary of Defense. It was widely believed that Deutch hoped to move from the CIA into the Defense job and therefore frequently took positions on policies as the DCI that were pro-military. CIA insiders believed Deutch was encouraging the shift of responsibilities to the Pentagon. Whether true or not, Deutch had enormous interests in military affairs and focused upon providing U.S. commanders with dominant battlefield awareness by better integrating satellite imagery, electronic intelligence, and human intelligence.

WASHINGTON, D.C., 1996: There was a bigger swagger in the walk of FBI director Freeh. He was winning the majority of the bureaucratic battles. The president endorsed the law enforcement approach in counterterrorism. Despite CIA objections, the FBI presence was growing overseas and taking the lead on many investigations. Freeh won a major battle when President Clinton decided to give the FBI the lead on the Khobar Tower bombing. Deutch objected, but did not prevail.

Conflicts between the FBI, the CIA, and the State Department were inevitable given the shift, and turf wars broke out over authorities and control. The CIA took umbrage over Legats (legal attachés) moving in on their contacts and not recognizing the CIA chief of station's authority over all intelligence activities overseas. The FBI clashed with the State Department, also on authorities, with it taking eight months to work out a memo of understanding on the relationship between the U.S. ambassadors and FBI agents overseas. The State Department was concerned that law enforcement activities would be undertaken without consideration of larger foreign policy issues. In certain cases, arrest and prosecution of a terrorist or drug trafficker might not be in the best overall interest of the United States. Ultimately, the State Department came out on top in the policy decision, but the battles over individual cases did not disappear. Sometimes the end result did not make very much sense.

JIFNA, WEST BANK, 1996: A notable example was the "reappearance" of the notorious terrorist Abu Abbas. Abu Abbas, a leader of the Palestine Liberation Front, masterminded the 1985 hijacking of the *Achille Lauro* cruise ship. U.S. citizen Leon Klinghoffer, a sixty-nine-year-old wheelchair-bound passenger, was executed during the operation, and his body was dumped in the water. International politics played into the hands of the terrorists, permitting Abu Abbas to evade prosecution in Italy. He took shelter with Saddam Hussein and stayed off the U.S. radar screen for almost a decade.

After the Oslo Accords were signed by Israel and the Palestine Liberation Organization (PLO) in 1993, a large number of expatriate Palestinians were allowed to return to the newly created Palestinian Authority in parts of the West Bank and Gaza Strip. Israel permitted Abu Abbas, who had renounced terrorism, to return. The Israeli agreement to grant amnesty to PLO members, who had been actively engaged in the liberation struggle, was part of a political package aimed at a historical reconciliation of the two peoples newly committed to live in peace, side by side. From the Israeli perspective, Abu Abbas was not the worst of the lot; at least he did not have Israeli blood on his hands.

Emboldened by the political agreement, Abu Abbas began traveling frequently from Baghdad to Amman and to the Palestinian Authority. At first there were rumors that he had been visiting Palestinian Authority officials discreetly. Then he began to be seen in public. The internal U.S. debate on what to do about Abu Abbas started after I found myself at a popular Palestinian restaurant in Jifna, seated at a table next to Abu Abbas. I joked with my lunch companion that it was too bad I did not have arrest powers, because the opportunity to bring him to justice was just too good.

I went back to the office and reported the incident, launching a fierce government debate on what to do about Abu Abbas. The FBI wanted to arrest him and the State Department advised against it, given the sensitive environment of the ongoing political negotiations. Achieving a final status agreement in the Palestinian-Israeli conflict was simply too important to jeopardize by the arrest of one terrorist. Support of the Palestinian security services was vital to maintain the security situation in the West Bank and Gaza Strip. The Palestinian security services were certain to oppose a U.S. rendition operation against Abu Abbas, who shared their credentials in the liberation struggle. Obviously, the issue was not important to the Israelis. If the Israeli government had a problem with Abu Abbas, they would either refuse him entry or arrest him at the Allenby Bridge when he crossed into the Palestinian Authority from Jordan.

Fresh in the diplomats' minds was the recent fiasco of Musa Abu Marzook, a Hamas political leader. In July 1995, the FBI and CIA rendered Abu Marzook in an elaborate operation of controlled domino deportations and refused entries, bringing him unwittingly without choice on a flight to New York City. Once in the United States, the FBI detained him for prosecution for funding terrorist groups. Five days after he was detained, Israel officially requested extradition. Abu Marzook stayed for two years in detention while the U.S. legal case against him floundered. At the time, the prosecutors did not have the laws to support a conviction against individuals providing material support to terrorist groups. Realizing that a U.S. court would not convict Abu Marzook, the Justice Department sought to have him extradited to Israel.

The Palestinian and Arab street became inflamed over the prospect of the United States, which claimed to be a neutral mediator in the conflict, "taking sides." There were street demonstrations and official protests against the United States, raising concerns that U.S. officials would become targets of violence if the extradition took place. In August 1995, the State Department was concerned enough about the growing anti-American feelings that it issued a travel warning to American citizens because of potential violence as a result of the detention of Abu Marzook. Ultimately, a deal was worked out whereby Israel withdrew its extradition request and the United States deported Abu Marzook to Jordan.*

---

* The story of Abu Marzook is a long one that is still in play. When he was deported from the United States, he agreed to give up his legal permanent-resident status. He lived in Amman for a time before being deported, along with rest of the Hamas external leadership, to Syria. After the September 11 attacks, Abu Marzook was indicted in Texas under the Patriot Act for funding terrorism.

The diplomats had no desire to repeat this incident and put pressure upon the Justice Department to prove in advance that it had sufficient evidence to convict Abu Abbas. With politics at play, the Justice Department decided it did not.* The legal action was dropped; thankfully, the government decision did not result in additional deaths of Americans. This was not always the case.

DOHA, QATAR, 1995: Sometimes a small intelligence break is all that is needed. In this case, a tidbit received late in the year revealed the location of wanted terrorist Khalid Shaykh Muhammad. Muhammad had been indicted in the United States for his involvement with Ramzi Yousef in the Bojinka Project, a botched terror operation in the Philippines. Yousef had recently been caught in Pakistan and the U.S. Justice Department was putting together the case against him. Apprehending Muhammad would be useful for the prosecution—plus there were lots of loose ends that needed to be tied. Yousef's trial would begin the following spring. Time was short.

U.S. intelligence discovered that Muhammad was living in Doha, Qatar. In the early and mid-1990s, certain Qatari officials were known for their sympathies for Islamic extremists, providing many safe havens, and funding Islamic charities, such as Human Appeal International, that were connected to terrorist groups. We began an operation to positively identify Muhammad as being the Muhammad described in the arrest warrant with the intent to render him to the United States for prosecution. However, when the FBI was briefed, the Legat based in Rome moved in and tried to take over the operation without concern for CIA equities on the ground or Qatari political tendencies.

The Legat wanted to conduct an open investigation, questioning the Qataris about Muhammad. He had a criminal investigation to pursue. I was concerned that because of sympathies for Islamic extremists, Muhammad would be warned off by Qatari officials and would flee. I cautioned strongly against the direct approach, instead proposing a snatch operation, luring Muhammad out of Qatar and interdicting him as he traveled. The FBI would still get their man. But the FBI was in a

---

* The second chapter on bringing Abu Abbas to justice closed. The third and final chapter came to a close after Abu Abbas was captured in Iraq in April 2003 during the war. While in U.S. custody, the legal eagles debated the validity of the Oslo Accords amnesty and its applicability to the United States. The debate was abruptly brought to an end when Abu Abbas died in custody, reportedly from a heart attack.

hurry, wanted to control the case and wanted to do it the "FBI way." It was pure vinegar and water when it came to the FBI special agent and me, with disastrous results.

Policymakers gave the nod to the FBI, and my assessment proved accurate. After formally requesting Qatari assistance in a handover, the Qatari government stalled on responding. Muhammad disappeared immediately after the request to the Qatari government was made. It was immediately obvious to me what had happened. There was no point in sticking around any longer; the operation was over. So I left.

When my husband picked me up at the airport, I was unusually glum. I usually did not share the details of my work with him, more out of ingrained security practices than anything else. However, this time I did. I told him that I just lost a key battle to bring a terrorist to justice. The battle was lost because of a turf battle with the FBI. How would I ever explain that to the American people? I could see myself sitting before Congress, testifying to a job not well done.

Subsequent to the failed arrest, the CIA determined that Muhammad was part of the al-Qa'ida network. His key al-Qa'ida role was not suspected until after the September 11 attacks. In March 2003, Muhammad was captured by Pakistani authorities and handed over to the United States. If Muhammad had been captured in 1996, a key player with ideas of using multiple aircraft in terrorist attacks would not have assumed a key leadership position in al-Qa'ida, possibly rewriting history.

WHITE HOUSE, WASHINGTON, D.C., 1995-96: The Clinton administration could not completely ignore foreign policy, but it was relegated to the back burner during the first four years, and "managed" when issues flared. Clinton's approach was ad hoc and, as a consequence, policies did not have deep roots of support, by either Clinton or his foreign policy team. When foreign policy initiatives backfired and became a source of criticism for the White House, the Clinton administration responses became increasingly risk averse.

In the mid to late 1990s, the threshold for risk taking dropped steadily in the National Security Council. CIA senior management opted to submit more operations for approval as the tolerance for flaps fell. Individual operations that would have been approved by the Seventh Floor in the 1980s were sent to the National Security Council for approval in the 1990s. When operations were not approved, which was frequent, it allowed CIA senior management wiggle room to pass the blame along to the National Security Council, saying that the CIA was willing to take risks, but not the politicos. In reality, risk aversion was pervasive throughout the Agency, in CIA senior management and in the administration.

For example, in early 1996, around the time of the shocking Dizengoff bombing in Tel Aviv, the Directorate of Operations was working against Palestinian extremists responsible for the string of suicide bombings in Israel and the Occupied Territories. One particular operation against a bomb maker was risky for a number of reasons and therefore was bumped up the chain of command, all the way to the Seventh Floor. The Seventh Floor, suffering from risk aversion, decided to send the proposal to the National Security Council.

The National Security Council proceeded to ask a stream of questions, being concerned that the bomb maker could be a U.S. person, or could be surrounded by U.S. persons, who would unwittingly become part of the operation. (The CIA is prohibited from using unwitting Americans operationally.) The National Security Council was also concerned what would happen to the bomb maker after detention. Would he be subject to extrajudicial execution or given a fair trial? If the bomb maker was killed in the process of being arrested, what was the likelihood of collateral deaths, and of the deaths of American citizens? The CIA and National Security Council went back and forth on these and other issues, with the CIA not being able to give definitive answers and guarantees to the National Security Council. Meanwhile, time passed, and the operational access to the bomb maker was lost.

The risk of doing something seemed greater to the politicians than the risk of doing nothing, regardless of the fact that this bomb maker was directly involved in terrorist operations that had killed Americans, Israelis, and Palestinians. The bomb maker would continue to run free for years, orchestrating more terrorist operations before the Israelis would take unilateral action, going after him in a "targeted killing" operation during the al-Aqsa Intifada. At the time of the CIA operational planning, the field chief who proposed the operation drafted a cable to Headquarters titled "Donovan Weeps," decrying the current state of inaction and risk aversion that would shame the CIA's founding father, Wild Bill Donovan.

Apparently the cable fell upon deaf ears.

21
The CIA Bites Back

SEVENTH FLOOR, LANGLEY, VIRGINIA, 1996: Deutch and almost all of his senior management left the Agency in December. His departure had been much anticipated, with the rumor mill reporting in August 1996 that he would depart at the end of the year. Deutch had his eye on the top job at the Pentagon. He was banking on being named to it by Clinton, and made it easy by being immediately available. His good friend Secretary of Defense William Perry was leaving the job that Deutch coveted so desperately. Deutch was certain it was his for the taking, having faithfully served as directed at the CIA. Deutch had carried out his tasking; he had ridden and tamed the tiger. He had made significant achievements during his nineteen months as DCI. He had cleaned house and restored the CIA's credibility with Congress and the White House. Indeed, the only complaint Congress voiced during his final hearing as DCI was that he was leaving too soon. He had worked closely with congressional oversight committees, in concert with them, not in conflict. He kept a low profile and tried hard to keep the CIA out of Clinton's in-box. He had done more than a good job. But, alas, it was not to be.

Deutch was disappointed on more fronts than one. Not only would he not win the president's nomination to the position of Secretary of Defense, but the tiger turned out not to be tamed. It bit him as he went out the door.

In August 1999, DCI Tenet suspended Deutch's security clearances for improper handling of classified information. In the Old CIA, there never would have been an investigation. DCIs were never held accountable for their actions, either while serving or in retirement. However, this target was just too good. The old boys could not let it go. Mr. Accountability would get a taste of his own medicine. Deutch's efforts to make peace with the Directorate of Operations, by later awarding medals to people he had fired, won him little goodwill. There was too much baggage in the relationship for small amends to bear much weight.

The payback started with the simple discovery of highly classified information on Deutch's computer at home several days after he had stepped down as DCI. According to the CIA inspector general's report, the information was related to covert action, top-secret communications intelligence, and the National Reconnaissance Program budget. It was a breach of security, but certainly not the first or the last time classified materials had been handled improperly by a senior government official.* The security violation was quietly reported to the CIA's Office of General Counsel—the functional equivalent to DCI's professional legal office. It was not reported to the Justice Department or the intelligence oversight committees as it would have been had a working-level CIA officer done the same thing. The rumor mill caught a whiff of the story when Office of Security officials began to complain that no action was being taken. E-mails began to fly. Slatkin tried to bury the issue by drowning the investigation with unending questions disguised as tasking. But e-mails continued to fly, many accusing Slatkin of trying to cover up the incident. When Deutch refused to be interviewed, a complaint was made to the CIA inspector general, who was "forced" to investigate.

The inspector general found that normal procedures had been violated during the initial investigation by those who did not wish to take action against Deutch. Eventually, Deutch admitted publicly that he had erred and that he respected Tenet's decision to suspend his CIA clearances. The real irony was that Deutch had declined to hold his predecessors accountable when he was meting out punishment for wrongdoing—Deutch considered accountability only a downward process. Acting DCI Tenet, the ultimate old boy, decided that in this

---

* For example, former U.S. Ambassador to Israel Martin Indyk had his security clearances suspended pending investigation of his mishandling of classified information. His clearances were restored, not because he was cleared of the charges, but because the peace process was taking a nosedive and he was needed back at post.

case, he (Tenet) was better served letting Deutch take the hit. The old boys had the last word.*

★ ★ ★ ★

Deutch arrived with a battle cry of reform. During his nineteen-month tenure, he would dramatically alter the way the CIA conducted its business. He introduced new limits on operational practices, transferred authority from the field to Headquarters, changed collection priorities and the CIA relationship with Congress. After operational flaps such as the Nicholson spy case, Guatemala, and the Paris Flap, CIA personnel and assets were scrubbed, with those not meeting the new and politically correct standards being terminated.

As the risk threshold in Washington policymaking circles dropped, the CIA view of risk taking switched from positive to negative. Operational activity slowed as the CIA focused on tearing up its innards rather than meeting its mission. Turf and policy battles with the FBI and State abounded, with the net effect of letting terrorists such as Khalid Shaykh Muhammad and Abu Abbas run free. Demoralized and demonized, CIA officers continued to jump ship and give exit interviews to the press on just how rotten the situation was.

Inside the embattled organization, those who stayed continued to believe in our sworn duty to protect national security. We worked long hours at low wages. The decade brought many intelligence successes, which fed our will to continue and a sense that our personal sacrifices were indeed worth it. I would be spurred along by participating in some incredible operations against Iranians, Arabs, Russians, North Koreans, and terrorists, the details of which I will remember forever but carry silently to my grave. It was still possible to see the impact of my work. I stole secrets and ran operations that saved lives and bolstered the security of the nation. The U.S. president read raw intelligence reports that I wrote and made decisions based upon these and other CIA intelligence reports. I found my work personally satisfying. Because I believed, I took risks. My colleagues took risks. I would survive the bureaucracy—but only for a few more years.

The CIA was not the only agency in transition. With great gusto, a

---

* When the Justice Department was poised to bring criminal charges against Deutch for improper handling of classified information, President Clinton granted Deutch a pardon. Just one more footnote to a broken accountability system!

presidential commission and congressional committee dove into the topic of intelligence community reform. Both recommended grand schemes for rationalizing the community, making it more efficient, smaller, and well-tooled for new requirements of the post–Cold War world. However, the recommended a redesign of the intelligence community would open bureaucratic internecine warfare, and at the end of the day, the administration and Congress judged the end result would not be worth the bloodbath. Instead of reengineering, bureaucratic tinkering prevailed.

While Washington focused on process and form, Usama bin Ladin's movement blossomed, spreading his *jihadi* ideology around the globe. The CIA was watching, but was slow to understand and react to this new phenomenon. Egyptian, Lebanese, and Iranian extremists remained the focal point, with bin Ladin being noticed just on the periphery. Al-Qa'ida's role in two attacks on Americans in Saudi Arabia was missed, as was the earlier attack in Somalia.

It took an al-Qa'ida defector to start to change the CIA's assessment of bin Ladin. Once upgraded from financer to terrorist mastermind, the CIA concentrated capabilities against bin Ladin, opening a special single-issue targeting station bearing his name. Although the issue station broke with tradition in order to work outside the box, the CIA proved itself unable to think outside the box, dangerously underestimating the force and appeal of this Islamic extremist ideology.[1]

PART

6

THE TENET YEARS
(JULY 11, 1997–JULY 11, 2004)

"If, in this new era, you confirm me as Director of Central Intelligence, you are not hiring me to observe and comment; you will be hiring me to warn and protect."

GEORGE TENET
Confirmation hearing, 1997

22
A Pleasant Surprise

SEVENTH FLOOR, LANGLEY, VIRGINIA, 1997: The confirmation of George Tenet as the next DCI was a surprise, a pleasant one. He had been at the CIA for twenty-two months as DDCI and for seven months as acting DCI. The Agency liked his style and his vision. We were glad to have him as DDCI, but were expecting the arrival of Anthony Lake, President Clinton's first choice, as Deutch's replacement. Lake's nomination crashed and burned because of partisan politics and Lake's involvement in controversial policies—especially giving the wink and nod to the Iranians to funnel arms to Bosnian Muslims, who were being massacred by well-armed Serbian forces intent upon wiping them off the face of the earth.

Even though on the National Security Council and tainted by the Bosnian arms "scandal," Tenet had not made a string of enemies on the Hill as Lake had done. Tenet was politically astute, building bridges through expanding networks and seldom burning any for a short-term gain. The fact that he spent seven years on the staff of the Senate Select Committee on Intelligence and was well known to most of the senators did not hurt either. He was an insider's insider. His confirmation hearing was a love feast. Tenet was broadly liked and respected by Congress, and was described by Senate Intelligence Chairman Richard C. Shelby as a "man of integrity and professionalism." While Shelby showered Tenet with praise at the time of his confirmation as DCI in July 1997, he would soon turn into Tenet's loudest congressional critic.

In his confirmation testimony to the Senate Select Committee on Intelligence, Tenet signaled his intent to change the CIA and intelligence community focus back to the core mission of keeping the nation safe. He said, "Stated simply, our mission is to ensure that the nation's leaders have the time and information they need to avert imminent danger, and, when it cannot be averted, the wherewithal to prevail." He wanted to tackle the problems within the intelligence community "at their roots in a systematic, comprehensive and strategic way, rather than one piece at a time."[1]

Tenet described his leadership style as straightforward: "people come first." Intelligence is primarily a human endeavor despite the use of sophisticated technology. He wanted to improve the capabilities of the workforce by focusing resources on better training, development of foreign language skills, and state-of-the-art technical skills. He wanted to deepen analytical expertise in all fields and reach out to specialists in universities and think tanks who could help fill critical gaps or bridge shortages. He identified his highest goal as "to assure that our people consistently are, and are recognized as, the nation's premier experts in their fields."[2]

In comparing Tenet's 1997 speech to his 1995 DDCI confirmation hearing statement, the shift in priorities was startling. In 1995, Tenet talked about reengineering the structure of the intelligence community, while in 1997 he focused on leading the community toward closer teamwork across the board. As the DDCI candidate, he talked about upon improving accountability, training, and awareness for counterintelligence. As the DCI-select, he talked about demanding the highest standards of personal integrity and professional performance, being independent and forthright, and taking risks to achieve mission. In 1995, Tenet said that the CIA Directorate of Operations must be revitalized, implying publicly that it was broken. In 1997, he did not single out problems in the Directorate of Operations, but instead highlighted the challenge of the mission. He said it was time to put aside the issue of whether there remained an intelligence mission, and focus on the more urgent question: "How can we ensure that our nation's intelligence capabilities are right for the twenty-first century?"[3]

The CIA liked Tenet immediately because he was focused on core issues: collecting, analyzing, and disseminating intelligence. In one of his early speeches as DCI to CIA employees, he stated clearly that the unending reform process had to come to an end. The CIA needed to put its energies into mission achievement and stop beating itself up over past wrongdoing. It was time to move on. Tenet had a clear vision on how and where the Agency was to move. Tenet was one of the principal drafters of the PDD-35 intelligence collection requirements while

he was at the National Security Council. Although these were introduced to the CIA when Tenet became DDCI, they became the mantra
under his leadership. According to Tenet, "Rather than doing more
with less, U.S. intelligence must do more of the more important."[4]
The problem with the approach would become apparent only a few
years later, when the definition of "more important" became what was
easily doable rather than what was a must-do.

That was another difference. Tenet was a leader of people, not a manager of bureaucracy. When he addressed the assembled masses in the
Bubble, you felt as if he was talking directly to you, whether you were
in the same room or watching him over the CIA network. He was clear
in articulating his expectations, sharing his vision, getting the troops on
board. While Deutch achieved much in his short tenure, he totally failed
to win the confidence of the troops. Therefore, every initiative of his was
resisted for one reason or another. Tenet was the kind of leader you
would follow out of the foxhole because you felt that he was really sure-
footed and loyal to his troops.

He liked to mingle with his officers and initially did not isolate himself on the Seventh Floor. At lunchtime, he occasionally ate in the
cafeteria with everyone else. He did not bring his senior managers along
for company, but chose a small table for himself. He would bring something to work on, such as draft testimony. Officers would walk past him
and greet him if he looked up, but not disturb him otherwise. He projected the image of someone wanting to be considered part of the larger
whole, a member of the team, not the isolated supreme leader. On road
trips, he would make a point to spend time with the more junior officers. After late-night meetings, when station officers were hanging
around the control room discussing final plans for the next day's
movements, Tenet would join the crowd, shoes kicked off, tie gone, a
cold beer in hand. He remembered officers' names and engaged them
in substantive issues on the matter at hand or larger ones facing the
Agency. Tenet demanded excellence but had that special way of bringing it out of his officers. When officers failed, he told them so. There
was never any question about where you stood with him. I greatly
respected Tenet for his leadership style and his focus on substance.

Tenet brought continuity of leadership to the CIA. The CIA had had
five directors in six years. That is a lot of change at the top. Change at
the top meant chaos at the bottom. Approved programs were disap-
proved overnight. Rules changed and then changed again. Tenet
brought an end to the turbulent first half of the decade by bringing stability in the second half. That is not to say that there were not changes;

there were, many significant in nature. The difference is that the changes were proposed, discussed, approved, implemented, and then tweaked. Gone was the reform whiplash caused by shifting vision. The period of drift was over and the new course was firmly set. The Agency was on an even keel, or so it felt.

DERA GHAZI KHAN, PAKISTAN, 1997: On June 17, the FBI arrested Mir Aimal Kansi in a cheap boardinghouse in the middle-of-nowhere, Pakistan, after a four-year hunt. He had been lured there by Afghan agents desirous of a cool $2 million bounty. In the joint statement by FBI Deputy Director William J. Esposito and Acting CIA Director Tenet, Esposito said, "The success of this investigation is primarily due to the dedication of the men and women of the CIA and FBI, as well as our partners in the State Department, who brought their skills to bear and successfully coordinated their efforts to make this arrest possible in the face of often overwhelming difficulties."[5]

This was no understatement. It was a tough operation; it required sustained support and a willingness to take risks. The New CIA suffered from the bureaucratic expectations of immediate results. The gains have to be immediate if the risks are to be weathered. Perhaps it was because the issue was so personal. Kansi had killed CIA officers on the Agency doorstep. CIA management in this case was willing to take the political heat of risky operations and have the bureaucratic patience to see the operation through from start to finish. It was proof that operations officers could still run operations even in a risk-averse environment. However, September 11, 2001, would show that they just couldn't do it enough. But for the moment, in those days just before Tenet's confirmation, the arrest was a much-needed success for the CIA and a shot in the arm for the Directorate of Operations. The look on Tenet's face when he announced the arrest to the workforce said it all. He beamed with pride.

OLD HEADQUARTERS BUILDING, LANGLEY, VIRGINIA, 1997: Tenet had a lot of repair work to do within the Agency once he took control. From his time as DDCI and acting DCI, he had a good idea of what was broken. He understood that Deutch's largest failing was that he had neglected the people of the CIA. A demoralized force could not be expected to produce at the level he expected. He took immediate action.

Like the much-revered DCI Richard Helms, Tenet forged an effective relationship with the Directorate of Operations as DDCI and expanded it as DCI. One of Tenet's first actions as DCI was the appointment of a legendary operations officer as Deputy Director of Operations. Tenet asked Jack Downing to come out of retirement to run the very troubled directorate. Morale was low. Operational activity was low. By appointing one of their own, Tenet signaled his respect and confidence in the directorate. It was a good start that was followed by many other initiatives that were well received.

Unlike his immediate predecessors, Tenet was not afraid of covert action. He just felt that covert action should "never stand alone, it should never be the last resort of a failed policy," as he put it in his confirmation hearing. While the number of covert action programs increased in quantity and scope during his early years, the programs were designed to minimize risk and to be well integrated in larger political programs. Most fell in the category of overt covert action and were to varying degrees controversial domestically.

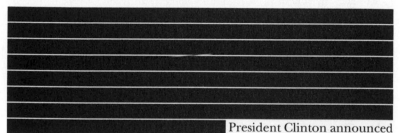

President Clinton announced at the Sharm el-Shaykh antiterrorism summit in March 1996 that the United States would provide resources to professionalize the Palestinian Authority security services to help them fight against terror emanating from inside the territories under their control. The United States would also provide additional intelligence and technical assistance to the Israelis.

agreements and agreements reached during trilateral security meetings. Playing the umpire, we mediated disputes around the table. As with everything, personalities and history play a role. The Palestinian terrorist/freedom fighter sat at the same table with his Shin Bet torturer/interrogator, sparring over the past, present, and future. Focused on security and security alone, we tried to forge a level of cooperation on the ground, separate from the political fray taking place between Ramallah and Tel Aviv.

The highly visible role of the CIA during political negotiations stirred a small storm within U.S. policy circles and in the U.S. press. Tenet's frequent visits to Israel and the Palestinian Authority, coupled with his presence at all the key Middle East Peace Process summits, opened a debate on whether the CIA was exceeding its mandate by crossing into policymaking. Indeed, security issues had become such an integral part of the Middle East Peace Process discussions that the line between security and political issues became blurred. It was argued at the time that the CIA had credibility with both the Israelis and the Palestinians, credibility that the State Department lacked.

Both the Israeli government and the Palestinian Authority frequently leaked information on CIA activities to suit their own political agendas. The local news was full of stories of secret trilateral security meetings or the lack thereof, of secret CIA training programs, and even secret CIA assessments on security agreement compliance and noncompliance.

The CIA field chief was "outed" when his name appeared in the local press, leading to a long debate on whether he needed to be recalled for his personal safety. Even a description of me (a flattering one, I must say) appeared, albeit without giving my name. Some of the stories were true, much was false, all of it unwelcomed by the CIA. We prefer to live and operate in the shadows.

With the outbreak of the al-Aqsa Intifada in September 2000, that phase of the covert action program effectively came to an end. The program could not stop the crisis caused by a failed political process. The renewed hostilities spelled failure for the Oslo peace process and the related covert action program. Watching five years of backbreaking work come unraveled once the Intifada started was one of the saddest parts of my career.

INDIA, 1998: While Tenet was getting the Directorate of Operations back to work, crisis was brewing on the other side of the house. In May 1998, India conducted a nuclear test, catching the intelligence community and policymakers by surprise. Deemed an intelligence failure and a failure of U.S. nuclear deterrence policy, the crisis was Tenet's first major test as DCI. CIA analysts assessed the situation, but assessed it 180 degrees wrong. The analysts predicted there would be no testing at that juncture. Tenet appointed an independent review board, named the Jeremiah Commission, to investigate. The Commission found poor analytical tradecraft of the worst kind, resulting in groupthink and mirror imaging. But there was much more to the story.

According to Mary Nayak, a former CIA analyst who worked on the Indian account at the time, the intelligence failure was caused by a complex set of factors. Speaking at the Eisenhower Series Conference in September 2003, Nayak stated that the CIA and the intelligence community were the victims of Indian denial and deception activities. The CIA knew that India had the capabilities and intentions to conduct a nuclear test. Long before 1998, the CIA had given the strategic warning to policymakers.

In the 1990s, the ascendant, extreme right-wing Hindu chauvinist Bharatiya Janata Party (BJP) became upset at the U.S. double standard for the nuclear club. It did not accept the policy of keeping out new members. The CIA assessed that if the BJP came to power, it would abandon the ambiguity surrounding the Indian program either by declaring India a nuclear state or by testing as a deterrent. The BJP won the national elections in February 1998. This should have been a red flag. In addition, BJP statements before the test indicated that India was seeking a strategic defense capability. This should have been another red flag.

However, Indian diplomacy was involved in an elaborate denial and deception campaign. The red flags were dismissed in light of arguments that appeared to have more weight—specifically, more political weight.

According to Nayak, there was a policy conflict that influenced analytical assessments. The United States was worried that India would test and trigger a regional nuclear arms race. The Clinton administration was confident that it could stop India. In late 1997, Clinton announced a new strategy of making India a linchpin for relations in the region, and initiated a strategic dialogue with India. He planned a state visit to India, and was putting together an economic and political package that the United States thought would deter India from muddying the waters by proceeding with testing. The assumption of the U.S. policymakers was not challenged by the intelligence community.

The reality was that the BJP felt it could have the political and economic benefits and finesse around the nuclear problem. Privately, Indian leaders told the United States that there would be no major steps in the nuclear program before a national security advisory board was set up. The United States saw India as receptive to the U.S. policy line. Indian diplomats engaged in a denial and deception program to squelch the perception that India might test. Statements played down the need and immediacy of testing. After each U.S. demarche, India improved its denial and deception activities. It took advantage of satellite coverage gaps and used shifting sands to cover up tracks at testing sites. There has been much made of then–Ambassador Frank Wisner showing imagery conclusively proving that India was preparing for testing in 1995; in fact a *New York Times* article had already exposed the fact that the United States was monitoring Indian testing sites by satellite. Because of the press leak, India learned to bury its cables.

After the fact, the Indian government told the United States that it was impossible for India to debate, discuss, and then test—hence the deception.

Why did the intelligence failure happen? According to Nayak, there were resource shortfalls and analytical shortfalls. Inadequate HUMINT and SIGINT made it hard to obtain inner-circle intelligence. Only a handful of Indians knew; the Indian president (who doesn't have the same powers as the U.S. president) was told only the day before the test. The Directorate of Operations did not have well-placed sources within the Indian nuclear or political establishments. Accusations that analysts did not consider a test are inaccurate; after the Pakistan missile test, the CIA considered the likelihood. Analysts had very little grist. According to Nayak, there was only diplomatic reporting and imagery. Imagery resources were also scarce, drawn off in support to military operations in Iraq and the Balkans. Imagery was taken only every three days, and many of the sites were later determined to be missile sites, not nuclear-testing sites.

The lack of information—was it denial and deception, or was it a true indicator that nothing was happening? The scarcity of intelligence put the onus on analysts to make their best call. Some thought the BJP wanted to test, and there was a technical need to test at that point in the program. Some argued that the BJP was pragmatic and that their statements before and during the elections were electioneering. India was a friend, which clouded the record. Open source information, often argued as clearly indicating there would be a test, was in fact ambiguous. India admitted after the fact that the Pakistani missile test was the deciding factor. According to Nayak, the CIA assessment did not give enough weight to the Pakistani missile test.

Senator Shelby called it a colossal failure. The Jeremiah Commission did not think it huge, but significant. The missed call torpedoed U.S. efforts to cap the spread of nuclear weapons. If policymakers had been warned, Nayak assessed, there was a chance India could have been persuaded to stop—especially if there had been presidential attention. The United States could have drawn upon the support of such allies as Japan. The relationship with Japan was crucial to the Indian economy. Furthermore, if testing had been made a topic of debate within the Indian coalition government, the other fourteen parties would have delayed—if not stopped—the testing. Indeed, some analysts thought that the decision to test then was because the coalition partners were still in disarray. The what-ifs did not change the reality that the CIA missed the call. Tenet was on the hot seat, and he used the occasion expertly to get what he wanted.[6]

SEVENTH FLOOR, LANGLEY, VIRGINIA, 1998: Tenet had been warning Congress for a year that collection and analytical capabilities were severely eroded, and he needed more and better people, more money, and more authority over community activities. The failure to predict the Indian nuclear test finally captured congressional attention. In 1998, Tenet began to get a portion of what he asked for in the first two areas; the last request—more authority—would remain unfulfilled until after September 11, 2001.

In May, before the Indian nuclear test, Tenet announced the DCI's Strategic Initiative to the CIA workforce. He stated that the primary goal was the strengthening of the two most fundamental capabilities of the CIA: clandestine collection and all-source analysis. The initiative included rebuilding field strength and increasing the tooth-to-tail ratio that had eroded since the beginning of the decade. He planned to increase the number of operations officers (the core field collection), increase the number of stations and bases, and augment existing stations.

Tenet planned to improve analytical tradecraft through training, rotational assignments, and outside interaction. As part of the Strategic Initiative, the new Sherman Kent School for Intelligence Analysis would open in 2000. In addition to training the next generation of analysts, the Kent School offered courses on managing and teaching analysis and an intelligence manager's seminar series, all geared to expand the skills of the current analytical corps. The Kent School also has academic outreach and intelligence-analysis studies programs to establish and expand links to resources outside the CIA.

Tenet's focus on core issues, coupled with a meaningful strategic vision, went a long way to turn the CIA around. Tenet had effectively fought the bureaucratic battle and had won more resources for two of the four directorates. The switch from downsizing and resource cuts to modest increases was duly noted by the workforce. Management practices continued to be the source of criticism, but Tenet was judged good for the Agency. While there continued to be significant intelligence failures under Tenet—such as the 1999 accidental bombing of the Chinese embassy in Belgrade, which resulted in three deaths, twenty-seven wounded, and a huge diplomatic snafu—there was a sense within the organization that a corner was turned in 1998.

The worst of the bad times were over, and the CIA was focused on the mission at hand and the future security of the U.S. government. For a change, the FBI was getting most of the bad press, not the Directorate of Operations. The CIA's image was improving among the new generation, which saw the Directorate of Operations as cool versus inherently evil. Jobs with the Clandestine Service ranked top billing in the *cooljobs.com* Internet job bank that caters to new college graduates. Life was looking up for most—but not all—Agency officers.

OLD HEADQUARTERS BUILDING, LANGLEY, VIRGINIA, 1999: By the late 1990s there was discussion on whether the Directorate of Science and Technology would survive. The directorate was only a marginal part of the strategic plan that Tenet introduced in the spring of 1998, which was focused on the operations and intelligence directorates. Tenet viewed the Directorate of Science and Technology as merely a tool to aid collection and analytical needs. Senior CIA management simply lacked vision on technology development and the critical role it could play in creating new means of collection. After the directorate's chief departed in September 1998, Tenet was slow to appoint a new deputy director. It was as if science and technology were nowhere on Tenet's priority list. When Tenet finally selected a new chief, it turned out to be a poor choice; Gary Smith lasted only nine months, leaving in January 2000. Morale plummeted.

Tenet was not ignoring the directorate, but was thinking outside the box on how to turn it into an arm that he felt useful to the business of intelligence. Rather than run a full in-house R&D program, Tenet authorized the directorate to create a technology-incubation organization, In-Q-Tel, to serve as an information technology (IT) portal from the private sector to the intelligence community. The CIA was significantly behind the curve in the area of IT. The IT industry was growing rapidly, with a large number of start-up firms pushing the edge of technology in interesting and potentially useful ways for the intelligence business. Given the high salaries start-ups were paying IT professionals, the directorate was unable to compete with the private sector in hiring the best and the brightest. So rather than compete, it decided to piggyback.

With initial funding of $28.5 million in CIA funds, the venture focused on building productive relationships with small firms involved in IT innovation. In-Q-Tel concentrated on technologies that integrate Internet technology and applications into intelligence work, that develop new security and privacy technologies, that nurture data-mining technologies to take better advantage of the CIA's vast storehouses of records, and that modernize the CIA's computer systems.

Through In-Q-Tel and other in-house programs, the directorate began developing tools to manage the volume problem. One computer tool, Oasis, converted audio signals from television and radio broadcasts into text, so that the information could be fused into searchable databases. Oasis, which was designed for English-language broadcasts, is being developed for other criteria languages, such as Arabic and Chinese. Furthermore, voice-recognition technology allowed the text to be labeled automatically.[7] This technology met current requirements for Foreign Broadcast Information Services, which was interested in capturing broadcasts by Usama bin Ladin, for example. Another computer tool, FLUENT, enabled a user to conduct computer searches of documents that were in a language that the user did not understand. Data-mining tools extracted and indexed all words. High-accuracy translation tools were developed to make up for the dearth of cleared translators in the CIA.

In-Q-Tel's start was risky. It opened its doors just as the IT bubble burst, with start-ups failing in rapid succession and venture-capital funds bailing out of the IT market as investors realized disappointing growth. By the end of 2001, In-Q-Tel reviewed nine hundred business plans, funded twenty-three companies and R&D projects, and introduced five technologies into the CIA.[8] While these numbers were impressive, the venture was not an immediate success. According to a review conducted by Business Executives for National Security in the first half of 2001, the CIA was slow to adopt the new technologies, due to cultural and bureaucratic obstacles. The review cited a 136-step review process by six different boards that was required before new hardware or software could be installed on CIA networks.[9] Without the technology being integrated into the CIA and used at the working level, it was clear that In-Q-Tel was having difficulty in achieving its primary mission. The same old obstacles cropped up: bureaucracy, stovepipes, and security-induced paralysis.

23
War on Terrorism

WHITE HOUSE, WASHINGTON, D.C., 1997: Politics of national security are a high-wire game. The winners assess the environment accurately and make it to safety. The losers catch the ill-fated wind and fall to their end. The CIA operates within this context and therefore has developed acumen for political survival. The political environment largely defines what the CIA can and cannot do. DCIs must gauge the willingness and capacity of the political leadership—that is, the president—to accept intelligence flaps as a cost of doing business. If the president places a premium on the capabilities of the CIA to deliver high-impact results, the DCI will be more willing to authorize risky operations and be confident that the president will accept blowback from failed ventures. If the president has little regard for the intelligence business, the potential-gains assessment will be low and the risk threshold even lower. The DCI will clear more operations with the political leadership to make sure that the CIA operates within acceptable (in other words, more limited) perimeters.

The Clinton administration, which was in the White House for most of the 1990s, was uninterested in intelligence and wary of the CIA. It was seen as an agency that was potentially dangerous to the White House and needed to be controlled tightly, kept on a very short leash. Other agencies, such as the Defense Department and the FBI, were viewed as more competent, more trustworthy, and more relevant and therefore were empowered at the expense of the CIA. As the Clinton administration stumbled in foreign policy initiatives and became increasingly cautious, it became less willing to authorize the CIA to take calculated risks. In effect, the CIA became the White House's policy tool of last resort.

Despite Clinton's lack of interest in intelligence matters, Tenet developed a solid relationship with him, breaking the mold of the previously established patterns. He had access to the White House and was included in key policymaking groups. The CIA was in Clinton's in-box— not because of scandals or wrongdoing, but in the form of intelligence briefs written in the way that Clinton liked his information. Tenet was nothing, if not a quick study. He understood that the president was risk averse on foreign policy issues and therefore kept CIA activities within Clinton's comfort zone. Tenet was diligent at highlighting the risks of certain kinds of activities—such as political blowback if field operatives are caught with their hands in cookie jars belonging to supposed allies, or potential retaliation against U.S. government officials by al-Qa'ida in response to rendition operations—so that Clinton would not be surprised. If Clinton did not like the risk factor, the CIA would not take the action, or would change course in midstream. With Clinton, Tenet acted more like a staffer than an advisor, allowing politics to trump substantive intelligence issues.

As their relationship developed, Clinton gained confidence in Tenet as a negotiator and presidential "hammer." Tenet assumed a very public role, quite unusual for a DCI, in the Middle East Peace Process. The political overtones were obvious to all. Tenet was televised at the president's right hand during important summits, causing an outcry on whether the CIA was exceeding its brief. Surely, the diplomats were better suited for such affairs, critics would exclaim with patent uneasiness. Tenet, with his excellent people skills, would cajole the ruffled diplomatic feathers, the concerned critics, and story-seeking journalists, saying just the right thing to the right audience. He always makes a blunt and straightforward impression, even if he is saying two different things to two different groups. What people do not realize immediately is that George Tenet is not just the chief spy, but also an able politician. It was this attribute that gave him staying power; it was also this attribute that led to his greatest failure.

The smartest political move Tenet made was naming the CIA Headquarters the George Bush Center for Intelligence in 1999. It was a stroke of brilliance, especially because the brilliance was not noticeable at the time. It was carefully scripted to not seem a CIA initiative, an organization that must strive for an apolitical reputation, but a congressional effort. Bush had been DCI from January 1976 to January 1977, just one year. The impact he had made in that one year was minimal, and he left behind an indistinct legacy. However, as president, Bush was a strong supporter of the CIA and a consumer of intelligence. He took care of Agency officers, pardoning those implicated in the fallout of the Iran-Contra affair. He rewrote his CIA legacy, *ex post facto.* Tenet paid the Agency's respect to Bush in a seemingly nonpolitical way. The benefits to Tenet would be significant a few years down the line.

Tenet understood how to read the political tea leaves. After Haiti, the Clinton administration would become very cautious on foreign policy issues. The administration's caution was evident in the types of activities the National Security Council Covert Action Working Group and the so-called White House Small Group would authorize. Covert action programs must be authorized by the National Security Council, and they are usually paid for by fenced National Security Council funds. Individual operations that were consistent with the language of the approved covert action program did not normally require additional National Security Council approval. However, if the operation is deemed risky, with potential political blowback, the CIA sought National Security Council approval for the operation. The rationale for this was to keep the administration informed, in control, and to avoid unpleasant surprises. From the CIA management perspective, it also spread responsibility for risk taking.

Tenet embraced the idea of risk management, referring a significant number of CIA operational proposals—counterterrorism and otherwise—to the National Security Council for vetting. To the troops, he would say that if the operational proposal was sound, it would be approved. In practice, approval had nothing to do with "operational soundness," but with political calculations usually based on the worst-case scenario. The result was that Tenet was successful in not getting caught out in front of Clinton. It also meant not getting out in front of rapidly emerging terrorist threats.

AFGHANISTAN, 1998: Because his first declaration of war had been ignored by the West, bin Ladin decided to repeat it. On February 23, he issued a new statement, under the name of the World Islamic Front. The statement was signed by bin Ladin and his key supporters within the international *jihadi* movement: Ayman al-Zawahiri of Egyptian Islamic Jihad, Abu Yasir Rifa'i Ahmad Taha of Egyptian al-Gama'at al-Islamiya, Shaykh Mir Hamzah of Jamiat-al-Ulema-e-Pakistan, and Fazlur Rahman, leader of the Bangladesh Jihad Movement.

Significantly less wordy and more to the point than his 1996 *fatwa*, bin Ladin delineated the crimes committed by Americans, including "occupying the lands of Islam in the holiest of places, the Arabian Peninsula, plundering its riches, dictating to its rulers, humiliating its people, terrorizing its neighbors and turning its bases in the Peninsula into a spearhead through which to fight the neighboring Muslim people." He condemned the "aggression against the Iraqi people using the Peninsula as a staging post." According to bin Ladin, the purpose of the war in Iraq was to "annihilate what is left of this people and to humiliate their Muslim neighbors. He condemned the American-Israeli alliance, saying that in addition to the United States having religious and economic aims, a third aim "is also to serve the Jews' petty state and divert attention from its occupation of Jerusalem and murder of Muslims there."

Having made the case of American evil deeds and intentions, bin Ladin went on: "All these crimes and sins committed by the Americans are a clear declaration of war on Allah, his messenger, and Muslims." Bin Ladin and his cohorts called upon supporters to defend Islam and the Holy places, issuing a *fatwa* for a defensive war against the United States. "The ruling to kill the Americans and their allies—civilians and military—is an individual duty for every Muslim who can do it in any country in which it is possible to do it, and in order to liberate the al-Aqsa Mosque and the holy mosque [of Mecca] from their grip, and in order for their armies to move out of all the lands of Islam, defeated and unable to threaten any Muslim."[1]

In other words, kill the Americans—wherever they can be found.

This simpler message caught Langley's interest. The CIA had been watching al-Qa'ida transform itself. Rather than being just one of many independent Islamic extremist groups, it was becoming a core around which other groups revolved. Bin Ladin was gaining more supporters unified behind targeting the United States as the first step in the global *jihad*. The list of cosignatories was not inconsequential. By early 1998, Egyptian Islamic Jihad began to merge into al-Qa'ida, and Ayman al-Zawahiri became bin Ladin's right-hand man. Egyptian Islamic Jihad had global terrorist capabilities. For example, in November 1995, its operatives destroyed the Egyptian embassy in Islamabad with a devastating car bomb. The merger could only mean increased threats to the United States.

Suspected al-Qa'ida and Egyptian extremist cells in Africa and the Balkans received more intensive scrutiny by the U.S. government. The level of activity was high. Threat reports against U.S. embassies in Africa increased dramatically, according to State Department Diplomatic Security reporting. The CIA did not know what was up, but opted to undertake disruption activities, getting local police services to detain and deport suspect cell members. In early 1998, a "walk-in"—an individual who volunteered information by walking into a U.S. facility overseas—told CIA officers in an African ████ (installation) about a plot to blow up the U.S. embassy in Nairobi. Judged a fabricator and rejected summarily, the walk-in would rejoin his al-Qa'ida cell and take his revenge upon the Americans.

Renditions continued to prove to be a tool of choice to disrupt al-Qa'ida operations. Cofer Black testified before Congress that in June 1998, the CIA worked with law enforcement and intelligence services to disrupt a cell with links to al-Qa'ida that was planning to blow up the U.S. embassy in Tirana.[2] According to Yossef Bodanski in his book *Bin Ladin*, the CIA worked with the Albanian National Intelligence Agency and Albanian police to arrest and "deport" four Egyptian Islamic Jihad terrorists from Albania to Egypt: Shawki Salama Attiya (aka Magid Mustafa), Ahmed Ibrahim al-Naggar, Muhamed Hasan Tita (aka Muhamed Hasan Mahmud), and Ahmed Osman Salah.[3]

According to press reports, they were handed over to the CIA for interrogation for several days before being flown to Egypt for a hand-off to Egyptian authorities. In early 1999, in the largest-ever mass trial of Islamic terrorists, Egyptian military court tried 170 Islamists, including members of the Albanian cell. Two of the "deported" individuals, Naggar and Salah, were executed in February 2000.[4] In a related operation, again according to Bodanski, Issam Abd al-Tawwab abd al-Alim, a senior Egyptian Islamic Jihad leader who previously operated from Albania, was rendered from Sofia, Bulgaria, to Egypt by American security officials.[5]

Meanwhile, the Justice Department finally decided there was sufficient evidence against bin Ladin to initiate legal action. In June 1998, the Southern District Court of New York issued a sealed indictment of bin Ladin and an unnamed coconspirator for a conspiracy to attack defense utilities of the United States. The indictment, which was unsealed in November 1998, traced the development of al-Qa'ida, citing overt criminal acts, including obtaining weapons and explosives for terrorist groups, providing training in Afghanistan and the Sudan for terrorist groups, producing counterfeit passports for use by terrorist groups, and recruiting American citizens to deliver messages and engage in financial transactions for terrorist groups.

The indictment stated that al-Qa'ida urged attacks on U.S. forces in Saudi Arabia and Yemen. Al-Qa'ida members participated with Somali tribesmen in an attack on U.S. military personnel during Operation

274 •   MELISSA BOYLE MAHLE

Restore Hope and provided training and assistance to these tribes. Bin Ladin had made efforts to obtain components of nuclear weapons and to produce chemical weapons. Coupled with the two *fatwas* to kill Americans, the indictment concluded that bin Ladin and the coconspirator conspired "to injure and destroy, and attempted to injure and destroy, national-defense material, national-defense premises and national-defense utilities of the United States with the intent to injure, interfere with and obstruct the national defense of the United States."[6]

NAIROBI, KENYA, AND DAR ES SALAAM, TANZANIA, 1998: The near-simultaneous blasts were horrifically spectacular. Timed to detonate at the same minute on the morning of August 7, two car bombings damaged the U.S. embassies in Nairobi and Dar es Salaam, killing more than 220 people, wounding 4,500 others, and causing significant damage to U.S. facilities and surrounding buildings. The Nairobi bombing was the more lethal of the two. As American and other search-and-rescue teams dug through the rubble, more dead than alive were pulled out. The stench of the rotting corpses would forever haunt the rescue and post-blast investigation teams. The latter, composed of FBI and CIA explosive experts, began to piece together the operational details.

The plots required careful, patient, and meticulous preparation, according to an in-depth CIA intelligence study of the attacks. The level of sophistication, the disciplined tradecraft, and compartmentalization for operational security was more typical of state-sponsored terror groups, thus startling when attributed to nonstate actors. Al-Qa'ida had taken the time to do it right. According to a senior U.S. intelligence official, bin Ladin began to build the terrorist infrastructure in East Africa as early as 1992. Key bin Ladin lieutenant Abu Ubaydah al-Banshiri selected Kenya to be the regional hub, with the business elements in Nairobi and the military cells in Mombasa, a populous Muslim port city. The large Muslim population provided good cover for the al-Qa'ida cells and offered ample recruiting possibilities. Slowly, the operation teams were put together, with most of the bombers engaged in low-profile, modest jobs in Mombasa. Once the infrastructure was in place, the targets were selected by bin Ladin. The operational cells surveilled and photographed the targets as part of the operational planning. It was a professional job.[7]

The full plot would begin to unravel days after the attacks with the arrest and extradition/rendition to the United States of two of the bombers, Mohammed Odeh and Mohamed Rashed Daoud al-Owhali.

Wadih el Hage would be arrested on October 17 in the United States. An earlier Kenyan police raid on his home had led to the confiscation of numerous records indicating that he was preparing three hundred activists for military activity, a good indicator of the size of the conspiracy. An al-Qa'ida defector also filled in key gaps on al-Qa'ida operational methods, fleshing out some of the gray areas.

It took three years and millions of dollars to conduct the investigation leading to indictments and convictions for the attacks on the U.S. embassies. In February 2001, the trial of four bin Ladin lieutenants opened in the Southern District of New York. In *U.S. vs. Usama Bin Ladin*, 308 charges were presented against 21 al-Qa'ida members, most still at large, with Usama bin Ladin topping the list. The lead charge, as reported by the press, was conspiracy to murder, bomb, and maim, in the attacks against the embassies. Two of the accused, Khalfan Khamis Mohamed and Mohamed Rashed Dauod al-Owhali, faced death sentences. Wadih el Hage and Mohammed Odeh faced life in prison.

According to the government case related to the embassy bombings, al-Qa'ida members began building their infrastructure in Kenya in 1993, first establishing business ventures to support al-Qa'ida members. In the latter part of 1993, cell members began discussing a possible attack against the U.S. embassy in Nairobi in retaliation for U.S. participation in Operation Restore Hope in Somalia. At that time, visual and photographic surveillance of the embassy took place. In 1994, cell members considered other targets for a possible attack, including a building housing the USAID office in Nairobi, and British, French, and Israeli targets in Nairobi.

Wadih el Hage, a Lebanese-American citizen, moved to Nairobi by 1994, and established business ventures. More importantly, he began to build up a military capability, working with Abu Ubaydah. He would take the place of Abu Ubaydah for a time, after Ubaydah died in a ferry accident in Lake Victoria in May 1996. In 1996, the Kenyan cell began acquiring explosives and detonators from Tanzania. In January 1997, Wadih el Hage traveled to Peshawar, Pakistan, to meet with al-Qa'ida leadership, including bin Ladin and Muhammad Atif (aka Abu Hafs). While there, he received instructions for the military East African cell. After this trip, there would be frequent contact and travel of planners to Peshawar, showing a pattern of increased operational activity and chatter.

In March 1998, operational planning went into its final stage. The planning and the execution teams were in place. Mustafa Mohamed

Fadhil was the operational commander for the Tanzania operation and Mohammed Odeh, a Jordanian-Palestinian, for the Kenyan attack. Ahmed Khalfan Ghailani and Khalfan Khamis Mohamed were Tanzanians of Arab origin from Zanzibar. Fahid Mohammad Ally Msalam and Shaykh Ahmed Salim Swedan were Kenyans of Arab origin from Mombasa. Abdullah Ahmed Abdullah was an Egyptian. These were pre-attack logistical cell members who rented the safe houses, purchased the vehicles used in the attacks, purchased the components, and constructed the improvised explosive devices. "Ahmed the German," an Egyptian, was designated the suicide bomber for the Dar es Salaam attack. Mohamed Rashed Daoud al-Owhali and "Azzam," an unidentified Saudi national, were designated the suicide bombers for the Nairobi attack. In early August, cell members who did not have a role in the execution of the plot began leaving Kenya and Tanzania; they included Swedan, Fadhil, Abdullah Ahmed Abdullah, Ghailani, Odeh, and Msalam.

On August 7, at 9:30 A.M., Fazul Abdullah Mohammed drove a pickup truck from the Nairobi safe house to the vicinity of the U.S. embassy. "Azzam" drove the Nairobi bomb truck, with Mohamed Rashed Daoud al-Owhali riding shotgun. At approximately 10:30 A.M. Owhali got out of the bomb truck as it approached the rear of the embassy building and threw a stun grenade in the direction of a security guard at the rear gate. As Owhali attempted to flee, Azzam drove the bomb truck into the rear of the embassy building. Seconds later, the bomb detonated, severely damaging the embassy building and the Cooperative Bank Building next door, and demolishing a multistory secretarial college also adjacent to the embassy. The blast killed more than 213 people and wounded 4,500 others.

Owhali was wounded, but survived the attack. After the attack, he made several calls to a cutout telephone exchange number in Yemen, passing and receiving messages to the al-Qa'ida leadership in Afghanistan. When he sought medical attention from a Nairobi hospital, he came under suspicion by Nairobi police. His story did not make sense. The FBI suspected he was involved and obtained his custody, transporting him to the United States. Fazul Abdullah Mohammed and other cell members went undetected and did the post-operation cleanup, clearing out the Nairobi safe house. On August 14 Mohammed left Nairobi for the Comoros Islands.

Meanwhile, in Dar es Salaam, Khalfan Khamis Mohamed and Ahmed the German drove the Dar es Salaam bomb truck to the U.S. embassy. Khalfan Mohamed left the truck along the route while Ahmed the

German drove the truck to the front gate of the embassy. At approximately 10:40 A.M., he detonated the bomb, killing eleven people wounding eighty-five others, and causing severe damage to the embassy building. Khalfan Mohamed returned to the safe house, cleaning it and removing evidence of bomb-making tools. On August 8, he escaped to Cape Town, South Africa.

The East African cells were a national hodgepodge—Egyptian, Palestinian, Saudi, Lebanese, Tanzanian, and Kenyan. They represented not "a loose affiliation of Islamic extremists angry at the U.S." as described by the 1995 NIE, but well-integrated operational groups that exploited capabilities across organizational, national, and sectarian lines. The embassy bombings served to make al-Qa'ida and bin Ladin household names, not just in the United States but around the world.

I was working in the Occupied Territories of the West Bank and Gaza Strip at the time of the bombings. The response from the Palestinian in the street was one of amazement. Most had never heard of bin Ladin before the bombings. Many condemned the attacks and expressed sympathy for the tragic human loss. However, bin Ladin struck a chord with many, especially younger Palestinians, who were impressed by the ability and the resolve of one man to take on the United States. They were awed by his feat and they saw him as the underdog champion, or the new Saladin, fighting to drive out foreign powers. Bin Ladin empowered them, awaking them to the possibilities of individual resistance.

Three years later, despite the absence of most of the conspirators and big holes in the details of the actual embassy-bombing plot—even after 92 witnesses and 1,300 exhibits—the conspiracy was unveiled to the satisfaction of a jury and judge. After three months of testimony and twelve days of jury deliberations, the four defendants were found guilty in U.S. Federal court. This time, there were no illusions that the case was closed.

FOGGY BOTTOM, WASHINGTON, D.C., 1998: The State Department accountability report of the embassy bombings found there was an institutional failure by State and embassies under its direction to recognize threats posed by transnational terrorism and vehicle bombs worldwide. Policymakers and operational officers were remiss in not preparing more comprehensive procedures to guard against massive truck bombs. Although the physical security systems and procedures met State Department standards, the standards were inadequate. They did not meet the "Inman Standards" developed by

Bobby Inman and his Advisory Panel on Overseas Security in 1985, following the bombing of the U.S. embassy in Beirut. Neither of the chancery buildings in Nairobi and Dar es Salaam had a one-hundred-foot setback/standoff zone.

The accountability report cited early intelligence reports on threats against several U.S. diplomatic and other targets, including the Nairobi and Dar es Salaam embassies. The reports had been discounted because of doubts about the sources. Indeed, the CIA inspector general's report would find that the Directorate of Operations too quickly discounted the information provided by the walk-in. The accountability report stated that actions taken by intelligence and law enforcement authorities to confront suspect terrorist groups, including the al-Haramain non-governmental organization and al-Qa'ida in Nairobi, were believed to have dissipated the alleged threats. This belief was obviously in error. Ultimately, however, the report concluded that the problem was insufficient defense, not insufficient intelligence. Nowhere in the report did the board suggest the development of a more aggressive counterterrorism policy. The threat could be managed by better defense.[8]

The State Department's focus on defensive measures would reinforce a trend within the policy and intelligence community that the best form of protection was a good defensive posture. After the embassy bombings, the Clinton administration requested $1.8 billion to upgrade security at diplomatic posts around the world and to build new embassies in Nairobi and Dar es Salaam. The State Department also dispatched Emergency Security Assessment Teams, Security Augmentation Teams, and Mobile Training Teams. State hired new guards, developed countersurveillance teams, and built vehicle barriers and blast walls. Bomb-detection equipment, X-ray scanners, closed-circuit recording cameras, and metal detectors were purchased and installed in missions throughout the world. Defensive security tactics for embassies and other official installations were changed in order to outwardly extend outer-perimeter security and harden middle-perimeter rings. Embassy officers practiced bomb drills, evacuation drills, and destruction exercises. If terrorist bombs could not be stopped, then facilities would be hardened to minimize damage and personnel trained to take immediate protective cover.

This trend—the focus on defensive measures—was particularly strong within the Defense Department, whose counterterrorism doctrine of the 1990s was limited to force protection. While the CIA would try to break out of the defensive mode and, for a brief moment, so would the White House, the so-called war on terrorism from 1998 to 2001 would lack an integrated offensive strategy.

COUNTERTERRORISM CENTER, LANGLEY, VIRGINIA, 1998: While the State Department focused on inadequate physical security, the Counterterrorism Center knew there had been an intelligence failure. There were so many indicators that an attack was in the works; the dismissed walk-in was only an important one of them. The pre-attack pattern of activity was documented thoroughly, and it would serve as an accurate template to predict later attacks. The bottom line was that there was no question that al-Qa'ida was responsible for the attacks. With evidence firmly in hand, the White House was briefed.

WHITE HOUSE, WASHINGTON, D.C., 1998: The U.S. retaliatory attack against bin Ladin and his organization was swift and fierce. On August 20, the U.S. military launched seventy cruise missiles targeted on al-Qa'ida training camps in Afghanistan. Other missiles targeted the al-Shifa pharmaceutical factory in Sudan. As President Clinton explained in his speech to the nation that same day: "Our target was terror. Our mission was clear—to strike at the network of radical groups affiliated with and funded by Usama bin Ladin, perhaps the preeminent organizer and financier of international terrorism in the world today. . . . There is convincing information from our intelligence community that the bin Ladin terrorist network was responsible for these bombings. Based on this information, we have high confidence that these bombings were planned, financed and carried out by the organization bin Ladin leads."[9]

In his speech, Clinton went on to say that the fight against terrorism did not start with the bombing of the embassies, nor would it end with the air strikes, and that the U.S. government was prepared "to do all that we can for as long as we must." These were strong words that proved very hollow. In reality, the willingness of U.S. political leaders to support and authorize risky operations was diminished significantly after the political fallout of the 1998 retaliatory attacks against bin Ladin and al-Qa'ida.

The strikes against the training camps and bases in Afghanistan and against the al-Shifa pharmaceutical factory in Sudan initially received strong support from the American public and Congress. A poll conducted by CNN found that 66 percent of the American public favored the strikes in response to the bombings of the U.S. embassies in Dar es Salam and Nairobi. Because the administration had consulted with

Congress prior to the attacks and the broad popular support even
Clinton's harshest congressional critics initially stood behind the presidential decision.[10] However, in the after-action political debate, spurred
on by press disclosures, the strikes became controversial and judged by
the administration as a foreign policy blunder.

The debate on whether or not al-Shifa was involved in the production of precursor chemicals for use in the manufacturing of VX nerve
gas raged for more than a year. The connection between bin Ladin and
the pharmaceutical factory was questioned. The Clinton administration
was criticized for not killing bin Ladin in the attack on the training
camp, on the one hand, and for even *trying* to kill him, on the other
hand. Clinton was also accused of launching the attacks as a political
maneuver to distract attention from the growing sex/candor scandal,
so-called Monica-Gate. The Small Group, responsible for making the
strike recommendations to the president was criticized for its secrecy
and exclusiveness and ultimately bore the rap for the "bad advice"
based on "weak intelligence" that the president, received. Somewhere
lost in the subsequent debate was the threat bin Ladin posed to the U.S.
government, as proved by the lethal bombings of the U.S. embassies in
Tanzania and Kenya.

The perceived "failure" of the 1998 strikes made the Clinton administration unwilling to respond aggressively to the growing threat as bin
Ladin developed his organization, building a loosely integrated global
network capable of striking inside the United States. Clinton's criteria
for authorizing operations were that the operation had to have a large
probability of success, could not risk the lives of U.S. servicemen, and
would not alienate important Arab allies. The target criteria also altered
from facilities where terrorists may be to facilities where bin Ladin was
proven to be. These criteria left few offensive operational options for
the CIA.

**COUNTERTERRORISM CENTER, LANGLEY, VIRGINIA,
1998:** The operational tempo of the issue station increased dramatically in 1998, after bin Ladin issued a *fatwa* stating that all Muslims have
a religious duty to kill Americans. If bin Ladin wanted war, he would get
war. And it was personal; there was now a new star on the wall in the CIA
Headquarters documenting the Agency's loss. The CIA provided the
target list for retaliatory attacks. Bin Ladin had drawn U.S. blood and
now it was his and his organization's turn to bleed.

Tenet declared war against bin Ladin. He really did. Those words
came out of his mouth—multiple times. They came out of his mouth

the same time he declared Kosovo a CIA surge priority. They came out his mouth the same time he declared support to the Middle East Peace Process a surge priority. They came out of his mouth the same time he declared counterproliferation operations against Iraq a high priority. In 1998, the Serbs were annihilating the Kosovars, the peace process was in a crisis of political stalemate, and Iraq had evicted the UN weapons inspectors. In other words, the CIA, which typically operates in crisis management mode, just added one more crisis to the pile.

Those officers in the Counterterrorism Center were totally committed to waging that war. It was their war. But because it was the Counterterrorism Center's war—not the CIA's war or the intelligence community's war—they faced one obstacle after another.

The Counterterrorism Center was hampered in its operations against bin Ladin by the mere fact that it was not the Agency's most important priority. First, the Counterterrorism Center and the bin Ladin issue group had staffing problems. There were never enough seasoned operations officers to go around. To operations officers, the Counterterrorism Center seemed controlled by the Directorate of Intelligence, and it was not viewed as a desirable assignment. When bin Ladin group officers would visit overseas stations to discuss operational opportunities, the field operations officers would find themselves talking to analysts, who had no real experience in what worked and did not work in the field. They did not speak the "language of ops." The Counterterrorism Center "owned" few operational slots in the field and was frequently in a negotiation mode with stations to put bin Ladin at the top of the collection priorities.

The Center was also critically short on experienced analysts. The available analysts, although hardworking and very smart, were mostly junior in rank and had insufficient analytical tradecraft training and experience. As a result of the crush of daily threat information, they spent their time on current analysis related to threat reporting and neglected strategic analysis.

None of these problems, in and of themselves, was insurmountable; with the attention of senior management, they could have been fixed. The CIA is a line organization. When management speaks, especially on personnel assignments, officers jump. Directed assignments are not unusual. If CIA management wanted a fully staffed, powerhouse counterterrorism center, all it had to do was speak. The DCI and the deputy directors of Operations and Intelligence obviously did not consider staffing the Center to be their highest priority.

Probably the most difficult problem that lay outside the control of the working level was the difficulty of taking action to disrupt bin Ladin. Any officer who ever served in the Counterterrorism Center will comment on the frustrations of having one's hands tied when it comes to doing something beyond collecting intelligence. In 1999, the CIA got rid of the puppy and hired a pitbull. With the assignment of Cofer Black as Chief of the Counterterrorism Center, the Agency made a concerted effort to move from the defensive to the offensive. Black had singular focus. He was committed to action, not collection for the sake of collection. Black made a tour of Near East and European stations, barking his intention to do things differently and to go on the offensive. He wanted to hear operational plans to take down terrorists, not to collect intelligence. He was not the kind of man who could be shrugged off, or taken lightly. His bulky figure, scowling face, and plain aggressive talk all projected the image of a man hell-bent on turning the wheels against the bad guys and bringing them down any way he possibly could.

The ban on assassination and the greater reliance upon the more politically acceptable practice of rendition did not mean that the CIA was banned from conducting lethal operations. The difference in definitions of lethal operations, targeted killings, and assassination is the subject of legal hairsplitting; the results are the same: somebody whom the government wants out of the way ends up dead, or at least is intended to, if the operation is a success. Always looking for the gray area, the CIA would note that the presidential ban on assassination does not make assassination illegal, because an executive order is not a law.

However, international law, according to the United Nations charter, states that political leaders or private individuals are supposed to be immune from intentional acts of violence by citizens, agents, or military forces of another nation in peacetime. In wartime, international law allows the targeted killing of a member of the enemy's chain of command, including a head of state, civilians, and military officers. The complicating factor here is that few recent wars have been declared formally. Terrorists fall into a special category, according to some experts, who argue that as "illegal combatants" they do not enjoy the protections of international law.

The lethal findings (technically called Memorandums of Notification [MONs]) that presidents signed in the 1990s had language avoiding the word "assassination," but authorized the CIA to use covert lethal force to accomplish a stated mission—that is, regime change in Iraq or destabilization of Slobodan Milosevic in Belgrade. In 1998,

Clinton signed a lethal finding targeting bin Ladin and his organization. A presidential writ authorizing lethal force does not mean the CIA had authority to launch a wet team and take out the target. The fine print limits CIA actions to capture and rendition. If the target is killed in the process of capture, the CIA is covered by the authority to use lethal force.

The CIA did not believe it had authority to straight-out assassinate Usama bin Ladin, according to Cofer Black's testimony before the National Commission on Terrorist Attacks upon the United States (i.e., the September 11 Commission). "The themes of the MONs were explicit—capture was the objective." Nor did Tenet request authority to assassinate bin Ladin, according to his testimony. Tenet tried to wiggle around this, saying that if the CIA had the capability, he would have requested additional authorities. In the world of operations, it does not work that way. As an operations officer, I find out what my mission and authorities are, and then I develop the capability to execute the mission without exceeding my authorities. The former drives the latter, not the other way around. Policymakers—namely, National Security Advisor Sandy Berger and Secretary of State Madeleine Albright—believed the CIA did have the authority to kill rather than capture. The testimony and the Q&A before the September 11 Commission showed just how murky the findings were.

When Clinton authorized the launch of cruise missiles against a training camp in Afghanistan, it was believed bin Ladin was there attending a high-level meeting. At the time, military spokesmen stated that bin Ladin was not the target of the attack, but there would not have been any grief if he had died as a result. What went unsaid was the timing and the target site was selected because bin Ladin was believed to be there, along with his senior lieutenants. Even in the course of a military action, the Clinton administration was mindful to avoid accusations of assassination operations.

U.S. intelligence had been collecting intelligence information on bin Ladin, al-Qa'ida, and Afghanistan for years, and intelligence sources identified and mapped the camps that bin Ladin operated in Afghanistan. The CIA had a good understanding of the high level of activities at these camps and the nature of the training. In other words, the al-Qa'ida infrastructure had been identified, a fundamental requirement for targeting. Furthermore, the CIA had the ability to keep rough tabs on bin Ladin as he lived in and moved around Afghanistan. U.S. intelligence had deployed considerable technical and human resources against bin Ladin, including listening to his satellite phone conversations, until this method was exposed by the press, according to Ronald Kessler in *CIA at War*.[11]

It was a difficult operational environment for U.S. intelligence, because there was no official platform, such as an ████████ from which CIA officers could deploy operationally. Furthermore, Afghanistan is sufficiently remote and isolated that strangers stood out. The Taliban regime was hostile to the United States and most U.S. allies. Those who did have diplomatic missions were denied freedom of movement outside Kabul. Allies that had good relations with the Taliban, like Pakistan and Saudi Arabia, would not work aggressively with the United States against bin Ladin because of domestic political interests and pressures. Thus, the United States found itself largely on its own in developing operations inside Afghanistan, depending upon the limited capabilities that the CIA planned and developed. That capability did not provide real-time around-the-clock tracking, but only intermittent spotting and tracking.

Reportedly, the CIA gained approval to work with the Northern Alliance in Afghanistan and the Uzbek government on operations to capture or kill bin Ladin.[12] While this sounds good, in truth the Northern Alliance and Uzbek governments did not have regular access to bin Ladin or the territory in which he operated, reducing the likelihood of success of such an operation. The CIA also reportedly had a surveillance team composed of Afghans whose mission was to track bin Ladin and to provide intelligence on his exact whereabouts.

If bin Ladin could be found, the U.S. government planned to launch a missile strike from nuclear-powered attack submarines on permanent station in the nearby waters of the northern Indian Ocean and the Gulf. Although strikes were considered and authorized, the final go was never given. President Clinton's main criteria for approving a strike was that there had to be "a substantial probability of success." A six-hour time lag from the final go for launch to strike was too long a window, as there was no guarantee that the mobile human target would remain in the same location. Despite the presidential findings, there remained a strong reluctance within the leadership of the CIA and in political circles to pursue operations that could be viewed as assassinations or indiscriminate killing.

In December 1998, when the CIA identified the specific whereabouts of bin Ladin in Kandahar and initiated an operational proposal to assassinate him with a predator missile, the proposal was viewed as too risky to be approved on the authority of the DCI. The proposal was bumped up to the National Security Council for approval while operational preparations continued. Ultimately, the operation was called off at the last moment, because the CIA could not give the National Security Council assurances that there would be no collateral deaths of civilians who might be in the area at the time of the attack. Potential collateral damage to a nearby mosque caused the National Security Council to reject the operation.

In May 1999, the Counterterrorism Center proposed a missile strike against the apartment building in Kandahar where the intelligence information indicated bin Ladin was and would probably spend several nights. The proposal was rejected because the CIA could not guarantee that there would be minimal collateral damage—that is, the death of civilians who might be in the apartment building at the time of the attack. There were other occasions that the CIA had intelligence on the specific whereabouts of bin Ladin in Afghanistan, but the authorization to proceed with a strike was not finally authorized, because there was no guarantee that bin Ladin would remain at the same location for the time required for the missiles to arrive. The probability of success was not high enough for the Clinton administration.

Frankly, the operational environment was restrictive. The CIA did what it considered doable. It used the tools it had and worked to get a few more. In 1995, President Clinton signed Executive Order (E.O.) 12947, which introduced a legal category of "specially designated terrorists," and it was specifically designed to stop the U.S.-based funding mechanisms of Hamas and the Palestinian Islamic Jihad, Islamic extremist groups that were disrupting the Middle East Peace Process. It also blocked all property and property interests in the United States or in the possession or control of a U.S. person belonging to entities named in the annex to the order. It prohibited U.S. persons from engaging in transactions with or making charitable donations to any entity named in the annex or otherwise designated under the order. The annex to the executive order listed specific groups and individuals to which E.O. 12947 applied.

After the embassy bombings, the CIA proposed expansion of the executive order to include bin Ladin and al-Qa'ida. On August 20, 1998, President Clinton signed E.O. 13099, which added bin Ladin and several of his close advisors to the annex. On July 4, 1999, E.O. 13129 was signed, expanding the authorities to include the Taliban, blocking all property and interests in property of the Taliban in the United States or in the control of U.S. persons. If the CIA couldn't put a bullet (or missile) in bin Ladin, then they would starve him and his friends to death.

Armed with these new legal tools to disrupt financial transactions in the United States that were previously watched passively and noted for the record, the CIA took aim at bin Ladin's wallet. With a war cry, CIA officers crossed the Potomac to confer with Treasury. However, the Treasury Department dragged its feet when it came down to freezing assets and shutting down the *hawala* financial system used by terrorist organizations. The reaction the CIA received led the Agency to conclude that Treasury's Financial Crimes Enforcement Center (FinCEN) was broken, unable and unwilling to engage against the nontraditional target that terrorism presented.

The *hawala* system operates on trust. If you disrupt the flows by shutting down the back end of the system—the repayment portion—the system becomes unreliable for the users. Tom is not going to give unsecured money to Dick for Harry if Dick has a reputation for not delivering. Delivery is everything; excuses don't count. Treasury had the capability of disrupting the flows electronically, making money disappear, but declined to do so out of concern for the integrity of the banking system. Making terrorist money disappear in an electronic black hole was just too much of a "dirty trick" for the staid watchdogs of the banking world.

Frustrated by interagency obstacles, the CIA opted to concentrate its efforts on foreign governments to disrupt cells, deport terrorists, or assist in rendition operations. They were not hung up on the niceties of playing by the rules in the war against terrorism. The CIA adopted a strategy of taking down al-Qa'ida cells in an ad hoc way—in other words, attacking them where they could be reached, through rendition and disruption operations, with partners who would play by CIA rules. The policy leash on the CIA was tight, with no tolerance for flaps. Within this context, the CIA could not be too aggressive, and had to make sure it operated in the shadows of deniability of U.S. involvement. The consensus was that Americans would not pay too much attention to the disappearance of a few terrorists, but nobody wanted to test the assessment. No scrutiny was preferable, because human rights issues could backfire on the administration and the Agency, as had happened in Latin America in the early 1990s.

EAST JERUSALEM, 1999: It was a beautiful night, the air clear and crisp, the stars burning bright, almost within reach. It was New Year's Eve, and I was hosting a group of friends for a dinner party and midnight toast on my rooftop garden terrace. Looking back over the past year, I had a deep sense of satisfaction. It had been a hard but good year. There had been no terrorist bombings in Israel and the Occupied Territories, but only because of concerted efforts on the part of the Palestinian and Israeli security services. The Middle East Peace Process was inching forward, but the obstacles were formidable. I had worked seven days a week for far too long. My baby daughter was thriving and bought us great joy, but I regretted all the hours I had missed because of work requirements.

The vast majority of my work time was dedicated to counterterrorism and security issues. Only occasionally did those issues include al-Qa'ida. When al-Qa'ida threat information came in, it was always a top priority. I recall one spring Saturday morning. I had helped planned a special community activity, taking American family members to the beautiful Palestinian town of Nablus for the day. Even in the best of times, travel to the West Bank was still done with caution. I made the security arrangements. Just as our convoy of cars was about to depart, I received a phone call instructing me to go see ███████████ Baby in tow, I went to Ramallah instead of Nablus. ████████████

██
██
██
██
██
██
██
██
██
██
██████████████████████████

Although it was a night of celebration, I was working that New Year's Eve. The millennium period had been fraught with threat information. Next door, the Jordanian authorities had uncovered a major plot to terrorize Western and Christian tourists gathered there to celebrate the millennium. The cell planned to attack tourist sites on Mount Nebo, where tradition says Moses saw the Promised Land. They also planned an attack against a Christian settlement along the Jordan River, where St. John the Baptist is believed to have baptized Jesus. Finally, the cell planned to attack a luxury Amman hotel during the New Year's Eve celebration. Jordanian security had raided the cell's safe house and found assault rifles, explosives, antitank rockets, artillery shells, detonators, and communications equipment.

As I mixed with my guests on my rooftop, I was well aware that not all the cell members had been arrested on December 12, and there remained the distinct possibility that the entire operation had not been disrupted. The links to al-Qa'ida were apparent from the outset, giving the threat more weight. Even more disturbing, there were links between the cell and suspected terrorists who might be in the United States.

As later described in the 9/11 Commission Report, authorities in the United States were on high alert. Two days after the Jordanian arrests, a U.S. Customs agent stopped Ahmed Ressam at Port Angeles, Washington, the border crossing from Canada. His rented vehicle was loaded with powerful explosives concealed in the spare tire well. He was planning to blow up the Los Angeles Airport in California as part of a larger campaign by al-Qa'ida during the millennium. Ressam was linked to the Armed Islamic Group, an Algerian terrorist group with ties to al-Qa'ida. That was all we knew at the time.

Ressam started cooperating with the FBI in May 2001, after he had been convicted on all charges related to the Los Angeles plot, according to Ressam's testimony against fellow conspirators in U.S. federal court (*U.S. v. Mokhtar Haouari*). He told U.S. officials that he developed the plan while he was in Afghanistan in 1998, training at al-Qa'ida camps, with fellow Algerian extremists. According to Ressam, other groups were planning attacks in Europe and the Gulf against Israeli and U.S. targets during the millennium. Ressam's group had decided upon an airport or consulate. Ressam testified that he trained on small arms, RPGs, manufacture of explosives, and improvised explosive devices, sabotage, surveillance, and operational security. He also learned how to launch a chemical attack and observed exercises using cyanide against dogs. According to Ressam, he ended up conducting the attack alone, because his other cell members were stopped in Europe and could not make their way to Canada, as had been planned.

There were also threats closer to my home in Jerusalem. Some extremist Christian groups believed that the new millennium was the time of judgment and the end of the world. Only those present in Jerusalem would be able to stand before God for judgment. The Second Coming would be ushered in by "blood flowing on the streets of Jerusalem." Some groups felt that the Second Coming could be triggered by making that blood flow. From a security perspective, we were concerned that an extremist group would stage attacks against non-Christian religious sites, such as the Muslim Dome of the Rock (Haram al-Sharif), in order to trigger sectarian violence. The Israeli government had been blocking entry into Israel of suspected "Millennialists" and deporting those already in the country. Again, there was no guarantee the threat was "under control."

Finally, there was the Y2K threat. For an entire year, we had been preparing for the possibility that as the date stamp turned from December 31, 1999, to January 1, 2000, computer glitches would shut down critical infrastructure around the world. I was tasked with monitoring the turnover for the West Bank and maintained scheduled contacts with officials to do so. My phone rang constantly as fireworks displays signaled the start of the New Year. In the distance, I could just make out the fireworks over Bethlehem. When I talked to my Palestinian contact in Bethlehem, he reported that the electricity remained on but they were having a problem with the doves. I did not understand and thought that I misunderstood his Arabic. No, he meant doves. The city authorities had released hundreds of doves to commemorate the peace process and the desire for a lasting peace in the new millennium. Immediately thereafter, the fireworks started. Soon, charred doves were dropping from the skies, to the dismay of the gathered crowds.

If I were more superstitious, I would say those charred doves were an omen for bad times to come. Ten months later, in late September 2000, the Middle East Peace Process collapsed. The anger and despair united, touching off the second Palestinian uprising, the al-Aqsa Intifada. Jerusalem burned as riots broke out spontaneously in the eastern part of the city. Palestinian suicide bombers blew up Jerusalem buses, killing schoolchildren, parents, and soldiers. Israeli tanks and hellfire missiles blew holes into Palestinian homes, killing the occupants inside and destroying all the small things that make up a family's life. Death and destruction replaced the doves of hope and peace.

GULF OF ADEN, YEMEN, 2000: It was a quiet morning in the Aden harbor on October 12. The USS *Cole* had pulled into the floating refueling station, taking its turn to fill up the tanks of the 505-foot destroyer. Operating under "Bravo" conditions—a slightly elevated threat condition—nothing appeared out of the ordinary. There had been threat information for the region, but it was old and not specific to the harbor.

The quiet was shattered when a small boat raced toward the *Cole*, the attackers detonating the explosive device on board as the craft pulled up alongside. The explosion killed seventeen U.S. crew members and wounded another thirty-nine sailors. Damage to the ship was extensive. As the crew struggled to aid the wounded and keep the ship from sinking, al-Qa'ida celebrated another victory.

The *Cole* Commission conducted an accountability review and found significant shortcomings in force protection procedures, including inadequate training and intelligence. While the U.S. State Department considered the threat level in Yemen to be "very high," the USS *Cole* was operating under only a slightly elevated threat condition. There was no good explanation for the two different postures. There were numerous threat reports for Yemen in the days and months preceding the attack; the USS *Cole* should have been on alert.

In many ways, the attack was inevitable; it was only a matter of time before al-Qa'ida identified weaknesses in force protection measures. The Defense Department was stuck in a defensive mentality. After the 1995 attack on the OPM/SANG building in Riyadh, the Defense Department assessments focused on making U.S. military facilities less vulnerable to terrorist attacks by increasing physical security and augmenting force protection practices. The accountability assessments following the 1996 Khobar Towers bombings again focused upon defensive measures. Although upgrades in physical security and force protection practices had been made, Secretary of Defense William Cohen found Brigadier General Terry Schwalier, Commander of the 4404th Wing, personally accountable for deficiencies in force protection. The terrorism threat was described as "unpredictable." The solution was better defense.

Unlike earlier reviews, the *Cole* Commission looked beyond force protection and called for a more aggressive stance toward fighting terrorism. The report found that the U.S. military was reacting too slowly to emerging threats after the Cold War and recommended that terrorists be viewed as a "relentless enemy" needing to be confronted "with the same intensity and discipline that [the U.S. military] used in the past to defeat conventional antagonists." The military was reacting to terrorism rather than focusing efforts to detect and deter threats before they could be carried out.[13] This call for a change in focus was not acted upon by the Defense Department. While there was a counterterrorism directorate in the Joint Chiefs of Staff, its mission focus was force protection against the terror threat—not counterterrorism.

Even after the CIA declared war on al-Qa'ida, the military was still playing defense. The Pentagon wanted no part in an offensive war on terrorism. After the 1998 retaliatory strikes against bin Ladin, senior military brass resisted follow-on military operations. Although follow-on strikes were planned, the utility of executing them was questioned. Secretary of Defense Cohen saw little positive effect of "pounding the dirt" in repeated air strikes on "jungle gym" training camps. Cohen assessed that repeated air attacks without killing bin Ladin made the United States look weak. Plus there was the cost issue of using very expensive missiles.[14]

The administration considered sending the U.S. military into Afghanistan to capture or take out bin Ladin. Having "boots on the ground" would give the United States greater command-and-control options. However, the deployed troops would likely come under fire by Taliban forces, which would treat the U.S. presence as an invading army. The history of Afghanistan, and costs to the Soviet and British armies that lost wars there, was not lost on the Pentagon decision makers.

The Pentagon played upon Clinton's fear of body bags. According to Pentagon recommendations, in order to "win" a military offensive, the United States would require a military force of significant size reinforced by pie-in-the-sky intelligence capabilities. Larger numbers meant the likelihood of significant American casualties. The risk-averse Clinton preferred the option of sending in a small special operations team to extract bin Ladin. The Joint Chiefs of Staff refused to support a small insertion team—cynically called "going Hollywood"—because of the risks. The military was unwilling to consider any middle ground between cruise missiles and a full-scale invasion of Afghanistan. As summed up by the Joint Congressional Intelligence Community report on September 11, "Senior U.S. military officials were reluctant to use U.S. military assets to conduct offensive counterterrorism efforts in Afghanistan, or to support or participate in CIA operations directed against al-Qa'ida prior to September 11."

FOGGY BOTTOM, WASHINGTON, D.C., 2000: The United States explored diplomatic pressures, albeit lightly. The United States first requested bin Ladin's extradition from the Taliban. When that did not work, the United States threatened the Taliban with the "hand-over-or-else" tactic. The problem was that the Taliban, highly confident of their fighting capabilities, called the U.S. bluff. With the military might of the Afghan *mujahadin* (holy warriors), the Taliban forced out the Soviet army and consolidated their control over most of Afghanistan.* The United States tried exerting pressure via Pakistan and Saudi Arabia. As they had created the Taliban, Pakistan was not interested and *muja-*

---

* The Afghans won the Afghan-Soviet war with a lot of covert military assistance from the CIA. In *their* worldview, however, the Afghans attribute their success to the will of Allah, not to the stingers and other machines of war generously provided by the U.S. government via the CIA.

hadin fighters continued to assist the Pakistani efforts in Kashmir. The U.S. efforts with Saudi Arabia were weak at best. On the range of issues of importance in U.S.–Saudi relations, terrorism fell somewhere toward the bottom in the 1990s.

COUNTERTERRORISM CENTER, LANGLEY, VIRGINIA, 2001: Officers in the Counterterrorism Center were totally focused on the mission at hand. They were winning some battles, but not all. The larger question was whether or not they were winning the war. In the October 21, 2002, testimony before a joint House-Senate intelligence committee, Tenet went into considerable detail (that is, for the CIA) in public session on past successes against al-Qa'ida—a good indicator of the level of pressure upon the Agency. Tenet outlined the following successes:

> The CIA-built collection infrastructure against al-Qa'ida, to include recruitment of sources, designed and built collection systems for use inside Afghanistan and expanded intelligence reporting from 600 reports in 1998 to 900 reports in the first nine months of 2001.*
>
> The CIA reduced its dependence on liaison reporting (reporting received from foreign intelligence services) by the recruitment of unilateral sources (agents recruited and controlled directly by the CIA), the reporting of the latter outnumbering the former starting in 1999.
>
> By September 11, 2001, the CIA had rendered seventy terrorists to justice around the world, working in cooperation with the FBI on those cases where the individuals were brought to the U.S.
>
> The CIA, working with friendly liaison services, disrupted planned operations. An operation in Jordan against a hotel and religious sites during the millennium period was disrupted and the planners brought to justice. An operation tar-

---

* Tenet's written statement stated that human intelligence sources reporting against the terrorist target grew by more than 50 percent between 1999 and September 11, 2001. This is a potentially misleading point because it refers to *all* human sources reporting on the terrorist target, as opposed to those focused *exclusively* on terrorism; furthermore, the Counterterrorism Center covers many other terrorist groups, in addition to Usama bin Ladin. The percentage figures mask the hard numbers, which were extremely low to start with.

geting U.S. military and civilian targets in the Persian Gulf was disrupted in the winter of 2000. A Hizballah network was taken down in East Asia. In the summer of 2001, a suspected al-Qa'ida cell in Jordan was taken down and a large quantity of weapons, including rockets and high explosives, were seized. Operations in Yemen and Saudi Arabia against U.S. facilities were thwarted. A planned operation against the U.S. Embassy or the cultural center in Paris was stopped. The CIA assisted another foreign government in rendering a senior bin Ladin associate, who planned to kidnap Americans in three countries and carry out hijackings.[15]

There were also attacks in Turkey, Italy, Austria, Belgium, Albania, Bosnia, India, Pakistan, Singapore, and Malaysia that were uncovered during the planning stage, resulting in arrests, renditions, seizure of weapons, and exposure of other al-Qa'ida networks and operatives. The arrest of Ahmed Ressam, who attempted to cross the Canadian border and execute an attack against the Los Angeles airport during the millennium celebrations, led to the exposure of the dissident faction of the Algerian Armed Islamic Group supported by al-Qa'ida.

If any of these operations had succeeded, the death toll of Americans and the destruction of U.S. facilities and interests would certainly have been higher. It is easy to count one's losses; it is far more difficult to estimate the costs of what did *not* happen. It is also easy to forget the successes in the face of one terrible failure: September 11. The CIA achieved many tactical successes overcoming a multitude of obstacles, internal and external. The operational momentum was gaining speed, but as history has shown, the Agency was behind the curve.

WHITE HOUSE, WASHINGTON, D.C., 2001: Why didn't Clinton engage the United States in a real war on terrorism? The answer lies in how Clinton viewed the threat. Former Assistant Secretary of State for Near Eastern affairs and former U.S. Ambassador to Tel Aviv, Martin Indyk, stated that Clinton's primary focus in the Middle East was the Middle East Peace Process. According to Indyk, Clinton felt that forging a comprehensive peace agreement would transform the whole region and resolve the issues that created an environment supportive of terrorism. An aggressive policy against terrorism emanating from the Middle East would upset the sensitive relationships that Clinton was building with Arab leaders in support of the peace process. While such a policy might have complicated these relationships, the reactions of Arab countries after the 1998 retaliatory attacks do not support the supposition that Clinton would have lost standing. While the Arab League rebuked the United States after the attacks, key Arab allies were more reserved in their reactions and quietly supported the United States for tackling a mutual threat. Clinton had leeway that he opted against exploiting.

Still others have argued that terrorism was not a priority for the Clinton administration. During his first term, Clinton was far more concerned with domestic issues, such as the economy and health-care reform. But in his second term, he spent significant time on foreign policy issues, including terrorism. He gave high-profile speeches about the threat of terrorism. He tripled the budget for counterterrorism programs. Two antiterrorism bills were passed while he was president. He authorized covert action findings against bin Ladin and other terrorists. While terrorism may not have been his first priority, he paid more attention to it than most presidents. The bottom line, however, was that the actions Clinton authorized and the scope of counterterrorism tools he endorsed were not working. Given additional options, all more risky and aggressive, he elected to not expand the criteria limiting operational activities.

Other Clinton administration officials argued that in the 1990s the threat of terrorism was seen as a threat distant from U.S. shores, and Americans would not have supported an antiterrorism policy that included broad military action and casualties. Only 32 percent of Americans viewed terrorism as one of the most important threats to world peace in January 1997. There is no doubt that the death of U.S. soldiers is a sensitive issue for Americans. The body-bag counts from the Vietnam War are inscribed permanently upon the memories and the cultural lore of America. Military adventurism is a negative concept in the United States. One-third of Americans did not support the 1998 retaliatory strikes against bin Ladin. The reaction to the deaths of the U.S. soldiers in Somalia was negative. This does support the felt need for the president to weigh the risks of engaging in a military battle with potential casualties against a distant and not widely accepted foe. In and of itself, it does not justify a reluctance to engage in a standoff military-attack posture, such as cruise missile attacks or a sustained air bombing campaign, or a more robust covert action program.

Clinton administration officials have stated that the intelligence on bin Ladin's whereabouts in Afghanistan was never solid enough to authorize cruise missile attacks. This is the heart of the issue, but not for the reason one might initially suppose. By limiting the operational scope to bin Ladin, the man, the U.S. government allowed al-Qa'ida, the organization, to continue to operate and to prepare terrorists for new operations against the United States. While the United States tried to get bin Ladin into its crosshairs, the scope ignored the other potential targets. All of the September 11 terrorists are believed to have been in Afghanistan in the late 1990s, training and preparing for their roles in the attacks against the United States.

By focusing upon having a clean hit against bin Ladin, and not on the operational headquarters, the United States failed to act to disrupt the central organ of al-Qa'ida. A sustained program of destroying al-Qa'ida bases would have denied the terrorists a safe haven for assembly, disrupted their training programs, destroyed some resources and capabilities, forced them to assume a greater defensive posture, tied up their remaining resources, and created a sense of greater vulnerability. Bin Ladin is just one man; destroying al-Qa'ida and the international network required more than the destruction of one man. Even Tenet admitted that the United States should have taken down the al-Qa'ida sanctuary "a lot sooner."[16]

But the problem was—and is—much larger than this. Destruction of al-Qa'ida headquarters alone would not destroy the ideology. A far broader campaign of political action to win away support from extremist Islamic movements (not just al-Qa'ida) was and is needed. The United States lacked a comprehensive and integrated strategy for countering the threat.

I believe that the source of Clinton's caution was his fear of failure of another foreign policy adventure rather than protection of a policy initiative, or a low priority on terrorism or reluctance to risk U.S. lives. His track record was weak, and there was no compelling reason to test the waters any further. The gain in getting rid of bin Ladin, or Saddam Hussein, was not worth the risk of negative political fallout that a failed attempt would bring. By 1998, Clinton recognized that terrorism was a growing threat that needed attention, but he did not recognize it as a strategic threat to the well-being of the nation. It was not the kind of threat that demanded risk taking that could endanger his presidency, which was already under impeachment threat. It was not the kind of existential threat for which a president could call upon Americans to make personal sacrifices. It was a threat that had killed U.S. soldiers and diplomats whose duties placed them in the line of fire. It was a threat that was geographically distant. It was a threat that could be managed and minimized. It was not a threat that required bold action. The attacks of September 11 were simply unimaginable when viewed from the Clinton White House of the 1990s.

The concept of unleashing the CIA and empowering the intelligence community to wage a real war on terrorism was not welcomed in the White House, in Congress, or with senior CIA management, for that matter. Clinton started off his presidency distrustful of the CIA and, eight year later, remained disinclined to use it as his action arm. Clinton was more inclined to use other policy arms first. As a last resort, he would call upon the CIA, but then would not authorize it to do what was necessary to achieve the mission. Congress reinforced the idea that the CIA was dangerous and needed to be kept on a short leash. In its recommendations for reforming the intelligence community, the House Permanent Select Committee on Intelligence described the activities of the Directorate of Operations as the operations that "inevitably land the DCI in trouble" and that this tendency "can be minimized if careful attention is paid to the command and control of clandestine operations."[17]

Tenet read the political tea leaves and pursued a conservative, risk-minimizing management strategy. He did not get in Clinton's face over terrorism. Tenet was willing to go to the mat over certain issues, but not the war on terrorism. For example, when Clinton proposed releasing Jonathan Pollard—a U.S. citizen convicted of spying for Israel—in order to sweeten the political deal between Israelis and Palestinians being worked out at Wye River, Tenet threatened to resign. The joint congressional intelligence committee found that "the U.S. Government's response to the bin Ladin threat was not the responsibility of the DCI or the Intelligence Community, but of the President and the National Security Council."[18] Ultimately, this is true, but it does not dissolve the responsibility of the DCI as the chief advisor to the president and the director of the intelligence community. In Tenet's own words, given at his confirmation hearing as DCI, he was hired to warn and protect the nation, not just to observe and comment.

So how important was fighting bin Ladin and the war on terrorism? It was not important enough to staff the CIA Counterterrorism Center properly. It was not important enough to change the prevailing mindset of risk aversion within the CIA and the political establishment. It was not important enough to break down stovepipes that separated the various arms of the Agency and the CIA from the rest of the intelligence community. It was not important enough to jeopardize bilateral relationships with Arab states. It was not important enough to risk the lives of American soldiers. It was not important enough to Tenet to risk his relationship with Clinton and his job as DCI. It was not important enough to Clinton to risk his presidency. From 1989 to 2000, it was important; it just was not the most-important-bar-none problem.

24
The Dark Side

LANGLEY, VIRGINIA, 2001: If one listened only to the hype of the Washington spin doctors, one might think that Tenet walked on water. Vocal critics have been far and few between, with the exception of Richard Shelby, former chairman of the Senate Intelligence Committee. Despite his overwhelming positive public image, Tenet did have his critics within the CIA. Complaints have been muted because of sheer contrasts, as opposed to specific conduct. Tenet was so much better than the preceding DCIs that his failings have been more readily overlooked or discounted. However, certain facts become unavoidable when examining performance. The Agency remained risk averse and senior management did not take the steps to rectify the problems. Tenet, always the political animal, chose to not make the necessary waves to engage in a real war on terrorism. Only after September 11 would Tenet's leadership and conduct be questioned externally. However, complaints of poor management and unfair personnel practices surfaced well before September 11.

NEW HEADQUARTERS BUILDING, LANGLEY, VIRGINIA, 1999: CIA counterintelligence officer Brian Kelley was about to get the surprise of his life. He thought that he was going to a routine meeting with a senior officer. Instead, he found himself the subject of a major counterintelligence investigation. In a small interview room not far from his own office, Kelley was greeted by two FBI agents who pronounced him a traitor. He was placed on administrative leave, his security clearance revoked.

298 • MELISSA BOYLE MAHLE

After Nicholson was arrested, the CIA remained convinced that there was another mole inside the Agency. The potential access to and information exposed by Ames, Nicholson, and former FBI agent Pitts did not explain certain operational losses. So much could not be explained by Ames alone. The CIA found highly sensitive intelligence reports in Ames's office on Soviet military issues to which Ames did not have approved access.[1] There were losses of technical operations against the Russians for which Ames did not have access. The CIA concluded that another Agency officer—a fellow mole—gave the reports to Ames and that he knew the identity of the other mole.

Ames was polygraphed repeatedly and asked one by one if so-and-so (all Agency officers) was a mole. When this tactic proved futile, Counterespionage staff abandoned the fishing operation. Counter-espionage staff had some information from sensitive reporting sources on the access of the mole, but the reporting sources stated that the SVR (formerly the KGB) did not know the name or position of their agent. From this access profile, the Agency looked at the assignments of a number of Agency officers, eventually determining that a particular Agency officer assigned to the Directorate of Operations in Counterespionage partially fit the profile. Therefore, the CIA notified the FBI of its suspicions of Brian Kelley.

The FBI initiated a covert investigation of Brian Kelley, including a covert search of his house and bugging of his phones, but was unable to develop any evidence against him. The CIA transferred him to a less-sensitive position, where he had minimal access to classified information. Kelley's daughter, who also worked for the CIA, was denied a sensitive and high-profile position on the basis of the suspicions of her father's loyalty. Kelley was subjected to a sting operation, in which an FBI agent posing as a Russian pitched him. Kelley reported the pitch to his superiors, who were in on the sting. He also successfully passed multiple polygraph examinations—one under false pretenses—all judged to have produced inaccurate results because the CIA and the FBI were certain that he was the mole.

Although there were CIA officers with access to the details who were convinced they had the wrong man, only one spoke up to senior management on his doubts. He was ignored. Everyone else was content to pass the ball to the FBI, holding up their arms, saying, "It is out of my hands." Some FBI officers involved in the investigation had their doubts. While these were shared with Counterespionage staff, management failed to report the information up the chain of command.

Once the investigation went overt, Kelley, as many before him, entered a special room in hell reserved for "problem employees." Most Agency officers do not know anything about this part of the Agency. Stories are dismissed as falsifications created by disgruntled former employees. It is just too hard to reconcile the unfair practices, official dishonesty, and purposeful humiliating treatment with the CIA that officers think they "know." A wall goes up between the employee and the Agency, immediately transforming the employee who was accustomed to being "one of us" into "one of them." With his security clearance revoked, the employee is no longer entitled to know the specifics of the case against him. Accustomed to dealing truthfully with colleagues, the employee is eventually shocked at the realization that he is receiving half-truths or outright lies in response to his questions—all in the name of security. It is a steep path downhill.

There is nothing worse than that feeling of having one's loyalty suspected. I am speaking from personal experience. As the target of a counterintelligence investigation that eventually forced me out of the Agency, I know exactly what Kelley went through. Turning over my badge meant being cut off from former colleagues and work about which I was passionate. I became a nonperson, isolated from everything that once was important. I was humiliated by having to call in to the Office of Security every day, checking in, letting my controllers know that I had not fled the country or committed suicide in despair. When summoned to the Office of Security, I was searched before entering a building that I used to enter freely. I was issued a visitor's badge that requires an escort. The badge was a scarlet letter, to be worn in shame before former colleagues.

The FBI harassed Brian Kelley and his family in order to provoke a confession. They followed him, questioned his friends and family, insinuating that they, too, could be arrested for protecting him. Meanwhile, Kelley tried to clear his name. He pointed out significant investigative failures on the part of the FBI. No one was interested in hearing his claims of innocence, because he was presumed to be lying. Only after FBI agent Robert Hanssen was arrested would the CIA clear Kelley of wrongdoing.

Kelley and Hanssen had similar professional backgrounds, both working in assignments involving counterintelligence and counterespionage work. Both focused on the Soviet Union and then Russia. Both lived in Vienna, Virginia, very near each other, and the dead-drop sites that Hanssen frequented. However, one was a deadly traitor and the other a loyal employee and citizen. Nevertheless, the similarities do not explain why the FBI and CIA failed to consider exculpatory evidence.

After twenty-one months of administrative leave, Kelley was restored to the workforce, returning to counterintelligence work. Due to the damage to his reputation, Kelley never really entertained the thought that he would ever be allowed to return. In his surprise, he was more cooperative than most would be. He accepted that he would no longer be assigned to the most sensitive work, work that would have required interaction with the FBI on sensitive matters—time was needed, said the powers that be. He accepted that his upward promotion into the Senior Intelligence Service would never happen, because he had been side-lined by suspicion for too long.

Kelley was content to be there, and to prove to all who would see his face that they were wrong. He was—and always has been—loyal to his organization and to his country. There would be no immediate official apology to Brian Kelley. Nor compensation for the pain and suffering caused to him by sloppy investigative work, intellectual arrogance, and a system with few checks and balances. At the CIA, even though he has been brought back into the fold, he will always remain suspect. His hall-corridor file will contain a big question mark.

Probably out of a psychological need, Kelley chose to focus his anger on the FBI, even though the CIA was responsible for starting the boulder rolling. The FBI conducted the investigation poorly, but was disinclined to admit this, even after the fact. An apology would come only after pressure was brought to bear on the FBI by Senator Pat Leahy, a college classmate of Kelley's. Furthermore, no one at the FBI or CIA has been disciplined for his or her role in allowing a seriously flawed investigation to continue for almost two years. The responsible CIA officers have subsequently been promoted and moved on to positions of greater authority. Once again, no one was held accountable.

Not all CIA employees are successful in clearing their names after becoming the focus of a counterintelligence investigation. The CIA increasingly practices a preemptive policy of revoking security clearances if the Agency begins to suspect divided loyalties. The threshold is very low, and the officer does not have to have crossed a line to have action taken against him or her. The mere *suspicion* that an officer might have divided loyalties, without any evidence of having done anything disloyal, is sufficient for termination. The DCI has this discretionary authority. Terminate the employee and let the FBI figure it out is the new policy.

In one case, a Jewish Agency lawyer was fired for "lack of candor" about his family's social and religious ties to right-wing groups in Israel. I was accused of lack of candor on my contacts with Palestinians.* Both of us lost our security clearances on the basis of what we might do in the future, not what we did in the past. Again, exculpatory evidence, past excellent performance histories, and contributions to national security were dismissed.

The fired lawyer is suing the CIA under Title VII anti-discrimination laws. He has been successful in keeping the venue in the District of Columbia, something that the CIA normally fights. The CIA has carefully cultivated the U.S. District Court for the Eastern District of Virginia in Alexandria, the district that has jurisdiction for Langley, the location of CIA Headquarters. This federal court—far more than the federal courts for Maryland and the District of Columbia—is sympathetic to arguments invoking national security interests and frequently rejects suits filed against the CIA on the basis of national security. It is no wonder that the CIA faces accusations that it operates above the law.

FEDERAL COURT, ALEXANDRIA, VIRGINIA, 1998: In a statement to the court, Douglas F. Groat admitted, "I put pressure on the government to resolve our dispute and I have used some of their own tactics against them. But I have paid dearly for standing up for my beliefs and fighting for fair and just treatment."[2] Groat was right, especially about paying dearly. He would spend the next three years in prison.

The press characterized the spying case of Douglas F. Groat as an oddity, but in fact it is an excellent example of oppressive CIA security action against an officer that ultimately pushed him over the edge. Groat was a sixteen-year veteran of the Directorate of Science and Technology, who worked in covert operations aimed at the penetration of cryptographic (communications) systems of foreign governments. These kind of covert operations are extremely hush-hush and can involve black-bag operations: breaking into foreign ███████ and facilities and compromising their communications.

This kind of work requires specialized skills and a certain kind of personality, with nerves of steel, meticulous work habits, and sharp focus. The risks of getting caught red-handed in a foreign embassy are high;

---

* Mine is a great story, but the CIA has done its best to keep me from telling it by advising me that portions of it are classified—without notifying me which portions. The CIA declined to respond to my letter asking for clarification.

there is no diplomatic immunity for operations outside the United States. If discovered during a break-in, if black baggers are fortunate not to get shot, they can expect a long period in a foreign jail. With conditions in many Third World jails inhumane, death can look preferable. Good interpersonal skills are nice but not really necessary for black baggers. The types of individuals who do this kind of work can be tough to manage because they want to do things their own way, since their asses are on the line. End of discussion.

Those who worked with Groat described him as difficult to get along with and set in his ways. Even before he joined the CIA, he had a history of being stubborn. His stubbornness got him in trouble when he worked as a police officer. After a disagreement with his supervisor, he was suspended for insubordination. Inflexible beyond the pale, Groat fought the charges to the bitter end. His perseverance paid off; he won his lawsuit against the Glenville Town Board and was reinstated.[3]

Groat's personality profile should have been well understood by the CIA, as an organization that relies on psychological assessments for officers doing stressful and highly secret work. When Groat came into conflict with CIA management, Office of Security opted to take the confrontational and threatening approach. Rather than backing down, Groat responded in kind and went on a war footing. Given Groat's history, this should have been anticipated. The consequences were negative for both the CIA and Groat.

In 1990, Groat became involved in a long battle with CIA management on operational methods that Groat considered flawed and a danger to his team's security. The conflict came to a head after an operation was exposed in early 1993. When management launched an internal investigation to determine what went wrong in the exposed operation against a foreign ████, Groat was not cooperative. He refused to take a polygraph test as part of the investigation, believing it a ploy to scapegoat him. His refusal to cooperate was sufficient grounds for Office of Security to revoke Groat's security clearance, which it did when the threat to do so did not result in Groat's acquiescence.

Groat became enraged that he was considered a security risk and was suspected of disloyalty. The CIA placed Groat on paid administrative leave in May 1993. Groat pursued an appeal, demanding reinstatement and compensation. Because the CIA is exempt for the Civil Service Protection Laws, Agency officers have no outside authority to challenge a personnel action, without resorting to legal action. There is an internal appeal process, but those doing the review are essentially the same people who make the initial determination. The appeal board almost never overturns the initial decision. Groat also took issue with the inspection done by the CIA inspector general's office, calling him "an extension of the CIA bureaucracy, primarily concerned with damage control and protecting management.[4] Not surprisingly, Groat lost his appeal and was fired in October 1996.

The CIA offered Groat a settlement worth $400,000 plus a pension based on his $70,000 salary, in an attempt to buy him off and ensure that he would go away quietly. A less confrontational person would have buried his pride, taken the money, and looked to the future for new beginnings. However, Groat was the kind of person who had to win, and this settlement did not meet his definition of winning. He wanted significantly more money for his silence—$1 million more.

Groat decided to do something that he knew would cause the CIA angst: he threatened to offer his services as a security consultant, trading on his professional knowledge, as a means of pressuring the CIA to see the cost of their intransigence. Groat got the CIA's attention—its full counterintelligence attention.

The FBI arrested Groat on April 2, 1998. According to court records, Groat carried through on his threat and revealed secrets to two foreign governments in 1997. Groat crossed the line and became disloyal, according to the government's case. On July 27, 1998, in a negotiated plea, Groat pleaded guilty to one count of attempted extortion, and the espionage charges were dropped.

While Groat bears full responsibility for his actions, the CIA role of pushing a troubled employee into a corner, and the tactics that it used, should not be ignored. Groat was not disloyal when the operation went bad in 1993; he was doing his job, albeit imperfectly. Groat became disloyal only in reaction to his treatment by the CIA Office of Security.

SEVENTH FLOOR, LANGLEY, VIRGINIA, 1999: When Tenet first arrived at the CIA, he indicated that security and accountability needed to be tightened up. Rather than improve the situation, under Tenet, the Agency adopted overbearing security practices and equally dysfunctional accountability procedures. The mission of the Office of Security is to keep the CIA secure, not to paralyze operations or to provoke officers into revengeful acts. It is a critical mission. The traumatic espionage cases of the 1980s and 1990s upset the equilibrium of the Agency. The bad old days of Angleton and destructive security and counterintelligence practices of that age have returned.

Employees are afraid to challenge the system out of fear of retribution, and management is not willing to address the problems out of fear of being called "soft" on security.

Retribution is a daily concern. Take the case of Johnny Michael Spann. Spann, a CIA paramilitary officer, was killed in the prison uprising at Mazar-e Sharif in the early days of the military offensive in Afghanistan. Normally, the death of a CIA officer is carefully kept out of the news because of cover issues. Tenet decided to make a large publicity play that CIA blood was the first spilled on the battleground, in what was interpreted within the halls of the CIA as a counteroffensive against perceived CIA inaction before the September 11 attack. Tenet's concern—and that of senior CIA management—for Spann's family was shown by high-profile attendance receiving the coffin from the military plane and at Spann's funeral.

What the public did *not* get to see was how Spann's death annuity was managed by the Agency. The past practice toward the families of officers killed in the line of duty was that the widow would receive an annuity for life (or until the time of her remarriage) based upon the salary level of the officer at the time of death. The knowledge of future financial security for the family was an important aspect freeing us to place ourselves in positions of mortal risk. The Agency policy of taking care of its own was well known and well appreciated. It was part and parcel of the lore of the organization and the band of brothers.

CIA management honored Spann in an in-house ceremony, announcing that he had received a postmortem promotion to a higher pay level. What went unmentioned was that the annuity to his wife was limited to one year. Details like this do not remain secret long within the halls of Langley. Directorate of Operations officers were outraged by the new and previously unannounced policy. If this was not tragic enough for Spann's family, Spann's first wife then died of cancer, orphaning their two daughters.

On their own, Spann's colleagues started a fund for the support of Spann's family. It was unofficial, and collection notices were sent out over the internal e-mail system. The response was tremendous—not only from colleagues, who gave generously, but from management. CIA senior management lashed back at the organizers, reprimanding them for misuse of Agency computers (e-mail) for personal business. Rather than address the problem, management sought to punish those highlighting the problem.

The change in the death annuity was not the only controversial personnel program under Tenet. Agency officers have been unhappy with

Executive Director Buzzy Krongard's initiatives on personnel practices. Dubbed Krongard's "Reign of Terror," the Executive Director has adopted an off-with-their-heads accountability program. Firing employees has more often become the personnel action of first resort, rather than matching the punishment to the misdeed.

Krongard apparently thinks that the CIA should have a personnel turnover rate the same as industry—approximately 15 percent. Krongard believes that the CIA treats its employees too well and therefore they stay too long. While turnover is important to keep new blood flowing through the personnel system, there is the reality that the skill sets employed by the Directorate of Operations and the Directorate of Intelligence are not developed overnight. It takes years for officers to reach their full potential. There is no natural spawning ground for mature officers with these skills outside the CIA. In early 2000, the CIA claimed it had an attrition rate of approximately 5 percent. To arbitrarily increase attrition through managed personnel actions, such as giving the boot to the bottom 10 percent, regardless of performance, hurts the Agency in the long run.

Agency officers are very distrustful of ongoing discussions to change the Agency compensation system and believe that the proposed changes would be to the long-term disadvantage of employees. The proposed compensation program would introduce a pay-banding system and reduce the number of compensation grades. Officers would remain in a pay band for an extended period of time. While promotions became fewer, officers would be compensated by salary bonuses for performance. The problem with the system is that the decision makers for the bonuses would be "paymasters" working in the chain of command of the officer being rated. Pay levels would become subjected to the power-and-influence game—in other words, the old-boy system.

This is not an idle concern; cronyism made a strong resurgence after Tenet became DCI. After being in his position for several years, Tenet began surrounding himself with his handpicked team, promoting those close to him out of sequence. One of his favorites jumped multiple grades in one promotion cycle. Officers who were fortunate to gain his attention were put on special lists and promoted rapidly. The assignment-transparency process put in place after the class action lawsuit by women operations officers was effectively undermined with Tenet's nod. "Needs of the service" became the new avenue for choice assignments to be given to protégés of the old boys. Although female officers had made significant inroads for senior assignments, the progress has eroded under Tenet.

As the practice of convening accountability boards has evolved under Tenet, there is great subjectivity on whether or not an infraction is referred to a board. The decision is influenced greatly by the old-boy network, where senior managers protect their protégés from administrative action. If a board is convened and the review is formal, there is already an informal consensus within management that punitive action will be taken.

Tenet reversed the trend of the 1990s for more openness and responsibility to the public on national security issues. As part of the "Reinventing Government" campaign, Vice President Gore initiated a review of security practices and procedures at the Defense Department and the CIA in an effort to get rid of unnecessary bureaucracy and secrecy. President Clinton signed an executive order in 1995 mandating the automatic declassification of government records—with specific exemptions—after twenty-five years.

Tenet embraced the declassification mandate with little enthusiasm. In 1998, he backed away from a program set up by Woolsey for "block review" for release of covert action programs of the 1940s, 1950s, and 1960s, as well as analysis on topics of special historical interest thirty years or older. Tenet claimed insufficient resources. The CIA had set up a secure warehouse where retirees and employees desiring overtime toiled at night reading old files, armed with black markers and a keen interest in history. It was a popular moonlighting job where one learned amazing things about the past and more than a few details on dirty tricks. Imagine being the one to review the Kennedy documents related to Oswald and the Soviets! These—along with all the major studies of the Soviet Union prior to 1960—were declassified in the early 1990s.

Tenet balked over the release of the Chile document, which covered CIA covert operations that undermined democratically elected socialist President Salvador Allende. After tremendous congressional pressure, he approved the release of seven hundred documents. In 1998, Tenet released the overall intelligence budget for 1997 and 1998, when it appeared that the CIA was about to lose a lawsuit that would set precedents for future disclosures. He fought the release of subsequent years' budgets, choosing his day in court when the odds for success were greater. Tenet prefers to play the public disclosure game only when it is to the overwhelming and immediate benefit of the Agency. His preference for secrecy reinforces self-destructive inclinations to use "national security" to cover up poor performance and wrongdoing.

25
Help Wanted

CIA RECRUITMENT CENTER, VIRGINIA, 1998: Slick new ads were just part of the new recruitment program. Pictures of young, attractive men and women of different races began to flood the print media, seductively calling America's youth to join an elite force and be more than they ever thought they could be. The CIA seal appeared boldly in ads, enticing applicants to call. The ads were everywhere, on posters on college campuses, in-flight magazines, prestigious national newspapers, trade journals, and minority recruiting fair programs. Gone were the days of a quiet recruiting, don't-call-us-we'll-call-you attitude. The CIA started its new recruiting drive with gusto, breaking all of the old rules.

The decision to resume hiring came as part of the DCI's Strategic Initiative. The last of the big hiring years was 1989. The personnel hemorrhaging of the early 1990s left the CIA woefully understaffed. It did not have the financial resources to maintain a steady stream of new-hires to maintain a normal personnel curve. As a short-term, cost-effective measure, the Agency turned to outsourcing certain types of work. Hiring contractors relieved the large financial burden of supplying benefits. Much of the support work could easily be outsourced. Analytical and operational work was more difficult to outsource, because the job requirements were not run-of-the-mill and because of security requirements. Outsourcing became an avenue for Directorate of Operations and Directorate of Intelligence retirees (called "annuitants") to return to the workforce, part-time or full-time, in accordance to their preferences. It was a good short-term fix for both the Agency and the retirees.

The Agency retained their expertise, while the retirees, who did not need the benefits, enjoyed keeping their hand in the game. However, it was not a sustainable solution.

In 1998, the Directorate of Operations realized that it was critically short on core intelligence collectors. By 1996, the Directorate of Operations had reduced the number of core collectors by over 30 percent. The number of deployed, officially covered operations officers had been declining at an average rate of almost 10 percent a year.[1] ▮▮

▮ Spread over the plan timeline, the Directorate of Operations planned to hire and deploy them overseas. In 1998, it was considered an ambitious plan that would be difficult to meet. Bottlenecks in the recruitment infrastructure were many, from insufficient recruiters to medical officers, background investigators, and polygraph operators. All applicants had to be interviewed multiple times, cleared medically, and issued top-secret-level security clearances. The Directorate of Operations had to compete with the other directorates, which were also hiring, for these scarce resources.

Up until 1998, the main obstacle was not finding the people within the organization to do the work, but getting the money out of Congress to pay for the salaries and benefits of new employees. Prior to 1998, Congress was not convinced that the CIA was understaffed. Congressional attitudes toward the intelligence community were stuck in the immediate post–Cold War perception that intelligence did not warrant the budget it had. Therefore, there were few members of Congress interested in championing increased funding for CIA infrastructure. It was relatively easy for the CIA to gain one-time funding for specific operations; obtaining long-term funding for new personal services contracts was nearly impossible.

Congressional attitudes changed after May 1998. The failure to predict the Indian nuclear test and the admission by the Directorate of Operations that it had no agents in place capable of reporting on India's plans was the catalyst for change. For too long, investments in technical collection means had been made at the expense of human operations. Technical collection, while extremely useful, has limited capabilities for providing intelligence on *intentions* of foreign leaders. Directorate of Operations was able to put the plan in motion because Congress finally became receptive to CIA's repeated warnings that human intelligence espionage capabilities had decayed to the point that the Directorate of Operations was becoming paralyzed.

The plan, which was considered ambitious in 1998, has been completely eclipsed by the new resource requirements as a result of September 11. I was working in the Recruitment Center before the attacks and was having difficulties meeting my hiring targets. After September 11, the target changed daily, always rising.

All directorates in the Agency developed new plans to significantly increase the number of new-hires over the coming years. In the weeks and months following the attacks, the CIA reassessed its human resources needs, with the numbers jumping higher and higher. Certain requirements were obvious. The CIA was short on linguists, especially native speakers of Urdu, Pashto, and Arabic. But that was just the tip of the iceberg.

The CIA realized that it would need to significantly gear up counterterrorism, counterproliferation, and paramilitary operations to support the war on terrorism. Five hundred officers were transferred immediately to the Counterterrorism Center. Whole groups were transferred, leaving enormous personnel gaps in the other area divisions and centers. Core collection officers in the field who were working "noncritical" issues were transferred back to Headquarters. The CIA found itself in a difficult position of having to staff new groups in counterterrorism and counterproliferation, and backfill those slots left empty by the surge to the Counterterrorism Center.

Planning to hire and actually hiring are two very different things. It is hard to find good people. It is very hard to find good people who are willing to work for a government wage, and harder still to find good people who are willing to work for a government wage and who can meet the existing security clearance requirements.

The September 11 attacks reinvigorated patriotism in the United States, and many Americans stepped up to the plate, volunteering their services to protect our national security. In the six months following the attacks, the CIA was swamped with résumés going from six hundred a week to two- to three thousand a week. Men and women from Wall Street and Corporate America wanted to do their part and join the ranks of the CIA. College students, who previously had been motivated by the prospects of making big money after graduation, rethought their priorities and sent in résumés. Retirees offered up their past experience and Rolodexes. There were résumés from CEOs, cowboys, bankers, bank robbers, doctors, lawyers, strippers, accountants, animal trainers—you name it. Some were very impressive; some were chilling, like the West Coast dentist who offered his knowledge of administering pain. The enthusiasm dampened as the applicants faced the reality of starting salaries ($40,000–$65,000) and the length of the application process. On a good day, it takes six to nine months from the time of the first interview to a job offer.

As the recruiting effort began to pick up in 1998, the CIA initially found itself in a tough employment market. Private sector salaries were significantly higher than starting salaries at the CIA. The CIA found it difficult to compete against the "Morgan Stanleys" of the world for a second-generation Arab-American with near-native Arabic-language ability willing to work in the Middle East in a commercial context. Patriotism was a relatively hard sale as compensation for the $100,000 the applicant would *not* make. However, patriotism was on the rise starting in 1998, as was the reputation of the CIA. There was a time that the CIA could not recruit on college campuses because of scandals resulting from the exposure of secret relationships between the CIA and research departments and scholars.

The times had changed; the CIA resumed a robust college recruiting program across the nation. During my time at the Recruitment Center, I spent a lot of time at universities, speaking to undergraduate and graduate students about career opportunities in the Directorate of Operations. I was always well received, even at universities known for their liberal politics.

The Directorate of Intelligence and the Directorate of Science and Technology forged new relationships with academia as they tried to tap into capabilities outside the Agency. Academics began moonlighting at the Agency, producing analysis on special issues for policymakers. The Directorate of Science and Technology funded research projects at universities. Academic openness remained an issue. Some prestigious universities declined CIA-funded research projects because of secrecy requirements. Also at issue was the CIA's new requirement to restrict research opportunities to U.S. citizens, even if the research is unclassified. Many universities were willing to compromise on secrecy requirements in order to obtain the government funding, as a counterbalance to private sector endowments, which have been declining throughout the decade.[2]

Having found that good applicant with the right qualifications and willingness to work for a government wage, the next hurdle is psychological suitability. This issue is far more important to the Directorate of Operations than the other directorates. Without going into the details of the suitability perimeters, it is sufficient to say that the Directorate of Operations looks for a specific psychological profile. The profile, which is fairly rigid, ensures that the applicant will fit well into the

Directorate of Operations culture, be a risk taker but not a rule breaker, an independent and action-oriented kind of person. The problem is that unless the applicant is an American raised in a middle- to upper-middle-class environment that embraces the major cultural icons of established America, he or she doesn't fit the profile.

The Directorate of Operations actively recruits ethnic minorities with native foreign language capabilities, only to lose them in the psychological screening process, or the security clearance process. I can't tell you how many minority applicants—Arab Americans, Chinese Americans, Korean Americans, Indian Americans, and others—whom I lost to security or suitability, because the number is classified; however, it was not an insignificant number. The problem was best illustrated by a panoramic view of the swearing-in of the first class to enter on duty to the Directorate of Operations after September 11; it was a sea of white faces.

Security clearance is perhaps the largest hurdle to obtaining employment with the CIA. In 2001, for every three applicants sent to Security for clearances, only one emerged cleared. The vast majority were rejected on the basis of the polygraph. According to information provided to the House Permanent Select Committee on Intelligence in 1979, approximately 75 percent of applicants denied security clearances by the CIA or National Security Agency resulted from the polygraph.[3] The clearance rate is a very difficult statistic to comprehend, because it suggests that two out of three Americans are engaged in a level of immoral, criminal, or counterintelligence behavior that exceeds the acceptable levels of the U.S. government national security requirements. While there is no doubt that the CIA has been damaged by hiring individuals who later defected, the security disqualification rate is outside the bounds of reasonable assessment.

A large part of the problem rests with overdependence on the polygraph, which has been discredited by the scientific community as inaccurate and unreliable. A conclusive 245-page report prepared by experts convened by the National Research Council, an arm of the National Academy of Sciences, stated that the scientific basis for polygraph testing was weak and that much of the research supporting its use lacked scientific rigor. The report found that polygraph testing was too flawed to use for security screening, that it did a poor job of identifying spies or other national security risks and was likely to produce accusations against innocent people.[4]

The Agency claims to weigh polygraph results with the results of background investigations before making a security determination. The

Agency also claims that it does not take personnel action on the sole basis of the polygraph. The Agency claims this because polygraphs are not admissible in court, except in very limited situations, and the CIA would theoretically be open to legal action if personnel action was taken solely as a result of a failed polygraph examination. The claims are just that: if the Agency was forced to open up its records, the statistics would prove otherwise.

Another problem is that there is no incentive to take risks, no matter how small. There is no such thing as the benefit of the doubt when it comes to clearances. Worse still, polygraph examiners are paid bonuses for catching people who lie when completing their SF-86 forms or during the polygraph. In order to recruit the number of people with specialized qualifications that the Agency requires, the security clearance system needs to be modified.

Tenet has been frustrated by the Agency's inability to hire and clear minority candidates, notably Arab Americans. Upon learning that there were no candidates in the pipeline for the first post–September 11 Career Service Trainee class, he went ballistic and dressed down his human resources team. He requested that Arab American candidates be brought on board without completing the standard security clearance process—notably the polygraph—in order to meet the "needs of the service." Security and counterintelligence staffs were apoplectic. While the needs are valid, so are the concerns, highlighting the quandary of the CIA. The screening system needs to be refined, not thrown out completely.

There is no new technology on the horizon that is ready for deployment that detects lies accurately. Meanwhile, the Agency considers the loss of personnel due to false positives as an acceptable cost of doing business, as the CIA is determined to never permit another Ames to burrow into the organization and destroy sources and methods again. Perhaps the costs are acceptable to the Agency, but they are not acceptable for the men and women who have been falsely labeled disloyal and security threats and have been denied the opportunity to serve their country. Once the CIA has denied or revoked a security clearance, it is virtually impossible to obtain a security clearance from another federal government agency, since federal government agencies routinely violate the privacy act and share the information.

Because of the personnel crisis, the practice of outsourcing has exploded since September 11, with some possible negative impact for the short and medium term. The demand in the intelligence community for individuals with special skills and existing security clearances has created a niche employment market. Workers who are in short supply have more leverage in the marketplace. The contract system allows workers greater mobility, and they can pick and choose between contracts to a far greater degree. This forces up the wage rate and erodes institutional loyalty. Agency employees are being wooed away from staff positions to contract positions because of greater financial rewards.

While allowing businesses to downsize or grow as the market changes might be a more efficient human resource management system in the private sector, in the intelligence business, it has the potential of creating a transient workforce with insufficient substantive expertise. For example, the pool of information technology (IT) specialists is large and growing with new graduates entering the workforce. The pool of seasoned operations officers with foreign language capabilities is small and homegrown (i.e., trained within the Agency). Assuming that this trend continues, the Agency will have increased difficulties in retaining staff and maintaining experts across the board in the short to medium term. In the long term, if the pool of trained professionals is enlarged significantly and the process for training professionals is expanded and regularized across the intelligence community, the system would be more efficient and better serve both the government and intelligence professionals.

Creating a national-level intelligence training center has been considered periodically over the past several decades. Proponents believe that providing a basic-level, multidisciplinary approach to training intelligence professionals through cross training would build linkages at the foundation of the intelligence community. These linkages currently do not exist. While intelligence professionals know a lot about their own organization, they tend to know little about other intelligence community agencies. This parochialism feeds bureaucratic turf battles that have plagued the intelligence community since its creation. A national-level training program would also increase the pool of trained intelligence professionals, easing the supply-and-demand equation in the long term.

Opponents argue largely along bureaucratic lines, highlighting the different missions and training needs of departmental and national programs. Currently, the only way to expose intelligence officials to the diverse capabilities and needs of the intelligence community is through on-the-job experience and the senior schools (i.e., war colleges). If the intelligence community is going to function more cohesively, changes need to be made at the bottom of the pyramid. The current system of top-down coordination is ineffective, as evidenced by unending turf battles.

26
Failure

WASHINGTON, D.C., 2000: With two feet firmly planted in the year 2000, looking back over a decade of reform initiatives, one can see at the intelligence-community level a lot of motion with limited structural impact and, at the Agency level, specifically within the CIA, tremendous flux with wide-ranging positive and negative impact in terms of policy and process. A report card issued in the year 2000 might have given the intelligence community a passing mark, especially for showing improvement.

The quality of intelligence had improved over the decade, being more relevant and useful to consumers and delivered more quickly through electronic-dissemination systems. Investment into collection, analytical, and production capabilities had produced dividends. Intelligence support during the Kosovo conflict compared to that during the 1991 Gulf War better met the needs of Total Battlefield Awareness doctrine. Turf battles between intelligence community members had quieted down as new divisions of labor were worked out behind closed doors rather than in the press. Turf battles did not disappear, but rather the individual agencies toned them down in the spirit of "corporateness" if not in its practice.

Yes, there were still areas needing improvement; there were still failures. Nonetheless, there was a sense in the community that the worst of it was behind us, that we had turned the corner and were on the right track and that policymakers and Congress were generally appreciative of our contribution and supportive of how the intelligence community was carrying out their mission.

Taking a harder look at which reform initiatives addressing intelligence community structure were actually implemented, it is evident that there was more talk than action. Integration of the command structure of the intelligence community did not come to pass. A position of intelligence czar or Director of National Intelligence was not created. The authorities of the Director of Central Intelligence were not expanded significantly. Initiatives to give the DCI expanded budgetary controls over Pentagon intelligence budgets were defeated in what was essentially a turf battle between the Senate intelligence committee and the Senate Armed Services Committee, as were the initiatives to increase DCI control over Pentagon intelligence collection, the right to approve the persons nominated to head the National Security Agency, National Reconnaissance Office, and the Defense Intelligence Agency, and the transfer of the Defense Department's clandestine human spy service to the CIA. Minor changes were legislated in 1996, such as the creation of four new presidentially appointed subordinates to help the DCI in his role as coordinator of the intelligence community—that is, a deputy director for central intelligence for community management, and assistant directors of central intelligence for administration, collection, and analysis/production.

One major structural realignment was achieved; the creation of the National Imagery and Mapping Agency, integrating all imagery collection, analysis, and dissemination into one organization. Significant rationalization within the Defense Department would not take place, and there would be no appointment of one officer responsible for intelligence, whether a Director of Military Intelligence or a focal point within the Joint Chiefs of Staff. Other recommendations to break down stovepipes were not implemented. Issue managers for the collection disciplines that would have authority across agencies were not established. Personnel management and training systems intended to facilitate rotational assignments between agencies were not integrated. There would be no systematic "right-sizing" legislation to adjust the size and skill set of the workforce in the intelligence community outside the established rules of reduction in force or early retirement programs.

On policy and process, especially within the CIA, reforms were far-reaching. How the CIA conducted business at the beginning of the 1990s was quite different from how it conducted business by the end of that decade. The concept of strategic planning was introduced. Mission statements were written for the first time, throughout the organization, which started the process of tightening up the structure of the organization. By the turn of the century, there was a more defined sense of mission, albeit reduced in scope when compared to that of previous times. The CIA went from a worldwide intelligence organization to one with global capabilities. The earlier reforms and process changes were conducted in an ad hoc manner and were not integrated into a long-term strategic plan, creating reform whiplash. By the end of the decade, efforts at integration began to pay off so that earlier reforms were reinforced rather than being in conflict with newer concepts or being reversed completely.

Authority and decision making were pushed upward, with senior management weighing in on—if not making—more decisions. In the Directorate of Operations, the center of power shifted from the field to Headquarters. The risk-gain calculation shifted in response to the risk-averse political environment. There were few agents, fewer operations, and fewer validated operational targets by the end of the decade. The face of covert action changed dramatically, moving away from the large paramilitary operations of the previous decades to more boutique programs to counter terrorism and the proliferation of weapons of mass destruction. New regulations governing all aspects of operational work were written, although enforced selectively. Documentation requirements proliferated, characterized by highly structured formats and reporting periods.

The organizational structure of the Directorate of Intelligence was streamlined, reducing the numbers of managers, returning them to the meat and potatoes of analytical work. Security and counterintelligence procedures were updated, empowering the two offices without appropriate checks and balances. The multitude of process reviews and reforms drove already-low morale downward, and the organization hemorrhaged, losing far too many quality officers. Staffing was reduced by 25 percent, but done so in a way that left a skewed workforce. Morale improved slowly as reforms took hold and officers saw their benefits. The hemorrhage slowed, and there was a needed infusion of new blood and new capabilities. Budget cuts flattened, and by the end of the decade, there were increases in funding, though most frequently in fenced funds—money that could be used only for very specific purposes. Counterterrorism budgets were relatively fat, while the rest of the organization remained on a starvation diet.

Views of Tenet's performance were positive. He inherited a weak organization, dysfunctional on many different levels. Under his wise and dynamic leadership, he helped the organization heal and refocus on the primary mission; protection of the national security of the United States through the collection, analysis, and dissemination of intelligence. Reform under Tenet was evolutionary; there was no attempt to take on the big structural problems. The CIA and the rest of the intelligence community were pronounced healthy, or at least on the path toward good health. Positivism had replaced negativism at last, after a long, hard decade, or so a year 2000 report card would have reported.

SEVENTH FLOOR, LANGLEY, VIRGINIA, 2001: Tenet badly wanted to keep his job as DCI. He loved the work, and there was so much more work to be done. There was a new man in the White House—George Walker Bush—and Tenet's future hung in the wind. As it turned out, one good turn would win another. Tenet's tribute to George Bush Sr. would be remembered favorably. George Bush Jr. kept Tenet on as DCI for what was understood to be an interim period. It made good political and personal sense. Keeping Tenet meant that the new president would have one "bipartisan" member on his team. It broke the recent pattern that the DCI position was political in nature. In the early and young-adult years of the CIA, the directors did not change with a change in administration. The chief spy was chosen for his intelligence and national security credentials, not his necktie. George Bush Sr. resented that he was dismissed as DCI when President Carter took over from Ford. Although a son may not always take his father's advice, he certainly does listen if offered. Also, Tenet's report card looked good. So Tenet stayed.

Tenet kept his job beyond the interim period because he became the DCI whom Bush wanted. Contrary to initial expectations, Bush turned out to be a foreign policy activist. Overnight, Tenet switched tracks, leading the charge. America felt the change after September 11, when President Bush declared war on all those against America. America would no longer react, but preempt. The CIA felt the change almost immediately after Bush became president, *long before September 11*. There was change in the air at Langley. Bush was serious about getting rid of Saddam Hussein. Bush was serious about stopping weapons proliferation. After September 11, Bush became serious about terrorism.

COUNTERTERRORISM CENTER, LANGLEY, VIRGINIA, 2001: By spring, operational activity of bin Ladin operatives had reached a high level, and intelligence tidbits indicating a spectacular operation was in the works were coming in from multiple sources. The then-chief of the bin Ladin issue group was working furiously, because he knew something was going to happen—something bad—but he did not know what it was. An experienced operations officer, with a string of successes on his record and a relaxed hands-off management style, pushed his small staff to the edge of their capabilities. He morphed into a different kind of a manager as fear of missing something haunted his every waking moment. He drove his staff incessantly by micromanaging, sending e-mails every morning, asking if they had followed up on one point or another. The stakes were too high not to do so.

The Counterterrorism Center conducted a review of all intelligence and operational information in its holdings related to bin Ladin in August 2001. The review caught some things previously overlooked, such as the failure to watch-list some bin Ladin operatives: putting their names on the border-control blacklist so that they would be detained—or denied entry at a minimum. The Agency notified the intelligence community and policymakers of its assessment that al-Qa'ida was planning a large-scale operation that was spectacular in nature and could cause mass casualties. The Agency warned that al-Qa'ida desired to strike inside the United States. The CIA made the strategic warning, but then missed the tactical moment: September 11.

There has been considerable after-action attention to the lack of information sharing within the intelligence community, with different agencies holding bits of information that could have led to the disruption of the September 11 attacks. Whether these "missed signals" would have made an appreciable difference is highly debatable. Better intelligence sharing certainly could not have hurt. The question that will never have an answer: would better sharing have stopped the attacks? Of those made public, none would have definitely exposed the plot. The Joint Congressional Committee on September 11 found no smoking gun.

If Abdallah al-Midhar or Nawaf al-Hazmi (two of the hijackers who were known al-Qa'ida members) had been denied entry into the United States, there is evidence that operational planning allowed for adjustments. The attack may have been postponed—as it appears that it had already once been—or proceeded without them. The cell showed great adaptability and ability to overcome obstacles, as evidenced by adjustments taken after the repeated failure of Ramzi bin al-Shibh (the Germany-based leader for operational planning) to obtain a U.S. visa and the arrest of alleged coconspirator Zacarias Moussaoui (the suspected hijacker for a second wave of attacks) just days before the attack. Better sharing of intelligence could not have hurt; the bottom line is that it may not have helped. The real deficiency lay elsewhere.

The most significant missed opportunities are the al-Qa'ida training camps. From 1996 to 2001, the CIA collected intelligence on the locations of the camps and the types of training given, but did not act to disrupt them. The CIA wanted to identify the leadership and take out the leadership—principally Usama bin Ladin—when the opportunity presented itself. Conceptually, the CIA was focused on the man, not the nature of the movement. Decapitate the network, and the network would dissolve, thought the CIA. Subsequent examination of the profiles of the September 11 hijackers indicates that they *all* received training in Afghanistan as part of the mission preparation. Rather than disrupt camp activity, the training simply proceeded under the watchful eye of the CIA.

Action—more specifically, coordinated interagency action—should have been taken to shut down these camps, denying the September 11 terrorists their base of support. The 1998 U.S. missile attack against al-Qa'ida camps was a reaction to an act of war against the United States—the bombing of the U.S. embassies in Africa. The missile attack should not have been the isolated response that it was, but part of a systematic effort to destroy the al-Qa'ida infrastructure in Afghanistan.

The key question is why did the U.S. intelligence community not move decisively and aggressively against the al-Qa'ida infrastructure in Afghanistan and thus deny al-Qa'ida organizational and operational assets and maneuverability? After all, the DCI had declared war on al-Qa'ida. The answer cuts to the core issue.

The CIA misassessed the fundamental nature of the threat. The CIA did not understand that it was dealing with an insurgency movement that required the use of counterinsurgency methods, not the common terrorist vulnerable to standard counterterrorism tactics.

Bin Ladin is a leader of an ideological movement sweeping the Muslim world. This movement holds that the Muslim world is under attack by the West, specifically by Christians and Jews under the banner of the United States. The United States, through the co-optation of un-Islamic and illegitimate Arab, African, and Asian governments, enacts policies designed to take Muslim land, soil Islamic values, desecrate Islamic shrines, steal Muslim raw resources, and otherwise subjugate Muslims to infidel control. Unlike some other adherents of this ideology, bin Ladin believes that by focusing on the United States first, and by defeating another superpower (the first was the Soviet Union), the corrupt and puppet Arab states will "wither away" and Islam will be restored to its rightful place. Bin Ladin is not a terrorist in the classical state-sponsored terrorist sense, but the leader of a movement that uses terror tactics to promote a social, religious, and political program.[1]

By failing to accurately assess the nature of the threat—a new ideology based on a militant religious interpretation that is bent on the destruction of the United States—the CIA failed to gain the attention and marshal the resources of the intelligence and policy communities to counter what should now be understood as an existential threat to the American way of life. With the right resources, interagency capabilities, and political support, the mission of taking down al-Qa'ida infrastructure is achievable, as the post–September 11 war on terrorism has proved. Countering the ideology itself is a battle the United States has not yet begun to fight. In the 1990s, the CIA had neither the capabilities and political support nor the conceptual framework to stop the growing threat of al-Qa'ida.

The CIA was too slow to move from a defensive (collection) mode to an offensive (takedown) position. The operational tools deployed were too limited in scope and too tactical in nature. When the CIA made the transition, it was in fits and starts and not in concert with the rest of the intelligence community, which the DCI is supposed to head. The intelligence community worked at cross-purposes, placing a premium on bureaucratic interests, rather than creating a corporate synergy against a strategic threat. It was a CIA war on terrorism—not an intelligence community war, and not a national security–establishment war. Finally, the DCI, as the president's chief advisor on intelligence, failed to impress upon the administration that a broader and more aggressive strategy against al-Qa'ida was required. The United States needed a strategic plan to take down a strategic threat.

As the CIA was in surge mode, resources were thrown into the Counterterrorism Center in an ad hoc way. With insufficient resources to build a systematic methodology for taking al-Qa'ida down through strategic blows, the CIA surged from one threat to another, cutting off the organization's dangerous tentacles. The brain of the organization remained largely intact in Afghanistan, while the ideology gained popularity in the Arab and Islamic world. Popularity and operational success fed the growth of more tentacles. The Counterterrorism Center was devoting resources to develop infrastructure in Afghanistan, including recruiting sources, building databases, and setting up listening platforms, but this, by nature, is slow going. There was no effort to counter the ideology of the movement through political action and classic counterinsurgency tactics—that is, winning hearts and minds.

The September 11 attacks and subsequent congressional investigations revealed critical weaknesses that still remain within the CIA. Although the Directorate of Intelligence implemented many reforms during the 1990s, the stovepipes, insufficient staffing, and long-term analysis problems remain. How the al-Qa'ida threat was analyzed illustrates the impact of these structural problems. The directorate has al-Qa'ida analysts, Hizballah analysts, Palestinian extremist analysts, and the like. They receive intelligence reports directly related to their accounts. Unless there is a direct link, they do not receive reporting on other terrorist groups, because they do not have a "need to know." Therefore, the bureaucratic structure—the stovepipes—impacts the analytical process. Furthermore, the barriers between the directorates of Intelligence and Operations deprive analysts from gaining the "ground truth" knowledge. If the directorate had been receiving more man-on-the-street reporting from the field or through direct contact with field officers, the insurgency pattern as well as the rapidly growing anti-American sentiment would have been more apparent to analysts.

The demise of the long-term analytical research papers results in a loss of opportunity for analysts to look at issues more deeply and with greater breadth. To say that policymakers are not interested in long-term analysis is not useful, because it assumes that everything the intelligence community does must have immediate relevance. If this were the case, the first satellite would never have been built. Long-term interdisciplinary thinking is not only useful, but vital. The congressional joint inquiry into September 11 identified a lack of strategic analysis as a key weakness leading to the failure to disrupt the attacks. The analytical weakness was not an exclusive CIA problem; the FBI functionally had no capability for strategic analysis. However, the CIA prides itself on its analytical capabilities, so it is worthwhile to examine the specifics of what went wrong.

The joint inquiry found that at the CIA there were only three analysts assigned to al-Qa'ida full-time between 1998 and 2000, and five analysts between 2000 and September 11, 2001. At a time when the CIA was "at war" with al-Qa'ida, these are meager personnel resource allocations, but they reflect how thinly stretched the analytical directorate was. In 1997, the Counterterrorism Center had created a career service for counterterrorism professionals in order to create a larger and more professional cadre of specialists. The career service was new, and therefore the newly hired analysts had limited experience under their belt, with three years of experience on average. The experienced analysts trained within the Directorate of Intelligence were fewer than the new analysts.

The press of business and the nonstop threat information put pressure upon the analytical group to focus on the immediate at the expense of the long term, meaning that the analysts spent their time writing current intelligence and targeting analysis (tactical analysis), not conducting strategic analysis to develop a broader understanding of the threat and of the organization. Counterterrorism Center senior management encouraged analysts to focus on analytical support to operations because of the widespread belief that operations saved lives.[2]

Before September 11, 2001, the prevailing assessment of bin Ladin and al-Qa'ida was that he was a terrorist mastermind and al-Qa'ida was a terrorist network. Bin Ladin spoke to the press frequently and issued communiqués of one sort or another (*fatwas*, letters, statements via the Internet, etc.), and these statements were viewed as a helpful indication of operational planning and execution in the near term. In other words, bin Ladin's words were examined on a tactical level. But a very different picture of him emerges when one focuses closely on what he was saying.

Bin Ladin clearly articulated his ideology and his methodology in his public statements: He is waging a religious war against the West. The war is defensive in nature, as bin Ladin attributes to Western civilization a continuation of its medieval crusades against Islam. Indeed, he calls Westerners "Crusaders" and "infidels." U.S. foreign policy, in particular, is anti-Islamic. The United States supports Israel, stealer of Arab lands, occupier of Islamic shrines, and subjugator of Palestinians. The United States attacks poor Muslim countries (Sudan, Iraq, Afghanistan, and Somalia) and allows others to be attacked (Bosnia, Kosovo, Chechnya). The United States supports cruel economic sanctions against the Iraqi people, and props up corrupt Arab leaders (Egypt, Saudi Arabia, Jordan). The United States defiles the major Islamic shrines by basing troops in Saudi Arabia who defile people and the governments with which they interact. Bin Ladin rejects Western values and considers them hostile to Islamic values. According to traditional Islamic law, all Muslims are required to participate in this defensive *jihad*. The intent is to destroy the United States and the corrupt regimes in the Muslim world and restore the dignity, glory and power of the *'umma* (the Islamic community).

Unfortunately, the words of bin Ladin find resonance and support in the Muslim world. Some U.S. policies are very unpopular with the masses. The advent of Arab satellite news transmits images of impoverished, besieged, and otherwise oppressed Muslims throughout the region. Local issues impact the entire region and regional politics.

Even the poorest Muslim has access to television and watches al-Jazeera TV. During the Balkans war, Muslims watched their "brothers" in Bosnia and Kosovo face ethnic cleansing. They watched their Palestinian brothers rise up in a new intifada, only to be crushed by overwhelming Israeli force. They saw their Iraqi brothers starve in the face of sanctions.

Bin Ladin's messages are mired in the tenets of Islam. As Islam encompasses religious, political, economic, and societal issues, providing a rich body of laws and guidance, bin Ladin's ideology draws upon this tradition and seeks legitimacy from it. Fundamentally, bin Ladin's movement is larger than himself and his immediate circle. It is an ideology that is sweeping the Muslim world in various incarnations. It is not a network that can be dismantled. It is a religious movement that will survive the death of bin Ladin. Shutting down al-Qa'ida bank accounts alone will not bankrupt it. Declaring it evil will not de-legitimize it. Merely rendering, arresting, and assassinating its operatives will not stop it.

In the aftermath of September 11, CIA senior management recognized the analytical deficiency, evidenced by the immediate and large-scale transfer of experienced Directorate of Intelligence analysts to the Counterterrorism Center. Not only did the experienced analyst take on the job of producing strategic analysis, but effort was immediately given to train the more junior counterterrorism analysts on Directorate of Intelligence tradecraft. In a joint inquiry hearing, Tenet stated, "The single lesson learned from all of this is the strategic analytical piece of this has to be big and vibrant to give you the chance to be predictive, even when you don't have much information to go on. I think it's a very important point. We've made a lot of progress [post–September 11]."[3]

Another key element for the analytical failure was the lack of grist for the mill. The Directorate of Operations did not have sufficient human reporting sources on the al-Qa'ida threat. The congressional investigation highlights the lack of reporting sources in the al-Qa'ida camps in Afghanistan, but this is really just the tip of the iceberg. The directorate did not have a handle on the extent of Islamic extremist activities in Europe, Africa, Asia, and the Middle East. Mosque watching had been deemed too low a priority for the CIA. Furthermore, reporting on basic sociopolitical issues in most Third World countries fell below the collection threshold. The State Department did not report on these topics either, as its resources were stretched far too thin.

The CIA has too few reporting sources, too few core intelligence collectors, and too restrictive reporting requirements to provide the kind of far-reaching intelligence that was needed. The native foreign language base of the directorate is shamefully small; professionally fluent speakers of Category 3 foreign languages and esoteric languages are too few as well.* The way the directorate is funded, with one-year funds and fenced funds, restricts the ability of management to support new initiatives within established programs. Furthermore, risk aversion, low morale, and poor management served to reduce the impact and capabilities of core intelligence collectors.[4]

The stovepipe culture of the directorate, with geography and discipline-based barriers, denied the CIA the ability to fuse collection capabilities and operate with a global perspective. The directorate did not understand the real nature of the threat from al-Qa'ida—that it was part of an insurgency movement sweeping across the Third World. Insufficient reporting divided along geographical lines contributed to the misassessment. Completing the circle, the Directorate of Operations applied the wrong tools to take down al-Qa'ida, using counterterrorism tools rather than counterinsurgency doctrine. The sad footnote is that even if the CIA recognized al-Qa'ida for an insurgency movement, it no longer retained the personnel with counterinsurgency skills and experience. The paramilitary cadre had been decimated during the 1990s. Covert action had changed in character, and counterinsurgency capabilities had been phased out.

WASHINGTON, D.C., 2001: If the year 2000 report card for the 1990s marked improvement in the performance of the intelligence community, with the focus on what had been achieved in terms of actionable, accurate, and timely intelligence, the watershed attacks of September 11, 2001, revealed what remained broken in the system and the cost of weak leadership. The conclusions of the 9/11 Commission and the joint congressional committee investigating the September 11 attacks reflect a renewed focus on both structure and leadership. The reports concluded that the structure, division of responsibilities, budgetary, and personnel authorities as currently exist deny the U.S. intelligence community to operate as a coherent whole.

The turf battles that have plagued the intelligence community since its earliest days played critical roles in the failure of the community to detect and deter the attacks of September 11. The late-1990s effort to

---

* Category 3 languages are Arabic, Chinese, Japanese, and Korean. The CIA language school teaches most major languages, but does not have programs for Pashto, Tadzhik, Kirghiz, Kazakh, and Uighur, languages from countries or locations that arise increasingly on the U.S. national security scope.

increase cooperation, or "corporateness" in the jargon of the moment, had limited impact. Most agencies just played lip service to the calls of greater cooperation.

The inability of the CIA and the Pentagon to work together continued under Tenet, despite the effort that Deutch put into the CIA–Defense Department relationship. When Tenet declared war on terrorism, the Defense Department was unwilling to follow the CIA lead or join the war effort as a partner. Before the chairman of the Joint Chiefs of Staff (JCS) would agree to become involved, he demanded a high level of actionable intelligence. The CIA was unable to meet the demanded threshold and felt that the threshold was purposely made high to keep the military from becoming involved.[5] There was no effort by the military to join the fray by adding collection resources to the table. Other than the 1998 cruise missile attack, there is no evidence that the military launched any kind of an offensive military operation against al-Qa'ida. The chairman of the JCS was against joint CIA-military operations, while the CIA supported the idea. After September 11, when the United States went into Afghanistan, there were joint operations, but complaints by the military continued to surface.

During congressional testimony, CIA officials made a point of highlighting the high level of cooperation between the CIA and FBI and minimizing the history of turf battles and noncooperation. Tenet discussed measures taken to improve cooperation on counterterrorism. In reality, cooperation did improve during the late 1990s, but there was nowhere to go but up. The beginning of the process was an FBI-CIA off-site in Rome in early 1996. The assembled FBI Legats and CIA chiefs of station met and discussed ground rules on how the two organizations would operate and cooperate overseas. The direction from then–DDCI Tenet was explicit. He did not want to hear about problems, but solutions. He demanded that his officers take the extra step to make the field relationships work. A similar message must have come down FBI channels, because there was a notable difference in the effort to get along. Problems persisted, but a real dialogue had begun in the field, and an ability to coexist in an ███████ (diplomatic) environment developed and even flourished at times. In the late 1990s, I had an excellent and productive relationship with the Legat in Tel Aviv.

Headquarters and U.S. field relationships remained spotty and largely dependent upon the personalities involved. At the senior level, in 1996, the FBI and CIA each seconded an officer to work in the other's counterterrorism section. Driving cooperation from the top down has its limitations, especially if the working level is not really on board. CIA officers working in the Counterterrorism Center worked hard to find good contacts at FBI headquarters with whom they could interface on a daily basis. A good contact would make the effort to get information that the CIA needed, often over objections within the FBI agent's team. If a good contact asked for something from the Counterterrorism Center, the CIA officer would do his or her best to come through. Essentially, the relationships were personal, not institutional. The institutional roadblocks were many, and included institutional needs to protect sources and methods and to maintain the integrity of the judicial process by not sharing investigative results of criminal cases. Forward-leaning individuals were able to overcome the institutional roadblocks, partly because the roadblocks frequently were excuses for not cooperating, or a poor understanding of the real legal limitations.

The joint congressional committee report and the 9/11 Commission showed in excruciating detail that the FBI was not sufficiently focused on counterterrorism issues and faced many structural, legal, and cultural restrictions that kept it from doing so. The failure to open investigations on lead information passed to or developed by the FBI meant that the FBI had no handle on al-Qa'ida cells in the United States before September 11.

Standard counterterrorism tactics identify the preparation stage as the most vulnerable to detection and disruption, and the execution phase as the most difficult to disrupt. The preparation stage, which includes recruiting, training, casing, and putting support assets in place, requires more people and more movement than the execution phase. Normally, those who conduct casings are not those who are involved in the execution phase. They tend to be lower-level operatives, with less training and poorer tradecraft. Al-Qa'ida had to conduct extensive casing operations in order to assess airport security and the specific practices of airports, airlines, and aircrews. The pilot-hijackers did not select flight schools out of the yellow pages. Al-Qa'ida operatives had to first assess the flight school's security awareness and acceptance policies. Would the hijackers stand out or fit in at the flight school? Do they check on visa status and biographical information? With multiple probing, alert security officials might notice a pattern, begin to ask questions, and assemble the pieces of the conspiracy. Safe houses had to be acquired and bank accounts opened. All of these activities required the movement of people and money and communication between cells, creating a hum of activity that intelligence assets are trained to pick up.

The FBI caught some pieces, but made no attempt to assemble them into a larger picture.

Fragility of the FBI-CIA cooperative spirit was highlighted in the investigations. As Congress began to delve into responsibility for the intelligence failure, finger-pointing between the CIA and FBI broke out quickly. Leaks, widely believed to be from the FBI, disclosed to the public that the CIA was aware of two of the hijackers' terrorist affiliation in 2000, but failed to advise the FBI. The implication was that if the FBI had known, the two would never have been permitted to enter the United States and the September 11 attacks would not have happened. The CIA struck back, issuing a "clarification," telling reporters that two FBI officials had been briefed and that there were e-mails to substantiate this. With Congress, the FBI, and CIA all pointing fingers at each other, the White House had to step in before the sandbox fight disintegrated into "mutually assured destruction." Since then, the official line is that cooperation could not be better. CIA officers have been assigned to work on FBI Joint Task Forces around the nation and cross-training and organizational familiarization programs have been expanded. However, CIA insiders comment quietly that the emperor has no clothes.

Cooperation with other intelligence community agencies, whose intelligence role is a relatively small portion of their overall mission, tended to be tactical. The CIA interfaces with Immigration and Naturalization Service, Treasury, and Commerce on a variety of issues. The CIA has cleared contacts in each of the agencies, as well as seconding CIA officials for intelligence support, in order to work issues such as export of controlled technology, maintaining watch lists at border crossings, and tracking terrorist financing.

When strategic-level cooperation was required, bureaucratic turf, domestic politics, and rival conceptions of national interest intervened. When the CIA wanted to go after the terrorist financial networks that were using U.S. banks, the Treasury Department opposed funding for a White House–sponsored National Terrorist Asset Tracking Center. At the same time, the Treasury Department declined to go after financial transfers in the United States, either those using banks or informal networks, such as the *hawala* system. The CIA has its own people at Treasury who are charged with working with the Financial Crimes Enforcement Center (FinCen) but found that the operation was unable and management unwilling to transition from 1980s-style money-laundering profiles to tracking those of terrorists. Treasury Department leadership opposed covert action programs that would disrupt bin Ladin's financial accounts, citing that cyberattacks on banks would undermine the integrity of the banking system and the U.S. standing in financial circles.[6] CIA officials equated this adherence to propriety to that of Secretary of State Henry L. Stimson at the dawn of World War II: "Gentlemen do not read each other's mail."

The joint congressional intelligence committee investigating September 11 found: "Prior to September 11, there was no coordinated U.S. Government–wide strategy to track terrorist funding and close down their financial support networks. There was also reluctance in some parts of the U.S. Government to track terrorist funding and close down their financial support networks. As a result, the U.S. was unable to disrupt financial support for Usama Bin Ladin's terrorist activities effectively." It would be long after September 11 before the Treasury Department would revamp its intelligence section, creating the Executive Office for Terrorist Financing and Financial Crimes. This office would oversee FinCen and the Office of Foreign Asset Controls, which enacts U.S. orders blocking bank accounts and freezing assets of terror groups and drug traffickers. After having lost two of its oldest agencies—Customs and U.S. Secret Service—to Homeland Security, Treasury finally took action to show that it was serious about being part of the war on terror.

DCI control over the intelligence community during the 1990s was weak, just as it had been weak during the previous five decades. Efforts to streamline, expand, or to make the intelligence community more effective were more often than not viewed within the framework of turf battles (win-lose situations) rather than building corporate synergies. Even though structural reform of the intelligence community was a topic of intense debate during the mid-1990s, the debate did not result in many tangible structural changes. Instead, the DCI attempted to manage the unruly community by expanding the community management staff structure within the Office of the DCI, with uneven results, as evidenced by the fact that the combined efforts of the intelligence community were insufficient to stop a major attack against the United States.

The investigation reports illustrated the nature of the stovepipes in the intelligence community that hindered the United States from getting on top of the al-Qa'ida threat. The findings were written from a counterterrorism perspective, but can and should be understood to impact all operations of the intelligence community. Stovepipes are barriers to communication between agencies. The FBI, National Security Agency, Immigration and Naturalization Service, and State Department all complained that the CIA policy to not share "operational" intelligence impacted their work. The CIA also complained that these agencies did not share their intelligence with the CIA.

Although the joint inquiry report found that there was no information that identified the time, place, and specific nature of the September 11 attacks, the intelligence community "did have information that was clearly relevant to the September 11 attacks, particularly when considered for its collective significance."[7] The 9/11 Commission identified a number of missed opportunities that—if caught—might have led to the unraveling of the plot. The bottom line is that the systematic failure to communicate reduced the ability of the intelligence community to achieve its collective mission: protecting the national security of the United States. The independent bureaucratic nature of the agencies of the intelligence community further undermined the ability of the intelligence community to act in a coordinated fashion. The joint inquiry report found that "the Director of Central Intelligence (DCI) was either unwilling or unable to marshal the full range of Intelligence Community resources necessary to combat the growing threat to the United States."[8]

The joint inquiry committee urged implementation of many past recommendations for reform, such as creating a Director of National Intelligence—who could not serve simultaneously as DCI—who would have the authority to establish and enforce priorities, control the community's budget and personnel, control community research and development, and manage intelligence–law-enforcement coordination.

Similarly, the 9/11 Commission, which went significantly beyond the joint inquiry investigation, had five major recommendations, four of which started with the word "unifying," and the fifth, "strengthening."* They were targeted to address six core problems within the

* The core recommendations of the 9/11 Commission were:
  • unifying strategic intelligence and operational planning against Islamic terrorists across the foreign-domestic divide with a National Counterterrorism Center;
  • unifying the intelligence community with a new National Intelligence Director;
  • unifying the many participants in the counterterrorism effort and their knowledge in a network-based information-sharing system that transcends traditional governmental boundaries;
  • unifying and strengthening congressional oversight to improve quality and accountability; and
  • strengthening the FBI and homeland defenders.

intelligence community: structural barriers to performing joint intelligence work, lack of common standards and practices across the foreign-domestic divide, divided management of national intelligence capabilities, weak capacity to set priorities and move resources; too many jobs for the DCI; and too complex and secret structures and procedures.

So, in many ways the United States had come full circle. The reformers of the mid-1990s had danced up a storm, but then found themselves and others in government and the intelligence community unwilling to weather the gales that would result from real structural reform. The changes in the world order and the failures in performance in the first half of the 1990s were enough to start a major reform initiative, but not enough to see it through. By the end of 1996, complacency had already set in and consensus had built to make what already existed work. The attacks of September 11 have stirred up these same winds and confirmed that jury-rigging was not the answer. Investigators of 2002–2004 reached conclusions similar to those of the earlier commissions: there is a pressing need to integrate the structures and procedures, strengthen capabilities, and destroy barriers of stovepipes and secrecy.

The results of the reform effort thus far have included the creation of the Department of Homeland Defense, the Patriot Act, the new position of Undersecretary of Defense for Intelligence, and the Terrorist Threat Integration Center (TTIC). The core concept of the creation of Homeland Defense was centralization and integration of domestic agencies with missions related to domestic security, with a goal of greater coordination across agencies involved in related activities.

The Patriot Act provided new authorities for law enforcement and foreign intelligence gathering purposes to track and intercept communications, combat financial crimes, control borders, and detain and remove from the United States those suspected of criminal activities. The legislation broke down some of the barriers to cooperation between law enforcement and intelligence. The target of the legislation is terrorism, but the language does not limit the targets exclusively to terrorists and those providing support to them.

The creation of one focal point in the Defense Department for intelligence is a step in the right direction to centralize, rationalize and make more effective the multitude of military intelligence capabilities.

TTIC, the new interagency clearinghouse for terrorism threat information, is designed to integrate community information on terrorism. Its challenge will be to overcome the bureaucratic shortcomings of the

CIA Counterterrorism Division by breaking down the stovepipes rather than just creating a new one.

These four reform initiatives, while having merit, are half-measures. They address only a small portion of the structural and policy problems that plagued the performance of the intelligence community. The joint inquiry made nineteen recommendations for change throughout the intelligence community, while the 9/11 Commission made a boat-load more. It remains to be seen if the outrage over September 11 and its causes will be of sufficient power and endurance to force a complete overhaul of the structure of the community.

It also remains to be seen whether the United States will hold the intelligence community accountable for the intelligence failure. It is an inescapable fact that September 11 occurred on Tenet's watch and was the worst intelligence failure since Pearl Harbor. Tenet cannot claim that he is the victim of the policies of previous directors, because he had been charting the CIA's course for the previous four years. It is true that he inherited a weak organization, and he improved the performance of the CIA during his tenure. However, the root causes of the failure were well known to Tenet. The causes of the intelligence failures of the 1990s were mirror images of those in 2001: insufficient reporting of human sources, poor analytical tradecraft, weak management practices, stovepipes, and turf battles.

Where Tenet failed as the chief spy is in the recognition that al-Qa'ida and ideologically related groups represent an existential threat to the American way of life. It was his job to know this and to take the actions necessary to wage a real war on terrorism, a war at the heart of the threat. It was his job to commission a National Intelligence Estimate on al-Qa'ida to focus the intelligence community on the threat. It was his job to create a counterterrorism strategy for the community. It was his job to advise the policymaking community on the threat and the required actions to counter it. It was a monumental job, given the risk-averse nature of the Clinton administration, and—perhaps one could argue—an impossible job. However, it was Tenet's job to do. Instead, Tenet played it safe and played politics.

Accountability is also good for the soul of America, not to mention good governance. America's call for accountability for September 11 should not be willed away. Too many mothers and fathers, sons and daughters died on September 11, 2001, for the U.S. government to say that no one was at fault, and no one will be held accountable. Perhaps the needs of the government require delayed response in an accountability review. There is a war to fight and win. Eradicating the roots of terrorism will take decades. The accountability process should not.

The joint congressional inquiry into September 11 recommended that the CIA, Defense Department, Justice Department, and State Department "should review the factual findings and the record of the inquiry and conduct investigations and reviews as necessary to determine whether and to what extent personnel at all levels should be held accountable for any omission, commission, or failure to meet professional standards in regard to the identification, prevention, or disruption of terrorist attacks, including the events of September 11, 2001."[9] The CIA does not have a good track record in deciding who should and should not be held accountable. It would be to the great benefit of the CIA to get it right this time. The indicators thus far are not encouraging. There have been no public announcements on individuals held accountable for their performance. The 9/11 Commission was quiet on the subject, saying that playing the "blame game" was outside their mandate. My heart went out to the families of the deceased, who must have been appalled to hear the functional equivalent of "Sorry, it's not my job."

27
Out of the Foxhole

LANGLEY, VIRGINIA, 2003: The attacks of September 11 did more than make the CIA surge; they fundamentally altered how the Agency perceived its mission. In the post–September 11 environment, counterterrorism has replaced anti-Communism as the lens through which the CIA views the world and national security threats. Like the Soviet Union in the past, the threat posed by terrorism is now seen as a major threat to the American way of life. As such, the threat warrants the full attention of the CIA.

New alliances and lines are being drawn, the criteria being, as President Bush stated forcefully, "You are either with us or against us in the war on terrorism." Intelligence relationships with foreign intelligence services (and governments) are judged on the basis of the level of cooperation that the services provide in countering terrorism. The battleground against terrorism has reverted back to the terrain that the CIA likes best: remote Third World countries where the CIA can exert more influence and operate extensively, away from the prying eyes of the press and public. The old methods—the "dirty tricks"—were dusted off and embraced once again. The gloves of political correctness were taken off and the image of the kinder, gentler CIA discarded.

Even counterintelligence is now viewed through the counterterrorism lens. No longer is the CIA focused upon foreign governments' attempts to infiltrate the organs of the U.S. government, but now the CIA's counterintelligence officers strive to know what activities foreign intelligence services are undertaking with or against terrorists but not telling the United States.

Political winds shift with changes in administrations and significant events. The view of what constitutes a strategic threat to the United States is different in 2004 than in 2000. The CIA has learned to ride the political winds. In the post–September 11 environment, the Bush administration has embarked on an aggressive campaign to root out terrorism. Calls to take the battle to the core of al-Qa'ida fell on receptive ears, and the United States launched a military offensive into the interior of Afghanistan.

There have been successes and failures. The Taliban had been unseated and the al-Qa'ida infrastructure in Afghanistan destroyed. Bin Ladin and many of his key lieutenants remain at large. American and allied soldiers, CIA officers and noncombatants have died as a direct consequence of the U.S. war on terror. These have all been judged in the court of public opinion as acceptable losses. Even more, the CIA is taking advantage of new access and influence with the White House and Congress that it has garnered post–September 11. The CIA has won support for increased funding, personnel, and authority within the intelligence community. As it has done so many times in the past, the CIA has capitalized upon a failure to remake itself.

In the new millennium, political action and paramilitary covert action capabilities within the CIA have been reconstituted. Afghanistan is a good case in point. Once it became clear that President Bush wanted to go after al-Qa'ida infrastructure, the CIA dusted off time-proven tools. CIA "bagmen" went into Afghanistan with suitcases of money to buy tribal allegiance during the U.S. military onslaught of al-Qa'ida. CIA officers with military experience were pulled together from all over the organization and deployed to Afghanistan to mobilize insurgency groups to support U.S. ground troops upon their arrival.

Covert propaganda operations are once again considered a useful tool. Indeed, the CIA geared up a large propaganda program in support of the covert action program against Iraq. Traditional covert action is back in force. Of the many recommendations of the joint inquiry, the committee recommended maximizing effective use of covert action and facilitating the ability of CIA paramilitary units and military special operations forces to conduct joint operations.[1] As art imitates life, James Bond has shed his wimp image and is back to using the old tricks of the trade.

President Bush signed a more encompassing finding broadening the kinds of activities that the CIA could take against al-Qa'ida, including the authority to hunt down and kill the terrorists, if capture is impractical and civilian causalities can be minimized. Reportedly, Bush authorized a list of al-Qa'ida members who have been sanctioned for targeted killing and has given the CIA authority to add names to the list and undertake operations without seeking further approval each time the Agency is about to stage an operation.[2] According to the *Washington Post*, the CIA was involved in the targeted killing of a senior al-Qa'ida leader in Yemen in November 2002. Qa'ed Salim al-Harithi and five companions traveling in the same car in the northern province of Marib were killed by a Hellfire missile launched from a Predator drone. Harithi, aka Abu Ali, was suspected of planning the al-Qa'ida attack against the USS *Cole* in October 2000. A U.S. citizen was in the car and died in the attack. Despite this fact, which was given very little press play at the time, the operation was considered "clean"—that is, having an acceptable level of collateral deaths. As is typical, the CIA declined to comment to the press when asked about its role in the attack. It is also noteworthy that there have been no further operations of this sort outside war zones.

Although marching along with their normal "can-do" approach, CIA officers are justifiably nervous. On one hand, there is the commander in chief who has directed the Agency to take off the gloves and destroy the enemy responsible for the deaths of innocent Americans and fellow officers of the U.S. government. On the other hand, these officers must sort through their own personal feelings about killing anyone. There is the knowledge that their career and personal standing in their society could be on the line sometime in the future if the operation did not go as planned and resulted in "unacceptable" collateral deaths. Or if another change in administrations could shift the rule book, *ex post facto*.

With CIA officers establishing the target list, where does one draw the line? Do only those directly responsible for deaths of Americans go on the list? Do the support cell members, such as the financiers, recruiters, and trainers, merit the list? Although the CIA has worked out specific rules of engagement for targeted killings and covert action in general, Porter Goss, when still the chairman of the House Permanent Select Committee on Intelligence, stated that he is not sure that the decision-making process is clear enough, saying, "I think there's still ambiguity."[3]

This cannot be comforting to CIA officers, who are already not confident that they will not be left hanging if the political winds shift again and targeted killings come to be viewed as an activity that the CIA should not have undertaken, regardless of political orders, because they are immoral or illegal or shortsighted fixes that caused unaccepted counteractions against U.S. interests. A nightmare scenario would be the assassination of a U.S. political leader in retaliation for the targeted killing of a terrorist, which brings back uncomfortable memories of the Kennedy assassination and the CIA's Operation Mongoose. Fact has no role when hysteria rules; CIA officers have learned this the hard way.

After September 11, 2001, renditions have continued and increased in tempo. The establishment of the Guantánamo Bay Naval Base detention facility in Cuba, operated by the U.S. military, provided an "offshore" location to incarcerate al-Qa'ida and Taliban fighters seized in Afghanistan. The CIA has been interrogating the prisoners, or "enemy combatants," alongside interrogators from Arab countries. The activities at Guantánamo Bay have been scrutinized closely by the American media, to the discomfort of the CIA. As a result, the CIA stopped rendering terrorists to this facility and has resumed the practice of sending them to third countries and other offshore military bases. As the scandal over the treatment of Iraqi prisoners grows, CIA officers should be concerned about blowback on Agency operations—specifically, handling of al-Qa'ida prisoners. The controversy is a good reminder that CIA actions must be defensible before the courts of law and public opinion.

Post–September 11, the phenomenon of anti-Americanism in Europe and the developing world has been acknowledged by policymakers. Anti-Americanism did not happen overnight, but has been developing steadily through the 1990s, moving into warp speed in 2001. There was a moment just after September 11 when the world's sympathy was with us. The Bush White House squandered it by acting like a bull in a china shop and pursued a policy of preemption and aggression, alienating traditional allies and needed supporters in the war on terrorism.

The view within the Bush administration is that the United States is simply misunderstood, having not marketed American lifestyle and foreign policies well. This is a myopic view, one that is blinded to the hard truth that our foreign policy choices have caused grave despair and hardship for others. Winning hearts and minds is important, but spin alone can only do so much. During the Cold War, the U.S. government went head-to-head with the Soviets in the battle for public opinion throughout the world. Recently declassified documents from the State Department on relations in the Middle East provide a window into the role of the United States Information Service on influencing public opinion through cultural and media outreach programs. These efforts were coordinated with and enhanced by CIA political action programs.

During the 1990s, the budget and role of United States Information Service was marginalized to the point that the independent agency was subsumed into the State Department and became the Office of Public Diplomacy. Cultural centers and libraries were closed due to lack of funding. Media and cultural events were neglected by ambassadors who were primarily concerned with "more substantive" political, economic, and military requirements.

Public diplomacy in intelligence work is considered akin to "white propaganda," true information disseminated to a specific target audience in order to influence as well as to inform. Historically, the CIA has engaged in the dissemination of propaganda, but, unlike the United States Information Service, did so covertly in order to hide the American hand. The CIA financed the Congress for Cultural Freedom and its subsidiary publications, the American Newspaper Guild, and radio stations in Europe in the 1950s and 1960s. The CIA also disseminated "gray and black propaganda"—that is, partially true and completely fabricated information, respectively, in support of operational objectives.

The CIA began to scale back its propaganda activities first in 1961, after public outcry and congressional hearings, as a result of an exposé in *Ramparts* magazine. Radio Free Europe and the Free Europe Committee continued to receive covert CIA funding, while other organizations transitioned to either open State Department or private philanthropic funding. After the investigation of the Church Commission, the CIA also began terminating its operational relationships with U.S. journalists and journalists working for U.S. news services. The CIA established a policy to no longer recruit U.S. journalists as agents or to use journalism cover, except in exceptional circumstances. The language banning their operational use includes an exception clause, which in practice has seldom been used.

In the budget crunch and the "asset scrub" of the 1990s, the CIA's ability to run propaganda operations in foreign media was significantly reduced. Press placement operations were given low priority, and the assets were terminated. The CIA was focused on "hard targets" and Tier 00 and 01 requirements; propaganda operations were considered marginal, at best. Influencing public opinion was left to the State Department, CNN, and MTV.

Post–September 11 debate within the intelligence community has raised the specter of resuming covert propaganda, both in context of the war on terrorism and anti-Americanism abroad. The Defense Department is revising its directive on information operations and is considering expanding the current policy of utilizing aggressive information tactics against adversary decision makers in the context of hostile engagement. Under discussion is a new policy that permits operations against allies and enemies alike to influence foreign perceptions and decision making. The Pentagon is debating the merits of providing news items, some true, others not, to foreign journalists to influence public opinion in friendly and neutral countries.[4]

The debate is not on whether such operations should take place, but on which organization(s) should be responsible. There is a growing understanding in the highest levels of the government that the United States needs a strategic communication coordinating body so that the U.S. government can better integrate its various voices and assess the impact of official communication. In late 2002, the National Security Council created a policy coordinating committee for strategic communication, jointly chaired by the State Department and the Defense Department. A representative of the CIA sits on this committee out of interest in linking covert propaganda activities to a broad communication initiative.

The Directorate of Science and Technology is also doing things differently. With yet another new chief, Donald Kerr, the directorate has found a new mission. September 11 ushered in new requirements and new funds. Kerr's vision of the directorate is that it is an operational organization that works hand in hand with the Directorate of Operations, not a research and development organization. As such, the directorate is actively involved in the war on terrorism with officers deployed to Afghanistan to support operations and the military. The directorate is not only providing support to collection activities, but is also providing personnel with the means to protect themselves.

The directorate management sees a need to switch from its traditional reconnaissance model to a surveillance model in the pursuit of terrorists. Existing databases offer a wealth of information that can be exploited to ferret out terrorists. Data mining or profiling of travel and financial databases can be used to "watch-list" certain patterns. A data-analysis approach, initiated by an investigative lead, can scan databases for links between a person under investigation and known terrorists, in terms of where they live, recent travel, and other behavior. Such talk gives privacy advocates chills. For the CIA, it is a potentially powerful way of putting technology to work to do the heavy lifting of sorting through millions of bits of information for the good of the American people.

According to Kerr, the directorate will maintain in-house R&D, led by a chief scientist, but the scale of the projects seems to be deliberately small. Instead, the directorate is looking to reestablish R&D relationships with academics, funding them to work as consultants for unclassified and classified research programs. Since fiscal year 2000, the Directorate of Science and Technology has sponsored $2 million a year of unclassified research at Sandia National Laboratories as well as at eighteen universities.[5] The directorate is looking to the private sector and academia for developments in digital signal processing, secure communications, language translation software, and sensors that can detect chemicals, sounds, or movement from a long distance that can be adapted for intelligence applications, in order to avoid sizable investments in new technologies.[6] The challenge is to use technology to find, mark, and track terrorists, working with human sources to take them out of operation before they strike.

There is broad national consensus for the war against terrorism, just as there was for the Cold War. Tenet rallied well after the September 11 attacks, bringing the CIA out of the foxhole to the front lines of the war. Officers of the CIA felt proud of Tenet and the Agency's performance in Afghanistan. Congress concurred. The CIA began to reap the benefits of being one of the primary weapons in the war on terrorism. The CIA was given additional budget and authorization to dramatically increase its staffing. The CIA has also been given new authorities, blurring the lines between overseas and domestic activities. Once again, life was looking up, or so it seemed to be.

SEVENTH FLOOR, LANGLEY, VIRGINIA, 2004: On June 3, George Tenet announced his decision to resign as DCI. Tenet said it was for personal reasons; perhaps, if you consider the personal reasons to be his knowledge that he would not be able to keep his seat at the big desk after the release of the investigative reports on Iraq prewar intelligence and the 9/11 Commission. His political capital had been eroding rapidly after the United States failed to find Iraqi WMD—the primary reason (according to President Bush) for waging a preemptive war—and by his decision to refer to the Justice Department a crimes report on the "outing" of a CIA officer under cover (the wife of Ambassador Joe Wilson). The first made the White House look incompetent; the second made it look criminal. Suddenly, everybody did not love George Tenet. The about-face was remarkable even for Washington.

But more important to CIA watchers is the horrific damage done to reputation of the CIA. Suddenly, there is a renewed crisis of confidence in the ability of the CIA to meet its core mission. Informed people are even asking such questions as: if the CIA got it wrong on Iraq, what's to say they have it right on Iranian WMD? The Iraq intelligence failure was a complicated one and outside the scope of this book. However, it should suffice to say that it was not the CIA's sole responsibility but was caused by many of the same problems that have plagued Agency performance: insufficient HUMINT reporting, poor analytical tradecraft (groupthink), and politicization. Coming so fast on the heels of September 11, with the reports on the two incidents coming within two weeks, there simply is no way to ignore the obvious: something has got to change—and change fast.

Personally, I believe that Tenet acted as a sacrificial lamb, resigning with the hope to preempt a full-scale attack on the Agency. He knew he could not win the battle as DCI and hoped that by removing himself from the helm, Congress and the public would not have an easy target in their scope. It was an act of loyalty to the people of the CIA—that is, a show of loyalty only once the political game was up. For some, it is easier to resign if you know that you are about to be fired. Those who wanted accountability will not get it; Tenet went out the door a hero without ever admitting his own leadership failure. Understandably, CIA officers have rallied behind him out of loyalty, despite the terrible circumstances in which Tenet has left them.

Where does that leave the CIA? Driverless at a very critical juncture. While the CIA is thoroughly engaged in the war on terror, the strategic challenge is daunting. It remains to be seen if the United States will develop an integrated strategy, encompassing diplomatic, economic, military, intelligence, and law-enforcement elements to counter the threat posed by virulent Islamic extremism. The CIA's current focus continues to be on bin Ladin as a terrorist, which is a grave misunderstanding. While having a new sense of mission is a great boost to the morale of Agency officers, mission alone will not solve the systemic problems that ailed the CIA through the 1990s. Without fixing these problems, the next intelligence failure is only a matter of time.

★ ★ ★ ★

For me, the Tenet years were both good and bad. My career was progressing spectacularly. I moved from one assignment in the Persian Gulf to another in the Occupied Territories—Gaza and the West Bank. I had the opportunity to be part of some incredible operations. And then I hit a brick wall in 2001. An operational mistake, which I freely admitted and accepted responsibility for—its details remain classified—brought a cloud of suspicion over me. With no willingness to consider

exculpatory evidence and my long record of exceptional performance, I was forced out of the Agency, one more living example of an
unfair accountability regime. I left the Agency in September 2002,
with very mixed feelings.

Tenet, the able politician, went out the door a hero, but with a rag-
ing fire burning all around him. Under his watch, three major intelligence failures occurred, all caused by the same endemic problems.
Instead of being remembered as a great leader, he should be remembered for having played it safe. He fought the battles he knew he could
win and played lip service to the others that seemed too hard or too
costly. He won many friends and supporters for playing the role they
wanted him to rather than the leader the nation needed. He did not
challenge the entrenched bureaucracies and old boys to complete the
reform process started in the early 1990s. He did not challenge the risk
aversion of the Clinton White House to take decisive and broad action
against emerging threats to national security. He did not live up to his
DCI duties, duties that he himself articulated in his confirmation
speech: that he was being hired to warn and protect the nation.

PART

7

THE YEARS AHEAD

"We must support our rights or lose our character, and with it, perhaps, our liberty."

JAMES MONROE
First inaugural address, 1817

28
Epilogue

WASHINGTON, D.C., 2004: The intelligence community finds itself at a new crossroads in the post–September 11 period. The crossroads offer an opportunity to adjust its course to meet the intelligence needs of the next decade and beyond. This requires an understanding of what those needs are and how best to transition to meet them. Much of the intellectual weight-lifting has already been done. It is now up to the policymakers and the intelligence community to seize the moment and implement the recommendations from the reform movements in the 1990s and the findings of the 9/11 Commission. It is also important to pay attention to the lessons learned from the reforms, the intelligence successes and failures of the 1990s.

The imperative to take immediate action has been deeply felt in Washington; all kinds of politically weird and unprecedented steps have been undertaken. In August 2004—the summer month when very little of substance happens in Washington—President Bush endorsed the establishment of a National Intelligence Director (NID), despite his own misgivings and those of his Secretary of Defense and acting DCI. Congress cancelled the summer recess and held extraordinary hearings on intelligence reform *and* congressional reform. Bush announced his choice to fill Tenet's shoes as DCI—Porter Goss, the serving chairman of the House Permanent Select Committee on Intelligence—triggering a confirmation hearing schedule that will provide critics and rivals a platform sure to garner national television coverage in the critical campaigning months before the November elections. Why are they doing this? The politicians are fearful of the next domestic terror attack and accompanying accusations of foot dragging on intelligence reform.

While it does not look good to be "soft" on reform, the challenge will be transcending form and focusing on substance. Will Porter Goss, as a former CIA case officer and congressional leader of the current system, have the right stuff to transform the CIA and the intelligence community? Will his background give him the tools, knowledge, and relationships to do things differently, or will they ground him in the traditional past ways of doing business? Will he even have a fighting chance to accomplish anything? Will the elections produce a Democratic administration with different personnel preferences for DCI? Or will the messiness of politics and reform bog down the best-intentioned folks so that the status quo forces seduce Washington into believing that the changes made in the immediate aftermath of September 11 are transformations sufficient for facing the next generation of national security challenges?

The next decade will bring a convergence of threats resulting from transnational issues, terrorism, and proliferation of weapons of mass destruction. Some of these threats will come from traditional "rogue nations." Others will come from unanticipated corners of the world, places where instability from failing states will encourage a myriad of other problems. In the past, the ills of the Third World stayed in the Third World. In the age of globalization, the United States must anticipate regional and global impact of local crises. These crises will not just be political, but economic, social, and environmental.

Anti-Americanism is a phenomenon that the United States dare not ignore. It is not enough to place the blame on those who hate, even though it is emotionally satisfying. The United States must understand the root causes of the hatred and embark on proactive programs to redress them. It is the element of anti-Americanism that makes the other threats converge against the interests of the United States. Extremist Islamic groups such as al-Qa'ida, Egyptian Gama'at al-Islamiya, and Indonesian Jamaah Islamiya have adopted extreme ideological programs, perverting the honorable religion of Islam, because of distinctly local issues. They grew out of environments in which there is great poverty, lack of political participation, and lack of personal freedom. They took on anti-American and anti-Western positions because of the belief that the United States and the West support unjust government(s) and are part of the subjugation process.

The Middle East has long been critical of U.S. foreign policy because of the negative impact the policy has had on their interests. Middle

Easterners previously have made the distinction between U.S. policy and American citizens. Americans are liked and welcomed in most Middle Eastern countries. America is respected for its freedom and opportunity. The emergence of extremist Islamic groups that target ordinary Americans marks the erosion of this distinction and the holding accountable of average Americans for disliked U.S. foreign policies and their perceived role in their oppression. Terrorism is the weapon of the weak. Al-Qa'ida proved to the watching world that the United States is indeed vulnerable to terrorism—not only overseas, but on its own shores.

It is not America's obligation to improve the lives of those in other countries. This is certainly not the mission of the national security establishment. It is the U.S. government's job to keep our nation safe and preserve the American way of life. However, when foreign crises caused by political, military, social, economic, health, and environmental factors converge into threats against the United States, it is in the U.S. national security interest to take action. The intelligence community's challenge is to identify these threats before they materialize so that policymakers can pursue strategic and tactical measures to render them harmless.

In the post–September 11 environment, the U.S. government must embark on a strategic program beyond a war on terrorism. This war is necessary, but it will not stop terrorism. Cutting off the fingers of terrorism by disrupting, arresting, or killing those active in the operational and support cells is a tactical measure. Discrediting the ideology, promoting and fostering alternative ideological frameworks, modifying foreign policies that provoke strong negative reactions, and addressing the societal and economic ills of the Third World within a broader strategic program will undermine the forces supporting the growth and spread of groups advocating anti-American terror. The 9/11 Commission got it right in the section of its report calling for a global strategy, accurately assessing the nature of threat posed by groups like al-Qa'ida. Hopefully, this portion of the report will garner the same amount of attention as the sections recommending intelligence community reform. It does not matter how strong the team is if the plan is wrong, or nonexistent.

The Bush administration has taken some steps in the right direction, such as the establishment of the Middle East Partnership Initiative. Public diplomacy, the remnants of the U.S. Information Service, needs to expand drastically its efforts in media, education, and cultural affairs. U.S. policy in the Third World needs to be closely reassessed and adjusted. The current perception that the United States is waging a crusade against the Islamic world needs to be countered. In many ways this is a hearts-and-minds campaign, much like what was waged during the Cold War.

The decision to occupy Iraq as part of the war on terrorism is a grave mistake. The occupation has confirmed the suspicions of the Arab people of U.S. neo-imperialist intentions, reinforced the blatant system of political double standards, and played into the strength of the radical Islamic groups. U.S. long-term strategic interests have been harmed by a precipitous policy to go beyond removing a tyrant to direct administration of post-Saddam Iraq.

The Arab and Islamic worlds have been traumatized by September 11. Their natural reaction has been defensive. Overly aggressive U.S. behavior, coupled with the complete dismissal of regional concerns and interests have transformed that reaction into passive aggression—not really what the United States wants in a hearts-and-minds campaign.

In this book, I have been critical of some of the leadership performance of Clinton—a right I feel I have because I voted for him. However, I note that Clinton had some special leadership skills that Bush lacks, and that is the ability—and desire—to reach out and connect on a multilateral and bilateral basis with world leaders and to speak directly to their constituencies in a nondictatorial, noncondescending manner. Clinton could always "feel the pain" and "understand the concerns" of his interlocutors. If the United States is to avoid a clash of civilizations—which we should do our utmost to avoid—we will need to show a great deal more understanding and empathy for the concerns of the region. As a covert operator, I fully see the merit of a sophisticated strategy of using soft power and influence rather than hard power exclusively.

The United States should not make the mistake that it made during the Cold War, by looking at all issues through a counter-Soviet lens—or, in this case, a counterterrorism lens. Some issues are distinctly local, and not all political violence is terrorism. There may be counterintelligence issues related to counterterrorism, but not all counterintelligence issues will be. A single-minded focus on counterterrorism will risk misassessment of situations or, worse, inappropriate responses that inflame situations. We already see that in the U.S. policy toward the Palestinian-Israeli conflict. The United States will ignore at its own peril issues not directly related to terrorism and weapons of mass destruction. For example, Russia and China pose challenges to U.S. access and influence in Central Asia and the Asian theater.

To face the challenges of the post–September 11 world, the United States will need a strong intelligence community that works together. The community will need sufficient resources to do the job. Intelligence capabilities need to be rebuilt. The surge strategy of the 1990s is neither efficient nor effective. The CIA must return to a worldwide organization. Intelligence collection requirements need to be expanded beyond the existing PDD-35 guidelines, but only in conjunction with expanding resources to cover the tasking. Collection guidelines and collection capabilities must have enough flexibility to adjust for new developments without robbing from traditional strategic requirements. Integration and centralization of the intelligence community must happen.

The September 11 attacks show all too painfully what can happen when the community does not move in the same direction, focus in tandem against strategic threats, and does not share information because of competing bureaucratic interests. Authority at the top must be increased, but top-driven centralization is not sufficient. The community needs to interact as a community with common missions rather than as a bureaucratic war zone. Interagency stovepipes that block flow of information need to be broken down as part of the integration and centralization process.

The Joint Congressional Intelligence Committee Report on September 11 accurately depicted how debilitating these interagency stovepipes are on the effectiveness of the intelligence community. Systemic Finding 9 found: "Within the Intelligence Community, agencies did not adequately share relevant counterterrorism information, prior to September 11. This breakdown in communications was the result of a number of factors, including differences in the agencies' missions, legal authorities and cultures. Information was not sufficiently shared, not only between different Intelligence Community agencies, but also within individual agencies, and between the intelligence and the law-enforcement agencies."[1]

It would be a grave mistake for our national leadership to give the intelligence community a pass, to say that the post–September 11 adjustments are sufficient and that no more substantial changes are needed. Without institutionalizing a different way of doing business, the CIA—and the intelligence community—will be destined to tread the path of future failure. We must decide on whether we want to plan for success or schedule failure.

It is not sufficient for the DCI to say that he needs more authority to manage a centralized intelligence community. Reform should begin at home. How can the DCI ask the intelligence community to smash china if the CIA is unwilling to break even a teacup? CIA internal stovepipes need to be broken down. Concept of corporateness is not sufficient; restructuring is required. The barriers, cultural and structural, that separate the directorates of operations, intelligence, and science and technology must be torn down, with the Agency endorsing fusion of the disciplines into issue and country teams. The Directorate of Operations will move into the current millennium only after its isolation is lifted. The CIA must get a grip on the accountability and corporate ethics issues. A rational system will inspire a rational system of risk taking. This also will positively impact counterintelligence and security behavior. Mistakes will be made. There will be future intelligence failures, operational flaps, and moles. The key is to have a rational system that works, with standard procedures and built-in checks to catch things when they go wrong.

To a certain extent, policymaking will always be ad hoc. The intelligence community must be responsive to the ebbs and flows; there must be a flexible system. What *cannot* be flexible are standards. Additionally, policymakers establish the environment in which the intelligence community must work. If the policymakers are risk averse, the national security environment will be risk averse. If policymakers view the intelligence community as something dangerous, they will not utilize the capabilities of the community. If policymakers treat the individual agencies of the intelligence community as their own personal domain or tool of power and influence, they will cripple the overall effectiveness of the community.

To keep a nation safe, it takes good leadership, not just good management. History has proven that it was a strategic mistake to cut the intelligence community capabilities to the bone in the 1990s, restricting coverage to an inch deep in many parts of the world. Successive DCIs warned policymakers of the potential consequences and the real impact of their decision making, warnings that fell on deaf ears. Simply put, Congress must act more responsibly in its role of keeping the nation safe. The White House should not play domestic political games when it comes to national security. Leadership does indeed matter.

While beefing up the capabilities of the intelligence community is in order, the risk of permitting the pendulum to swing to the other extreme needs to be checked. Americans do not want to live in a police state. Integral to the American identity are the concepts of liberty and justice. If America is going to remain the great nation that she is, sacrificing these in the name of security cannot become an acceptable idea.

Notes

CHAPTER 1: INTELLIGENCE FAILURE

1. "Tenet's Testimony before Senate Committee," *New York Times*, February 6, 2002.

CHAPTER 2: IRAN-CONTRA LEGACY

1. For the details pertaining to the Iran-Contra scandal, except where otherwise noted, I drew extensively on the Independent Counsel's investigation report, "Final Report of the Independent Counsel for Iran-Contra."
2. James McCullough, "Personal Reflections on Bill Casey's Last Month at CIA," *Studies in Intelligence* 39, no. 5 (1996).

CHAPTER 4: SETTING NEW STANDARDS

1. Wise, *Nightmover: How Aldrich Ames Sold the CIA for $4.6 Million*, p. 203*n*.
2. John Pomfret, "Polish Agents Rescued 6 U.S. Spies from Iraq," *Washington Post*, January 17, 1995.
3. Marc Fisher, "Embassy Staff Leaves Kuwait; U.S. Ambassador, 4 Others End 4 Months under Siege," *Washington Post*, December 14, 1990; Steve Twomey, "For Weary Families Back in US, 'We Have to Keep Being Strong,' " *Washington Post*, August 29, 1990; and Lisa Leff, "Quiet but Happy Scene at Andrews as Last of Embassy Staff Arrives," *Washington Post*, December 15, 1990.

CHAPTER 5: CONFIRMATION OF AN INSIDER

1. L. Britt Snider, "Sharing Secrets with Lawmakers: Congress as a User of Intelligence," Center for the Study of Intelligence (Spring 1989).

CHAPTER 6: A NEW VISION

1. Senate Committee on Foreign Relations, *The BCCI Affair: A Report to the Committee on Foreign Relations*, 1992, p. 102–350.
2. Commission on the Roles and Capabilities of the U.S. Intelligence Community, *Preparing for the 21st Century*, 1996.
3. Robert Gates, "Comments at University of Virginia on CIA Brand of Non-Partisan Intelligence Still Needed," October 18, 1993, Charlottesville, VA.
4. George Lardner, "Gates Rejects Overhaul of Spy Agencies: CIA Head to Install 'Evolutionary' Plan," *Washington Post*, April 9, 1992.

CHAPTER 7: RETHINKING COVERT ACTION

1. Jeffrey-Jones, *The CIA and American Democracy*, p. 41.
2. Zegart, *Flawed by Design*, pp. 188–89.
3. Wyden, *Bay of Pigs*, p. 311.
4. For background on pre-1980s covert action programs, see Blum, *The CIA: A Forgotten History*, and Agee and Wolf, *Dirty Work: The CIA in Western Europe*.
5. Jeffreys-Jones, *The CIA and American Democracy*, p. 87.

CHAPTER 8: THE DIRECTORATE OF INTELLIGENCE

1. George Bush, "Speech at the Bush School of Government and Public Service, Texas A&M University," November 19, 1999, College Station, TX.
2. House Permanent Select Committee on Intelligence, *IC21: The Intelligence Community in the 21st Century*, Staff Study, 1996.
3. Senate Select Committee on Intelligence, *Nomination of Robert M. Gates, 1991*.

CHAPTER 9: POST–COLD WAR CONVULSIONS

1. Bodanski, *Bin Ladin*, p. 63.
2. Gup, *The Book of Honor*, pp. 354–59.

CHAPTER 10: THE TECHNOCRAT AND THE NEW WORLD ORDER

1. *U.S. v. Ramzi Ahmed Yousef, et al.*, Lead No. 98-1041 (2nd Cir. Filed August 25, 2000); *U.S. v. Omar Ahmad Ali Abdal Rahman, et al.*, 189 F.3d. (2nd Cir., August 16, 1996); and J. Gilmore Childers and Henry J. DePippo, *Senate Judiciary Committee, Subcommittee on Technology, Terrorism, and Government Information, Hearing on Foreign Terrorists in America: Five Years After the World Trade Center*, 1998.
2. J. Daily, "Bin Ladin Trial Highlights U.S. Intelligence Problems," *Jane's International Security News*, April 20, 2001.
3. Vernon Loeb, "The CIA in Somalia: After Action Report," *Somalia Watch*, February 27, 2000.
4. Ibid.
5. Ibid.; and Bowden, *Black Hawk Down*, pp. 20–28.
6. Halberstam, *War in a Time of Peace*, pp. 248–65; and Ibid.; Loeb, "The CIA in Somalia: After Action Report," *Somalia Watch*, February 27, 2000.
7. Halberstam, *War in a Time of Peace*, pp. 267–73.
8. "Iran Linked to Buenos Aires Blast," *International Counterterrorism Center*, May 5, 1998; "Argentina Issues Warrant in Israeli Embassy bombing," *International Counterterrorism Center*, September 4, 1999; "Suspect in Bombing of Israeli Embassy Held in US," *International Counterterrorism Center*, August 20, 2000; "Report: Former Argentine President Linked to Cover-up of AMIA Bombing," *International Counterterrorism Center*, July 22, 2002; and Marc Perelman, "Iran Leader is Fingered in Bombing, By Defector," *Forward*, November 9, 2001.

CHAPTER 11: NEW DIRECTIONS

1. CIA, "Task Force on Greater CIA Openness," 1991, declassified version.
2. "CIA to Open up Secrets, 'Warts and All,' Director Says, *Reuters*, September 29, 1993.
3. R. James Woolsey, "Comments to the Center for Strategic and International Studies on National Security and the Future Direction of the Central Intelligence Agency," July 18, 1994, Washington, D.C.
4. Walter Pincus, "CIA and the 'Glass Ceiling' Report; Female, Black Operatives Report Harassment," *Washington Post*, September 9, 1994.

5. Pincus, "A 21st Century Intelligence Test," *Washington Post,* February 20, 1995.

CHAPTER 12: ALDRICH AMES

1. CIA, "Unclassified Abstract of the CIA inspector general's Report of the Aldrich H. Ames Case," October 21, 1994.
2. Weiner, Johnston, and Lewis, *Betrayal,* p. 86.
3. Walter Pincus, "Soviet Letter Warned Ames in 1989 about Using CIA Computers, Sources Say," *Washington Post,* March 15, 1994.
4. Senate Select Committee on Intelligence, *An Assessment of the Aldrich H. Ames Espionage Case and Its Implications for U.S. Intelligence, 1994.*

CHAPTER 13: DOING LESS WITH LESS

1. Walter Pincus, "CIA Struggles to Find Identity in a New World," *Washington Post,* May 9, 1994.
2. House Permanent Select Committee on Intelligence, *IC21: The Intelligence Community in the 21st Century, Staff Study,* Chapter IX, 1996.
3. Vise, *The Bureau and the Mole,* p. 147.

CHAPTER 14: WOOLSEY'S UNDOING

1. CIA, "Unclassified Abstract of the CIA inspector general's Report of the Aldrich H. Ames Case," October 21, 1994.
2. *United States v. Ramzi Ahmed Yousef, et al.,* Appeal, No. 98-1041 (2nd Cir. Argued May 3, 2002), pp. 12–16, 76-91; Miniter, *Losing Bin Ladin,* pp. 78–82; Brendan Lyons, "Terrorist foretold 9/11 Towers Plot," *Timesunion.com,* September 2, 2002; "Sept 11 Mastermind Identified: US Officials: Khalid Shaikh Linked to Ramzi Youssef," *Dawn.com,* June 6, 2002; and Phil Hirschkorn, "Convicted Bomb Conspirator Linked to Plots," *CNN.com,* September 20, 2001.
3. *United States v. Omar Ahmad Ali Abdel Rahman, et al.,* 189 F.3d. 6-18 (2nd Cir., Appeal, August 16, 1999).
4. *United States v. Ramzi Ahmed Yousef, et al.,* Appeal, No. 98-1041 (2nd Cir. Argued May 3, 2002); pp. 72–73.
5. *United States v. Omar Ahmad Ali Abdel Rahman, et al.,* 189 F.3d. 6-18 (2nd Cir., Appeal, August 16, 1999).

CHAPTER 15: THE RELUCTANT SPY

1. Senate Select Committee on Intelligence, *Nomination of John M. Deutch, 1995.*

CHAPTER 16: POLITICALLY CORRECT ESPIONAGE

1. "Who knew what and when did they know it? Harbury/Bamaca Case Update," Global Exchange.
2. Tim Weiner, "Report Faults CIA on Hiring of Informers in Guatemala," *New York Times,* June 29, 1996.
3. Intelligence Oversight Board, "Report on the Guatemala Review," June 28, 1996; Weiner, "Report Faults CIA on Hiring of Informers in Guatemala," *New York Times,* June 29, 1996.
4. Walter Pincus, "Deutch under Pressure to Punish CIA Agents," *Washington Post,* July 31, 1995.
5. Senate Select Committee on Intelligence, *Special Report of the Select Committee on Intelligence, January 4, 1995 to October 3, 1996,* 1997, 11.
6. Pincus, "Relaxed CIA Covert Action Rules Urged: Blue-ribbon Panel Wants More Risk-taking within the Limits of the Law," *Washington Post,* January 30, 1996.

CHAPTER 17: AL-QA'IDA DAWNS

1. State Department, "Patterns of Global Terrorism, 1996."
2. Senate Select Committee on Intelligence, *Current and Projected National Security Threats to the United States and its Interests Abroad,* 1996, 4–12.
3. Cofer Black, "Testimony before the Joint Inquiry into Intelligence Community Activities before and after the Terrorist Attacks of September 11, 2001," September 26, 2002.
4. State Department, "Significant Incidents of Political Violence against Americans," 1996.
5. Anne Gearan, "Freeh Blames Iran for Khobar Bombing," *Associated Press,* December 18, 2003.
6. Senate Select Committee on Intelligence, *Current and Projected National Security Threats to the United States and its Interests Abroad,* 4–12.
7. *Peterson, et al. v. Islamic Republic of Iran,* Civil Action No. 01-2094 (US District Court for the District of Columbia, 2003).
8. Richard Armitage, "Testimony before the National Commission on Terrorist Attacks Upon the United States," March 24, 2004.

9. Senate Select Committee on Intelligence, *Current and Projected National Security Threats to the United States and its Interests Abroad*, 1997, 3–11.
10. Clark, *Against All Enemies*, pp. 120–21.
11. National Commission on Terrorist Attacks upon the United States, *Staff Statement No. 5: Diplomacy*, 2004; and ibid, *Staff Statement No. 11: the Performance of the Intelligence Community*, 2004.
12. For the role Jamel Ahmed al-Fadl played in changing the intelligence community's assessment, see National Commission on Terrorist Attacks upon the United States, *Staff Statement No. 11: The Performance of the Intelligence Community*, 2004; the 9/11 Commission Report, pp. 79, 129, 202. Also see *US v. Usama Bin Ladin, et al.*, S(7)98 Cr. 1023 (S.D.NY), February 6–7, 2001 (transcript pp. 158–410) for detailed testimony given by Fadl on the birth of al-Qa'ida, its ideology and range of activities.
13. Anonymous, *Through Our Enemies' Eyes*, p. 179.
14. Ibid., pp. 170–77.
15. Kessler, *Inside the CIA*, pp. 69–71.
16. George Tenet, "Testimony before the Joint Inquiry into Intelligence Community Activities before and after the Terrorist Attacks of September 11, 2001," October 17, 2002.
17. Dana Priest and Barton Gellman, "U.S. Decries Abuse but Defends Interrogations: Stress and Duress Tactics Used on Terrorism Suspects Held in Secret Overseas Facilities," *Washington Post*, December 26, 2002.
18. Bodansky, *Bin Ladin*, pp. 156, 257; Mohamad Bazzi, "Covert War Waged with Egypt's Help," *Newsday*, October 21, 2001; and Rijiv Chandrasekaran and Peter Finn, "U.S. Behind Secret Transfer of Terror Suspects," *Washington Post*, March 11, 2002.
19. "Message from Osama bin-Muhammad bin-Laden to His Muslim Brothers in the Whole World and Especially in the Arabian Peninsula; Declaration of Jihad against the American Occupying the Land of the Two Holy Mosques; Expel the Non-believers from the Arabian Peninsula," *al-Islah* 2, September 1996.

CHAPTER 18: MISSION ALIGNMENT

1. Mike Causey, "Forced Early Retirement," *Washington Post*, April 3, 1995.
2. Ibid.; Causey, "Forced Early Retirement," *Washington Post*, May 5, 1995; and Causey, "Don't Count Clinton In," *Washington Post*, May 19, 1995.

3. Randy Stearns, "The CIA's Secret War in Iraq," *ABCNews.com*, February 1998.
4. Tim Weiner, "Baghdad's Foes: Opponents Find That Ousting Hussein is Easier Said Than Done," *New York Times*, November 16, 1998.
5. Weiner, "CIA Drafts Covert Plan to Topple Saddam," *New York Times*, February 26, 1998.
6. Stearns, "The CIA's Secret War in Iraq," *ABCNews.com*, February 1998.
7. Weiner, "CIA Drafts Covert Plan to Topple Saddam," *New York Times*, February 26, 1998; R. Jeffrey Smith and David Ottaway, "Anti-Saddam Operations Cost CIA $100 Million," *Washington Post*, September 15, 1996; and Weiner, "Yet Again, Saddam's Foes Pay Price for Foiled U.S. Plot," *New York Times*, September 11, 1996.
8. Weiner, "Iraqi Offensive into Kurdish Zone Disrupts U.S. Plot to Oust Hussein," *New York Times*, September 7, 1996, and Weiner, "Yet Again, Saddam's Foes Pay Price for Foiled U.S. Plot," *New York Times*, September 11, 1996.
9. Walter Pincus, "Intelligence Community Faulted by House Panel," *Washington Post*, June 19, 1997.
10. Stephen Marrin, "CIA's Kent School: A Step in the Right Direction," *International Studies Association Conference*, University of Virginia.

CHAPTER 19: UNETHICAL SPIES

1. Tim Weiner, "The C.I.A.'s Most Important Mission: Itself," *New York Times*, December 10, 1995.
2. Walter Pincus, "CIA Chief Castigates 7 Agency Officials; Deutch's Criticism Excludes 3 Former Directors," *Washington Post*, November 1, 1995.
3. Weiner, "CIA Traitor, Saying He Wanted Cash for Family, Gets 23 Years," *New York Times*, June 6, 1997.
4. House Permanent Select Committee on Intelligence, *IC21: The Intelligence Community in the 21st Century*, Staff Study, Chapter IX, 1996.
5. Kent Pekel, "The Need for Improvement: Integrity, Ethics, and the CIA," *Studies in Intelligence* (Spring 1998).
6. George Lardner, "Witness Weeps about Scandal's Impact on CIA Career," *Washington Post*, July 30, 1992.

CHAPTER 21: THE CIA BITES BACK

1. George Tenet, "Testimony before the National Commission on Terrorist Attacks upon the United States," *Staff Statement No. 7: Intelligence Policy*, 2004.

CHAPTER 22: A PLEASANT SURPRISE

1. Senate Select Committee on Intelligence, *Nomination of George J. Tenet to be DCI*, 1997, 52–57.
2. Ibid.
3. Ibid.; Senate Select Committee on Intelligence, *Hearing on Nomination of George J. Tenet to be DDCI*, 1995, 10–18.
4. Senate Select Committee on Intelligence, *Hearing on Nomination of George J. Tenet to be DDCI*, 1995, 10–18.
5. CIA, "Statement by CIA and FBI on Arrest of Mir Aimal Kansi," June 17, 1997.
6. Mary Nayak, "Intelligence Failure—Indian Testing of a Nuclear Device in 1998." (Speech presented at the Eisenhower Series Conference.) September 23, 2003, Washington D.C.
7. "CIA Using Data Mining to Keep Smart," *Reuters*, March 5, 2001.
8. Justin Hibbard, "Mission Possible: The CIA Is Increasingly Dependent on Its Fledgling Venture Capital Arm," *Red Herring* 108, December 11, 2001.
9. Ibid.

CHAPTER 23: WAR ON TERRORISM

1. "World Islamic Front Statement Urging Jihad against Jews and Crusaders," *al-Quds al-Arabi* (Arabic), February 23, 1998.
2. Cofer Black, "Testimony before the Joint Inquiry into Intelligence Community Activities before and after the Terrorist Attacks of September 11, 2001," September 26, 2002.
3. Bodansky, *Bin Ladin*, pp. 253–55.
4. Mohamad Bazzi, "Covert War Waged with Egypt's Help," *Newsday*, October 21, 2001; Andrew Higgins and Christopher Cooper, "CIA-backed Team Used Brutal Means to Break Up Terrorist Cell in Albania," *Wall Street Journal*, November 20, 2001; "Third Egyptian Accused of Terrorism Arrested in Tirana," *Albanian Telegraphic Agency*, July 21, 1998; Barbara Plett, "Egypt Sentences Militants to Death," *BBCNews.com*, April 18, 1999; and Rajiv Chandrasekaran and Peter Finn, "U.S. Behind Secret Transfer of Terror Suspects," *Washington Post*, March 11, 2002.
5. Bodansky, *Bin Ladin*, pp. 253–54.

6. *U.S. v. Usama Bin Ladin,* Indictment, No. 98 Cr. (S.D.N.Y. unsealed November 4, 1998).
7. Anonymous, *Through Our Enemies' Eyes,* pp. 127–28, 200.
8. U.S. State Department, "Report of the Accountability Review Boards: Bombings of the U.S. Embassies in Nairobi, Kenya and Dar es Salaam, Tanzania on August 7, 1998," January 8, 1999.
9. "President Clinton's Speech on Terrorist Attacks," *Conservative New Service,* August 20, 1998.
10. Ryan C. Hendrickson, "The Clinton Administration's Strikes on Usama Bin Ladin: Limits to Power," *Contemporary Cases in U.S. Policy,* pp. 196–216.
11. Kessler, *CIA at War,* p. 226.
12. Bob Woodward, "CIA Paid Afghans to Track Bin Ladin: Team of 15 Recruits Operates Since 1998," *Washington Post,* December 23, 2001.
13. "Lessons from the *Cole,*" *ABCNews.com,* January 9, 2001; and Army Sgt. 1st Class Kathleen T. Rhem, "Commission Stresses Beefing up Intel, Changing Focus," *American Forces Press Service,* January 11, 2001.
14. William Cohen, "Testimony before the National Commission on Terrorist Attacks Upon the United States," March 24, 2004.
15. George Tenet, "Testimony before the Joint Inquiry into Intelligence Community Activities before and after the Terrorist Attacks of September 11, 2001," October 17, 2002.
16. House and Senate Intelligence Committees, *Joint Inquiry into Intelligence Community Activities before and after the Terrorist Attacks of September 11, 2001,* Development of U.S. Counterterrorism Policy Before September 11, 2001, p. 228.
17. House Permanent Select Committee on Intelligence, *IC21: The Intelligence Community in the 21st Century,* Staff Study, 1996.
18. House and Senate Intelligence Committees, *Joint Inquiry into Intelligence Community Activities before and after the Terrorist Attacks of September 11, 2001,* Development of U.S. Counterterrorism Policy Before September 11, p. 234.

CHAPTER 24: THE DARK SIDE

1. Walter Pincus, "Soviet Letter Warned Ames in 1989 about Using CIA Computers, Sources Say," *Washington Post,* March 15, 1994.
2. Bill Miller and Walter Pincus, "Ex-CIA Agent Given 5 Years in Extortion Case," *Washington Post,* September 26, 1998.
3. Tim Weiner, "A Straight-Arrow Policeman Turns Loose Cannon at CIA," *New York Times,* April 12, 1998.

4. Miller and Pincus, "Ex-CIA Agent Given 5 Years in Extortion Case," *Washington Post,* September 26, 1998.

CHAPTER 25: HELP WANTED

1. House Permanent Select Committee on Intelligence, *IC21: The Intelligence Community in the 21st Century,* Staff Study, Chapter IX, 1996.
2. Ibid.
3. Mark S. Zaid, "Testimony before the Senate Committee on the Judiciary," April 25, 2001.
4. William J. Broad, "Lie-Detector Tests Found Too Flawed to Discover Spies," *New York Times,* October 9, 2002.

CHAPTER 26: FAILURE

1. For an excellent assessment of the nature and intentions of Usama bin Ladin, see Anonymous, *Through Our Enemies' Eyes.* The author of the book, whose identity must for the time remain masked, is a senior CIA analyst who followed bin Ladin issues closely. Neither his assessment of bin Ladin nor the publication of his book was welcomed by the CIA. I worked with him for a while. He is one of those great analysts who think outside the box and therefore is not favored by the CIA.
2. House and Senate Intelligence Committees, *Joint Inquiry into Intelligence Community Activities before and after the Terrorist Attacks of September 11, 2001,* Strategic Analysis, pp. 336–43.
3. Ibid., Strategic Analysis, p. 337.
4. Ibid., Abridged Findings and Conclusions, p. xvii.
5. Ibid., Covert Action and Military Operations against Bin Ladin, p. 306.
6. Barton Gellman, "Struggles inside the Government Defined Campaign," *Washington Post,* December 20, 2001.
7. House and Senate Intelligence Committees, *Joint Inquiry into Intelligence Community Activities before and after the Terrorist Attacks of September 11, 2001,* Abridged Findings and Conclusions, p. xi.
8. Ibid., Abridged Findings and Conclusions, p. xvi.
9. House and Senate Intelligence Committees, *Joint Inquiry into Intelligence Community Activities before and after the Terrorist Attacks of September 11, 2001,* Recommendations, pp. 15–16.

CHAPTER 27: OUT OF THE FOXHOLE

1. House and Senate Intelligence Committees, *Joint Inquiry into Intelligence Community Activities before and after the Terrorist Attacks of September 11, 2001,* Recommendations, p. 5.
2. "Bin Ladin Reportedly Heads White House 'Hit List'," *Reuters,* December 15, 2002.
3. Doyle McManus, "A U.S. License to Kill," *Los Angeles Times,* January 11, 2003.
4. Thom Shanker and Eric Schmitt, "Fight against Terrorism; Pentagon May Push Propaganda in Allied Nations," *New York Times,* December 16, 2002.
5. Daniel Golden, "After Sept. 11 CIA Becomes a Growing Force on Campus," *Wall Street Journal,* October 4, 2002.
6. Ibid.

CHAPTER 28: EPILOGUE

1. House and Senate Intelligence Committees, *Joint Inquiry into Intelligence Community Activities before and after the Terrorist Attacks of September 11, 2001,* Abridged Findings and Conclusions, p. xvii.

Glossary of Intelligence and National Security Terms

ACCOUNTABILITY. As public servants, CIA officers are accountable to the government for their actions, including management of government funds, upholding of rules and regulations, and conducting themselves in a manner consistent with government expectations. Accountability boards are committees that review allegations of wrongdoing and make personnel action recommendations.

AGENT. Agents are individuals recruited by the CIA to collect intelligence or provide intelligence support services in a clandestine manner. CIA employees are not called agents, but officers.

AGENT ACQUISITION CYCLE. This is the cycle that CIA operations officers use to find, employ, and manage agents. The cycle includes targeting/spotting, assessing, recruiting, handling, and terminating.

AFGHAN ARABS. Arabs who went to Afghanistan to fight with the Afghanis in the Afghan-Soviet war. Afghan Arabs formed extensive networks and stayed in contact after the war, with some returning to their countries of origin and others going off to fight in other *jihads*, such as in Bosnia and Chechnya.

ASSET. A clandestine source or method. When referring to sources, the term is used interchangeably with "agent." There are reporting assets (those that provide intelligence) and support assets (those that provide other kinds of services). **STABLE OF ASSETS** is the collective term.

ASSET SCRUB. Scrubs are the process of reviewing all aspects of operational activities, to include effectiveness, security, counterintelligence, and production. Assets are scrubbed periodically to weed out the poor performers or problem assets, and to validate the good ones.

ASSET VALIDATION SYSTEM. Abbreviated AVS, this is the system that the CIA uses to determine if its assets are who they say they are, have the access to intelligence that they claim they have, report information reliably, and are not secretly working for another foreign intelligence agency against the CIA.

BUBBLE. A futuristic-looking secure auditorium located in the CIA Headquarters compound at Langley.

BUGS. Audio devices used for eavesdropping.

BUREAU OF INTELLIGENCE AND RESEARCH. Abbreviated INR, the State Department intelligence analysis and research office.

CHIEF OF STATION. Abbreviated COS, this is the senior CIA officer in charge of a field station.

CLANDESTINE SERVICE. Abbreviated CS, this is an alternative name for the CIA Directorate of Operations.

COLD TURNOVER. When an operations officer is replaced by another officer who will manage the case, normally there is a personal introduction of the incoming officer to the agent by the departing officer, called a warm turnover. However, sometimes circumstances dictate that there can be no personal introduction and the new officer will meet the agent on his or her own, a cold turnover.

COMMUNICATIONS INTELLIGENCE. Abbreviated COMINT, this involves the interception of foreign communications, typically voice or data. It is a subcategory of signals intelligence (SIGINT).

COMPARTMENTALIZATION. A process of restricting access to intelligence. Intelligence is placed in a compartment whose access is controlled by a bigot list.

COMPROMISE. Exposure of an operation or information.

CONTRACT EMPLOYEES. Employees who are hired to do a specific job for a specific period of time under a contractual agreement. In CIA history, these typically have been individuals working in covert action programs, of which the CIA wishes to deny direct involvement. More recently, contract employees have assumed the place of providing services previously provided by CIA staff employees.

CORPORATENESS. Jargon used by the CIA meaning to work with a team orientation.

COUNTERESPIONAGE. The defensive discipline of protecting U.S. secrets from compromise by foreign intelligence services.

COUNTERINTELLIGENCE. The offensive discipline of targeting foreign intelligence services, trying to compromise their sources and methods.

COVER. A false identity or affiliation that intelligence officers use to hide their true employers and activities. Also called a **LEGEND.**

COVERT ACTION. A special category of operations that does not involve the collection of intelligence that is done clandestinely with the explicit intention of providing political deniability to the sponsoring state or entity.

CRYPTS. Substitute word(s) to encode plain text. In the CIA, crypts are used for agents, collection methods, operations, and foreign and domestic agencies. Some crypts are composed of a two-letter digraph to indicate geographical location or operation type, and words to identify the specific operation, agent, or method.

CURRENT INTELLIGENCE. A category of intelligence production that is done on a daily basis to provide consumers with a rapid assessment of daily events.

DANGLE. A controlled source that is "dangled" before a foreign intelligence service, with the operational plan of the foreign intelligence service recruiting the dangle without realizing that the source is already under the control of an intelligence service. Dangles are used in double-agent operations and counterintelligence operations in order to obtain intelligence on the operating sources and methods of foreign intelligence services.

DEAD DROPS. A form of impersonal communication that permits agents and handlers to pass information back and forth without the two being in the same place at the same time, reducing the operational risk of exposure from being sighted in a personal meeting.

DEFECTOR. A government official (diplomat, intelligence officer, scientist) who abandons his/her own country for another country, and who cooperates with the adopted country's government by providing intelligence and other services against the interests of the country of former residency.

DEFENSE INTELLIGENCE AGENCY. Abbreviated DIA, the centralized U.S. military all-source intelligence and analysis organization.

DENIED AREA. A country or area of a country that is under hostile government control in which conducting clandestine operations is very difficult. Intelligence officers are denied free movement in the area and/or are subjected to extensive surveillance that restricts operational activity.

DIRECTORATE OF INTELLIGENCE. Abbreviated DI, the analytical arm of the CIA.

DIRECTORATE OF OPERATIONS. Abbreviated DO, the overseas arm of the CIA that collects foreign intelligence and conducts clandestine operations.

DIRECTORATE OF SCIENCE AND TECHNOLOGY. Abbreviated DS&T, the technical and scientific side of the CIA.

DIRTY TRICKS. Jargon referring to a variety of clandestine operational activity to disinform, disrupt, or damage foreign governments, entities, and individuals. Dirty tricks include propaganda operations, assassination, rendition, false-flag recruitment, blackmail, bribery, and the like.

DOUBLE AGENT. An agent who works simultaneously for two intelligence agencies, working secretly for one against interests of the other.

FARM (THE). The CIA training facility located in the Virginia Tidewater area.

FENCED MONEY. Funding to agencies that is specially provided and restricted in the ways it can be spent. Fenced money cannot be reprogrammed to other activities or spent on related support activities not specifically outlined in the initial granting.

FEDERAL BUREAU OF INVESTIGATION. Abbreviated FBI, the federal law enforcement agency in the Justice Department.

FINDING. An authorization by the U.S. president to the CIA for the conduct of covert action.

FINISHED INTELLIGENCE. Intelligence reports written by analysts that consider a range of information, frequently from multiple sources (raw human reporting, intercepts, imagery, and open source information) providing analysis of the intelligence.

FLAP. The consequences caused by an operational or analytical failure. Flaps can be operational or political, or both.

GLASS CEILING. A promotion barrier that is unwritten but exists in practice in the senior services of government and private industry.

GROUPTHINK. A condition where a group of analysts follows, without challenge, one particular analytical line, with analytical rigor breaking down due to pressures of forming an analytical consensus.

HANDLING. The process of running and managing an agent. The operations officer is the agent's direct handler. Within the agent-acquisition cycle, the handling stage follows the recruitment stage.

HARD TARGETS. A category of operations that includes the most difficult cases, either in terms of access and/or hostility toward the United States.

HAWALA. An informal banking system popular in the Middle East, Africa, and East Asia. Money transfers are transacted through exchange houses or private individuals with little to no formal paper trail. A person in one country will give money to a middleman and another middleman will give the equivalent amount of money (less fees) in another country. The system is based on trust and the reputation of the middlemen. The system is most popular in locations where the formal banking system is weak or nonexistent.

HOME BASING. A personnel management process for the care and feeding of CIA officers. CIA officers have a career assignment to a particular directorate and component for personnel management responsibilities (promotion, training, benefits, and so on). For example, an officer will be home-based in the Directorate of Operations/ Latin America Division. He will serve in the division primarily, but will also take rotational assignments outside the division, directorate, or even the Agency.

HOSTILE. Designation for countries, organizations, activities and agents that work actively against the United States—i.e., the enemy.

HOUSE PERMANENT SELECT COMMITTEE ON INTEL-LIGENCE. Abbreviated HPSCI, the House of Representatives committee responsible for intelligence oversight.

HUMAN INTELLIGENCE. Abbreviated HUMINT, the category of collection by means of human sources.

IN-COUNTRY OPERATIONS. Operations that are conducted inside the country in which an operations officer or an agent resides.

INTELLIGENCE COMMUNITY. A term for a group of U.S. government agencies that have missions related to intelligence, national security, and law enforcement. The main agencies include the CIA, FBI, National Security Agency, National Security Council, Defense Department (and military service branches), Defense Intelligence Agency, National Reconnaissance Office, National Imagery and Mapping Agency, Treasury, Commerce, State Department (INR), Energy, and Homeland Security.

INTELLIGENCE CZAR. A proposed new position creating one focal point for the U.S. government responsible for the intelligence community.

INTERNAL OPERATIONS COURSE. A specialized training course given to CIA officers who are scheduled for assignments to the former Soviet Union.

KGB. Soviet Committee for State Security (*Komitet Gosudarstvenoy Bezopasnosti*) is the former Soviet external intelligence agency. With the dissolution of the Soviet Union, it was replaced by the Russian SVR. The KGB was the archrival of the CIA.

LEGAL ATTACHÉ. Abbreviated "Legat," FBI officers assigned to U.S. embassies.

LETHAL FINDING. A presidential finding that authorizes the use of lethal force in covert action operations. A lethal finding does not necessary authorize assassination, but provides authorization to take certain actions that might result in deaths, such as hostile renditions.

LIAISON. A cooperative relationship between the intelligence or law enforcement services of two countries. Liaison officers are those who are designated to work in official cooperation with officers of foreign intelligence (or law enforcement) services.

MEASUREMENT AND SIGNATURES INTELLIGENCE. Abbreviated MASINT, intelligence collection using technical means for metric, angle, spatial wavelength, time-dependence modulation, and hydromagnetic data, air samples, and water samples.

MIRROR IMAGING. The risky methodology of predicting foreign behavior based on one's own cultural expectations and mores—e.g., expecting foreign leaders to act like U.S. leaders.

MISSION SUPPORT OFFICES. Abbreviated MSO, these are the offices that provide administrative support within the CIA. MSO previously was named the Directorate of Administration.

MOLE. A spy who has burrowed his way into a government agency and is falsely believed to be loyal to that agency but is in fact working on behalf of a foreign government, stealing secrets or influencing decision making.

MOSSAD. Israeli foreign intelligence service.

MUJAHADIN. A Muslim waging *jihad,* or a *jihadi.* Also a collective reference for the Afghan fighters.

NATIONAL IMAGERY AND MAPPING AGENCY. Abbreviated NIMA, the U.S. agency responsible for imagery collection and production, as well as production of military maps for operations and planning.

NATIONAL FOREIGN INTELLIGENCE PROGRAMS. One of three intelligence community budgets and the only one under the control of the DCI.

NATIONAL RECONNAISSANCE OFFICE. Abbreviated NRO, a joint Air Force-CIA research, development, and procurement agency for remote collection platforms.

NATIONAL SECURITY AGENCY. Abbreviated NSA, the U.S. agency responsible for the collection, exploitation, and production of signals intelligence and information security.

NATIONAL SECURITY COUNCIL. Abbreviated NSC, an executive branch agency responsible for policy formulation for the U.S. president on national security issues and managing the execution of national security policy.

NEED TO KNOW. The guiding principle for limiting access to intelligence.

NEEDS OF THE SERVICE. The principle that organizational requirements take priority over everything else, including standard practices, regulations, and personal needs.

1985 LOSSES. A shorthand reference to the CIA operational compromises in the Soviet and East European Division that started in 1985. CIA agents were arrested and technical collection operations exposed.

NON-OFFICIAL COVER OFFICER. Abbreviated NOC, a CIA officer operating under non-U.S. government cover.

NUMBERS GAME. The practice of inflating the number of agents by recruiting marginal producers in order for operations officers to look good at promotion time—at least on paper.

OFFICE OF STRATEGIC SERVICES. Abbreviated OSS, the wartime intelligence organization established at the beginning of World War II and dissolved at the end of the war. The OSS is considered the predecessor organization for the CIA.

OPEN SOURCE INTELLIGENCE. Abbreviated OSINT, intelligence that is gleaned from public sources of information.

OPERATING DIRECTIVE. The written guidelines that direct the collection focus of CIA field stations.

OPERATIONS OFFICERS. Formerly called **CASE OFFICERS,** operations officers target, recruit, and handle agents.

OUTED. The act of purposely exposing the identity of an intelligence officer under cover.

PERSONA NON GRATA. Abbreviated PNG, the government act of declaring a foreign official no longer welcome in the country and advising of the intent to deport the official.

PITCH. An operational proposal to a candidate for work as an agent for a foreign government or entity. Also called a **RECRUITMENT PROPOSAL** or **RECRUITMENT PITCH.**

PLAUSIBLE DENIABILITY. The concept of obscuring the origin or the responsibility for operational activity so that if the operation is exposed, the originators or the responsible governing authority can claim no connection or knowledge, thus protecting them from embarrassment or political damage.

PRESIDENTIAL DECISION DIRECTIVE-35. Abbreviated PDD-35, the policy guidelines for intelligence collection priorities as directed by President William Jefferson Clinton.

PROPAGANDA. Information operations meant to influence. Propaganda can be completely false (black propaganda), partially false (gray propaganda), or true information attributed to a false source (white propaganda).

RAW INTELLIGENCE. Intelligence information that has not been analyzed.

RECRUITMENT. The operational process of obtaining the agreement of an individual to work as an agent for an intelligence organization. The recruitment stage follows the agent-development stage in the agent-acquisition cycle used by the CIA.

REDUCTION IN FORCE. Abbreviated RIF, the traditional way the U.S. government downsizes by laying off employees on the basis of seniority.

RENDITION. Extrajudicial detention and transportation of an individual to judicial or security authorities—or, in other words, extradition outside the legal process.

SENATE SELECT COMMITTEE FOR INTELLIGENCE. Abbreviated SSCI, the Senate committee responsible for intelligence oversight.

SEVENTH FLOOR. In-house CIA reference to senior management, whose offices are located on the seventh floor of CIA Headquarters.

SIGNALS INTELLIGENCE. Abbreviated SIGINT, intelligence derived from all electronic emanations and transmissions, including communications intelligence (COMINT) and electronic intelligence (ELINT).

SPOT REPORTING. Intelligence and operational reporting that is brief and meant to quickly alert senior-level CIA management (the Seventh Floor) on significant developments as they become known.

STAFF OFFICERS. CIA full-time and part-time employees who are not employed on a contractual basis. also called **BLUE-BADGERS.**

STASI. Formerly, the East German secret police and foreign intelligence service.

STATION. The name of the principal CIA office in a field location.

STATION EQUITIES. The parochial interests of a station that are invoked to either support or object to operational activities proposed by other stations or CIA Headquarters.

SURGE. Rapid movement of personnel and operational resources to meet a new and unplanned requirement.

SVR. The Russian Foreign Intelligence Service (*Sluzhba Vneshney Razvedki Rossii*).

STOVEPIPES. Bureaucratic organizational structure and equities that restrict flexibility to work across organizational lines.

SUPPORT TO MILITARY OPERATIONS. Provision of intelligence to military field commanders during wartime or peacetime operations.

TARGETED KILLING. A legal category in international law that permits the purposeful targeting and killing of a member of the enemy's chain of command during wartime.

THIRD-COUNTRY OPERATIONS. Operations that are conducted outside the United States (the first country) and in a country other than the one to which a CIA officer is permanently assigned (the second country).

TOTAL BATTLEFIELD AWARENESS. Military doctrine of providing military field commanders all-source intelligence so that the commanders can "see" everything that is happening on the ground and in the air during a military operation.

TRADECRAFT. Methods used by intelligence officers to conduct their operations or analysis.

WALK-INS. Individuals volunteering information or services who walk into embassies or other government facilities, usually without prior notice. Frequently, walk-ins want something in return, such as political asylum or money.

WATCH LIST. A list of people of intelligence or law enforcement interest.

Bibliography

BOOKS

Adams, James. *Sell Out: Aldrich Ames and the Corruption of the CIA*. New York: Viking, 1995.

Agee, Philip, and Louis Wolf. *Dirty Work: The CIA in Western Europe*. New York: Dorset Press, 1978.

Anonymous. *Through Our Enemies' Eyes: Osama bin Ladin, Radical Islam and the Future of America*. Washington, DC: Brassey's, 2002.

Baer, Robert. *See No Evil: The True Story of a Ground Soldier in the CIA's War on Terrorism*. New York: Crown Publishers, 2002.

Bearden, Milt, and James Risen. *The Main Enemy: The Inside Story of the CIA's Final Showdown with the KGB*. New York: Random House, 2003.

Bennett, Richard M. *Espionage: An Encyclopedia of Spies and Secrets*. London: Virgin Books, 2002.

Blum, William. *The CIA: A Forgotten History*. London: Zed Books, 1986.

Bodansky, Yossef. *Bin Ladin: The Man Who Declared War on America*. Rocklin, CA: Forum, 1999.

Bowden, Mark. *Black Hawk Down: A Story of Modern War*. New York: Atlantic Monthly Press, 1999.

Clarke, Richard A. *Against all Enemies: Inside America's War on Terror*. New York: Free Press, 2004.

Gates, Robert M. *From the Shadows: The Ultimate Insider's Story of Five Presidents and How They Won the Cold War*. New York: Simon & Schuster, 1996.

Gup, Ted. *The Book of Honor: The Secret Lives and Deaths of CIA Operatives*. New York: Doubleday, 2000.

Halberstam, David. *War in a Time of Peace: Bush, Clinton, and the Generals.* New York: Scribner, 2001.

Jacobsen, David. *Hostage: My Nightmare in* Beirut. With assistance of Gerald Astor. New York: Donald I. Fine, 1991.

Jeffreys-Jones, Rhodri. *The CIA and American Democracy.* New Haven, CT: Yale University Press, 1989.

Kessler, Ronald. *Inside the CIA: Revealing the Secrets of the World's Most Powerful Spy Agency.* New York: Pocket Books, 1992.

———. *The CIA at War: Inside the Secret Campaign against Terror.* New York: St. Martin's Press, 2003.

Maas, Peter. *Killer Spy: The Inside Story of the FBI's Pursuit and Capture of Aldrich Ames, America's Deadliest Spy.* New York: Warner Books, 1995.

Mangold, Tom. *Cold Warrior: James Jesus Angleton: The CIA's Master Spy Hunter.* New York: Simon & Schuster, 1991.

Mendez, Antonio. *The Master of Disguise: My Secret Life in the CIA.* With assistance of Malcolm McConnell. New York: William Morrow & Co., 1999.

Mendez, Antonio, and Jonna Mendez. *Spy Dust: Two Masters of Disguise Reveal the Tools and Operations That Helped Win the Cold War.* With assistance of Bruce Henderson. New York: Atria Books, 2002.

Miniter, Richard. *Losing Bin Ladin: How Bill Clinton's Failures Unleashed Global Terrorism.* Washington, D.C.: Regnery, 2003.

Odom, William E. *Fixing Intelligence: For a More Secure America.* New Haven, CT: Yale University Press, 2003.

Pillar, Paul R. *Terrorism and U.S. Foreign Policy.* Washington, DC: Brookings Institution Press, 2001.

Richelson, Jeffrey T. *The Wizards of Langley: Inside the CIA's Directorate of Science and Technology.* Boulder, CO: Westview Press, 2001.

Riebling, Mark. *Wedge: The Secret War between the FBI and CIA.* New York: Alfred A. Knopf, 1994.

Rositzke, Harry. *The CIA's Secret Operations: Espionage, Counterespionage, and Covert Action.* New York: Reader's Digest Press, 1977.

Rudgers, David F. *Creating the Secret State: The Origins of the Central Intelligence Agency, 1943-1947.* Lawrence: University Press of Kansas, 2000.

Shannon, Elaine, and Ann Blackman. *The Spy Next Door: The Extraordinary Secret Life of Robert Philip Hanssen, the Most Damaging FBI Agent in U.S. History.* Boston, MA: Little, Brown, 2002.

Vise, David A. *The Bureau and the Mole: The Unmasking of Robert Philip Hanssen, the Most Dangerous Double Agent in FBI History.* New York: Atlantic Monthly Press, 2002.

Weiner, Tim, David Johnston, Neil A. Lewis. *Betrayal: The Story of Aldrich Ames, an American Spy.* New York: Random House, 1995.

Wise, David. *The Spy Who Got Away: The Inside Story of Edward Lee Howard, the CIA Agent Who Betrayed his Country's Secrets and Escaped to Moscow.* New York: Random House, 1988.

————. *Nightmover: How Aldrich Ames Sold the CIA to the KGB for $4.6 Million.* New York: HarperCollins, 1995.

Wright, Robin. Sacred Rage: The Wrath of Militant Islam. New York: Simon & Schuster, 1985.

Wyden, Peter. *Bay of Pigs: The Untold Story.* New York: Simon & Schuster, 1979.

Zegart, Amy B. *Flawed by Design: The Evolution of the CIA, JCS, and NSC.* Stanford, CA: Stanford University Press, 1999.

ARTICLES, DOCUMENTS, HEARINGS, AND SPEECHES

Ackerman, Robert K. "Intelligence Technology Development Accelerates." *SIGNAL Magazine,* June 2002. Available: http://www.cartome.org/cia-scitech.htm.

Armitage, Richard. "Testimony before the National Commission on Terrorist Attacks Upon the United States." March 24, 2004.

Armstrong, Fulton T. "Ways to Make Analysis Relevant But Not Prescriptive." *Studies in Intelligence,* 46, no. 3 (2000).

Babcock, Charles R. "Gates Passed Panel's Test on Lessons Learned From Casey's Controversies: Matured is Intelligence Committee Code for Changed Ways." *Washington Post,* October 19, 1991.

Bazzi, Mohamad. "Covert War Waged with Egypt's Help." *Newsday,* October 21, 2001.

Berkowitz, Bruce. "Failing to Keep Up with the Information Revolution: The DI and 'IT'." *Studies in Intelligence* 47, no. 1 (2003).

"Bin Ladin Reportedly Heads White House 'Hit List.'" *Reuters,* December 15, 2002.

Black, Cofer. "Testimony before Joint Inquiry into Intelligence Community Activities before and after the Terrorist Attacks of September 11, 2001." September 26, 2002.

Brant, Daniel. "Journalism and the CIA: The Mighty Wurlitzer." *NameBase NewsLine* 17 (1997). Available: http://www.namebase.org/news17.html.

Broad, William J. "Lie-Detector Tests Found Too Flawed to Discover Spies." *New York Times,* October 9, 2002.

Broder, David S. "Countering Critics, Defending Decisions 'I'm Not Going to be Rushed to Judgment' in Spy Case, Woolsey Declares." *Washington Post,* May 12, 1994.

Bush, George. "Speech at the Bush School of Government and Public Service, Texas A&M University." November 19, 1999, College Station, Texas. Excerpts Available: http://www.cia.gov/csi/studies/summer00/art02.html

Bushinsky, Jay, and Jon Immanuel. "Ross Pushes for Joint Security." *Jerusalem Post,* August 12, 1997.

Butler, Desmond. "Terror Suspect's Departure from Germany Raises Concern in Other Nations." *New York Times,* December 24, 2002.

Cannistraro, Vincent. "The CIA Dinosaur." *Washington Post,* September 5, 1991.

Causey, Mike. "Buyouts at the CIA.," *Washington Post,* June 14, 1993.

———. "Buyouts a Popular Goal." *Washington Post,* July 8, 1993.

———. "Forced Early Retirement." *Washington Post,* April 3, 1995.

———. "Forced Early Retirement." *Washington Post,* May 5, 1995.

———. "Don't Count Clinton In." *Washington Post,* May 19, 1995.

Central Intelligence Agency. "Task Force on Greater CIA Openness." 1991 (declassified version). Available: http://www.namebase.org/foia/pa01.html.

———. "Unclassified Abstract of the CIA inspector general's Report of the Aldrich H. Ames Case." October 21, 1994. Available: http://www.nsi.org/Library/Espionage/Hitzreport.html.

———. "Fifteen DCIs' First 100 Days," *Studies in Intelligence* 38, no. 5 (1995).

———. "DCI Announces Senior Personnel Appointments." May 17, 1995. Available: http://www.cia.gov/cia/public_affairs/press_release/1995/pr51795.html.

———. "Restructuring the DS&T." June 27, 1996. Available: http://www.gwu.edu/~nsarchiv/NSAEBB/NSAEBB54/st43.pdf.

———. "Key Excerpts from the DI Strategic Plan." Unclassified Version, August 1996. Available: http://www.politrix.org/foia/cia-stuff/cia-di.htm.

———. "Statement by CIA and FBI on Arrest of Mir Aimal Kansi." June 17, 1997. Available: http://www.cia.gov/cia/public_affairs/press_release/1997/pr61797.html.

———. "Press Statement by the Director of Central Intelligence George J. Tenet on the Release of the Jeremiah Report." June 2, 1998. Available: http://www.cia.gov/cia/public_affairs/press_release/1998/pr060298.html.

———. "Inspector General Report on Improper Handling of Classified Information by John M. Deutch." February 18, 2000 (unclassified version). Available: http://www.cia.gov/cia/reports/deutch/deutch.pdf.

————. "Tenet Dedicates New School for Intelligence Analysis." May 4, 2000. Available: http://www.cia.gov/cia/public_affairs/press_release/2000/pr050400.html.

————. "DDCI Actions RE Deutch Investigation." May 25, 2000. Available: http://www.cia.gov/cia/public_affairs/press_release/2000/pr05252000.html.

————. "Central Intelligence Agency Concludes Investigation of Inappropriate Use of Computer Systems." November 30, 2000. Available: http://www.cia.gov/cia/public_affairs/press_release/2000/pr11302000.html.

Chandrasekaran, Rijiv, and Peter Finn. "U.S. Behind Secret Transfer of Terror Suspects." *Washington Post,* March 11, 2002.

Childers, J. Gilmore and DePippo, Henry J. *Senate Judiciary Committee, Subcommittee on Technology, Terrorism, and Government Information, Hearing on Foreign Terrorists in America: Five Years After the World Trade Center,* 105th Cong., 2nd sess., 1998, S. Hrg 105-0703.

"CIA Defends Decision to Identify Officer Killed in Afghanistan." *InsideDefense.com,* December 4, 2001. Available: http://www.fas.org/sgp/news/2001/12/id120401.html.

"CIA Looking to Hire Spies." *USA Today, October* 19, 2001. Available: http://www.usatoday.com/news/sept11/2001/10/19/cia.htm.

"CIA to Open up Secrets, 'Warts and All,' Director Says." *Reuters,* September 29, 1993.

"CIA Officials to Meet with Israeli, Palestinian Security Chiefs." *New York Times,* March 8, 1996.

"CIA Using Data Mining to Keep Smart." *Reuters,* March 5, 2001.

"CIA Weighs 'Targeted Killing" Missions." *Washington Post,* October 28, 2001.

Clark, Timothy B. "Editor's Notebook." *Government Executive Magazine,* July 1, 1999. Available: http://www.govexec.com/features/0799/0799edit.htm.

Clinton, William J. "Remarks at the Signing Ceremony for the U.S.-Israel Counterterrorism Accord." May 1, 1996, Washington D.C. Available: http://www.yale.edu/lawweb/avalon/mideast/mid036.htm.

————. "Remarks at the 50th Anniversary of the Central Intelligence Agency." September 16, 1997, Mclean, VA. Available: http://www.fas.org/irp/offdocs/pdd35.htm.

Cohen, William. "Testimony before the National Commission on Terrorist Attacks Upon the United States." March 24, 2004.

Commission on the Roles and Capabilities of the US Intelligence Community. *Preparing for the 21st Century.* 1996.

"Conclusions of the Majority Report." *New York Times*, December 12, 2002.

Congressional Research Service. "The USA Patriot Act: A Legal Analysis." April 18, 2002.

Council on Foreign Relations. "Assassination: Does it Work? Should America Try?" Terrorism Q&A, n.d. Available: http://www.terrorismanswers.org/home.

————. *Making Intelligence Smarter: The Future of U.S. Intelligence – Report of an Independent Task Force*, 1996. Available: http://www.fas.org/irp/cfr.html.

Daily, J. "Bin Ladin Trial Highlights US Intelligence Problems." *Jane's International Security News*, April 20, 2001.

"Deputy CIA Director Meets Arafat in Gaza." *Jerusalem Post*, March 10, 1996.

Deutch, John M. "Remarks at CIA Town Meeting." May 11, 1995. Available: http://www.fas.org/irp/cia/product/dci_speech_51195.html.

————. "DCI Statement Concerning Class Action Settlement." June 9, 1995. Available: http://www.cia.gov/cia/public_affairs/press_release/1995/ps6995.html.

————. "Speech at National Defense University." June 14, 1995. Available: http://www.cia.gov/cia/public_affairs/speeches/1995/dci_speech_61495.html.

————. "Statement to the Public on the Ames Damage Assessment." October 31, 1995. Available: http://www.cia.gov/cia/public_affairs/press_release/1995/ps103195.html.

————. "Worldwide Threat Assessment Brief to the Senate Select Committee on Intelligence." February 22, 1996.

Dizikes, Peter. "Analyze This: In Terror Fight, CIA Leans on Analysts to See Big Picture." *ABC News.com*, June 10, 2002. Available: http://abcnews.go.com/sections/business/DailyNews/ciaagents020610.html.

Drozdiak, William. "The Cold War in Cold Storage: Washington Won't Part with East German Spy Files, Bonn Wants Them Back." *Washington Post*, March 3, 1999.

Erlanger, Steven. "CIA's Role in Mideast Peace Prompts Outcry and a Call for Senate Hearings." *New York Times*, October 26, 1998.

"FBI Probed Alleged CIA Plot to Kill Saddam." *Reuters*, February 15, 1998.

Federation of American Scientists. *PDD-35 Intelligence Requirements*. March 2, 1995. Available: http://www.fas.org/irp/offdocs/pdd35.htm.

"Feds Indict Seven in Dallas-Area Terror Probe." *Associated Press*, December 19, 2002.

Finn, Peter. "At CIA, a Vocation of Imitation." *Washington Post*, September 8, 1997.

Fisher, Marc. "Embassy Staff Leaves Kuwait; US Ambassador, 4 Others End 4 Months under Siege." *Washington Post*, December 14, 1990.

Fletch, Michael A. "Black Caucus Urges Probe of CIA-Contra Drug Charge; Newspaper Articles Fan Conspiracy Suspicions." *Washington Post*, September 13, 1996.

Gates, Robert M. "CIA Brand of Non-Partisan Intelligence Still Needed." (Speech at University of Virginia, Miller Center for Public Policy.) October 18, 1993. Available: http://www.virginia.edu/insideuva/textonlyarchive/93-10-29/9.txt.

———. "The CIA's Little-Known Resume." *New York Times*, October 29, 1998.

Gearan, Anne. "Freeh Blames Iran for Khobar Bombing." *Associated Press*, December 18, 2003.

Gellman, Barton. "Broad Effort Launched after '98 Attacks." *Washington Post*, December 19, 2001.

———. "Struggles inside the Government Defined Campaign." *Washington Post*, December 20, 2001.

Golden, Daniel. "After Sept. 11 CIA Becomes a Growing Force on Campus." *Wall Street Journal*, October 4, 2002.

Greenberg, Joel. "Palestinians Denounce Arafat's Forces." *New York Times*, October 27, 1998.

Gurule, Jimmy. "Testimony before House Committee on Financial Services." October 3, 2001.

Hall, Charles W., and Walter Pincus, "Spy Suspects Refusing to Go Quietly: Prosecutors Don't Have Leverage Used in Past To Get Tough Plea Deals." *Washington Post*, January 23, 1997.

"Hamas Leader Deported to Jordan." *CNN World News*, May 6, 1997. Available: http://www.cnn.com/WORLD/9705/06/marzook.

Harris, John F. "President Expands Role for CIA Nominee; Deutch to Receive Cabinet Status and Be Involved in Setting National Security Policy." *Washington Post*, March 12, 1995.

"Hearings Held on Middle East Role." *Associated Press*, October 26, 1998.

Hendrickson, Ryan C. "The Clinton Administration's Strikes on Usama Bin Ladin: Limits to Power." *Contemporary Cases in U.S. Policy* (2002), pp. 196–216. Available: http://www.cqpress.com/context/articles contemp8.html.

Henry, Marilyn. "Jewish Lawyer Plans to Sue CIA for Anti-Semitism." *Jerusalem Post*, April 11, 1999.

Hibbard, Justin. "Mission Possible: The CIA Is Increasingly Dependent on its Fledgling Venture Capital Arm." *Red Herring* 108, December 11, 2001. Available: http://www.redherring.com/mag/issue108/908.html.

Higgins, Andrew, and Christopher Cooper. "CIA-backed Team Used Brutal Means to Break Up Terrorist Cell in Albania." *The Wall Street Journal*, November 20, 2001.

Hirschkorn, Phil. "Convicted Bomb Conspirator Linked to Plots." *CNN.com*, September 20, 2001.

Hitz, Frederick P. "The Incredibly Shrinking Spy Machine." *New York Times*, September 15, 1998.

Horowitz, Jason. "Italy Seeks Extradition of Captured Cruise Ship Hijacker." *New York Times*, April 16, 2003.

Hutman, Bill. "Ayalon, Dahlan Meet in Gaza." *Jerusalem Post*, April 3, 1996.

Intelligence Oversight Board. *Report on the Guatemala Review.* June 28, 1996. Available: http://www.gwu.edu/~nsarchiv/NSAEBB/NSAEBB27/04-02.htm.

International Counterterrorism Center. "Iran Linked to Buenos Aires Blast." May 5, 1998. Available: http://www.ict.org.il/spotlight/det.cfm?id=78.

———. "Argentina Issues Warrant in Israeli Embassy Bombing." September 4, 1999. Available: http://www.ict.org.il/spotlight/det.cfm?id=318.

———. "Suspect in Bombing of Israeli Embassy Held in US." August 20, 2000. Available: http://www.ict.org.il/spotlight/det.cfm?id=472.

———. "Report: Former Argentine President Linked to Cover-up of AMIA Bombing." July 22, 2002. Available: http://www.ict.org.il/spotlight/det.cfm?id=807.

Johnston, David, and Tim Weiner. "On the Trail of a CIA Man: Trips and Big Cash Transfers." *New York Times*, November 21, 1996.

Johnston, Rob. "Integrating Methodologists into Teams of Substantive Experts." *Studies in Intelligence* 47, no. 1 (2003).

Kindsvater, Larry C. "The Need to Reorganize the Intelligence Community." *Studies in Intelligence* 47, no. 1 (2003).

Lardner, George. "CIA to Look for Criminal Activities outside Agency; Gates Approves Procedures to Make Agents More 'Vigilant' in Intelligence Gathering." *Washington Post*, January 26, 1992.

————. "Clearance Sought for New CIA Network; Agency Would Transmit Latest Intelligence Only to Select to Officials." *Washington Post,* February 5, 1992.

————. "Gates Rejects Overhaul of Spy Agencies: CIA Head to Install 'Evolutionary' Plan." *Washington Post,* April 2, 1992.

————. "CIA Report on Openness Classified Secret." *Washington Post,* April 23, 1992.

————. "Witness Weeps about Scandal's Impact on CIA Career." *Washington Post,* July 30, 1992.

Leff, Lisa. "Quiet But Happy Scene at Andrews as Last of Embassy Staff Arrives." *Washington Post,* December 15, 1990.

"Lessons from the Cole." *ABC News.com,* January 9, 2001. Available: http://abcnews.go.com/sections/world/DailyNews/yemen010109_cole.html.

Lichblau, Eric. "US Weighs Trial of Terror Suspect in '85 Ship Killing." *New York Times,* April 16, 2003.

Lobe, Jim. "War on Terror: Pentagon Ponders Disinformation Campaign." *Asian Times,* February 26, 2002.

Loeb, Vernon. "Where the CIA Wages Its New World War; Counterterrorist Center Makes Many Arrests, Pursues Bin Ladin with Aid of FBI, NSA." *Washington Post,* September 9, 1998.

————. "CIA Emerges to Resolve Mideast Disputes; Out of Shadows, Agency Is Directly Involved in Israeli-Palestinian Security Talks." *Washington Post,* September 30, 1998.

————. "Director of CIA Plays Key Role in Peace Pact; Israeli, Palestinian Security Concerns Thrust Tenet into an Unsought Limelight." *Washington Post,* October 24, 1998.

————. "Saddam's Iraqi Foes Heartened by Clinton." *Washington Post,* November 16, 1998.

————. "Wanted: A Few Good Spies." *Washington Post,* November 27, 1998.

————. "CIA Won't Disclose Total Intelligence Appropriation for Fiscal Year." *Washington Post,* December 25, 1998.

————. "Bush Affiliation No Secret at Langley; Former Director and President is Honored in Naming of CIA Headquarters." *Washington Post,* April 27, 1999.

————. "Deutch's CIA Clearance Suspended; Home Computer Security Lapses Led to Unprecedented Action against Ex-Director." *Washington Post,* August 21, 1999.

————. "At Hush-Hush CIA Unit, Talk of a Turnaround; Reforms Recharge Espionage Service." *Washington Post,* September 7, 1999.

———. "Intelligence Budget Can Be Secret, Judge Rules." *Washington Post,* November 23, 1999.

———. "CIA Director May Keep Post in Interim." *Washington Post,* December 1, 2000.

———. "CIA Is Faulted for Not Probing Deutch's Actions; Secret Report Criticizes Tenet for Delaying Criminal Review." *Washington Post,* February 2, 2000.

———. "Ex-Spy's Mission at CIA: Buying the Bureaucracy as Agency Administrator, Deputy Means Business." *Washington Post,* February 4, 2000.

———. "Back Channels: The Intelligence Community in House of Mirrors, a Bad Reflection." *Washington Post,* February 18, 2000.

———. "CIA to Release Chile Documents." *Washington Post,* October 24, 2000.

———. "The CIA in Somalia: After Action Report." *Somalia Watch,* February 27, 2000. Available: http://www.somaliawatch.org/archivejuly/000927601.htm.

———. "Tenet, Krongard Alter CIA Power Structure." *Washington Post,* May 1, 2001.

———. "CIA Resurfaces, in the Oval Office Tenet, Bush Develop Close Relationship." *Washington Post,* July 29, 2001.

Loeb, Vernon, and Josh White. "CIA Reports Officer Killed in Prison Uprising." *Washington Post,* November 29, 2001.

Lohr, Steve. "Data Expert Is Cautious about Misuse of Information." *New York Times,* March 25, 2003.

Lose, James M. "National Intelligence Support Teams." *Studies in Intelligence* (Winter 1999–2000).

Lumpkin, John J. "CIA Ramps up Presence at FBI Offices." *Associated Press,* October 23, 2002.

Lunney, Kellie. "CIA Reorganization Will Not Cut Agency Jobs." *Government Executive Magazine,* May 2, 2001. Available: http://www.govexec.com/dailyfed/0501/050201m1.htm.

Lyons, Brendan. "Terrorist foretold 9/11 Towers Plot." *Timesunion.com,* September 22, 2002. Available: 2003. http://www.timesunion.com/AspStories/storyprint.asp?StoryID=57896.

Makovsky, David. "Clinton pledges $100m in Anti-terror Aid." *Jerusalem Post,* March 15, 1996.

Markoff, John. "C.I.A. to Nurture Companies Dealing in High Technology." *New York Times,* September 29, 1999.

Marrin, Stephen. "CIA's Kent School: A Step in the Right Direction." *International Studies Association Conference, University of Virginia*, n.d. (Adaptation from Marrin's Masters thesis). Available: http://www.isanet.org/noarchive/marrin.html.

Mason, Barnaby. "CIA Returns to Mid-East Role." *BBC News.com*, April 26, 2001. Available: http://news.bbc.co.uk/1/hi/world/middle_east/1298290.stm.

Mayer, Jane. "The Search for Osama." *New Yorker*, July 28, 2003.

McCullough, James. "Personal Reflections on Bill Casey's Last Month at CIA." *Studies in Intelligence* 39, no. 5 (1996).

McManus, Doyle. "A U.S. License to Kill." *Los Angeles Times*, January 11, 2003.

"Message from Osama bin-Muhammad bin-Laden to His Muslim Brothers in the Whole World and Especially in the Arabian Peninsula; Declaration of Jihad against the Americans Occupying the Land of the Two Holy Mosques; Expel the Non-believers from the Arabian Peninsula." *al-Islah* 2, September 1996.

Miller, Bill, and Walter Pincus. "Ex-CIA Agent Given 5 Years in Extortion Case." *Washington Post*, September 26, 1998.

Miller, Laura, and Sheldon Rampton. "The Pentagon's Information Warrior: Rendon to the Rescue." *PR Watch* 8, no. 4 (2001). Available: http://www.prwatch.org/prwissues/2001Q4/rendon.html.

Narrett, Eugene, "CIA Brings its 'Kiss of Peace' to Israelis." *The Radical Academy*, December 11, 2000. Available: http://radicalacademy.com/genarrettessay3.htm.

National Commission on Terrorist Attacks Upon the United States. *The 9/11 Commission Report*. GPO, 2004.

Nayak, Mary. "Intelligence Failure—Indian Testing of a Nuclear Device in 1998." (Speech presented at the Eisenhower Series Conference.) September 23, 2003, Washington D.C. Available: http://www.eisenhowerseries.com/Final_04/compendium.pdf.

Page, Susan. "Why Clinton Failed to Stop bin Ladin." *USA Today*, November 12, 2001.

"Palestinians Wail over Agreement, CIA Monitoring of Israeli-Palestinian Security Relations." *ArabicNews.com*, August 22, 1997. Available: http://www.arabicnews.com/ansub/Daily/Day/970822/1997082216.html.

Pappas, Aria A., and James M. Simon Jr. "The Intelligence Community: 2001–2015." *Studies in Intelligence* 46, no. 1 (2000).

Pekel, Kent. "The Need for Improvement: Integrity, Ethics, and the CIA." *Studies in Intelligence* (Spring 1998).

Perelman, Marc. "Iran Leader in Fingered in Bombing, By Defector." *Forward,* November 9, 2001.

Perl, Raphael, and Ronald O'Rourke. "Terrorist Attack on USS Cole: Background and Issues for Congress." *Congressional Research Service,* January 20, 2001.

Peterson, et. al. v. Islamic Republic of Iran, Civil Action No. 01-2094 (US District Court for the District of Columbia, 2003).

Pincus, Walter. "Beyond Glare of Hearings on Gates, CIA Analysts Get Pep Talk from the Chief." *Washington Post,* October 12, 1991.

————. "East German Files Helped in Ames Arrest." *Washington Post,* March 6, 1994.

————. "Soviet Letter Warned Ames in 1989 about Using CIA Computers, Sources Say." *Washington Post,* March 15, 1994.

————. "CIA Struggles to Find Identity in a New World." *Washington Post,* May 9, 1994.

————. "White House Labors to Redefine Role of Intelligence Community." *Washington Post,* June 13, 1994.

————. "CIA Plans to Close 15 Stations in Africa Pullback." *Washington Post,* June 23, 1994.

————. "Many Female CIA Officers Allege Bias; Agency Negotiates to Avoid Lawsuit over Treatment in Spy Branch." *Washington Post,* July 20, 1994.

————. "CIA and the 'Glass Ceiling' Report; Female, Black Operatives Report Harassment." *Washington Post,* September 9, 1994.

————. "Tough Internal CIA Report Cites Failures That Helped Shield Ames, Officers Who Overlooked Signs Criticized, Punishment Left to Woolsey." *Washington Post,* September 18, 1994.

————. "CIA's Woolsey Disciplines 11 in Ames Spy Scandal." *Washington Post,* September 29, 1994.

————. "CIA Chief's 'Judicial' Approach in Ames Case Irks Hill Critics; Reprimands Meted Out by Woolsey are Called Too Timid." *Washington Post,* October 1, 1994.

————. "Two CIA Officers Choose Retirement over Demotion; Woolsey Ordered Punishment after Subordinates Gave Award to Colleague Involved in Ames Case." *Washington Post,* October 14, 1994.

————. "Ex-CIA Chief Backs Smaller Spy Agency." *Washington Post,* December 10, 1994.

————. "FBI Expands Training of Police from Abroad." *Washington Post,* December 14, 1994.

————. "Ex-CIA Officer Settles Sex Discrimination Suit." *Washington Post*, December 24, 1994.

————. "Woolsey Resigns from the CIA after Troubled Tenure." *Washington Post*, December 29, 1994.

————. "President Launches 13-Month Review of Post-Cold War Intelligence Needs." *Washington Post*, February 3, 1995.

————. "Clinton, Deutch Discussed Top Job at the CIA, Sources Say." *Washington Post*, January 4, 1995.

————. "A 21st Century Intelligence Test: Chairman Sets Study of Needs to Help Panel Reshape Network." *Washington Post*, February 20, 1995.

————. "Accused Agent Withdrawn before Espionage Publicity." *Washington Post*, February 24, 1995.

————. "Carns Withdraws as CIA Nominee, Abusive Accusations Cited; Deutch New Choice." *Washington Post*, March 11, 1995.

————. "CIA Agrees to Settle Discrimination Charges by Female Case Officers." *Washington Post*, March 30, 1995.

————. "CIA Operations Chief to Retire at Week's End." *Washington Post*, May 3, 1995.

————. "CIA Steps Up Scrub Down of Agents." *Washington Post*, July 28, 1995.

————. "Deutch under Pressure to Punish CIA Agents." *Washington Post*, July 31, 1995.

————. "Pentagon to Spy More Overseas." *Washington Post*, October 30, 1995.

————. "CIA Chief Castigates 7 Agency Officials; Deutch's Criticism Excludes 3 Former Directors." *Washington Post*, November 1, 1995.

————. "CIA Chief Reconsiders Disclosure; Spy Operation Balks at Naming Agents." *Washington Post*, November 5, 1995.

————. "Pentagon Gaining Turf from the CIA; Intelligence Aides Deny Accounts that Deutch Lets Langley Lose Ground to Military." *Washington Post*, November 16, 1995.

————. "CIA, Pentagon Back NIMA Concept, Combining Spy Satellite Photo Units." *Washington Post*, November 29, 1995.

————. "Tainted Moscow Data Swayed US, CIA Says: Information Concealed Soviet Decline, Hill Told." *Washington Post*, December 9, 1995.

————. "CIA's Spies Watching Deutch's Disciplinary Decision on Paris Station Chief." *Washington Post*, December 27, 1995.

————. "Agencies Debate Value of Being out in the Cold." *Washington Post*, January 12, 1996.

————. "Relaxed CIA Covert Action Rules Urged: Blue-ribbon Panel Wants More Risk-taking Within the Limits of the Law." *Washington Post,* January 30, 1996.

————. "FBI, CIA Try to Set Turf Rules as Bureau Branches Out; State Department Is Concerned about Possible Conflicts between Law Enforcement and Foreign Policy Goals." *Washington Post,* March 18, 1996.

————. "Intelligence Battleground: Reform Bill." *Washington Post,* May 30, 1996.

————. "Panels Continue Impasse on Intelligence: Senate Armed Services Bars Plan to Strengthen role of CIA Head." *Washington Post,* June 7, 1996.

————. "Curtain Is Falling on Another Intelligence Drama: Reform." *Washington Post,* July 8, 1996.

————. "Deutch Shelves $10 Million CIA Field House." *Washington Post,* July 31, 1996.

————. "Internal CIA Study to Ask Why Officers Are Quitting." *Washington Post,* November 26, 1996.

————. "Crossword Puzzle Palace." *Washington Post,* October 16, 1996.

————. "CIA Trims a Little off Middle: Higher-pay Senior Slots Added to Keep Analysts around." *Washington Post,* March 26, 1997.

————. "Panel Says Battlefield Intelligence Still Late." *Washington Post,* June 12, 1997.

————. "Intelligence Community Faulted by House Panel." *Washington Post,* June 19, 1997.

————. "In Clandestine Service, Not So Secret Strains." *Washington Post,* May 1, 1997.

————. "CIA Turns to Boutique Operations, Covert Action against Terrorism, Drugs, Arms." *Washington Post,* September 14, 1997.

————. "A Low Profile for CIA Chief; Behind the Scenes, Tenet Gains Growing Respect." *Washington Post,* January 13, 1998.

————. "CIA's Espionage Capability Found Lacking." *Washington Post,* May 10, 1998.

————. "Berlin to Get CIA Copies of 320,000 Stasi Files." *Washington Post,* October 27, 1998.

————. "Cold War Footnote: CIA Obtained East Germany's Foreign Spy Files." *Washington Post,* November 22, 1998.

————. "CIA Workers Ask ACLU Aid on Polygraph Issues." *Washington Post,* January 13, 1999.

————. "U.S. Won't Hand Over E. German Spy Files; CIA Obtained Data Sometime after '89." *Washington Post,* January 20, 1999.

Pincus, Walter, and Bob Miller. "Ex-CIA Operative Pleads Guilty to Blackmail Attempt at Agency." *Washington Post,* July 28, 1998.

Pincus, Walter, and George Lardner. "Gates Strikes Back at Critics in CIA: Charges of Politicizing Agency 'Ridiculous.'" *Washington Post,* October 4, 1991.

Pincus, Walter, and R. Jeffrey Smith. "East German Files Helped in Ames Arrest." *Washington Post,* March 6, 1994.

Pincus, Walter, and Roberto Suro. "Rooting Out 'Sour Apples' inside the CIA." *Washington Post,* November 19, 1996.

Plett, Barbara. "Egypt Sentences Militants to Death." *BBC News.com,* April 18, 1999. Available: http://news.bbc.co.uk/1/hi/world/middle_east/322362.stm.

Pomfret, John. "Polish Agents Rescued 6 U.S. Spies from Iraq," *Washington Post,* January 17, 1995.

Powers, Thomas. "The Trouble with the CIA." *New York Review of Books,* January 17, 2002.

Priest, Dana. "CIA Killed U.S. Citizen In Yemen Missile Strike." *Washington Post,* November 8, 2002.

Priest, Dana, and Barton Gellman. "U.S. Decries Abuse but Defends Interrogations: Stress and Duress Tactics Used on Terrorism Suspects Held in Secret Overseas Facilities." *Washington Post,* December 26, 2002.

Regoler, Arnon. "How the CIA Operates in Israel and in the Territories." *Israeli Kol ha- ir,* November 24, 2000. Available: http://www.kokhavivpublications.com/israel/0612002.html.

Rhem, Kathleen T. "Commission Stresses Beefing up Intel, Changing Focus." *American Forces Press Service,* January 11, 2001. Available: http://www.af.mil/news/Jan2001/n20010111_0040.asp.

Richelson, Jeffrey T. "Science, Technology and the CIA." *National Security Archive,* September 10, 2001. Available: http://www.gwu.edu/~nsarchiv/NSAEBB/NSAEBB54/.

Risen, James. "Getting Back to Basics, C.I.A. Is Hiring More Spies." *New York Times,* June 27, 1998.

———. "Militant Leader Was a U.S. Target Since the Spring." *New York Times,* September 6, 1998.

———. "Bin Ladin Was Target of Afghan Raid, U.S. Confirms." *New York Times,* December 14, 1998.

———. "To Bomb Sudan Plant, or Not: A Year Later, Debates Rankle." *New York Times,* October 27, 1999.

———. "Gaps in CIA's Ames Case May Be Filled by FBI's Own Spy Case." *New York Times,* February 21, 2001.

————. "Intelligence; U.S. Pursued Secret Efforts to Catch or Kill bin Ladin." *New York Times,* September 30, 2001.

————. "Qaeda Diplomacy: Bin Ladin Sought Iran as an Ally, U.S. Intelligence Documents Say." *New York Times,* December 31, 2001.

————. "Investigators at Odds over Extent of FBI Spy's Cooperation." *New York Times,* May 7, 2002.

————. "CIA and FBI Agree to Truce in War of Leaks vs. Counterleaks." *New York Times,* June 14, 2002.

————. "CIA's Inquiry on Qaeda Aide Seen as Flawed." *New York Times,* September 23, 2002.

Risen, James, and Benjamin Weiser. "US Officials Say Aid for Terrorists Came through Two Persian Gulf Nations." *New York Times,* July 8, 1999.

Risen, James, and David Johnston. "The Wrong Man: CIA Officer Mistaken for Spy Down the Street." *New York Times,* August 11, 2001.

————. "Split at CIA and FBI on Iraqi Ties to al-Qa'ida." *New York Times,* February 2, 2003.

————. "Qaeda Aide Slipped Away Long before Sept. 11 Attack." *New York Times,* March 8, 2003.

Robinson, Clarence A. "Intelligence Agency Adjusts as Mission Possible Unfolds." *SIGNAL Magazine,* October 1998. Available: http://www.us. net/signal/Archieve/Oct98/intel-oct.html.

"Rumsfeld Promises No Torture of Suspect." *MSNBC,* April 3, 2002. Available: http://www.suite101.com/discussion.cfm/investing/ 68672/625408#message_3.

Sanger, David E., and Tim Weiner. "Emerging Role for the C.I.A.: Economic Spy." *New York Times,* October 15, 1995.

Schemo, Diana Jean. "The Burial; Agent Praised as Patriot in Graveside Ceremony." *New York Times,* December 11, 2001.

Sciolino, Elaine. "Violence Thwarts CIA Director's Unusual Diplomatic Role in Middle Eastern Peacemaking." *New York Times,* November 13, 2000.

"Sept 11 Mastermind Identified: US Officials: Khalid Shaikh Linked to Ramzi Youssef." *Dawn.com,* June 6, 2002. Available: http://dawn. com/2002/06/06/int5.htm.

Serlin, Michael D., and Timothy B. Clark. "The Company Goes Commercial." *Government Executive Magazine,* July 1, 1999. Available: http://govexec.com/features/0799/0799s1.htm.

Shanker, Thom, and Eric Schmitt. "Fight against Terrorism; Pentagon May Push Propaganda in Allied Nations." *New York Times,* December 16, 2002.

Sherman, Lee. "Corporate Espionage." *Knowledge Management*, May 9, 2001. Available: http://www.destinationkm.com/articles/?Article ID=547.

60 Minutes II. "How the FBI Gets Its Man." *CBSNEWS.com*, October 10, 2001. Available: http://www.cbsnews.com/stories/2001/10/10/60II/main314283.shtml.

Smith, R. Jeffrey. "Woolsey: A Washington Insider in Every Way: CIA Director-Designate Boasts of His Links with Both Political Parties." *Washington Post*, December 23, 1992.

———. "An Insider Who Shunned the Spotlight: CIA Designee Woolsey Seen as 'Realist' with Penchant for Consensus." *Washington Post*, February 2, 1993.

———. "Administration to Consider Giving Spy Data to Business: CIA Designee Says Topic Is 'Hottest' in Field." *Washington Post*, February 3, 1993.

———. "3rd Security Review Is Out of Shadows; Administration Presses Overhaul of Cold War–era Secrecy Rules." *Washington Post*, May 27, 1993.

———. "Senators, CIA Fight over $1 Billion; Key Democrats Want Big 'Peace Dividend' from Espionage Community." *Washington Post*, July 16, 1993.

———. "As Woolsey Struggles, CIA Suffers; Director Finds Himself at Odds with Capitol Hill, White House." *Washington Post*, May 10, 1994.

———. "Deutch Vows to Clean out Top of CIA; New Generation to Take over Covert Operations, Nominee Tells Panel." *Washington Post*, April 27, 1995.

———. "The CIA Puts on a New Face; Deutch Marks 1st Day Trying to Calm Staff." *Washington Post*, May 12, 1995.

———. "CIA Director Pledges Swift Reform; Deutch Predicts Guatemala Study Will Spur Serious Concerns." *Washington Post*, May 16, 1995.

———. "Punishment in Guatemala Affair Sparks Angry Backlash at CIA." *Washington Post*, October 3, 1995.

———. "After 15 Years, CIA Obeys Order to Give Congress Sensitive Secrets." *Washington Post*, October 11, 1995.

———. "Deutch Leaving No Doubt Who's In Charge of Intelligence." *Washington Post*, December 10, 1995.

———. "Deutch Outlines Plan to Centralize Control of Intelligence Community." *Washington Post*, December 20, 1995.

———. "Clinton to Sign Bill Giving CIA Three New Managers; Measure Also Expands Powers of FBI, CIA." *Washington Post*, October 5, 1996.

————. "Spy Case Hurts at the CIA; Morale Devastated, Agency's Chief Says." *Washington Post,* November 21, 1996.

————. "CIA Drops Over 1,000 Informants." *Washington Post,* March 2, 1997.

————. "By Way of Hill and NSC Staff, Tenet is Unconventional Choice for CIA." *Washington Post,* March 20, 1997.

————. "Espionage Budget Totaled $26.6 Billion, Under Pressure, CIA Breaks Overall Figure Out of Fog of Secrecy." *Washington Post,* October 16, 1997.

Smith, R. Jeffrey, and David B. Ottaway. "Anti-Saddam Operations Cost CIA $100 Million." *Washington Post,* September 15, 1996.

Snider, L. Britt. "Sharing Secrets with Lawmakers: Congress as a User of Intelligence," *Center for the Study of Intelligence.* (Spring 1989).

"Spy Agency Changes Its (Dress) Code." *Reuters,* July 21, 1994.

Stearns, Randy. "The CIA's Secret War in Iraq." *ABC News.com,* February 1998. Available: http://www.defencejournal.com/oct98/cia_secret war.htm.

Tamayo, Juan O. "War on Terrorism around the World." *Miami Herald,* September 8, 2002.

Tenet, George J. "Statement by Acting Director of Central Intelligence before the Senate Select Committee on Intelligence, Hearing on Current and Projected National Security Threats to the United States." February 5, 1997. Available: http://www.cia.gov/cia/public_affairs/speeches/1997/dci_testimony_020597.html.

————. "Statements on the Need to Strengthen the Directorate of Operations." May 5, 1998. Available: http://www.cia.gov/terrorism/strenghtening_the_do.html.

————. "What 'New' Role for the CIA?" *New York Times,* October 27, 1998.

————. "Statement on the Belgrade Chinese Embassy Bombing before the House Permanent Select Committee on Intelligence." July 22, 1999. Available: http://www.cia.gov/cia/public_affairs/speeches/1999/dci_speech_072299.html

————. "Statement to CIA Workforce." September 12, 2001. Available: http://www.cia.gov/cia/public_affairs/speeches/2001/dci_speech_09122001.html.

————. "Testimony before the Joint Inquiry into Intelligence Community Activities before and after the Terrorist Attacks against the United States." June 18, 2002. Available: http://www.cia.gov/cia/public_affairs/speeches/2002/dci_testimony_06182002.html.

————. "Testimony before the Joint Inquiry into Intelligence Community Activities before and after the Terrorist Attacks of September 11,

2001." October 17, 2002. Available: http://www.cia.gov/cia/public_affairs/speeches/2002/dci_testimony_10172002.html.

"Tenet's Testimony before Senate Committee." *New York Times*, February 6, 2002.

"Terror Plot Foiled." *ABC News.com*, September 27, 2001. Available: http://abclocal.go.com/kfsn/news/092601_nw_wedneday.html.

"Third Egyptian Accused of Terrorism Arrested in Tirana." *Albanian Telegraphic Agency*, July 21, 1998. Available: http://www.hri.org/news/balkans/ata/1998/98-07-21.ata.html .

"This is Not Just an Intellectual Food Fight Among . . . Analysts." *Washington Post*, October 4, 1991.

Thomas, Pierre. "Interagency FBI-CIA Tensions Defy Decades of Efforts to Resolve Them." *Washington Post*, May 3, 1994.

Twomey, Steve. "For Weary Families Back in US, 'We have To Keep Being Strong.'" *Washington Post*, August 29, 1990.

Travers, Russ. "The Coming Intelligence Failure." *Studies in Intelligence* 1, no. 1 (1997).

U.S. v. Ahmed Ressam, No. Cr99-666C JCC (W.D. Wash).

U.S. v. Mokhtar Haourari, No. S4 00 Cr. 15 (S.D.N.Y.), July 3, 2001.

U.S. v. Omar Ahmad Ali Abdel Rahman, et. al, 189 F.3d. (2nd Cir, August 16, 1996).

U.S. v. Ramzi Ahmed Yousef, et. al, Lead No. 98-1041 (2nd Cir. Filed August 25, 2000).

U.S. v. Usama Bin Ladin, et al., S(7)98 Cr. 1023 (S.D.N.Y.).

U.S. Congress. House and Senate Intelligence Committees. *Joint Inquiry into Intelligence Community Activities before and after the Terrorist Attacks of September 11, 2001*. 2002, 107th Cong., 2d Sess., H. Rept. 792. S. Rept. 351.

———. House Permanent Select Committee on Intelligence. *IC21: The Intelligence Community in the 21st Century*. 1996.

———. House. *Intelligence Authorization Act for Fiscal Year 1998*. 1997, 105th Cong., 1st sess., H. Rep. 105-35.

———. Senate Committee on Foreign Relations. *The BCCI Affair: A Report to the Committee on Foreign Relations*. 1992, 102nd Cong., 2nd sess., S. Hrg., 102-350.

———. Senate Select Committee on Intelligence. *Nomination of Robert M. Gates*. 1991, 102nd Cong., 1st sess., S. Hrg. 102-0799.

———. Senate Select Committee on Intelligence. *An Assessment of the Aldrich H. Ames Espionage Case and Its Implications for U.S. Intelligence*. 1994, 103rd Cong., 2nd sess., S.Rep. 103-90.

———. Senate Select Committee on Intelligence. *Nomination of John M. Deutch*. 1995, 104th Cong., 1st sess., S. Hrg. 104-160.

————. Senate Select Committee on Intelligence. *Nomination of George J. Tenet to be DDCI.* 1995, 104th Cong., 1st sess., S. Hrg. 104-203.

————. Senate Select Committee on Intelligence. *Current and Projected National Security Threats to the United States and its Interests Abroad.* 1996, 104th Cong., 2nd sess., S. Hrg. 104-510.

————. Senate Select Committee on Intelligence. *Special Report of the Select Committee on Intelligence, January 4, 1995 to October 3, 1996.* 1997, 105th Cong., 1st sess., S.Rep. 105-1.

————. Senate Select Committee on Intelligence. *Current and Projected National Security Threats to the United States and its Interests Abroad.* 1997, 105th Cong., 1st sess., S. Hrg. 105-201.

————. Senate Select Committee on Intelligence. *Nomination of George J. Tenet to be DCI.* 1997, 105th Cong., 1st sess., S. Hrg. 105-314.

U.S. Department of Defense. "Independent Review of the Khobar Towers Bombing." by Lt. General James F. Record, October 31, 1996. Available: http://www.au.af.mil/au/awc/awcgate/khobar/recordf.htm.

————. "Secretary of Defense Report: Personal Accountability for Force Protection at Khobar Towers." July 31, 1997. Available: http://www.au.af.mil/au/awc/awcgate/khobar/cohen.htm.

U.S. Department of State. "Patterns of Global Terrorism." April 1996.

————. "Significant Incidents of Political Violence against Americans." 1996.

————. "Report of the Accountability Review Boards: Bombings of the US Embassies in Nairobi, Kenya and Dar es Salaam, Tanzania on August 7, 1998." January 8, 1999. Available: http://www.fas.org/irp/threat/arb/board_overview.html.

"U.S. Welcomes News of Abu Nidal's Death." *CNN.com,* August 19, 2002. Available: http://www.cnn.com/2002/WORLD/meast/08/19/mideast.nidal/.

U.S. White House. *A National Security Strategy of Engagement and Enlargement.* February 1996. Available: http://www.fas.org/spp/military/docops/national/1996stra.htm.

————. Office of the Vice President. "National Performance Review of the Intelligence Community." http://nsi.org/Library/Intel/npr1.html.

Walcott, John. "Mission Impossible? Anthony Lake Takes on a Demoralized, Recalcitrant CIA." *Washington Post,* December 8, 1996.

Walker, Martin. "Czechs Retract Terror Link." *UPI,* October 20, 2002.

Walsh, Lawrence E. *Final Report of the Independent Counsel for Iran/Contra Matters.* December 3, 1993.

Watson, Dale. "Testimony before the Joint Inquiry into Intelligence Community Activities before and after the Terrorist Attacks of September 11, 2001." September 26, 2002.

Weiner, Tim. "The C.I.A.'s Most Important Mission: Itself." *New York Times*, December 10, 1995.

———. "U.S. Plan to Change Iran Leaders Is an Open Secret before It Begins." *New York Times*, January 26, 1996.

———. "Report Faults CIA on Hiring of Informers in Guatemala." *New York Times*, June 29, 1996.

———. "Iraqi Offensive into Kurdish Zone Disrupts US Plot to Oust Hussein." *New York Times*, September 7, 1996.

———. "Yet Again, Saddam's Foes Pay Price for Foiled U.S. Plot." *New York Times*, September 11, 1996.

———. "Spy Suspect Seemed Like the Best and the Brightest." *New York Times*, November 19, 1996.

———. "Careers Are among the Casualties of CIA's Latest Security Breach." *New York Times*, November 20, 1996.

———. "CIA Traitor, Saying He Wanted Cash for Family, Gets 23 Years." *New York Times*, June 6, 1997.

———. "CIA Severs Ties to 100 Foreign Agents." *New York Times*, March 3, 1997.

———. "CIA Officer Admits Spying for Russians." *New York Times*, March 4, 1997.

———. "U.S. Diplomat Leaves Austria after Being Caught Wiretapping." *New York Times*, November 6, 1997.

———. "CIA Drafts Covert Plan to Topple Saddam." *New York Times*, February 26, 1998.

———. "CIA Officers Teach Tricks of Their Trade to Palestinians." *New York Times*, March 5, 1998.

———. "A Straight-Arrow Policeman Turns Loose Cannon at CIA." *New York Times*, April 12, 1998.

———. "Bail Is Denied for Former CIA Officer Accused of Being a Spy." *New York Times*, April 17, 1998.

———. "The Mideast Talks: Cloaks and Daggers: the US Intelligence Chief Steps up to the Plate." *New York Times*, October 23, 1998.

———. "Baghdad's Foes: Opponents Find that Ousting Hussein Is Easier Said Than Done." *New York Times*, November 16, 1998.

———. "The CIA's Domestic Reach." *New York Times*, January 20, 2002.

Weiner, Tim, and James Risen. "Decision to Strike Factory in Sudan Based on Surmise Inferred from Evidence." *New York Times*, September 21, 1998.

Weiser, Benjamin. "The Once and Future Spy Mission for Gates, CIA Sits at a Critical Juncture." *Washington Post*, November 2, 1991.

"Who Knew What and When Did They Know It? Harbury/Bamaca Case Update." *Global Exchange*, n.d. Available: http://www.global exchange.org/campaignes/guatemala/harbury/documents.html.

Wright, Robin, and Richard A. Serrano. "U.S. Identifies al-Qaida Leader in Custody as Cole Mastermind." *Los Angeles Times*, November 22, 2002.

Woodward, Bob. "Secret CIA Units Playing a Central Combat Role." *Washington Post*, November 18, 2001.

————. "CIA Paid Afghans to Track Bin Ladin: Team of 15 Recruits Operated Since 1998." *Washington Post*, December 23, 2001.

Woolsey, R. James, "Comments to the Center for Strategic and International Studies on National Security and the Future Direction of the Central Intelligence Agency," July 18, 1994, Washington, DC. Available: http://www.fas.org/irp/cia/ciafut.htm.

"World Islamic Front Statement Urging Jihad against Jews and Crusaders," *al-Quds al-Arabi* (Arabic). February 23, 1998, English translation from Federation of American Scientists Web site, www.fas.org/irp/world/para/docs/980223-fatwa.htm.

Yannuzzi, Rick E. "In-Q-Tel: A New Partnership between the CIA and the Private Sector." *Defense Intelligence Journal* 9, no. 1 (Winter 2000).

Zaid, Mark S. "Testimony before the Senate Committee on the Judiciary." April 25, 2001. Available: http://www.fas.org/sgp/congress/2001/042501_zaid.htm

Index

I

Impersonal Communications, 54, 222
In-Q-Tel, 267–68
India, 263–65, 308
Indyk, Martin, 252, 293
information technology (IT), 267–68, 313
Inman, Bobby, 278
Inman Standards, 277
intelligence, 38–39, 90
    community, 239–43
    current, 94–95
    failure of, 2, 7, 11–12, 279, 332
    foreign, 38
    future of, 347–52
Intelligence Organization Act of 1992, 75
Intelligence Oversight Act of 1980, 69
Intelligence Oversight Board, 175–76
Internal Operations Course, 54
internet, 73, 222–23
interrogation techniques, 204
Iran, 21–23, 119, 194–97
Iran-Contra, 17–32, 83–84, 225
    See also Nicaragua
Iranian Ministry of Information and Security (MOIS), 195
Iranian Revolutionary Guard Corps (IRGC), 21, 195
Iraq, 57–60, 93, 109, 214–17, 350
Iraqi National Accord, 217
Iraqi National Congress, 215
Islamic Amal, 195
Islamic Army, 199
    See also al-Qa'ida
Islamic Jihad, 100, 192, 200, 271–73
Islamic Movement for Change, 190, 194
Ismoil, Eyad, 109
Israel, 24–25, 97, 112, 161, 178, 245–46, 249, 262

J

Jacobsen, David, 28
Jamaah Islamiya, 348
Jamiat-al-Ulema-e-Pakistan, 271
Jenco, Lawrence, 28
Jeremiah Commission, 265

Jewish Community Center (AMIA), 118
Jewish Defense League, 160
jihad, 98–100, 103, 116, 200, 271–72
John Paul II, Pope, 159
Joint Inquiry Congressional Committee on 9/11. *See* September 11th
Joint Military Intelligence Program, 241
Jordan, 11, 108, 109, 178, 199, 200, 203, 217, 246, 276, 287–88, 292, 323
Justice Department (DOJ), 74

K

Kahane, Meir, 160
Kansi, Mir Aimal, 102, 260
Kelley, Brian, 297–300
Kennedy, John, 82, 85
Kenya, 274–77
Kerr, Donald, 340–41
Kerry, John, 74
Kessler, Ronald, 202
KGB, 55, 134, 136
Khatami, Mohammad, 197
Khobar Towers bombing, 194, 226, 244, 290
Khomeini, Ayatollah Ali, 119
Kimche, David, 23
Klinghoffer, Leon, 25, 245
Krongard, Buzzy, 305
Kurdistan, 215
Kuwait, 57–60, 93

L

Lake, Anthony "Tony", 198, 216, 257
Leahy, Pat, 300
Lebanon, 21, 24–25, 28–29, 196
Legion of the Martyr Abdullah al-Huzaifi, 194
letterhead incident, 182
Libyan Fighting Group, 200

M

Madrid Peace Conference, 97
Maghniyah, Imad, 21
Mahmud, Muhamed Hasan (aka Muhamed Hasan Tita), 273

Office of Strategic Services, 8, 81, 231
Office of the Program Manager/
Saudi Arabian National Guard
(OPM/SANG), 190, 194, 290
Operation Desert Storm, 58
Operation Restore Hope, 273–74
Operation Southern Watch, 193
operational training, 44
Operations Advisory Group, 82
Orion spy planes, 113
Oslo Accords, 112, 245, 247
outsourcing, 312
al-Owhali, Mohamed Rashed Daoud,
274–76

P

Pakistan, 159–60
Palestine, 97, 112, 161, 246
Palestine Liberation Organization
(PLO), 97, 245
paramilitary officers, 87, 112
paramilitary training, 44
Paris Flap, 180
Parry, Robert, 86
Patriot Act, 331
Patriotic Union of Kurdistan, 215
Pavitt, Jim, 184
Pearl Harbor, 8
Pekel, Kent, 234–35
pensions, 214
Pereira, Fernando, 34
Performance Appraisal Reporting
System (PARS), 142
Perry, William, 251
Philippines, 158–59
Pitts, Earl E., 137, 298
Poindexter, John, 32
Pollard, Jonathan, 296
polygraph, 143–45, 311–12
Pope, Robert, 215–16
Powers, Francis Gary, 82
Presidential Daily Brief, 157
Presidential Decision Directive-24
(PDD-24), 142
Presidential Decision Directive-35
(PDD-35), 12, 209–10, 258
Presidential Decision Directive-39
(PDD-39), 110–11

propaganda activities, 339
public diplomacy, 339

Q

al-Qa'ida
beginnings, 13–14, 198–203, 254
CBRN, 76
CIA intelligence, 283–88, 319,
322–25, 329
FBI information, 327
Finances, 198–200, 285–86
ideology, 321–23, 325, 332, 348
and Khalid Shaykh Muhammad,
248
military offensive against, 326, 336
pre–September 11th attacks, 111,
226, 254, 272–79, 289–91
al-Shifa Pharmaceutical factory, 280
training, 294–95, 320, 327
Qatar, 247–48
Qatari Charitable Association, 200
Quality of Life program, 226
al-Quds Forces, 21

R

Rafsanjani, Ali Akbar Hashemi, 22, 28
Rahman, Fazlur, 271
Rahman, Omar Abdel (aka Blind
Shaykh), 110, 160, 162, 190, 199, 204
Rainbow Warrior, 34
Reagan, Ronald, 22–23, 29–30, 83–85
reduction in force (RIF), 122, 213
Reed, Frank, 28
reform initiatives, 239–43, 315–18
Reinventing Government campaign,
306
rendition operations, 202–4
Ressam, Ahmed, 288, 293
retirement, 213–14
risk management, 173, 184–86, 225,
237, 248, 343
Rodriguez, Felix (aka Max Gomez),
20, 28, 31
Russia House, 57

S

Sadat, Anwar, 100, 110, 190
Salah, Ahmed Osman, 273

USS *Cole*, 289–90, 337
USS *Harlan County*, 118

V

Velasquez, Efraim "Bamaca" (aka
Comandante Evarardo), 174–75, 178
VEVAK, 119

W

Walsh, Lawrence, 66, 77
War on Terrorism, 13, 87, 95, 238,
269–96, 297, 309, 321, 326, 332, 335,
338, 339, 340–41, 349, 350
Webster, William
beginnings, 15–17, 32, 36
polygraph, 143
public speaking, 122
reforms, 41, 48–49, 51–52, 56
resignation, 60–61
Weir, Benjamin, 24
Wisner, Frank, 264
women in the CIA, 124–31
women's class action lawsuit, 126–29
Woolsey R., James
and Bill Clinton, 105, 107–8,
116–17, 119–20

confirmation hearing, 162
downsizing, 122–24, 148
polygraph, 143
public speaking, 121–22
reforms, 153–58
World Islamic Front, 271
World Trade Center bombing, 108–11,
160–62, 204
World Wide Web, 73, 222–23
Worldwide Threat Assessment, 192,
194

Y

Y2K threat, 289
Yasin, Abdul, 109
Yemen, 289–91
Yemeni Islamic Group, 200
Younis, Fawaz, 202
Yousef, Ramzi, 109–11, 159–62, 247
Yurchenko, Vitaly, 55

Z

al-Zawahiri, Ayman, 100, 271–72
Zenawi, Meles, 98